JUÁREZ

PROFILES IN POWER

General Editor: Keith Robbins

ELIZABETH I
Christopher Haigh

RICHELIEU
R.J. Knecht

GUSTAVUS ADOLPHUS (2nd Edn)
Michael Roberts

OLIVER CROMWELL
Barry Coward

JUÁREZ
Brian Hamnett

NAPOLEON III
James McMillan

LLOYD GEORGE
Martin Pugh

HITLER
Ian Kershaw

CHURCHILL
Keith Robbins

NASSER
Peter Woodward

DE GAULLE
Andrew Shennan

CASTRO
Sebastian Balfour

JUÁREZ

Brian Hamnett

LONGMAN
London and New York

Longman Group UK Limited,
Longman House, Burnt Mill,
Harlow, Essex CM20 2JE, England
and Associated Companies throughout the world.

Published in the United States of America
by Longman Publishing, New York.

First published 1994

ISBN 0582 05054 5 CSD
ISBN 0582 05053 7 PPR

British Library Cataloguing-in-Publication Data
A catalogue record for this book is
available from the British Library

Library of Congress Cataloging in Publication Data

Hamnett, Brian R.
Juárez / Brian Hamnett.
p. cm. – (Profiles in power)
Includes bibliographical references and index.
ISBN 0-582-05054-5 (CSD). – ISBN 0-582-05053-7 (PPR)
1. Juárez, Benito, 1806-1872. 2. Mexico – History – 19th century.
3. Presidents – Mexico – Biography. I. Title. II. Series:
Profiles in power (London, England)
F1233.J9H36 1993
972'.04'092 – dc20 92 – 46296
[B] CIP

Set by 14P 11/12 Linotron Baskerville

Produced by Longman Singapore Publishers (Pte) Ltd.
Printed in Singapore

CONTENTS

	List of Maps	viii
	Abbreviations	ix
	Preface	xi
CHAPTER 1	Nineteenth-century Mexico: the world of Juárez	1
	The geo-politics of Mexico	1
	Mexican constitutionalism	9
	The aims of Mexican Liberalism	12
	The politics of fragmentation	13
CHAPTER 2	The provincial origins: Juárez and Oaxaca	18
	Oaxaca: culture and society	19
	The Institute of Science and Arts	22
	The Liberal experiment of 1833–34	23
	The Centralist Republic (1836–46)	26
	The restoration of federalism in 1846	32
	State governor of Oaxaca (1847–52)	34
	The crisis in the Isthmus	40
CHAPTER 3	Juárez and Liberalism	49
	Juárez: broadening horizons	51
	Juárez in the Liberal constellation	53
	The Revolution of Ayutla	56
	Deepening divisions in the Liberal Party	62
CHAPTER 4	Juárez, the Constitution of 1857 and the collapse of the Liberal regime	71
	State-level politics	75
	The breakdown of the constitutional experiment	79

CHAPTER 5 Juárez and the Catholic Church 86
Early Liberalism and the revival of the Church 87
Governor Juárez and the Church 91
The Juárez Law 96
Disamortization: the Lerdo Law 98
Governor Juárez and the bishop of Oaxaca 100
The escalation of conflict and the civil war of the Reform 101
The Veracruz Reform Laws 104
Nationalism, secularism and pluralism 110

CHAPTER 6 Juárez and the state governors 116
The state governors and the civil war 117
The Juárez regime in Veracruz 121
Juárez and Congress 125
The struggle with Vidaurri 130
The impact of the French Intervention 132
Juárez in Chihuahua 135
The decrees of 8 November 1865: Juárez's *coup d'état*? 138

CHAPTER 7 Juárez and the United States 145
Territorial cession and transit rights 145
The issue of recognition 148
Mexico and the American civil war (1861–65) 152
The victory of the *juaristas* 158

CHAPTER 8 Juárez and the European Powers 166
The debt question and the Allied intervention of 1861–62 167
The establishment of the Mexican Empire 171
Juárez's policy of uncompromising resistance 175
Marshal Bazaine and the French response 182
The collapse of the empire 184
The execution of Maximilian 189

CHAPTER 9 The last period of Juárez: party, Constitution and power 198
The later Juárez 199
The *convocatoria* of August 1867 and the controversy over constitutional reform 201
The growth of opposition 203
Liberal divisions in Puebla 208
The civil war in Guerrero 211
Social movements and the agrarian question 214
Nayarit and the agrarian movement of Manuel Lozada 216

CHAPTER 10 Juárez, the Díaz brothers and the Rebellion of La Noria 220
Félix Díaz in control of Oaxaca (1867–71) 222
The Rebellion of La Noria and the destruction of Porfirio Díaz (1871–72) 225
Constitutional reform revived 232
The death of Juárez – July 1872 233

Conclusion 236
Bibliographical essay 244
Chronology 252
Glossary 261
Dramatis personae 267
Maps 281
Index 286

LIST OF MAPS

1. Mexico, 1821–53 282
2. The State of Oaxaca, 1857 283
3. The Mexican Republic in 1867 284

. . . .

ABBREVIATIONS

AGEO	Archivo del Estado de Oaxaca
AGN	Archivo General de la Nación (Mexico City)
APBJPS	*Archivo Privado de D. Benito Juárez y D. Pedro Santacilia* (ed. J. Puig Casauranc, Mexico 1928)
BBSHCP	*Boletín Bibliográfico de la Secretaría de Hacienda y Crédito Público*
BEO CMMG	Biblioteca del Estado de Oaxaca, Colección Manuel Martínez Gracida
BJDOCS	*Benito Juárez. Documentos, discursos y correspondencia* (ed. Jorge L. Tamayo) 15 vols (Mexico 1964–71)
FJ	Fondo Juárez, Archivo General del Estado, Oaxaca
HAHR	*Hispanic American Historical Review*
UNAM	Universidad Nacional Autónoma de México

PREFACE

Benito Juárez (1806–1872) was one of the outstanding Latin American political figures in the two centuries since the struggles for Independence. Controversial during his lifetime and subject to contradictory interpretations thereafter, Juárez has proved to be a most elusive personality when it comes to assessing his career. This is a study of Juárez and political power. It is not a biography, of which several already exist. Here we shall concentrate on the context, both national and provincial, out of which he emerged. We shall examine how he became the centre of a provincial circle of professional men wedded to the Liberal Party in the Indian south of Mexico. From there we shall explore his route to power at the national level at a time of great danger for his country, beset by irreconcilable divisions and external pressures. In many respects, the career of Juárez accompanied and reflected the formative period of Mexican nationalism four decades after political independence from Spain in 1821. Juárez bound the Liberal cause to that of nationalism during the 1860s in response to the French Intervention and the establishment of a monarchy under the Archduke Maximilian of Habsburg. Juárez's clarity of vision in defining the issues at that time contributed not only to his own survival as a political leader but also to the eventual expulsion of the French and the collapse of Maximilian's empire in 1867. This was Juárez's finest hour.

The struggle of Juárez against the European Intervention was watched closely in the United States, in the rest of Latin America, and in Europe itself. The French opposition to the Emperor Napoleon III supported Juárez and the Mexican republicans and used the débâcle of the Intervention as a weapon with which to undermine the regime at home. Bismarck and the Prussian government learned from the inability of the French army to hold down a weak and divided American country. Latin Americans saw in Juárez's stand a second struggle for independence, a second defeat for the European powers, and a second reversal of the Conquest. Juárez represented the struggle of the conquered, non-white population against the contemptuous European or North American. His victory in 1867 was a triumph of anti-colonialism in an age of dominant empires. As such, it anticipated the struggles of the mid-twentieth century in an exemplary manner. Juárez, furthermore, proved himself to be a skilful politician, who pursued power as ruthlessly and unsentimentally as any of his European contemporaries. For that reason, contemporaries, who had generally underestimated him because of his Indian origins, recoiled, stunned and horrified at the ease with which they were outmanoeuvred.

The literature on Juárez reveals less the man, less the capable politician, than the symbol, the statue of bronze or stone that stands in so many Mexican towns. This symbol, as remote as the pre-Columbian gods, detracts from the historical reality. The cult of Juárez forms a central part of Mexican political mythology. On one side, he stands alongside the secular saints in the official hagiography; on the other side, he is execrated in a demonology of opponents of the Church. Juárez himself contributed greatly to this mythology even during his own lifetime. Always conscious of the powerful impact of image, he was careful to create and cultivate a unique persona for himself, even down to the clothes he wore. He saw himself as the embodiment of national sovereignty and republican virtue. In that sense, he preferred to stand alone. His ethnic origin, his provincial background and the need to work upwards from the bottom to the highest political position in the land isolated Juárez from other men. Beyond a few intimates mainly from Oaxaca, his home state, Juárez trusted no one. Never a great writer or brilliant speaker, he may well have suffered a sense of inferiority towards his many brilliant contemporaries. Few of them, however, possessed Juárez's political aptitude. In the end, Juárez's capacity for survival made him the most excoriated figure in the Republic, the object of numerous unsuccessful rebellions.

No one ever said less than Juárez. He hardly ever expressed his inner thoughts and feelings. Effusive he was not. Yet Juárez was not a man devoid of emotion, as his intimate letters to his wife and son-in-law reveal, above all concerning the fate of his children during the long periods of separation from his family. Juárez overcame most of the disadvantages placed before him by means of a successful education and subsequent law practice, an early entry into provincial politics, a successful marriage, and the cultivation of a long-lasting circle of intimates of Oaxacan origin. He rose in politics and maintained himself therein through tactical alliances. These were by nature shifting. Accordingly, it is often difficult to determine where exactly Juárez stood in the ideological spectrum. Even so, he was not primarily an ideologist, in spite of his frequent adoption of a high moral tone. He was essentially a pragmatist, increasingly dedicated to the survival of the state and the discovery of the most practical means of administering it. As President from 1858 to 1872, he did not depend exclusively upon any particular individual or group. He dispensed with whatever allies he had whenever it became politically necessary to do so. Increasingly, Juárez was portrayed by disgruntled contemporaries as a threat to the democratic institutions that they portrayed themselves as defending. He himself in the later years (1867–72) undoubtedly saw himself as greatly misunderstood. There is a clear element in Juárez's career that reveals a fascination for power and a love of the game of securing and retaining it.

My sources are partly archival and partly published documents. I have used state and notarial archives in Oaxaca and the Archivo Juárez in Mexico City. I am grateful to their respective directors for all the assistance given to me. In Oaxaca, the help and friendship of Angeles Romero and Manuel Esparza contributed to successful and enjoyable research. The British Academy provided generous funding. Latin Americanist colleagues in three Oaxaca Workshops, held in London, Oxford and Essex, have helped me mull over my ideas on the Juárez era. Recent research in the Mexican National Archive and the Condumex Foundation has enabled me to deepen my knowledge of the Second Empire. Conversations with Héctor Martínez, Leticia Reina, Jean Starr and Ross Parmenter in Oaxaca and with Cristina Torales, Josefina Vázquez and Jan Bazant in Mexico City helped define the issues presented herein. I owe a debt of hospitality to José Antonio Serrano and the late Alberto Cuervo in Mexico City in 1988 and 1989. The topic itself really originated in the first course I ever gave as a university teacher, which was a Reading Seminar in Modern Mexican History at the State University of New York at Stony Brook, USA, during the academic year 1968–69. The present work is dedicated to those who were my students at that time, wherever they may be now.

Chapter 1

NINETEENTH-CENTURY MEXICO: THE WORLD OF JUÁREZ

Many issues in the political and social history of nineteenth-century Mexico had European parallels. Mexican uniqueness and diversity ensured that conflicts and consequences would differ from those in Europe. Nevertheless, central issues such as political legitimacy, constitutional government, relations between centre and region or Church and state, the impact of Liberalism, types of social organization and landownership, and problems of political economy, all could be seen not only throughout the rest of Latin America, but also in Europe during the same period. There is no reason to regard Mexico as in any way isolated from these mainstream currents. The specific characteristics of Mexico, however, provide the distinctions and the interpretative difficulties. This former Spanish colony had been the centre of sophisticated indigenous civilizations that long predated the Aztec Empire encountered by the Conquistadores in 1519. Its cultural richness and ethnic diversity help to explain both its fascination and its complexity. Benito Juárez was formed by that society and reflected many of these complexities. We shall explore some of them in the following pages.

· ·

THE GEO-POLITICS OF MEXICO

By the middle of the nineteenth century, Mexico's total population reached around 9 million. It had risen from 6 million at the time of the Wars of Independence in the 1810s – comparable to the 6.8 million living in the United States at that time – and would rise again by the outbreak of the

Revolution of 1910 to more than 15 million. The distribution of population, however, remained uneven. The overwhelming majority remained concentrated in the temperate higher altitude zones, rather than in the tropical coastal zones or in the arid lowlands of the far north. Nevertheless, the general tendency was a northward advance of population during the nineteenth century. This tendency had already been evident as far back as the sixteenth century with the opening of the silver mines of Guanajuato, San Luis Potosí and Zacatecas. It was more marked in the course of the recovery of the mining economy during the eighteenth century and the development of large livestock estates in Coahuila, and became an irreversible process in the last decades of the nineteenth century.

In the Spanish colonial era (1521–1821), the territory included in the Viceroyalty of New Spain extended well beyond the spheres of influence of the Aztec Confederation that preceded it. Even so, the colonial capital, Mexico City, was constructed right on top of the Aztec capital, Tenochtitlán. The focal point of Hispanic power lay in the heartland of Indian Mexico. Hispanic Catholic Mexico was grafted on to the pre-Columbian society that became transformed in the process. Several other principal Hispanic cities, such as Puebla and Guadalajara, arose in the midst of areas settled and farmed for centuries by Indian communities.

In the province of Oaxaca, where Benito Juárez was born in 1806, the Aztecs founded a number of settlements, which may have been initially little more than trading posts or garrison positions. One of them, Huaxyacac, formed the basis for the Hispanic settlement of Antequera de Oaxaca, shortly afterwards the seat of a bishopric. Juárez did not come from Antequera, the centre of Hispanic wealth and influence, but from the Zapotec village of Guelatao in the northern highlands beyond the city, an intermediary zone between the central valleys and the tropical lowlands of the Gulf of Mexico.

Several cities had no claim to indigenous origins and lay beyond the principal areas of pre-Columbian settlement. Among them was Guanajuato in the highlands above what in the eighteenth century became the rich cereal-producing plateau of the Bajío. The towns of the Bajío lay beyond the northern frontier of the Aztec Empire on the River Lerma. The contrast between Oaxaca, where some 90 per cent of the population was of Indian origin in the middle of the nineteenth century and controlled the greater part of usable land, and the Bajío, where a Hispanic and mestizo population predominated, could not be more striking.

During the eighteenth century colonial Mexico reached the apogee of its cultural development and prosperity. Even so, population recovery after the catastrophes of the Conquest and economic growth were highly regionalized. Silver-mining continued to provide the main impetus for growth, but many provinces remained predominantly rural. The economic transformation of the Bajío from livestock-raising to cereal agriculture was one of the most striking phenomena of the eighteenth century. It was closely related to the expansion of the mining communities of Guanajuato, San Luis Potosí and Zacatecas. At the same time, the woollen textile industries of Querétaro, Acámbaro and San Miguel el Grande supplied not only these areas, but also the northern livestock zones. The Bajío cities played a decisive role in defining the cultural characteristics of early-nineteenth-century Mexico. Centres of learning, channels for the reception of European Enlightened ideas, and cradles of popular Catholicism, they shaped the responses and reactions of the leading political and religious figures of the independent Republic.

From the middle of the eighteenth century, the city of Guadalajara rose to the position of major cotton textile producer and political centre for the north-west. The ecclesiastical and bureaucratic establishments in the city were already formidable. Although not itself a major mining zone, Guadalajara remained linked to the northern mines of Bolaños and Rosario. The resident landed and commercial elite, several of whom had acquired noble titles and founded entailed estates, expanded its sphere of activity throughout the surrounding zones of Indian peasant-artisan culture. From the latter part of the eighteenth century onwards, ethnosocial relations in the central zone of what after 1823 would become the state of Jalisco remained uneasy. At times, as in 1810–15 and again during the Liberal Reform era after 1855, they exploded into violent conflict. In contrast to Guanajuato, where the mining economy suffered greatly during and after the War of Independence, Guadalajara recovered rapidly from the dislocation. It became a centre of federalist support for much of the nineteenth century. Guanajuato's mining industry did not begin to recover until at least the 1850s, and its political influence remained diminished.

The silver economy of Zacatecas, on the other hand, recovered quickly after 1817. Ten years later, this zone produced two-thirds of Mexican silver output. Accordingly, its influence within the federal system established under the Constitution of 1824 was considerable. Always a centre of federalist support, Zacatecas under its state governor, Francisco García Salinas, became the show-piece for the Liberal experiment of the post-Independence era. State educational establishments, a state library and an agrarian development bank were the hallmarks of García's administration between 1829 and 1835. The state authorities, however, resisted central government pressures on their revenues. Federal institutions created barriers to the exploitation of provincial resources by the national government. Accordingly, as some states, such as Zacatecas, prospered, and some individuals grew rich on commerce and credit, the federal government languished in poverty and ineffectiveness. State governments, moreover, sought to protect their interests by forming civil militias – in the case of Zacatecas some 3,000 strong. In such a way, they sought to protect the federal system and deter the national government from employing the army to reduce their autonomy.

While some regions rose, others declined. Yet even when decline proved to be the case, it had distinct local features. Within the state of Puebla, for instance, the traditional Hispano-Indian central valleys remained largely stagnant in demographic and economic terms from the early eighteenth to the late nineteenth centuries. The landed estates seemed incapable of overcoming the problems of soil erosion, indebtedness and labour resistance to coercion. In contrast, the sugar sector of the southern, peripheral zone expanded until the 1810s and recovered again by the 1840s. There, ethnosocial relations between planters and village communities remained strained, as they did in the contiguous zone of Cuautla-Yautepec (now in the state of Morelos) and the Oaxacan Mixteca. The northern highlands of Puebla, a transit zone between Veracruz and the Valley of Mexico, increased in population and importance during the first three-quarters of the nineteenth century. Their fluid, racially mixed population provided the social base for Liberal support and the manpower for the Puebla National Guard during the Reform era.

A similar sub-regional divergence could be seen in the state of Oaxaca between the central valleys and the northern sierra, which became the core area of *juarista* support until the 1870s. In the central valleys, the position of the predominant Hispanic elite of merchants and owners of relatively small (often rather impoverished) estates remained weak. The dye-export boom from the 1760s had petered out in the 1790s, and attempts to stimulate a mining sector had proved elusive. The collapse of the Spanish hegemony of merchants, administrators, army officers and bishops left the provincial families, which moved into office after 1821, perilously exposed in an Indian state. They were obliged to form alliances with educated mestizos and Indians in order to maintain their position. The search for a new economic base for the state provided a common bond among these socially divergent groups. Nevertheless, the attempt to revive business and use what power the state could count upon to reinforce the position of private property-owners led to the insurrection of the Zapotec villages of the southern Isthmus of Tehuantepec during the period of Juárez's first state governorship from 1847 to 1852.

Puebla's business community remained closely linked to Veracruz, the principal port and line of contact with Europe and the eastern seaboard of the USA. Several leading Puebla entrepreneurs, such as Pedro Escandón and Estéban de Antuñano, had been originally Veracruz merchants. Cotton for Puebla's textile industry was produced on the Gulf and Pacific coasts. The Puebla elite in the 1830s and 1840s saw in mechanization of production the solution to economic stagnation. Mexico's early attempt at industrialization came to a halt, however, with the cotton shortage at the end of the 1840s and the insoluble problems of capital, technology and market. While Puebla businessmen pressed for protectionism and were prepared to contemplate the demise of federalism in order to achieve it, the political elite of Veracruz, in which merchant houses played a major role, remained wedded to the import trade and by the mid-1850s confirmed their position among the leading supporters of Liberalism.

Federalism and provincial Liberalism marched hand in hand. The political elites of the geographical peripheries of the Republic tended in the main to sustain the federal idea. This was not always uniform or consistent. In Chihuahua, for instance, the rising Terrazas family hovered between parties in the 1850s. Governor Luis Terrazas, who would eventually become the protector of Juárez during the French Intervention (1862–67), took a considerable time to commit himself. As in the case of other regional leaders, such as Santiago Vidaurri in Nuevo León-Coahuila, Terrazas continued to usurp federal revenues and use them for state-level purposes. Nevertheless, once this dispute was resolved, Juárez's support enabled the Terrazas family to complete its control of property, business and political life within the state by the 1880s.

During the War of Independence, which began in September 1810, the economic and political linkages which had bound together the Spanish colonial Viceroyalty of New Spain unravelled. From the 1810s, we are witnessing the disaggregation of central government in Mexico. At the same time, regimes of differing ideological complexion failed to discover how to reconstitute it. This process took place during most of the lifetime of Juárez. When Juárez recovered national political power in 1867, following the collapse of the French Intervention, he inherited this problem in no uncertain terms. Regional diffusion of power greatly impeded Juárez's aim to reconstruct a viable central government with an effective presidential authority.

For this reason it is essential that we examine throughout this book the regional base of political life. This in itself introduces a number of difficulties: it means that we should constantly be aware of divergent patterns of economic and political life, social structure and agrarian usage, as well as ethno-cultural differences across the vast territory of the Mexican Republic. Focus on central government politics alone is inadequate. It will not tell us what we need to know; it will not show us how political movements operated at their local base. At the same time, the localization and regionalization of politics led to the predominance of personality – 'personalism'. In nineteenth-century Latin America, this took many forms. In Mexico, its most characteristic feature was clientelism through the form of broadly ranging patron–client networks. These frequently represented a type of surrogate for formal political institutions. Nevertheless, they did not exist in opposition to political ideologies and movements. On the contrary, the latter operated through them and in concert with clearly identifiable local chieftains (*caciques*). The regionalization of political life, above all in the period

1810–67, emphasized this tendency towards personalism. Some commentators have described Mexican federalism as the institutionalization of *caciquismo*.

Regional sentiment already existed before Independence. Civil strife did not create it, but the weakening of central government and bureaucracy provided the political opening for regionalism at the national level in 1823. Mexico had two federal constitutions, in 1824 and 1857, in the nineteenth century, and a third (in force at present) in 1917. Topography alone did not produce regions: the element of local consciousness was the decisive factor. Distinct ethno-cultural origins, social structures, economic relationships and interests, relations with the official power, with other areas, and sometimes directly with the external market – all of these factors helped to influence the shaping of a region as well. The collapse of Spanish colonial power in 1821 stimulated provincial pressures for an effective political voice at the centre. The failure of Mexico's first monarchy in 1823 and with it the disintegration of the national army opened the way for several regions, notably Jalisco, Zacatecas, Puebla, Oaxaca and Yucatán, to proclaim themselves free, sovereign states, only loosely federated with one another and the diminished central government. Regionalism, then, was not identical to separatism: in essence, it represented the demand from the provinces for greater participation in national affairs. Only in exceptional instances, as the cases of Texas and Yucatán in 1835–36 showed, was a separatist course chosen.

Much of nineteenth-century Mexican history revolved around the competition of regional elites for predominance at the centre. Yet, at the same time, the regional factor should not be overemphasized. At no stage did Mexico cease to exist as a political entity. The nineteenth century, a period of almost continuous crisis for the new Republic, demonstrated Mexico's capacity for survival and coherence at a time of decline and in a dangerous world. Mexico managed ultimately to maintain its cohesion, because the colonial past contributed a number of centripetal elements to the new nineteenth-century Republic. Three were of overriding importance. First, there was the economic unity which derived from the second half of the sixteenth century onwards. We are not referring here to an integrated national market linked by the type of modern infrastructure brought by the railways from the 1880s onwards. It would be wrong to suppose that before then connections did not operate. An infrastructure of trade certainly existed, but the principal linkages were those forged by merchant-financiers whose interests radiated outwards from Mexico City, an effective economic centre, and the provincial capitals. These importers, exporters and domestic investors forged a unity out of the principal economic resources of the colonial Viceroyalty. Although agriculture remained the base of the economy (until the middle of the twentieth century), silver-mining provided the dynamic that determined the rhythm. Second, colonial Mexico's administrative structures, imperfect as they were, bound together divergent territories into a functioning whole. The focus of power lay with the viceroy and *audiencias* (the supreme administrative and judicial body) in Mexico City and Guadalajara. In view of the close association of the mercantile guild with the sources of peninsular power, the economic and political linkages remained complementary until the period of the Bourbon reforms after 1765. Thirdly, the Viceroyalty of New Spain had a distinct ecclesiastical structure, also centred upon Mexico City, the seat of the archdiocese established in 1528. There were ten dioceses when the First Federal Republic was established in 1824. These integrating factors helped to ensure that Mexico did not disintegrate after Independence into its component parts as the Kingdom of Guatemala (later the Central American Federation) would do by 1840.

From the 1830s the rise of the United States provided a further element making for Mexico's cohesion as a political entity. After the shock of the loss of Texas in 1836, relations with the USA never ceased to be an overriding factor not only in Mexico's external relations but also in its domestic politics. The shadow of the United States extended over the Mexican Republic from the second decade of its existence. The problem of Mexico's relationship with the USA still remains essentially unresolved at the end of the twentieth century. In spite of regionalism, then, nineteenth-century Mexico had somehow to respond cohesively to the constant pressures from the north, in a way that no other Latin American country had to in the same period. The economic difficulties of Mexico during the first three-quarters of the century occurred at the same time as the development of the USA. The shifting relationship between the two societies was particularly galling for Mexicans, who somehow had to deal as well with a deeply wounded pride. The defeat of the Mexican army by the USA in the War of 1846–47 made matters worse. Mexico lost half its national territory, and sank deeper into weakness and division. Some observers compared Mexico in the mid-nineteenth century, caught between the United States and the European Powers, to Poland, caught between Imperial Russia and Prussia. They feared that Mexico might share the fate of the obliterated Polish state.

Throughout the nineteenth century, then, the relationship between region and centre remained crucial. An intimate interrelation existed between regional-level politics and the national level. Mexican political culture cannot be understood without bearing that in mind. Even so, the defeat of 1847, followed by the civil war of the Reform (1858–61) and the War of the French Intervention reopened all the centrifugal elements in Mexican political life. Regionalism and personalism, frequently and powerfully combined, frustrated successive attempts to establish constitutional government in the country. Realization of the ideal of representation, which had first germinated in response to Bourbon centralization after 1765, proved elusive. Accordingly, Mexico, departing from the United States in terms of economic development, also departed from it in terms of the successful establishment of representative, republican government. This had, for the most part, been the goal of the founders of the Mexican Republic in the 1810s and 1820s: it remained the objective of Juárez throughout his career. The study of Juárez reveals the full extent of this dilemma. It highlights the obstacles encountered by Latin American states, a few decades after independence from Iberian rule, in attempting to establish a legal basis of government, discover a policy for economic development, and at the same time work out their relationship with the outside world. Mexico is in many respects an exemplary case, ruled as it was by Juárez from 1858 to 1872, a non-white member of the colonial subject race.

. . .

MEXICAN CONSTITUTIONALISM

The problem of how to establish constitutional government is the underlying theme of nineteenth-century Mexican history. Even so, there are no constitutional histories of Mexico to which we can confidently refer. Given the magnitude of Mexico's political failure during the nineteenth century, it is perhaps understandable that the historiography has largely been preoccupied with fragmentation, conflict and personal power. Needless to say, none of those three elements will be absent from the present book. However, it is essential to recognize that the career of Juárez represented, for all its limitations, a concerted attempt to establish constitutional government, the supremacy of the civil power and the rule of law, in what had been Spain's richest colony. The career of Juárez cannot be understood except in that context.

The transition from colonial absolutism to constitutional government formed part of Mexico's post-imperial readjustment. The problem was common to virtually all the other Ibero-American territories, newly independent in the 1810s and 1820s. It has similarly preoccupied newly independent states in the latter half of the twentieth century as well. The earlier case of Mexico, then, is both relevant and illustrative. Essentially, the problem was how to re-establish the supremacy of the civil power and the law. This had characterized the long colonial era, but had been lost in the wars of independence both in Spain and the Indies. The Spanish Cortes of 1810–14 had attempted to address the issue by placing a written Constitution at the apex of the political process. In this system population rather than corporate status defined the form of representation. Under the Constitution of March 1812, the imperial parliament or Cortes would be unicameral. This reflected the deputies' distrust of an upper house composed of senior noblemen and clerics. Yet rejection of bicameralism exposed the Cádiz Liberals to the charge of Jacobinism. It made it easy for conservatives to brand them as servile imitators of the French Revolution. Furthermore, the relationship of the new organs of representation to the Bourbon monarchy had not been clearly defined. As a result, the restored monarch, Ferdinand VII, found the Constitution unacceptable and in May 1814 dissolved the Cortes. The reversion to absolutism did not remove the problem of representation: it delayed its resolution.

The 1812 Constitution provided much of Spanish America with its first experience of representative government. Many of its provisions were controversial, especially since they attempted to formulate new political structures on the basis of abstract principles rather than inherited practice. The absence of political participation during the colonial period would have, then, a transcendent significance throughout the nineteenth century. The Spanish Liberals and their American allies, who formed the principal pressure group in the Cortes until 1813, sought to take advantage of the departure of the Bourbons in 1808, in order to restructure the entire political system. They claimed the legitimacy to do so through the adoption by the Cortes of the doctrine of sovereignty of the nation in September 1810. The deputies in Spain, however, conceived of this nation in entirely different terms from the American separatists, who had already launched their territories on the road to independence during the same year. The Cortes defined the nation as the full extent of the Hispanic dominions in both hemispheres. They envisaged a unitary state under a constitutional monarchy, with American electors sending their representatives to the parliament in the Spanish capital.

Newly independent American territories dispensed with that definition, but, at the same time, retained much of the constitutionalism inherited from Cádiz. They applied the doctrine of sovereignty of the nation to their own polities as a means of legitimizing armed insurrection against what had formally been regarded as a divinely instituted monarchy to which they had owed obedience. In that sense, the conditions existed for the entry into the Spanish American political tradition of the ideas associated with the North American and French Revolutions. These came after the event, as it were, in order to legitimize actions already taken and brought to fruition. For such a reason, the early constitutional experience of Spanish America reflected a multiplicity of influences, both internal and external. The overriding urgency of the definition of sovereignty helps to explain the early impact of Liberalism throughout the Spanish American world.

Cádiz constitutionalism and the early Liberalism which sprang from it owed much of their shape to the Enlightenment. The political battles of the nineteenth century had their roots in the eighteenth-century contradiction between resurgent absolutism or 'Enlightened Despotism' and political philosophies of representative government. There would be much in the mid-nineteenth-century Liberalism of the Juárez era that would reflect this paradox of state-building and liberalization. The Liberal debt to the Enlightenment could be seen most especially in the case of the Catholic Church. Mexican Liberals demonstrated a marked readiness to employ the power of the state, in order to promote their cherished objective of reducing the role of the Church in society. In the tradition of the absolutist ministers of the Bourbon era, Liberal leaders and polemicists rapidly identified the Church as their outstanding obstacle. Despite their professed constitutionalism, Liberals in the Hispanic world inherited the statist politics of the absolute monarchy they sought to supersede. Their proposed subordination of the Church, the appropriation of its remaining properties, and their projected secularization of society principally through the means of lay education, all revealed those roots. This process reached its culminating point in the Juárez era, during the period known as the *Reforma* (1855–76).

. . .

THE AIMS OF MEXICAN LIBERALISM

Liberalism in Latin America responded to the struggle to rise out of the colonial past and throw off the inheritance of the *ancien régime.* Latin America shared with most of Europe a common experience of absolute monarchy and a common attempt to find a viable alternative to it. Yet the need to justify armed rebellion in the struggle for Independence had led to two remarkable developments: the insurgent adoption of the doctrine of sovereignty of the people – above all in Mexico, and the recruitment (spontaneous or otherwise) of non-elite social groups into the revolutionary struggle. The continuity of ideas between Spanish and American Liberalism could not disguise the fact that the new states came into existence between 1816 and 1826 as the result of an armed struggle. For that reason the doctrine of sovereignty of the people had complex implications in Spanish America. It was the first principle of Liberalism, but nowhere in the continent did the 'people' or the 'nation' actually exist. First imagined, they had then to be created after the event.

Liberals in Mexico, and their growing body of Conservative opponents, sought to work out in their different ways the legal and political implications of the revolutionary origins of the new sovereign state. Liberal political philosophers, such as

José María Luis Mora (1794–1850), a former cleric, regarded the corporate survivals of the colonial era as the main obstacles to the emergence of a 'national spirit'.

Mexican historians and political writers of the nineteenth century examined their country's past and attempted thereby to determine the nature and purpose of the new sovereign state created in 1821. In the main, two currents emerged: one consisted of writers highly influenced by the Spanish Enlightenment and Cádiz constitutionalism, such as Mora and the more radical Lorenzo de Zavala; the other, of which Lucas Alamán became the principal representative, saw in the colonial era the real origins of modern Mexico. This tradition argued that the new state should have been established on Hispanic Catholic foundations and not on their rejection. Mora and Zavala viewed the colonial inheritance as the obstacle to what they regarded as progress. They urged a wide-ranging series of reforms designed to uproot it. Although both advocated liberal representative government, they differed in type. Mora was anxious to avoid extremes. He did not wish to see the constitutional experiment in Mexico go the way of the French Revolution: he favoured a moderate Liberalism. Zavala, in alliance in 1828–29 with Vicente Guerrero, who had been the insurgent leader during the latter stages of the War of Independence, embarked upon what moderates came to view as a dangerous, radical course, in seeking to incorporate the popular classes into the movement.

. . .

THE POLITICS OF FRAGMENTATION

The ideas that germinated during the 1820s responded to Mexico's political problems in the aftermath of Independence. They gave rise to the principal issues of the following fifty years, encompassing thereby the entire span of Juárez's political life. Factional struggles and personal rivalries, however, frequently had a greater impact than intellectual debate, as we shall see. The political structure established by the federal Constitution of October 1824 was shaken only shortly afterwards by the Rebellion of Tulancingo in 1827. Vice-President Nicolás Bravo, who had also been one of the insurgent leaders, led a conspiracy to impose a form of centralism on the country. Guerrero put down the rebellion.

Thereafter, Bravo conceived a deepening hatred of Guerrero, whom he sought to destroy. The perceived threat to federalism radicalized the provincial wing of Liberalism, which was organized through the medium of the masonic lodges of the newly established *yorkino* rite. Moderates adhered, increasingly precariously, to the older *escocés* rite. They managed, however, to defeat Guerrero in the presidential elections of 1828. That defeat provoked a radical Liberal insurrection, directed by Zavala, which broke the constitutional order for the first time. The Rebellion of the Acordada imposed Guerrero as President in 1829, with Zavala as Finance Minister.

Political failure and financial weakness brought down the Guerrero regime, which was removed by Vice-President Anastasio Bustamante, formerly a Royalist commander during the counter-insurgency, acting as the candidate of a tactical alliance of moderate and conservative forces within the elites. Bustamante, in close collaboration with Alamán, established a type of centralizing, neo-Bourbon regime between 1830 and 1832. Moderate opinion rapidly moved away from the administration, and searched for leaders sufficiently powerful to remove it. This was brought about through the intervention of General Antonio López de Santa Anna in 1832. The reaction within the elites to the Bustamante–Alamán regime provided the context for the first Liberal experiment under Vice-President Valentín Gómez Farías in 1833–34. The Liberal regime attempted to put into effect policies derived from the Spanish Enlightenment and Cádiz constitutionalism. Its rapidly deteriorating relationship with the Church amply illustrated that. The influence of Mora and Zavala could be seen at different stages. The polarization of opinion that resulted opened the way for a second intervention by Santa Anna, who extinguished the regime in May 1834. Liberal anticlerical policies were held back thereby for an entire generation, until the *Reforma* of the later 1850s. The collapse of early Liberalism and the disintegration of the federal system in 1834–36 led to the first centralist experiment of 1836–46. The *Siete Leyes* of 1836 attempted to codify the constitutional basis for this new system.

At every stage, then, intellectual debate and constitutional politics in Mexico were intercepted by factional conflicts and personalism. The actions of Bravo, Guerrero, Bustamante and Santa Anna exposed the fragility of the new order, which finally collapsed in 1836, the year of the secession of both Texas and Yucatán. The politics of faction and personalism should not be seen in opposition to constitutional conflicts, though in theoretical terms they certainly were. On the contrary, they functioned within the constitutionalist context. Few, if any, interventions sought the overthrow of the constitutional order.

Dictatorship, in any case, signified a very different thing in 1840 from what it would in 1940. The classic Latin American dictator of the first decades of the nineteenth century was Simón Bolívar. In the tradition of the Roman Republic, his dictatorships represented attempts to salvage the republican system in times of crisis. Throughout his career, Bolívar had sought to establish a constitutional basis for the political life of independent Spanish America. He had never sought to found a personal regime above the Constitution and the law. Bolívar's career itself represented a profound reaction to colonial absolutism. Santa Anna in his wilder moments may have aspired to a dictatorship in Mexico, but no military base existed to substantiate it. The army had broken into rival factions after Independence. In any case, Santa Anna himself lacked consistency of purpose. Whenever able to take power, he withdrew from the political centre, leaving day-to-day administration to a Vice-President, an interim President or a strong minister. Santa Anna's dictatorship of 1842–44 was scarcely oppressive. Within a year, a new centralist constitution, the *Bases Orgánicas* (1843), came into effect. The attempted dictatorship of General Mariano Paredes y Arrillaga, in January–August 1846, collapsed with the outbreak of the war with the United States. Paredes, initially the candidate of Guadalajara federalists, apparently held monarchist views and sought to dispense with political parties. Santa Anna's last regime of 1853–55 dispensed with any Constitution at all and, in its brusque treatment of opposition, more resembled a dictatorship. Leading Liberal figures, such as Juárez and Melchor Ocampo, former governor of Michoacán, were dispatched into exile. The deteriorating financial situation, however, coupled with political failure, undermined the regime. Military weakness exposed it to escalating popular resistance.

Personal politics had its roots in Latin American political culture. Patron–client relationships in commerce and on the land had characterized colonial society. In Peru and Bolivia, where party development remained weak, or in Paraguay and Ecuador, where it was virtually non-existent, personalism could function independently of party struggles. In Mexico, however, party conflict intensified from the mid-1830s to the mid-1870s. Ideological polarization, party politics, social conflict and personalism remained inseparable in that period. Bustamante, Paredes or Santa Anna intervened less to promote their personal ambitions than in response to overtures from civilian politicians. The latter, without the opportunity or skill to remove incumbent administrations, resorted to extra-parliamentary means to attain their objectives. The readiness of Gómez Farías to collaborate with Santa Anna amply demonstrated that Liberals as well as Conservatives succumbed to this temptation. Liberals, at the same time, were in no way averse to cooperation with the former insurgent caudillo, Guerrero, as Zavala did in 1828–29. Similarly, a later generation cooperated with Juan Álvarez, Guerrero's spiritual heir and *cacique* of the Pacific hinterland zone since the 1820s. This close association enabled the construction of the coalition of forces which would bring the Revolution of Ayutla (March 1854) to power after the flight of Santa Anna. From August 1855, the pathway to the Liberal Reform lay open.

After 1821, we are no longer dealing with the relationship between crown and subject, viceroy or *audiencia* and corporative institution, judicial bureaucracy and Indian communities. The basic political relationships thereafter became those between circles of influential individuals – powerful through their capacity to mobilize men or ideas. This was very much the reality at all levels beneath the competing ideologies of Conservatism and Liberalism, centralism and federalism, republicanism and monarchy, secularism and defence of religion. In fact, it was the usual manner in which these higher struggles were expressed. For this reason, we have to deal in this book with an array of names, not for their own sake, but because personal rivalries were frequently the means through which the political issues were disputed. Ambition and pique coloured ideological conflict.

We are not dealing solely with naked struggles for power. Many of the political figures of the Reform era passionately believed in the ideas that they defended. These ideas were held not for their own sake, not because they had respectable

European pedigrees, but because they were seen as instruments with which to resolve the complex, pressing problems of Mexico. These issues concerned the role of the state in society, its relation to the regions and to the individual, its moral purpose – hence the urgency of defining its legitimacy at the outset, and its relationship to the Church. None of these issues, however, could be worked out in Independent Mexico without reference to the growing importance of the United States.

Chapter 2

THE PROVINCIAL ORIGINS: JUÁREZ AND OAXACA

Juárez was born to a Zapotec peasant family in 1806, a subject of the Spanish crown. Oaxaca, a distant southern province on the frontier of the Kingdom of Guatemala, had become one of the nine Intendancies into which the Viceroyalty of New Spain had been divided in 1786 by the late Bourbon administrative reforms. During those twenty years, between 1786 and 1806, Oaxaca had already passed the peak of its colonial prosperity as a dye and textile producer. It was moving into a long recession that would last until the 1880s. The ethnic and linguistic disparities of Oaxaca made for a cultural diversity that mid-nineteenth-century Liberals scarcely appreciated in their desire for what they perceived to be modernization.

Oaxaca epitomized the rich and deeply rooted regional differences within the Mexican Republic, which, even after the loss of half the national territory to the United States in 1848, was still the size of France and Spain combined. Within Oaxaca, as elsewhere in the Republic, topographical and meteorological variations reinforced these differences. The province contained sub-regions of very distinct character. These ranged from the temperate central valleys at around 5,000 feet above sea-level to the tropical Pacific coast and the lowlands of the Gulf zone beyond the northern sierra. The central valleys were virtually enclosed on all sides by mountain ranges, spurs of the Sierra Madre Oriental, which terminated at the Isthmus of Tehuantepec. The Isthmus linked the Gulf of Mexico and the Pacific Ocean, but in the nineteenth century there was still no easy route across it. Many Oaxaca politicians, including Juárez, saw in this transit route the great hope of a future recovery for their state. Foreign powers, such as the United States and Imperial France, also had designs on the Isthmus. Unfortunately for all parties concerned, the Isthmus remained one of the most politically turbulent areas in the Republic. Juárez himself discovered this when he became governor of Oaxaca for the first time between 1847 and 1852.

. . .

OAXACA: CULTURE AND SOCIETY

Zapotec and Mixtec cultures traditionally predominated in Oaxaca. The focal point of early Zapotec culture had been in the central valley at Monte Alban from *c.* 400 BC until the end of the ninth century AD. Thereafter a series of smaller states, such as Yagul and Lambityeco, superseded it. In the Mixteca in western Oaxaca, urban centres arose in the period from 200 BC to 300 AD and predominated there until the tenth century. The Aztec presence in Oaxaca was relatively recent. The principal Zapotec town in the central valley, Zaachila, was subordinated in 1495, and shortly afterwards Aztec power reached the Isthmus. The Aztec objective was the imposition of tribute upon the native Oaxacan lordships: otherwise, they were left undisturbed. The Spanish Conquest after 1520 was relatively pacific in Oaxaca, with the exception of Pedro de Alvarado's bloody destruction of the rich Mixtec Kingdom of Tututepec on the Pacific coast and the long campaign to reduce the Zapotec communities of the northern highlands.[1]

During the colonial era, the predominance of the central valleys in the political and economic life of Oaxaca was affirmed through the outward-ranging financial and commercial networks of the Spanish merchants resident in the provincial capital. The dye-trade boom from the 1760s to the 1790s considerably improved their position. Oaxaca's cochineal and indigo commanded a broad international market, while its cotton textiles reached northwards beyond Mexico City to the main silver-mining towns of the colony. During the course of the eighteenth century, the economic importance of some of the geographical peripheries of the province increased. This was particularly the case with regard to the Mixteca Alta, where in the Tlaxiaco area a number of merchants had turned to sugar cultivation and refinement, and the northern sierra. In the sierra districts of Ixtepejí,

Ixtlán and Villa Alta, several city merchants began investing in the mining sector, perhaps in response to Bourbon government attempts to break open the monopolies enforced in the dye and textile trades by district administrators acting on behalf of their merchant-financiers. Juárez was born in the tiny village of Guelatao in the vicinity of Ixtlán. This was a different Zapotec world from the central valleys or the Isthmus. While the Oaxaca mining sector could never yield the great profits of Guanajuato, San Luis Potosí or Zacatecas, it did attract capital in the late colonial period and it did give the sierra an atmosphere of upward mobility.[2]

In Oaxaca, ethnicity defined social relations. Indian land retention reinforced ethnic identity. Juárez, however, did not come from an area in which Indian communities possessed substantial tracts of arable and pasture lands. Sierra communities, when able to do so, subsisted more from commerce than from farming. Ixtepejí and Villa Alta, for instance, depended upon the dye and textile trades. Oaxaca's lack of a dominant white landowning caste ensured that the key factors in economic and political life would be the merchants and the district administrators. In parishes where priests existed and commanded respect, they, too, formed part of the structure of authority. In accordance with Spanish colonial law, Indian towns (*pueblos*) possessed their own internal governments and their own civil and religious hierarchies. In some areas, such as the Mixteca Alta, Indian communities contained land worked by individual families or rented to non-Indians, such as the sugar-planters of Tlaxiaco. Many communities in the eighteenth century were transferring communal lands to their religious confraternities, in order to preserve them from acquisitive district administrators. A network of local markets not only linked villages together but also joined them to the wider market and encouraged local specialization.[3]

The rise of non-elite individuals to political predominance in Oaxaca in the decades after Independence resulted from the absence of a racially homogenous and strongly entrenched ruling class in the period after 1820. Leading creole politicians, such as the moderate conservative, José López Ortigoza, governor on several occasions between 1830 and 1846, and Ramón Ramírez de Aguilar, acting governor during the first Liberal years (1833–34), were ecumenical in their attitudes to newcomers. They acted as their patrons and assisted their entry into the lower-level positions of the state administration. Juárez began his rise in precisely that way. His chief associates from the sierra mining zones, Marcos Pérez, Miguel Castro and the Meijueiro family rose during the same period. The importance of the geographical peripheries of Oaxaca in the politics of the post-Independence decades could be seen in the emergence of their leading figures on the provincial stage. Colonel Antonio de León, who had brought Oaxaca into line behind the cause of Independence in 1821, came from the Mixteca Baja: his influence proved decisive at several instances until his heroic death in 1847 in the war against the United States. Similarly, Castro and the Meijueiros dominated the northern sierra and upheld the *juarista* cause until the 1870s.

At first sight the association of Juárez with Liberalism is problematic. He had no intellectual roots in creole politics; he had no educational or family contacts with Independent Mexico's leading reformers. Other prominent Mexicans of Indian origin, such as Tomás Mejía or Manuel Lozada, gravitated towards the Conservative camp. Another Indian, of a later generation, Victoriano Huerta, led the counter-revolutionary regime that followed the murder of Francisco Madero in February 1911. Saturnino Cedillo, the Indian political boss of the state of San Luis Potosí, aspired in the later 1930s to become the General Franco of revolutionary Mexico. Many Indian communities in Mexico had rallied to the Conservative cause during the civil wars of the mid-nineteenth century and a significant number had professed their allegiance to the Emperor Maximilian. The Liberalism of Juárez, then, needs explanation.

Initially, Juárez had been destined by his bookbinder benefactor for a career in the Church, largely on the grounds that a person of his background could expect to attain a position of social distinction only by that route. The reluctant ordinand attended the Seminary College of Oaxaca in the mid-1820s along with other aspirants, usually the sons of respectable city families. At that time, the principal families of Oaxaca in common with their counterparts in the other provinces were in the process of forming the state-level institutions through which they themselves would play the roles of state governors, department authorities, sub-prefects, senators, congressmen, magistrates and senior officials of the judicial and fiscal bureaucracies within the federal system. It seemed as though the prospects for the young Juárez could stretch no further than a country parish, or, at best, a position in a city parish.

. . .

THE INSTITUTE OF SCIENCE AND ARTS

Much has been made in the hagiographical literature of the impassivity of Juárez, but he does not seem at any decisive stage to have accepted his fate impassively. In August, 1828, when the Institute of Sciences and Arts of the State of Oaxaca, a secular college of higher education, was opened under the sponsorship of the moderate liberal state governor, José Ignacio Morales, Juárez withdrew from the seminary college and enrolled. The abandonment of an ecclesiastical career inevitably meant a transfer to law, which, in turn, generally led to politics. In Oaxaca, it also meant passage through a controversial local institution anathematized by the clergy. At the institute, Juárez came under the influence of the brilliant Miguel Méndez, Professor of Logic, Mathematics and Ethics, then the central figure in Oaxacan Liberalism. Méndez (b. 1804) was also a fellow *serrano,* a Zapotec from the highland mining town of Capulalpan, who had been sent by his parents to Oaxaca in order to train for the priesthood. Instead, he had moved to the institute. At his advice, both Juárez and Pérez, who came from Teococuilo, abandoned theology for law. Méndez admired the ideas of the French Revolution. The institute's first director, Fray Francisco Aparicio, a Dominican, had been Morelos's principal supporter among the city clergy during the insurgent occupation of Oaxaca in 1812–14. In that sense, the institute symbolically combined the revolutionary tradition of Morelos with Liberal ideas derived from the Enlightenment and the Spanish Cortes and developed in a Mexican context by Gómez Farías and Zavala. Méndez drew from both these elements. He attracted talented potential reformers to the institute.[4]

In the sharply contested presidential elections of 1828 Méndez championed the cause of Vicente Guerrero, Morelos's heir in the insurgent leadership after 1815. The Oaxaca state legislature, however, supported the candidacy of Manuel Gómez Pedraza, a moderate, who represented the respectable classes and who had fought against the insurgency as a Royalist army officer. This presidential campaign marked Juárez's *prise de conscience.* His support for Guerrero clearly identified him with local Liberals and with the revolutionary inheritance of Morelos. Méndez was elected to the legislature in October 1828 and acted as its president in July 1829, during the period of the Guerrero administration at the national level. Among the Oaxaca elite, the principal figure associated with Liberalism was Ramírez de Aguilar, owner of a seventeenth-century entailed estate and a militia officer who had cooperated with León in 1821. Two years later, he supported León's attempt to establish a Free Sovereign State of Oaxaca. Ramírez de Aguilar was Morales's vice-governor in 1825 and held the governorship from January 1829 until February 1830, roughly corresponding to the duration of the Guerrero administration at the national level. Oaxaca Liberalism, then, cut across the social and ethnic divide: it also included the sons of prominent colonial merchant families, such as Victor Manero Embides and Manuel Iturribarría, and lawyers such as Lope San Germán and Tiburcio Cañas. The state's leading businessmen, José Santiago Hernández and José Joaquín Guergué, however, remained aloof.

Méndez provided the intellectual centre of provincial Liberalism and in his house the younger generation met to argue over ideas. In that way, the Oaxaca Liberal Party was born, the institute its official voice. The party stood for the removal of clerical control of education and for the promotion of secular learning and civic virtue. This early promise, however, came to nothing. The Guerrero administration was overthrown at the end of 1829, and the new proto-Conservative administration of General Anastasio Bustamante began the process of installing sympathetic state governors. By the end of March 1830, Méndez was dead, and the nascent Liberal Party leaderless.[5]

· · ·

THE LIBERAL EXPERIMENT OF 1833–34

The Conservative administration's alienation of moderate opinion encouraged Santa Anna to remove Bustamante in 1832. This turn of events prepared the way for his own election to the presidency in the following year and for his sponsorship of a second Liberal experiment under his Vice-President,

Gómez Farías. In Oaxaca, Ramírez de Aguilar took office again from January 1833 until June 1834, when the Liberal regime collapsed at the national level. During the intervening years, Juárez completed his training as a lawyer and began a political career, first as city councillor and then as state legislator. In 1830 he had become substitute Professor of Physics at the institute, a position that came with a small salary sufficient to pay for the completion of his course in jurisprudence during the following year. He was then able to gain practical experience in the law office of Tiburcio Cañas, who was another product of the institute. Support from Governor López Ortigoza, son of one of the province's wealthiest late colonial merchants, secured his election to the city council for the year 1832. Ramírez de Aguilar sponsored the election of Juárez, at that time secretary of the institute, to the state legislature early in 1833. As a result, Juárez participated directly in the experience of the Gómez Farías regime. Already a substitute magistrate of the State Court of Justice, Juárez took his final law examination in January 1834. That involved the resolution within forty-eight hours of a test case prepared for him by the court. Passing with distinction, he was thereupon authorized to practise in any court of law within the state. Juárez was the first person to receive the official qualification of lawyer in the state of Oaxaca, rather than, as was the traditional custom, from a court outside the state. Juárez's matriculation, then, represented a vindication of the new state institutions established in accordance with the federal Constitution of 1824. In February 1834 he became one of the official magistrates of the State Court.[6]

As a member of the Chamber of Deputies, Juárez worked closely with the governor for the rehabilitation of Guerrero, who had been betrayed to his Conservative enemies and judicially murdered by them in the grounds of the convent of Cuilapan outside the city of Oaxaca in February 1831. Juárez and two of his colleagues proposed that Cuilapan should be renamed Ciudad Guerrero in honour of the Consummator of Independence. Finally, on 12 April 1834, Governor Ramírez de Aguilar provided for the solemn transfer of Guerrero's remains to the Rosary Chapel of Oaxaca's Dominican convent. In the same month, in Mexico City, Guerrero's political heir, Álvarez, initiated legal proceedings against the ministers of the Bustamante regime, allegedly the originators of the crime against Guerrero. From these events two significant elements emerge. First, Juárez's intimate association with the institute did not preclude political alliances with sympathetic notables, whose assistance the small Liberal group needed. Second, the symbolic linkage between Juárez and Guerrero, and thence to Morelos and Hidalgo, was already established. This linkage had a practical aspect, since it extended also in the direction of Álvarez, ever determined to keep central government out of his *cacicazgo* (fiefdom). Álvarez's hatred of the Conservatives made him a potential ally for the southern Liberals.[7]

Writing three decades later, Juárez looked back on the events of 1833–34, as the first steps of the Reform – measures taken, albeit abortively, to diminish the position of the Church in society, which anticipated the more far-reaching decrees of 1855–59. Juárez's identification with the regime of Ramírez de Aguilar makes nonsense of the claim by Francisco Bulnes, writing in 1905, that he had no clear political views, was associated with no political grouping, and acquired his secularizing Liberalism only through association with Melchor Ocampo, anticlerical governor of Michoacán (1846–48; 1852–53) in their common exile in New Orleans during Santa Anna's last regime. Even so, the direction of events in the early 1830s was not as clear at the time as it would seem in retrospect. Ideological lines had not yet been irrevocably drawn and the irreconcilable parties of the late 1850s were not then confronting each other over a widening divide. Army officers, such as Santa Anna, Bustamante or Mariano Paredes Arrillaga, stood above or between parties and factions, and on occasions behind one or other of them to promote a complicated series of goals, partly personal and partly party. Such figures and their lesser counterparts at the provincial and sub-regional levels could count on their own clientele, attached to their person rather than to any particular ideology.[8]

Furthermore, there were a considerable number of figures whose ideas reflected aspects of both Liberalism and Catholicism. One such figure, Canon Florencio del Castillo, had been an early influence on Juárez. He became director of the Oaxaca Institute on several occasions between May 1830 and November 1834. Castillo had represented his native Costa Rica in the Cádiz Cortes, wherein he had worked for the extinction of the Inquisition throughout the Spanish Empire.

As governor of the vacant diocese of Oaxaca, it fell to Castillo, however, to defend the rights of the Church in 1833–34 against increasing state pressure on its financial resources. The rift between the two authorities deepened into open conflict. Castillo firmly opposed attempts by the Gómez Farías administration to subordinate the Church to the state. He rejected the argument that the Mexican sovereign state had legitimately inherited the royal patronage over the Church granted to the Spanish monarchy by the papacy at the time of the discoveries. The conflict in Oaxaca, however, was superseded by Santa Anna's intervention at the national level and the removal of the Liberal administration. In response to those events, León at the head of militia forces from Huajuapan personally loyal to himself took control of the state capital on 21 June 1834 under the terms of the Plan of Cuernavaca, which called for the defence of religion and the corporate prerogatives of Church and army. By September, López Ortigoza was back in power, and in November, the sixth state Congress nullified most of the decrees of its predecessor, the president of which had been Juárez.[9]

. . .

THE CENTRALIST REPUBLIC (1836–46)

Scarcely commented on at all is Juárez's statement that the collapse of the regimes of 1829 and 1833–34 was due to the political immaturity of their partisans. That remark helps to explain his circumspection during the following decades and more especially at the time of the Comonfort administration of 1855–57. For the young Liberal generation of 1834 the extinction of the Gómez Farías regime was an unpleasant and deeply conditioning shock. Juárez was briefly exiled across the Puebla state border to Tehuacán. Thereafter he dedicated himself to his legal practice, but an indication of the unfavourable political atmosphere was the Loxicha affair. The attempt to take up the grievances of this Pacific hinterland village against the parish priest resulted in a further imprisonment for a nine-day period. Most of the other cases that Juárez dealt with in the period concerned the properties and monies of the prominent families of Oaxaca, such as those of Ramírez de Aguilar. By 1838, however, Juárez and other Liberals resumed their ascent through the judicial organs of what had become the Department of Oaxaca.[10]

Although the overthrow of federalism in 1836 and the establishment of a centralist system brought Bustamante to the presidency in the following year, the Oaxaca Liberal circle, though excluded from power as a group, could, nevertheless, count on the presence of several individuals in the principal departmental organs. In April 1838 Juárez, for example, became secretary of the Superior Tribunal of Justice and in December 1839 one of the seven substitute magistrates, re-elected again at the end of 1840. Evidently a well-known Liberal past was not a disqualification. Cañas was the court's president and Pérez one of its secretaries.[11]

It was, in fact, precisely during this time that Juárez delivered a discourse in the city on 16 September 1840 to commemorate the Hidalgo uprising for Independence thirty years previously. His identification with Hidalgo clearly emerged. He distinguished the Spain of the Conquistadores from the Liberal Spain of the Cortes, rejecting along with Hidalgo the former, but embracing the latter. Several notes entered this discourse, however, which revealed the influence of an Oaxacan of the older generation, Carlos María de Bustamante, who had been a close associate of Morelos in the south in 1812–14. Bustamante had always argued that Independence was the reverse of the Conquest, and that thereby the proponents of the new nationhood were the avengers of Moctezuma: a direct continuity existed, then, between the Mexican nation of 1521 and that of 1821. This position Juárez adopted in his discourse of 1840. Spain had maintained its rule over 'our forefathers' partly by superior force and partly by inducing religious belief in the vanquished, so that domination would become venerated as if from God. Consequently, the modern legacy of the colonial era was 'intolerance and fanaticism'. Juárez's discourse upheld the idea of 'nation' as the correct object of veneration. He appealed for loyalty to the nation above private political objectives, so that Mexico should not be the plaything of foreign powers. The speech developed these themes and began to resemble a not very thinly veiled diatribe against all the principles sustaining the clerical-conservative reaction of 1836. Juárez denounced the colonial era as a three-hundred-year period of 'degradation', and contrasted 'the progress of enlightened learning' to the abuse and ignorance of tyranny. He reminded his audience that the Mexican sovereign nation had chosen to become a republic of free men. Accordingly, 'we ought to follow the guidelines of a just and enlightened politics; we ought to remove all obstacles to the free exercise of the rights of man' and reward virtue and merit, disdaining ambition, servility and infamy. His dream was that Mexico should be 'the classic land of honour, moderation, and justice', in which 'the holy tree of liberty will put down the deepest roots'. Existing evidence tells us nothing of responses to this kind of language. It can only be assumed that by 1840 the political climate had moderated.[12]

The lull in political activity provided Juárez, at the age of 37, with the chance to contemplate marriage and raise a family. At the time of his marriage to Margarita Maza he had already been Civil Justice in the First Instance for the previous two years, earning a respectable annual salary of 1,200 pesos. The marriage has been invested with symbolic significance in the hagiographic literature as the union of Indian and European blood, the personification of mestizo nationality. Yet the plain fact was that the illegitimate daughter of an immigrant Genoese merchant was prepared at the age of 17 to contract matrimony with a middle-aged lawyer in political eclipse, a Zapotec from a little-known highland village, who was publicly identified with the Liberal cause.

Antonio Maza had moved from Genoa to Cádiz, where he had married Micaela Yela, a woman from Ronda, though no children had resulted from the marriage. Maza, unaccompanied by his wife, had subsequently transferred his business activities to Oaxaca, where he formed part of the mercantile community. In his will in August 1833, Maza had made provision through the medium of Manuel del Solar Campero for his wife in the event that she might still be alive in Cádiz. Solar Campero had been one of Oaxaca's leading Spanish merchants, but returned to the peninsula after Independence. Maza's choice of Estéban Maqueo as co-executor points to a business connection with a fellow Italian immigrant later to be the partner of Guergué in the purchase of the Cortés estates in the Isthmus of Tehuantepec in 1836. Once in Oaxaca, Maza made the acquaintance of Pertrona Parada and lived with her outside marriage. Again, the evidence tells us nothing of social responses to this situation, which may have been countenanced at this time of questioned traditional values. They had four children, the second of whom, Margarita Eustacia, married Juárez. She must have known Juárez from childhood, since his sister had worked in the household as a cook. The Maza house had been the 12-year-old Benito's destination when he walked down from Guelatao to the city in search of her and escape from his uncle and the life of a shepherd boy.[13]

Under centralism a Department Assembly had replaced the state Congress of the Federal Republic of 1824–36. In October 1843 the electoral committee chose Juárez for one of the substitute positions in the assembly. Again he was not the only Liberal to be associated with a basic institution of centralism. His future collaborator, Colonel Luis Fernández del Campo, was one of its secretaries. Late in May 1844, when death provided a vacancy, the Department Assembly requested Governor León (September 1841 to September 1845), to allow Juárez to fill it. During the governorship of León, the Liberal circle emerged from the wilderness. León's capture of power in 1841 corresponded to Santa Anna's regime of 1841–44 at the national level, following the removal of Bustamante in a rebellion of the three generals, Paredes Arrillaga, Valencia and Santa Anna.[14]

It has been said, by Bulnes among others, that León was Santa Anna's 'proconsul' in Oaxaca. The clear implication – that Juárez would collaborate with anyone in order to hold office – has no foundation. In the first place, León had led the federalist movement in 1823, which had proclaimed the Free Sovereign State of Oaxaca. In that enterprise, one of his close allies had been Ramírez de Aguilar. In April 1828 León had founded the Yorkist branch of the masonic order in Oaxaca, a series of lodges usually identified with radical Liberalism and federalism. When Guerrero took office at the national level in 1829, León once more became Military Commander of the State. When a section of the military, led by General Valentín Canalizo, who had been implicated in the execution of Guerrero, attempted in 1833–34 to overthrow the second Ramírez de Aguilar regime in the state, León refused to cooperate. In that way, he contributed to the collapse of the rebellion in the name of Religion and Corporate Privilege, which formed part of an attempt to bring down Gómez Farías. León's two interventions in 1834 and 1841 mitigated the impact of centralism in Oaxaca.

The León family's influence derived from herds of migrant goats in the Mixteca Baja in the west of the state, with the focus in the town of Huajuapan. León does not appear to have had political ambitions at the national level. During the period 1821–47 he remained one of Oaxaca's most influential figures. The probability is that, as the Santa Anna regime disintegrated, León needed to broaden his political base, in order to attempt to survive the impending crisis. The influence of his son, José María, a colleague of Juárez in the Supreme Tribunal of Justice, seems to have secured the latter's selection in 1844 as secretary to the governor. During the year that he held this office, Juárez presided over a definitive reorganization of the state judiciary.[15]

At virtually every decisive stage of Mexican politics during the nineteenth century the interrelation of provincial and national events is apparent. Recurrent destabilization of political life at the national level, and its repercussions in the provinces, ensured that governments, whatever the ideology they professed, would be weak. They were generally unable to enforce their authority over large areas of national territory. The First Federal Republic had broken down in 1836 because of its inability to raise sufficient tax resources to sustain itself. Resolute opposition within the elites to direct taxation had been the principal cause. Given the economic dislocation following the War of Independence, the state was poorer and less effective than it had been in the late colonial era. The country itself, in spite of the general contraction of its economic activities from the 1810s, was not poor, and certainly a number of wealthy merchant-financiers, such as the Escandón family, were able to extend their influence over a large sphere. Governments, however, found themselves unable to tap this wealth, and, as a result, they became increasingly reliant upon credits from such sources. Future tax revenues, generally from the sales tax, the tobacco revenue or customs duties, were mortgaged as guarantee of repayment of loans. The Mexican state's default on the two London loans of 1824 had ensured that no further credits were available abroad. In the mean time, an internal and external debt mounted with every year.[16]

National government poverty combined with repeated instability to provide opportunities for local communities to maintain whatever gains they had made at the expense of the official power during the insurgency of the 1810s, to assert their rights, and to recover what had been previously lost. During the Centralist era (1836–46), however, this position began to alter. Although the Centralist Republic proved in the long run to be no more capable of putting national finances on a sound footing than the execrated federalist predecessor, its leading figures, Mexico's principal military politicians and businessmen, did lend support, where they could, to local proprietors anxious to assert control over lands they considered to be their properties, push back village claims, and to subordinate the free, peasant labour force. The impact of such pressures was felt at its maximum in areas which produced a commodity with significant market demand and high value. This occurred in the case of the vanilla-producing district of Papantla in the Veracruz coastal zone and in the broad belt of sugar cultivation stretching from Cuernavaca and Cuautla in the west across to Putla in western Oaxaca. Sugar-producers were attempting to expand at the expense of the peasant communities at a time of increased central government efforts after 1842 to establish a uniform direct tax known as the capitation. Local and outside pressures at the same time combined to inflame opposition into outright rebellion in many such areas during the mid-1840s, and the official power at both national and departmental levels found it difficult to deal with so many outbreaks. Furthermore, the resistance movements in the south were located perilously close to the territory under the control of Álvarez. Always an opponent of centralism, Álvarez played a double game: on the one hand, he acted as responsible broker between dissident peasant villages and the official power, while, on the other hand, he sought to exploit the widespread discontent, in order to destabilize the regime of Santa Anna. These activities formed a major part of the events which brought about the collapse of the regime and its replacement in December 1844 by a moderate liberal administration under General José Joaquín de Herrera, with whom Juárez greatly sympathized.[17]

The political transformation in Mexico City ultimately made León's position in Oaxaca untenable. On 2 September 1845 he handed over power to Juárez's associate, Fernández del Campo. The apparent drift towards Liberalism and possibly even a restoration of federalism was halted by the seizure of power by Paredes Arrillaga in Mexico City in January 1846.

Herrera had tried at all costs to stave off an impending conflict with the United States over the annexation of the independent Texas Republic, still claimed by Mexico. Paredes, for his part, was anxious to employ the Mexican army not on the frontier with Texas, but for the purpose of installing a military dictatorship in Mexico, a strongly centralist system which might at some stage be presided over by a monarch drawn from one of the European Catholic royal families. Paredes sought to dispense altogether with the political parties, which he saw as the cause of the country's disastrous national history. The war with the USA, however, brought about the collapse of Paredes's policies and led to the recall of Santa Anna, who began preparations for resisting invasion. Santa Anna took power in August 1846 in alliance with Gómez Farías, national leader of the Liberal Party, a situation which augured a repetition of the events of 1833–34. With the disintegration of the Centralist Republic, the federal Constitution of 1824 was restored in the same month.[18]

. . .

THE RESTORATION OF FEDERALISM IN 1846

The Oaxaca garrison adhered to the federal movement and on the collapse of the Paredes regime the Department Assembly dissolved itself. The outgoing members appointed a 'junta of notables', which, in turn, designated a 'legislative committee' that took office on 11 August. This body was entrusted with the institutional transfer to federalism. One of its first actions was to appoint a triumvirate to exercise executive power in the newly restored state. These three men were Fernández del Campo, José Simeón de Arteaga, one of the institute's professors, and Juárez.

Strictly speaking this transitional body, which derived its position ultimately from a garrison rebellion, was illegal. The morality of the political transition troubled liberal politicians greatly, since they were anxious to legalize their return to power as quickly as possible and thereby create lasting institutions which could give effect to their policies. With the formal restoration of federalism in Oaxaca on 22 August, the matter of legitimacy became vital, since the Oaxaca State Constitution of 1825 recognized as legal only civil governments that had come to power as a result of elections. The impasse was broken, however, by executive action at the federal level. President Mariano Salas ordered Arteaga to assume the state governorship. With the dissolution of the 'legislative committee' on 11 September, Arteaga formally took office. He wasted little time before appointing Juárez President of the State Court of Justice.[19]

With the restoration of federalism, Juárez for the first time moved beyond the provincial sphere to the national Congress. In the elections for federal deputies, he was one of the seven Liberals who formed the majority of the state's ten deputies. This federal Congress appointed Santa Anna interim President and, in his absence on campaign, authorized Gómez Farías to form an administration. Arteaga wrote a letter of introduction for Juárez in November 1846 to present to Gómez Farías after arrival in Mexico City. In this letter he described Juárez as a thorough-going federalist and Liberal. At this time he also made the acquaintance of Mariano Otero, then the principal intellectual figure of moderate Liberalism. Although in a minority in Congress, the Liberal group managed to push through a controversial wartime measure. This provided for the auction of ecclesiastical properties to the total value of 15 million pesos, in order to raise funds for the continuation of the war. The decree, passed on 11 January 1847, provoked the *polko* clerical rebellion in Mexico City. A parallel rebellion took place in the city of Oaxaca and led to the removal of Governor Arteaga on 15 February, and his replacement by Guergué. This insurrection also sought to undermine the position of the Oaxaca deputies in the federal Congress, who had voted for the decree. According to Arteaga, the 'mob', rushing through the streets crying, 'Long Live Religion and Death to the Heretics', had been egged on by army officers. Ramírez de Aguilar, Governor of the Central District at that time, had been forced to flee to the safety of the Augustinian convent.[20]

The *polko* regime in Oaxaca provided only the meagre sum of 350 pesos each for the full expenses of the federal deputies. Juárez complained acerbicly on two occasions and asked why the state treasurer claimed to have no available funds, when Oaxaca had not actually been invaded by enemy forces:

> the explanation is because the present Oaxaca deputies protested in the body of the congress, as was their duty, against the scandalous sedition of 15 February, when the legitimate authorities in the state were overthrown – events in which you yourself played such a significant role and which resulted in the administration which drove Arteaga from office and which you now serve.

He continued in the same vein,

> Is it because we the deputies here have not prostituted our principles and forfeited our dignity by recognising as legitimate an administration we have by our vote in congress condemned as illegitimate? Or is it because the administration wants to demonstrate that only the wealthy classes should be allowed to represent the nation, and thereby enable the realisation of the anti-national policy begun during the disastrous administration of General Paredes?[21]

Such remarks foreshadow the stance taken by Juárez during the early stages of the *Reforma* in the mid-1850s.

In Oaxaca, a military intervention removed the *polko* regime and transferred power back to the Liberal group. José María Castellanos, commander of the city garrison, took as his authorization the federal Congress's decree of 11 May, referred to by Juárez, which had declared the *polko* administration in the state illegal. For the second time, then, Liberal military had acted to install politicians of their party. The latter's task, then, was to find some way of legitimizing an action, which in principle they condemned. Liberalism frequently benefited, however, from actions by its military sympathizers. The history of Spain and Spanish America from the 1820s amply testified to that. Pérez, first magistrate of the Supreme Court, became acting governor on 23 October 1847. Pérez used his position to reconvene the state legislature, which on 29 October designated Juárez governor of Oaxaca.[22]

. . .

STATE GOVERNOR OF OAXACA (1847–52)

Technically, Pérez was the first state governor of Indian origin. He and Juárez were the first Indians to rule in Oaxaca since the time of Cosijoeza, the last Zapotec king, in the 1520s. Their reflections on this matter do not appear to have survived. They may not, perhaps, have seen their position in quite that light. Few mid-nineteenth-century Mexican Liberals had any serious interest in the pre-Columbian past and scarcely any sympathy with the distinct ethno-cultural traditions of the Indian communities, which formed the overwhelming majority of the inhabitants of states such as Oaxaca, Chiapas or Yucatán. Pérez and Juárez were first and foremost Liberals rather than Indians. Apart from the brief introductory remarks of the *Apuntes, para mis hijos,* there seem to be no further references by Juárez to Zapotec origins or to any distinct political consciousness derived from them. On the contrary, everything that Juárez and the Liberal circle stood for militated against such an identification. Their aim was the integration of all corporate entities and distinct linguistic groups into one common civic identity within a nation-state governed as a republic in accordance with the principles of sovereignty of the people, equality before the law, representation according to population, and supremacy of the civil power.[23]

In spite of these high-minded principles, the accession of Juárez remained highly irregular. Nevertheless, as interim governor, Juárez's initial proclamation stated that 'the free and spontaneous vote of the representatives of the people has raised me to the first magistracy of the state'. In effect, he attributed his position not to the military intervention which had removed the *polkos* but to the actions of the reconvened state legislature. He appealed for general support on the basis of a clean record in judicial and administrative service:

> dedicated to the public service for many years here in Oaxaca, I am already known for constant application, a passionate love of liberty, and a determination to uphold the rights of man. Do not fear, then, that the immense power placed in my hands today will either be transformed into the instrument of your oppression or be used in order to give favour to any family, party, or class.

In his address to Congress, Juárez maintained that power held no intrinsic attraction for him and that he was not the candidate of any faction or interest group. Not until 12 August 1848 did Juárez formally take office as constitutionally elected state governor. The interim period lasted ten months. The elections gave him a four-year term due to end on 12 August 1852. There was no guarantee, given past experience, that he or any other governor would survive that long.[24]

Elections for the national Senate had been held under the federal electoral law of 3 June 1847, which reflected the principles established in the Constitution of 1824. President Herrera's decree of 2 September 1848 used this law as the basis for elections within the states; accordingly, Juárez twelve days later called for elections in Oaxaca. The method was the indirect, or tier, system, inherited from the Cádiz Constitution of 1812, a provision that owed its origins to the French Revolutionary Constitution of 1791. All Mexicans by birth or naturalization had the right to vote if they were 20 years of age or over (and male), 'providing they had an honest means of livelihood and had not been condemned under the criminal law for any ignominious crime'. After the primary stage at parish level, electors would then convene in the district head towns in order to choose the final representatives. The Senate in September 1848 consisted of six members, at least two of them lawyers, one an entailed property-owner, and another a cleric, Bernardino Carvajal, who was a leading Liberal and personal friend of Juárez. There were ten congressmen, at least half of them leaders of the Liberal Party, including Miguel Castro, Manuel Iturribarría, who had been a federal deputy along with Juárez in 1846–47, Estéban Calderón and José María Díaz Ordaz. The majority of congressmen were members of the legal profession. The legislative branch, then, consisted of sixteen individuals and an equivalent number of substitutes. There were seven ministers of the Court of Justice, eight Department Governors, some twenty Sub-Prefects of the districts and thirty-eight Justices of the First Instance. The governor had a cabinet of four individuals. In political terms, this small group of men constituted the regime, which sought to preside over the destinies of more than half-a-million inhabitants, most of whom were probably unaware of or indifferent to their existence.[25]

The elections of 1848 provided the Juárez administration with the legitimacy it sought. That in itself, however, reflected the liberal constitutionalist view of the Oaxaca world. Beyond this limited group the authority of the state government and the principles of the Liberal order were neither universally accepted nor obeyed. It was one thing to satisfy the scruples of constitutionalists, but quite another to enforce compliance with the new form of law. The aim of Juárez was to inculcate a popular awareness of the obligations required of the citizen by the civil authorities and of the advantages that could accrue thereby. This he sought to do primarily by moral example and through changes in institutions. For the long-term strategy, he saw lay primary education as the means of transforming a society primordially loyal to corporate and ethnic identities, kinship ties, and patron–client networks into one consisting of citizens undertaking their civic obligations in a republic. The attainment of such an objective would require an extraordinary use of state power, far beyond the resources available to government at that time, especially in view of repeated popular resistance to taxation. It presupposed a single-minded readiness to view the world through the perspectives of Liberal ideology, rather than in accordance with contemporary realities. Against these stood the laicizing Liberal group, which proposed to transform the political culture of Oaxaca through the medium of the laws and representative institutions created under the terms of the state Constitution of 1825.[26]

The immediate requirement of the new governing group was for an armed force capable of giving effect to its political decisions. One of the first actions of the triumvirate of 1846 had been the decree of 12 August for the establishment of a National Guard battalion in the city of Oaxaca in anticipation of the restoration of federalism. A civil militia had originally been projected under the federal Constitution of 1824, and derived as an idea from the Cádiz Cortes. It was to be the state government's instrument for the defence of the federal system and the representative institutions associated with it. State-level politicians had seen in the militia a counter-balance to the regular army. For that reason army commanders disliked it from the start. The war with the United States made the reconstitution of a state-level force imperative. Governor Juárez saw the National Guard as a means of defence from within the states against the national ambitions of military leaders. Furthermore, the National Guard, as the instrument of the state government, had an important internal function as well: the maintenance of order as defined by the political authorities.[27]

Relative to the state population, the available armed force

remained puny. On taking office, Juárez reported that the National Guard in his state consisted of no more than some 300 ill-disciplined men, even though the threat of US military action still remained. The decree of 30 October 1847 set about remedying this state of affairs, in the first place by strengthening the significantly named Guerrero Battalion. By July 1848 this consisted of 410 men. At the same time Juárez organized armed companies in outlying districts where state government control continued to be weak, in Tehuantepec, where the situation was rapidly deteriorating, Pochutla, Tlaxiaco, Huajuapan, Teotitlán and Tuxtepec. The importance that he attached to the National Guard could be seen by his establishment of a hospital for guardsmen early in 1848. In the state budget estimates for 1849, the estimated cost of the Guard came to 94,468 pesos, that is between one-quarter and one-third of the state revenue. By May 1849 there were said to be 761 men under arms and a further 2,512 available for prompt service. Juárez implemented in Oaxaca President Herrera's regulations of July 1848 imposing on all citizens the obligation to enlist in the militia, with the sole exception of certain specified occupations.[28]

Juárez intended to base his government on what he hoped would be an effective and steadily expanding armed power exclusively loyal to the regime. At the same time, he undertook to honour the state's obligation to supply a requisite number of recruits for the federal army. His particular fear was the continued presence in the state of a federally appointed Commander-General with regular forces at his disposition. The governor regarded this office as a potential instrument in the hands of ambitious army politicians who might use such a force to overthrow the federal system and representative institutions. He feared that unscrupulous officers, whether through opposition to Liberal principles or for personal motives, might exploit the deepening tensions in the Isthmus in an attempt to bring down his regime. Juárez distrusted General José María Malo, in particular, since he had been one of the leading *polkos*; he had included him in his cabinet in order to watch over him. He requested the federal government to remove Malo from the state and to abolish the office of Commander-General for good. Although willing to remove Malo and appoint Castellanos, the national government balked at abolition, since relations with the USA remained unsettled. Even so, Malo had to be forced from office in November 1847.[29]

Juárez was fortunate in having federal government backing for his position, especially since Castellanos, until his death from cholera in 1851 while on campaign in the Isthmus, proved to be a mainstay of the Liberal regime. Castellanos stood by Juárez's decision to refuse Santa Anna, in flight from his enemies, entry into the state in March 1848. The administration feared that the perennial adventurer's presence in the city would stimulate army commanders into supporting an attempt to use Oaxaca as a base for recovering power and create the same havoc there that happened during his previous intervention in 1828. Santa Anna later commented, 'That little Indian has not forgiven me for waiting on me barefoot when I was in Oaxaca in 1828'. Juárez could count on Castellanos to sustain his position, but that resulted not from the nature of the office but from the loyalty of one individual. For this reason Juárez continued to argue for the abolition of the office. Since, as he saw it, few military commanders had been prepared to guarantee 'the inviolability of democratic institutions', he regarded his own position as highly vulnerable to military intervention. In his view, army commanders founded their ambitions on the 'absence of republican virtues and any substantial enlightenment among the majority of our society'.[30]

Even so, Juárez survived his full term of office, in spite of the fact that the years 1847–52 were among the most turbulent in Oaxaca's history, not least because of the crisis in the Isthmus. Part of the explanation for Juárez's uninterrupted four years lay in the fact that some form of military power reinforced his civil authority, even though armed force was not necessarily always effective. At least, it was continuous. This element, however, has generally been overlooked. That is not to argue that Juárez was ever the tool of any army or militia commander or the candidate of any military faction. However, it is to say that the self-styled defender of the supremacy of the civil power, the wearer of the lawyer's frock-coat, was careful at all stages of his career to ensure that his position was sustained by available armed contingents and loyal commanders. Perhaps Juárez's own self-portrayal as the incarnation of legality has obscured these deeper calculations, whether intentionally or accidentally. Castellanos, in fact, held office as acting governor during Juárez's three short absences from the capital. Similarly, the support of Fernández del Campo (briefly governor from 21 January to 4 February 1853) and Ignacio Mejía, Senator in 1851 and successor to Juárez from 16 August 1852 until his overthrow on 17 January 1853, was vital in upholding the Liberal regime. When Juárez himself departed for the Isthmus, in order to attempt a final settlement of the turmoil there, he took a body of troops with him. Similarly, when he left Mexico City at the end of December 1855 to take up appointment as governor of Oaxaca for the second time, following the termination of his period as Minister of Justice and Ecclesiastical Affairs, he was accompanied by a small force placed as his disposal by President Ignacio Comonfort.[31]

. . .

THE CRISIS IN THE ISTHMUS

Two measures gravely aggravated social tensions in Oaxaca. They were symptomatic of the general developments at the national level in the aftermath of Independence. In 1825 the federal government, anxious for revenue, sold the state monopoly of the salt deposits of the Isthmus Pacific coast to a private individual, Francisco Javier Echeverría. Local Zapotec, Chontal and Zoque communities depended upon the trade in salt for income, especially since the dye trade was in decline. This revenue helped them to maintain their economic freedom. In 1836 the situation in the southern Isthmus worsened, when the eight livestock estates originally founded by Hernán Cortés were sold to Guergué and Maqueo. These new proprietors were particularly concerned to define the legal status of lands disputed with the neighbouring communities. By the early 1840s tensions reached boiling point. National politics at that time entered a disastrous period of turmoil, which resulted in the loss of effective control over the Isthmus by the national government.[32]

Lower socio-ethnic groups in Oaxaca and elsewhere in the Republic were ready and able to exploit national-level crises and factional state-level politics, in order to promote their own objectives. The widespread popular rebellions of the 1840s and 1850s amply demonstrated this. During these decades popular mobilization reached a scale not seen since the insurgency of the 1810s. In contrast to the decade of the Wars of Independence, however, no national leadership was available to coordinate the localized rebellions. National and provincial administrations dealt with them as best they could, which was not very well, since factionalism disrupted all levels of government. Spontaneous localized movements were able to take root and ineffective government repression ensured in several cases a long duration. Such was the case with regard to the rebellions across the Puebla–Oaxaca border, particularly in the Tlapa-Chilapa-Putla zone in 1842–44. Land conflicts in the sugar belt from Cuernavaca to Izúcar between peasant communities and expanding plantations reflected earlier conflict in the 1780s and foreshadowed later struggles from the 1890s to the 1930s. Of similarly long duration was the conflict in the Isthmus.[33]

Commercial agriculture had developed in the Tehuantepec zone early in the colonial period. Indian communities constantly regarded European ranchers as intruders and violators of their traditional rights. The crisis in the Isthmus assumed national importance, when Santa Anna in 1842 awarded a concession to José Garay, a businessman associated with the regime, to construct either a railway or a canal from the Gulf to the Pacific Ocean. Juárez inherited the problem of the Isthmus in 1847. Although a Zapotec himself, Juárez came from a different culture and a distinct linguistic group from the Isthmus Zapotecs. Accordingly, no necessary identification existed between them. The new Liberal administration rapidly discovered that it could not enforce payment of the capitation tax in the Isthmus. Pérez, who became Sub-Prefect of Petapa in August 1849, complained of a concerted opposition to the tax throughout the area. In his view, the inhabitants of Petapa, Tehuantepec and Juchitán viewed the state government's fiscal needs with the 'utmost indifference'. The situation in the Isthmus became the most formidable test of the Juárez administration. It exposed to the full the precarious nature of state authority in an area where central government control had traditionally been weak.[34]

The *polko* rebellion in the city of Oaxaca provided the opportunity for outright rebellion in the Isthmus. A leader of military expertise and political cunning emerged: José Gregorio Meléndez, locally known as 'Che Gorio Melendre', played a major part in the politics of Juchitán and

Tehuantepec until poisoned in 1853. The rebellion of 1847 took place when US forces were still campaigning on Mexican territory. Governor Juárez saw the danger immediately, in view of US designs on the Isthmus transit route, and sought to defuse the conflict before it escalated further. Instead, he experienced defeat and humiliation. He encountered a situation that would not yield to his particular combination of principle and flexibility. Juárez had no roots in the Isthmus and no personal experience of its politics. He made serious miscalculations. He appointed Meléndez Colonel of the Tehuantepec National Guard, with the specified object of repelling any US invasion force. At the same time, he made Máximo R Ortiz, bitter personal enemy of Meléndez, interim Department Governor. Juárez's motives were complex. He wanted to distance the state government from the private business interests in the Isthmus, neutralize Meléndez by giving him office, and play him off against Ortiz. None of these aims succeeded. Meléndez and Ortiz had their own specific objectives in local politics, and both adopted a hostile stance towards Juárez and the central valley politicians. Thereupon, Juárez dispatched an armed force into the area in December 1847.[35]

The Juárez administration found itself caught in the middle. On the one hand, it sought to uphold the law and thereby the rights of private property. On the other hand, it attributed the cause of the rebellion to the new property administrators' high-handed enforcement of their claims. Juárez remained determined to prevent what he described as a 'terrifying caste war'. For that reason, he took his stand on the principle of enforcement of the law. That implied the use of armed force to impose a solution on the Isthmus. In the mean time, the degenerating situation there was destabilizing politics in the state capital. The violence that accompanied Meléndez's rebellion in Juchitán in March 1850 explained Juárez's decision to send down a second military expedition on 19 May. He had reluctantly concluded that the *juchitecos* had mistaken leniency for weakness: 'I can condone offences committed against my person, but it is not at my discretion to allow the dignity of government to be insulted with impunity and that it should become the object of mockery and jeering by the insolent'. As if to justify further its intervention, the state government portrayed the *juchitecos* as drunken vagrants, thieves, contrabandists and tax-dodgers. A three-hour battle took place in the outskirts of Juchitán, during the course of which a section of the town's houses, normally with thatched palm roofs, caught alight in the rifle and artillery fire. The military intervention cut short the rebellion.[36]

Eight months later, Meléndez issued a Plan calling for the separation of the Isthmus from the state of Oaxaca. He denounced the 'war of desolation' inflicted by the official power on the *juchitecos.* Juárez expressed his intention to 'terminate the custom of compromising with criminality and vice'. After a rebel attack on a government detachment stationed in Ixtaltepec and the murder of the Sub-Prefect, the federal government authorized Juárez to deliver the 'final blow'. Castellanos led the third expedition into the Isthmus that November. The outbreak of cholera, however, aborted operations and led to the death of Castellanos and the disintegration of government forces. Meléndez, unexpectedly saved, issued a second Plan on 10 January 1851.[37]

Anxious to resolve the crisis, Juárez secured congressional authorization on 13 September 1851 to proceed to Tehuantepec in person. Once again he attempted a policy of conciliation. For a time, this appeared to work. As soon as he returned to the capital, however, Ortiz joined forces with Meléndez and renewed operations. Juárez vacated office at the expiry of his constitutional term on 12 August 1852 with the situation in the Isthmus still unresolved. After a short interlude, his political associate, Ignacio Mejía, took office. The rebellion of Ortiz and Meléndez, however, gained unexpected momentum from the rebellion of disaffected Conservative interests in Jalisco against the moderate Liberal administration of General Mariano Arista in Mexico City. The Plan of Jalisco on 20 October 1852 led to a movement for the return of Santa Anna to power. The extension of the Jalisco movement left the Liberal administration in Oaxaca increasingly isolated. Accordingly, the Isthmus rebels declared in favour of the military revolt. Mejía sent the Military Commander of Oaxaca, General Ignacio Martínez Pinillos, to check them. Martínez Pinillos, who was in no way committed to Liberalism, found himself cornered by the rebels in Tehuantepec. Accordingly, when the Arista administration collapsed on 5 January 1853, Pinillos defected to the rebel camp and proclaimed the Plan of Jalisco.[38]

Juárez's warnings concerning the unreliability of military commanders in the state had proved accurate. Pinillos, at the head of rebel forces, marched on the city of Oaxaca. The state Congress on 4 February had little option but to recognize him as interim governor. In Tehuantepec, Meléndez formally recognized Santa Anna as 'General-in-Chief of the Army of Liberation'. When Santa Anna resumed office in Mexico City, the decree of 29 May 1853 created the Federal Territory of the Isthmus of Tehuantepec, separate from the state of Oaxaca. The Oaxaca Liberals had been powerless to prevent the overthrow of the regime established in October 1847 and the dismemberment of the state by the national government. In terms of provincial politics, the unresolved crisis in the Isthmus contributed to that. The consequence of the return of Santa Anna and the establishment of the Pinillos regime in Oaxaca was the dispersal of the Liberal group and their counterparts elsewhere in the Republic. Juárez was arrested on 27 May 1853, his third arrest so far. Escorted to Jalapa, the state capital of Veracruz, he was banished from the Republic on 5 October, and remained in exile in New Orleans until 20 June 1855.

Juárez's failure in the Isthmus stemmed from three causes: his misunderstanding of the real intentions of dissident leaders, his underestimation of the intensity of community hostility to the private business interests and to government interference, and to the contradictions inherent in the nature of Oaxacan Liberalism.Liberals sought unsuccessfully to balance the interests of entrepreneurs in the name of progress with those of the peasant-artisan villages in the name of justice. Here, too, the contradictions in Juárez's personality and political position were also revealed. At one and the same time he identified with individual enterprise and community autonomy, obedience to the law and Indian advancement. He strove to cut a way through these contradictions. However, his defence of the law exposed him to the charge of using the armed power of the state, disguised as law, to promote the interests of private parties. From such a dilemma there could be no successful outcome. Although Juárez's survival in office between 1847 and 1852 bore witness to his political skills, he was unable to dominate events. It proved to be more a question of tacking a way through them, in order to avoid sinking altogether. His efforts to defuse the crisis in the Isthmus had met with failure, because the issues were too long-standing and the conflicts already far too advanced for one administration to cope with them, however well-intentioned. Nevertheless, Juárez learned a great deal from the experience of his first governorship. He learned, in particular, how to avoid dangerous errors, and who to trust and who not to trust. Many of the techniques of politics learned the hard way in the Isthmus were applied more successfully by Juárez at the national level.

In less than twenty years, Juárez had risen from the position of student at the Oaxaca Institute to become governor of the state. National political circumstances were for the most part not conducive to such a rise, as the eclipse during the years 1834 to 1841 testified. The young Juárez identified with the nascent Liberal Party from its inception. He formed part of a circle of friends and political allies, several of whom, such as Mejía and Castro, remained with him throughout his national career, the former as Minister of War after 1867 and the latter as governor of Oaxaca and principal monitor of local affairs. He had broken with the indigenous world in which his family had lived. He had adopted the world-view of the Hispanic city of Oaxaca and pursued a career in the professions with remarkable success. That is not to say, however, that he had rejected the Indian population from which he sprang. His efforts on behalf of Loxicha testified to that. He saw Indian interests, though, through Liberal eyes. He identified not with the defence of village perspectives, community institutions and local religious practices, but with the attempts of Hidalgo, Morelos and Guerrero to construct a Mexican sovereign state on liberal, republican principles out of a Spanish colony founded upon Indian realms and governed for nearly three hundred years in accordance with the precepts of monarchical absolutism.

. . .

NOTES AND REFERENCES

1. See Whitecotton Joseph W 1977 *The Zapotecs: Princes, Priests, and Peasants.* Norman, University of Oklahoma Press. Spores Ronald 1984 *The Mixtecs in Ancient and Colonial Times*, Norman, University of Oklahoma Press. Chance John K 1989 *Conquest of the Sierra: Spaniards and Indians in Colonial Oaxaca.* Norman, University of Oklahoma Press.

2. Hamnett Brian R 1971 *Politics and Trade in Southern Mexico 1750–1821.* Cambridge University Press, pp. 41–94.
3. Taylor William B 1972 *Landlord and Peasant in Colonial Oaxaca.* Stanford University Press, CA. Beals Ralph 1975 *The Peasant Marketing System of Oaxaca, Mexico.* University of California Press. Chance John K 1978 *Race and Class in Colonial Oaxaca.* Stanford University Press, CA.
4. Sánchez Juan (1902) 1972 *Vida literaria de Benito Juárez.* Mexico City, UNAM (Universidad Nacional Autónoma de México), pp. 6–8. Fernández Ruiz Jorge 1986 *Juárez y sus contemporáneos.* Mexico City, p. 28
5. Sierra Justo (1905–06) 1948 *Juárez: Su obra y su tiempo.* Mexico City, UNAM, pp. 51–52.
6. Tamayo Jorge L (1964–72) (ed.) *Benito Juárez: Documentos, discursos y correspondencia.* 15 vols, Mexico City, Secretaria del Patrimonio Nacional, 1, pp. 107, 382–95. Hereafter cited as *BJDOCS.*
7. BEO CMMG vol. 72, Ramón Ramírez de Aguilar, Oaxaca, 12 April 1834.
8. *BJDOCS* 1, pp. 107, 109. Bulnes Francisco (1905) 1967 *Juárez y las revoluciones de Ayutla y de la reforma.* Mexico City, pp. 104–11.
9. Berruezo María Teresa 1986 *La participación americana en las Cortes de Cádiz (1810–1814).* Madrid, pp. 194–200. BEO CMMG vol. 39, Castillo, Oaxaca, 15 July 1834.
10. *BJDOCS* 1, pp. 81, 109–33. Fernández Ruiz, *Juárez y sus contemporáneos,* pp. 32–33.
11. *BJDOCS* 1, pp. 397–400, 475–84.
12. Mendieta Alatorre Angeles 1972 *Margarita Maza de Juárez: Antología, iconografía y efemérides.* Mexico City, pp. 68–70. Velasco Pérez Carlos 1986 *Margarita Maza de Juárez: Primera dama de la nación.* Oaxaca, p. 113.
13. Archivo de Notarías (Oaxaca) Protocolos de Francisco Mariscal (Centro), no. 458, ff. 114–117, Oaxaca, 3 August 1833.
14. Noriega Elío Cecilia 1987 *El Constituyente de 1842.* Mexico City, UNAM, pp. 34, 41.
15. Bulnes *Juárez y las revoluciones* pp. 104–11. Tamayo, Jorge L 1947 *El General Antonio de León: Defensor del Molino del Rey.* Mexico City, pp. 26–27.
16. Tenenbaum Barbara 'El poder de las finanzas y las finanzas del poder en México durante el siglo XIX', *Siglo XIX,* ano III, no. 5 (enero–junio 1988), pp. 197–221.
17. Reina Leticia 1980 *Las rebeliones campesinas de México (1819–1906).* Mexico City, Siglo XXI, pp. 83–120. Tutino John 1986 *From Insurrection to Revolution in Mexico: Social Bases of Agrarian*

Violence, 1750–1940. Princeton University Press, NJ, pp. 215–58. Hart John M 'The 1840s Southwest Mexico Peasants' War: Conflict in a Transitional Society' in Katz Friedrich (ed.) 1988 *Riot, Rebellion and Revolution: Rural Social Conflict in Mexico.* Princeton University Press, NJ, pp. 249–68.

18. Urías Margarita 'Militares y comerciantes en México 1830–1846' in Florescano Enrique (ed.) 1985 *Orígenes y desarrollo de la burguesía en América Latina 1700–1955.* Mexico City, Siglo XXI, pp. 73–103.
19. Archivo del Estado de Oaxaca (AGEO) Fondo Juárez (FJ) I/13744, Juárez to Arteaga, Oaxaca, 13 September 1846.
20. *BJDOCS* 1, pp. 147, 149, 1085. Costeloe Michael P 'The Mexican Church and the Rebellion of the Polkos' *HAHR* 46, 2 (May 1966), pp. 170–78.
21. AGEO FJ I/13744, exp. A7a, Alcance al no. 29 de *La Voz Popular*: Juárez to J M Núñez, Oaxaca, 16 September 1847.
22. Ibid. exp. 7a *El Espíritu de la Independencia* I, no. 8, 28 October 1847.
23. Until the time of Manuel Orozco y Berra and José Fernando Ramírez, both of whom served the empire of Maximilian, C M Bustamante remained an exception.
24. AGEO FJ I/13744 Juárez to Oaxaqueños, 29 October 1847.
25. AGEO FJ 10/13788 *La Crónica: Periódico del Gobierno del Estado Libre de Oaxaca* I, no. 24, 1 September 1848.
26. Guerra François-Xavier 1985 *Le Mexique: De L'Ancien Régime à la Révolution.* 2 vols, Paris, Publications de la Sorbonne, I, pp. 166, 174, 184–85, 225, 273–74; II, pp. 305–11.
27. AGEO FJ 3/13746, decree of 12 August 1846.
28. Juárez Benito 1848 *Exposición al Congreso del Estado.* Oaxaca, pp. 29–30, nos 25, 28, 30. Juárez Benito 1849 *Exposición al Congreso del Estado.* Oaxaca, no. 29.
29. Juárez *Exposición* (1848), pp. 6–9.
30. Ibid.
31. *BJDOCS* 1, pp. 237–45.
32. Juárez *Exposición* (1848) pp. 9–10. Reina Leticia (et al) 1988 *Historia de la cuestión agraria mexicana: Estado de Oaxaca.* 2 vols, Mexico City. Juan Pablos Editor S A, I, pp. 181–267.
33. Bustamante Carlos María de (1845) 1986 *Apuntes para la historia del General D. Antonio López de Santa Anna.* Mexico City, Fondo de Cultura Económica, pp. 58, 236.
34. Garay J de 1846 *An Account of the Isthmus of Tehuantepec.* London, pp. 59–60, 69–71. Gutiérrez Brockington Lolita 1989 *The Leverage of Labor: Managing the Cortes Haciendas in Tehuantepec, 1588–1688.* Durham, NC, and London, Duke University Press.

35. Martínez Gracida Manuel 1883 *Cuadro sinóptico de los pueblos, haciendas y ranchos del Estado Libre y Soberano de Oaxaca.* 2 vols, Oaxaca, Gobierno del Estado, 1, Tehuantepec (no page numbers). AGEO FJ 4/137447 and BEO CMMG 73 (1847–48) for ample documentation.
36. BEO CMMG 41 (1851–52) for correspondence. Juárez Benito 1850 *Exposición al Congreso.* Oaxaca, pp. 5–9, 11. Juárez Benito 1851 *Exposición al Congreso.* Oaxaca, pp. 4–5.
37. AGEO Diversos Históricos 1850B, José Esperón to State Secretary, Oaxaca, 26 July 1850.
38. Archivo Juárez Mss J. Supl. 427–430. Vázquez Mantecón Carmen 1986 *Santa Anna y la encrucijada del estado: La dictadura (1853–1855).* Mexico City, Fondo de Cultura Economica, pp. 28–29.

Chapter 3

JUÁREZ AND LIBERALISM

The objective of three generations of Liberals from the 1820s to the 1870s was to transform post-colonial society into a 'popular, representative, federal republic', terms used by Juárez, for example, in 1847 when taking office as state governor. The republic would consist of individual citizens owing their prime allegiance not to village, community, corporation or privileged body, but to the nation. Such citizens were to be equal before the law and have the right of representation at all levels from municipality to federal Congress. They also had obligations – to pay state and federal taxes and to serve in the civil militia, generally known after 1846 as the National Guard, formed to defend republican institutions. Such principles,with their clear French Revolutionary and Spanish Liberal resonance, frequently ran into conflict with Mexican realities. This is not to suggest that Liberalism was an entirely alien creed that a myopic political elite of urban professionals sought to superimpose on a resisting and uncomprehending society. Such a view is tempting. It fails to take account, however, of the fact that Liberalism took distinctly Mexican forms and that its intellectual make-up emerged equally out of Mexican origins. It provided a doctrinal expression for regional sentiment, for instance, at a time of growing resistance in the provinces to the traditional dominance of the centre-core elite of merchant-financiers and viceregal bureaucrats.[1]

Liberals, Juárez among them, frequently denounced the 'privileged classes', by which they meant essentially those groups which had inherited their social and legal predominance from the colonial era, protected themselves with corporate privilege, and sought to re-create the political structure of the defunct viceregal regime. Corporate privilege, however, was not solely the prerogative of the highly placed and the rich; it sheltered many humble persons from loss of status, land or income. Not least of these were the many who found a refuge within the ecclesiastical estate, which extended well beyond the priesthood, and the peasant-artisans of the numerous Indian communities throughout the Republic. Liberalism, with its anti-corporate bias, stood in full opposition to those privileged groups as well. The real danger, one that never fully materialized, in spite of conscious efforts during the empire of Maximilian, would be the coming together of the privileged elites and the privileged poor in a common opposition to Liberal measures.[2]

Liberalism had to forestall such a menacing combination. Accordingly, it had to appeal to significant elements among the non-professional and non-educated sectors of the population. In order to survive and to function as a political force at the national level, Liberalism required a working popular base. Given Mexico's social and ethnic disparities, its wide geographical variations, and the differing histories of its component populations, Liberalism required several distinct categories of popular base, which taken together often appeared to be contradictory. It had to bring into its fold aspiring groups that saw in its constitutional provisions both a guarantee of their position and a means of advancement. Legal position and perceived status determined allegiances as much as thought of material gain. Sub-regional rivalries played a major part in forming the popular base of Liberalism, as the cases of the northern sierras of Puebla and Oaxaca clearly illustrated from the 1850s into the 1880s.

A number of authors have stressed the disparities between the Liberal project and Mexican realities, and the degree to which the latter frustrated its fulfilment. This is the theme of a study by Laurens Ballard Perry. It also forms the continuing thread throughout François-Xavier Guerra's examination of the origins of the Mexican Revolution. For Guerra, Liberalism was a minority creed; it could be imposed only by dictatorship: the Díaz regime, accordingly, represented the culmination of modernizing Liberalism. John Tutino views Liberalism as the doctrine which enabled private property-owners to strike at village landownership and a free peasantry. For John Hart,

Liberalism represented an aspect of the advance of capitalism into the rural areas, with consequent disruption of traditional relationships. He also points out, however, that in its defence of municipal autonomy, Liberalism commanded a profoundly popular appeal. All of these views make important contributions to the debate concerning the nature of Latin American Liberalism. They testify to the rich bibliography on the subject. Nevertheless, each in its own way distorts the picture by over-systematization. The most useful approach is to examine what Liberalism meant in the provincial contexts where it had its greatest impact.[3]

. . .

JUÁREZ: BROADENING HORIZONS

The Liberal movement produced leadership cadres at several levels that sprang from lower ethno-social groups. One such figure was, of course, Juárez. To all intents and purposes the political rise of Juárez had come to an abrupt end in 1853. With the return of Santa Anna to power in alliance with Alamán and the Conservatives, the 1824 Constitution lay in abeyance. Santa Anna governed between April 1853 and August 1855 with no constitution at all. Leading Liberals were forced into exile in New Orleans, as Alamán struggled against time to recreate the institutions of the late viceregal era.

Three figures became crucial to Juárez during his New Orleans exile. Two of them were well-known Oaxaca allies and friends, Castro and Mejía, who looked after his wife and children during those eighteen months. Since the family owned no land, Margarita Maza de Juárez found herself obliged to set up shop with Mejía's aid in the small valley town of Etla, in order to maintain the family. The third figure was a Cuban separatist, Pedro Santacilia, who had been deported to Spain in 1852 but had escaped through Gibraltar to New York. Santacilia married Manuela ('Nelita'), Juárez's eldest daughter, in May 1863. Reduced to the meagrest of livelihoods, since he had not enriched himself while governor, Juárez earned his keep by making cigarettes. At one transaction in Bourbon Street, Juárez met Santacilia, who took him to a meeting of Cuban exiles. In this way, the Cuban connection of Juárez, which began in October 1853, when he sighted the first foreign country he had ever visited, began to take shape. It is often overlooked, since the emphasis usually placed in discussion of the period of exile is on the role of Melchor Ocampo, who had been governor of Michoacán in 1846–48 and 1852–53.[4]

In the opinion of Bulnes, Juárez was a virtually apolitical nonentity, who became 'ideologized' by Ocampo at that time. Justo Sierra, by contrast, saw a coming together of politicians, who reached similar conclusions on ecclesiastical questions. Ocampo, though, was by far the more radical. In the view of Richard Sinkin, Ocampo was the leader of a 'revolutionary government in exile' and Juárez the second in command. Ocampo is portrayed as a more advanced reformer, who brought out Juárez's latent radical tendencies. Such interpretations have been perpetuated throughout the literature, though they have been based more on conjecture than on evidence. They perpetuate the idea of Juárez the gullible novice, the simple Oaxacan shamed into the background in the presence of superior intellects. Essentially, the conclusion drawn is that Juárez throughout his career relied on the ideas of more brilliant men such as Ocampo, Miguel Lerdo de Tejada, and finally his brother, Sebastián Lerdo. Juárez's own early Liberal credentials and his experience as state governor are either unknown altogether or given no serious consideration. While it may be said that Juárez was not an intellectual, he was, nevertheless, an independent political mind.[5]

Mexican Liberals saw in continued Spanish control of Cuba a threat to the independence of their country. During the 1850s the Captain-General of Cuba, Francisco Serrano, was proposing to use the island as a springboard for a renewed Spanish expansion in the Americas. The three Cubans close to Juárez at this time, Santacilia, Domingo de Goicuría and Juan Clemente Zenea, all argued for insurrection as the only way of securing Cuban independence. As we have already seen, the younger Juárez of 1840 stood in the tradition of Hidalgo and Morelos in opposition to the Spanish imperial tradition, while, at the same time, identifying himself with the contemporary Spanish Liberal experiment.

Santacilia played a leading role in the life of the Juárez family from the New Orleans exile onwards. Santacilia and Goicuría, who had inherited a fortune in Cuba, operated a commercial house in New Orleans at that time and sent arms to the state of Guerrero during the civil war of the Reform, for which Álvarez consistently acknowledged his gratitude. Santacilia took care of Margarita and the children during their difficult exile in New York between 1863 and 1867 at the time of the French Intervention. Goicuría became commercial agent of the Veracruz Liberal regime during the civil war of the Reform and had played a significant part in frustrating the Mexico City Conservative regime's efforts to bring ships from Cuba to blockade the port in 1859. He became *de facto* special envoy in the United States for the Juárez government after 1862. Two of the leaders of the Cuban struggle for independence which began in 1868, Carlos Manuel de Céspedes and Manuel Quezada, had fought in the civil war of the Reform and against the French Intervention. Manuel and Rafael Quezada took part in the successful defence of Puebla in 1862. The former escorted Juárez and his itinerant ministers to San Luis Potosí and Saltillo in 1863, when the French threatened Mexico City. The Cuban revolutionaries received full moral and political support from President Juárez in 1868. Mexico, in any case, had severed all diplomatic relations with Spain as a result of the Intervention. Congress in 1869 voted to declare the Cuban insurgents belligerents, a nation in arms against another nation. The Liberal press, with *El Siglo XIX* in the forefront, championed the Cuban cause. Margarita Maza de Juárez, for long ill and confined, attended a celebration of the first year of the Cuban struggle in October 1869. When Goicuría was captured and garroted in May 1870, there was intense grief in the Juárez family at the loss of this companion of the New Orleans exile. Juárez's readiness to trust these Cuban revolutionaries and admit one of them into his family has received little comment. Perhaps as a Oaxacan, he had difficulty trusting Mexicans. Certainly his wife, a fellow Oaxacan, warned him from her New York exile to be wary and to trust no one in his long peregrination during the Intervention.[6]

. . .

JUÁREZ IN THE LIBERAL CONSTELLATION

The international dimension of Liberalism, then, was expressed not merely in ideas, themselves flimsy and shifting, but more especially in commitments, personal loyalties and actions. Juárez, as in so many other instances, stood at the centre of these linkages, both as man and as symbol. Charles Berry sees Juárez as essentially the reconciling element within the politics of Oaxaca during the period from his second governorship until the French Intervention, that is between 1856 and 1863. The local party had divided into 'moderate' and 'radical' factions, known respectively as *borlados* and *rojos.* Loyalty to Juárez held the two factions together. The former tended to be civilians, such as the businessman, José Esperón, and the lawyer, Manuel Dublán, who had married a sister of Juárez and who acted as head of the governor's secretariat. Yet Juárez was also closely allied from an early age with Marcos Pérez, one of the leading 'radicals' and mentor of Porfirio Díaz, who was one of the *rojos* in the Liberal army. Even so, the principal figure, Miguel Castro, remained above faction altogether. In Berry's view, 'Such a complex of political, personal, and family ties and friendships served to bind together the two extreme factions and those in between into a cohesive party while Juárez was present in the state as governor.'[7]

Juárez never held any position in the literary nationalism of mid-nineteenth-century Mexico, in which Ignacio Altamirano, for instance, featured so strikingly. He was a practical administrator with a wide range of interests in government, most notably education, and a readiness to pay close attention to detail. His gifts were political in that he sought to hold together as best he could an uneasy coalition of dissident factions, ideological purists, prima donna literati, ambitious military commanders, state governors determined to retain control of federal resources, and local *caciques* with their personal armed following. These were the principal components of the Liberal Party. According to Guillermo Prieto, writing in the aftermath of the collapse of Comonfort's administration at the end of 1857, 'The speciality of the Liberals is the talent for prefaces; the works remain incomplete, but the prefaces are divine'.[8]

Since Juárez did not himself write political tracts, it is often difficult to place him in the spectrum of Liberal politics. Much confusion has resulted from trying to pin him down as either a 'moderate' or a 'Jacobin', the term devised by Sierra to describe the radical or 'progressive' wing of Liberalism. Was he conciliatory or a revolutionary? The answer is neither, since he cooperated with whomever it was necessary, as he saw it, to cooperate at the time and with whatever faction of the party.

This clearly emerges from a study of Juárez's relationship to the party made by the jurist, León Guzmán, at one time an ally and subsequently a strong opponent.

Guzmán identified himself as part of the 'progressive' wing of the party, which, after the promulgation of the Constitution of 1857, described itself as the 'constitutional party', in that it sought to carry out its provisions to the letter. He described the Juárez administration during the civil war of the Reform as 'progressive'. The principal influence he saw as Ocampo – 'he was always superior to anyone else'. In 1861, when Juárez remodelled his cabinet, the emphasis remained 'progressive', with 'such well-known constitutionalists' as Francisco Zarco, Ignacio Ramírez and Prieto as ministers. The elections of that year were free, and returned 'a substantial majority of progressives' to Congress, as well as 'a group of Liberal extremists, and a small minority of moderates'. Congress, however, refused to work with the administration and the extremist wing pressed for the establishment of a committee of public safety, on the lines of the French Revolution. This apparently was too much even for the 'radical' Guzmán, who saw at that time the prudence of Juárez as the only guarantee of rationality. He was alarmed at the deterioration of Mexico's foreign relations, and the deepening threat posed not only by Spain but also the France of Napoleon III. Once the Intervention had taken place, however, Juárez's alliance with the 'progressives' ceased, according to Guzmán. Thereafter, the defenders of the 1857 Constitution were consigned to the wilderness, as Juárez aligned with the 'moderates', whom they so greatly distrusted. The principal culprits were Sebastián Lerdo and Ignacio Mejía. Lerdo's influence became decisive during the War of the Intervention – 'the favoured minister whose voice was overriding and final in the national government.'[9]

In Oaxaca, however, a quite different set of circumstances from that outlined by Guzmán prevailed. In 1863, as the French army threatened the central plateau, Juárez began to fear that the moderate Liberals in control of Oaxaca might attempt to seek a compromise on the basis of non-compliance with Reform legislation. Accordingly, he instructed his chief military ally in the state, Porfirio Díaz, to remove Governor Ramón Cajiga and his secretary, José Esperón, from office. This he did in December, and took over the civil authority himself at Juárez's request. This regional divergence from the supposed national norm illustrates Juárez's response to distinct situations by differing methods. The tactical alliance with the Oaxaca radicals neither committed him to their interpretation of Liberalism nor subordinated him to their objectives. By 1867 this alliance had already broken down.[10] Juárez attempted as best he could to stay above factional strife, or, at worst, tack a careful way through it. He was a politician who could see clearly above the basic conflicts of the day to the broader issues at stake. He was capable of understanding what the essential nature of the struggle was about, as we shall see when we come to examine his role during the Intervention. At the same time, Juárez was not a visionary. Nevertheless, he stood for a few strongly held principles. Their defence ran as a unifying element throughout his career. These principles were that government should be constitutional, that the law should be upheld and obeyed, and that the civil power should be supreme. To only the most limited extent had such principles been applied in Mexico since Independence. Juárez attributed the disastrous early decades of the Mexican sovereign state to failure to observe them. He regarded them as absolutes, above party altogether. There is considerable evidence to suggest that, in spite of Juárez's clear Liberal affiliation, he sought to identify with the national interest, as he perceived it, above party and beyond the narrow circles of the articulate, political elite. This may well be the key to explaining the complex last years of Juárez, which we shall deal with in Chapter 9. If such a view is correct, then it must be concluded that one of the principal obstacles encountered by Juárez after 1867 was precisely the Liberal Party.

. . .

THE REVOLUTION OF AYUTLA

Juárez emerged as a national figure in the aftermath of the Revolution of Ayutla, which began in March 1854. This movement originated in the south, and, accordingly, not only encapsulated the inheritance of Morelos and Guerrero but also formed a continuation and extension of the earlier localized rebellions that had been taking place in the zone between Cuernavaca and the Pacific coast during the 1840s and early 1850s. This gave the Ayutla movement a certain popular appeal and provided it with a base in the villages and among non-elite social and ethnic groups. The Plan of Ayutla, however, emerged from a traditional *cacique* hostility to the central power. Some kind of pronouncement had been contemplated by Álvarez and his close associate, the retired militia colonel, Ignacio Comonfort, an hacienda-owner of Puebla who had become administrator of the Customs House of Acapulco. The Plan itself resulted from a meeting held at Álvarez's Hacienda La Providencia. It was then sent to Colonel Florencio Villarreal, Civil Governor and Military Commander of the Costa Chica, who proclaimed it on 1 March with the support of his 400 racially mixed forces (*pintos*) in the district of Ometepec.[11]

The Plan reacted in general terms to Santa Anna's attempt to rebuild a centralist system after the defeat of 1846–47, and in particular to military recruitment and the capitation tax, which weighed so heavily upon the villages. The Plan of Ayutla, however, made no mention of Liberalism and said nothing concerning any reduction of corporate privilege or any changes in Church–state relations. Liberalism appeared when Comonfort issued a revised version of the Plan in Acapulco on 11 March. This time liberal institutions were described as the only ones suited to the country to the exclusion of all others. The Comonfort modifications suggested the possibility that reforming measures such as those identified with the Gómez Farías administration of 1833–34 might be resumed. Yet, in order to remove Santa Anna and the circle of business and landed proprietors that had formed around him, a broad consensus would have to be formed. Comonfort represented the 'moderate' wing of Liberalism, and had been influenced by the ideas of Mariano Otero and the Liberal generation of the 1840s, which had become increasingly sceptical of federalism. Comonfort favoured constitutional government and reforms, but not the dissolution of the regular army and a direct onslaught on the Church. Although frequently associated with the 'radicals', Álvarez himself was not a *puro* but rather the able forger of flexible popular alliances that incorporated lower social and ethnic groups, though usually in order to pre-empt their own autonomous actions and defuse their radical potential. This 'caste' element, however, was feared by 'moderates' and Conservatives alike, though it is quite clear that Juárez did not feel intimidated by it.[12]

The Revolution of Ayutla opened a power struggle that lasted sixteen months. It was not itself a popular movement, though it contained marked popular elements. Santa Anna proved incapable of effective counter-insurgency warfare and the guerrilla movement spread across the south into the Oaxaca Mixteca and to Michoacán in the west, where it merged with the uprising by the *cacique*, Gordiano Guzmán, who, like Álvarez, had fought in the War of Independence and controlled thereafter a vast territory in the Pacific hinterland. These popular undercurrents ran throughout the Reform era. Local issues of land, water, labour, customary rights, recruitment, taxation, ecclesiastical dues, religious customs and municipal autonomy emerged as they had done during the 1810s and would do again in the 1910s. Popular participation, however, was only Liberal to the degree that Liberals at state and national levels were prepared to respond to lower class aspirations and attempt a redress of grievances. Skilful local leaders could build by such means a lasting popular base capable of challenging national or regional Liberal leaderships unwilling to sacrifice consensus or alienate 'moderate' opinion.

The great chieftains of Liberalism did not adhere to the Revolution of Ayutla until it had become clear that Álvarez and Comonfort had successfully immobilized the regular army. Juárez and part of the Liberal intelligentsia were, as we have seen, in exile in New Orleans. On the news of the revolution in the south, Ocampo in company with Ponciano Arriaga and José María Mata, moved to Brownsville, Texas, where they set up a Revolutionary Junta on 22 May 1855. They quickly established contact with Santiago Vidaurri, political boss of Nuevo León-Coahuila, who had risen with the National Guard five days previously. The Ayutla movement, thereupon, became an alliance of southern and northern *caciques*, with the intellectuals hurriedly trying to establish their credentials as camp-followers. In such a way, Vidaurri, subsequently a bitter enemy of Juárez and a partisan of the empire, whom Díaz would execute for treason in July 1867, became a founding father of the Mexican Reform movement.

The New Orleans exiles delegated Juárez to proceed directly to Acapulco in order to link up with Álvarez. The Brownsville Junta raised his fare of 250 pesos. He was seen off by Santacilia on 20 June, and after arrival in Mexico, by way of the Isthmus of Panama, Álvarez appointed Juárez to be his secretary. After the advance northwards to Iguala, Álvarez formed a council of representatives of the states: Juárez was selected for Oaxaca. Four other notable figures declared for the Revolution of Ayutla. Félix Zuloaga, Santa Anna's military commander in Michoacán, persuaded by Comonfort, defected; Antonio Haro y Tamariz, a former Finance Minister in the Santa Anna regime, pronounced in San Luis Potosí on 1 August, and in Guanajuato and Jalisco respectively Manuel Doblado and Santos Degollado rose against the Mexico City administration. Both Haro and Doblado, however, specifically called for the protection of Church and army, and supported not the restoration of the federal Constitution of 1824, but the Centralist regime's *Bases Orgánicas* of 1843. Comonfort drew these disparate elements into the Ayutla coalition. It was he, rather than Álvarez, who held them together. This coalition, always fragile, collapsed during the last six months of 1857. To Juárez fell the task that Comonfort had abandoned.[13]

Seen in its full complexity, the Revolution of Ayutla represented the tactical alliance of all those forces in the country anxious to terminate the personalist style of government associated with Santa Anna. It was not, then, uniquely either a revolution of the south or a Liberal insurrection. Had it not been for Vidaurri's northerners and then the actions of Zuloaga and Haro, both subsequently identified with the Conservative opposition, and then Doblado and Degollado, and finally the mutiny of the Mexico City garrison in August 1855, the revolutionaries of Ayutla would have been confined to a war of attrition in the southern, tropical hinterland. All these disparate elements should be taken into consideration when assessing the often contradictory course of events that led to the collapse of the Liberal regime in December 1857 and to the ignominious fall of Comonfort. Out of that disaster came the presidency of Juárez. Above all, it should be recognized that the Ayutla coalition took power in the national capital on the sufferance of the regular army, following the flight of Santa Anna on 8 August 1855.

Ultimately, the success or failure of the Reform movement would depend on the army's view of it. For precisely that reason, Juárez, along with Ocampo, pressed for the abolition of the army in favour of state militias committed to the new system. Comonfort, concerned to hold the coalition together, strongly opposed such a course of action. His overriding aim was to incorporate the army into the Reform movement but gradually to reduce its size. For a reasonable time he was able to contain armed rebellions and hold back the army, but he could not restrain the ideological war waged within the Liberal camp. Radical predominance in 1857 accounted for Comonfort's attempt to come to an arrangement with Zuloaga, then commander of the Mexico City garrison, in order to defuse the political situation.[14]

Two distinct influences immediately became apparent in Álvarez's cabinet, that of the New Orleans exiles and that of Comonfort. The leading returned exile was Ocampo, who wanted to exclude the clergy from any participation in the political processes. Álvarez selected him for foreign affairs, and kept the more circumspect Juárez for the Ministry of Justice and Ecclesiastical Affairs. This was Juárez's first ministerial appointment. Arriaga took Interior, while Prieto became Finance Minister and Comonfort War. The *puros*, then, were strongly represented in the Álvarez circle, and included Ignacio Ramírez and the elderly Gómez Farías. The moderates grouped around Comonfort, who became the senior figure in the government. On 21 October, however, Ocampo resigned in protest at Comonfort's opposition to radical measures.

Juárez's actions as Minister of Justice had profound significance for the future course of the Liberal Reform. It should be recalled that no federal Congress was in session and that, accordingly, the Álvarez regime governed as a result of its capture of power by means of revolutionary action. The celebrated Juárez Law on the Administration of Justice, issued on 23 November, was imposed by executive decree. This law had two aspects, one of which has occasioned widespread comment while the other has been virtually ignored. The law restricted the jurisdiction of ecclesiastical and military courts. This aspect had received much comment, and we shall deal with it in Chapter 5, which discusses the relationship between Juárez and the Catholic Church. The other aspect was Juárez's assault on the Supreme Court. This has been examined recently by Linda Arnold, who has stressed the unusual nature of the measures taken by Juárez under the terms of his Law. Furthermore, no prior public discussion seems to have taken place concerning its provisions.

In accordance with the Law of 23 November, the federal government received the right to nominate the members of the Supreme Court. This innovation violated the specifications contained in the Constitution of 1824 and flew in the face of contemporary practice. Previously the state legislatures had nominated candidates, which would then be elected by the federal Congress. Juárez's action, then, struck a blow not only at the independence of the judiciary but also at the role traditionally played by the legislative branch (at state and federal levels) in the selection of magistrates. The law also altered the structure and function of the Supreme Court. The new court would convene three days after the executive had designated its new members, all of whom would be required to swear allegiance to the Plan of Ayutla. This duly took place on 30 November, in the face of protests from outgoing members of the court. This swift and deeply political measure imposed by Juárez overrided requests made from the magistrates to restore judicial independence and integrity following Santa Anna's attempts to pack the Supreme Court with supporters. Instead, Juárez subordinated the court to the requirements of the Liberal Reform. His action clearly revealed a belief that only strong executive authority could carry through the Liberal programme. It suggested, furthermore, a distinct willingness to move from the subordination of the judiciary to that of the legislative branch as well. Although the rapid disintegration of Liberal unity prevented any immediate realization of such a project, the measures taken in November 1855 foreshadowed those adopted after the final triumph of Liberalism in 1867.[15]

The divisions that characterized the Liberal Party during the following decades dated, then, as far back as these early weeks of the Álvarez cabinet. They would play a disastrous and destructive role, ultimately contributing to the construction of a self-perpetuating authoritarian regime by Porfirio Díaz after 1884. The final failure of the Liberal Party to become an effective party of government undermined the possibility of the lasting establishment of representative government in Mexico during the second half of the nineteenth century.

In his *Apuntes* Juárez made great play of two distinctions, the first was between the moderates and the Liberals, and the second was between the privileged classes and the unprivileged majority. This account, written some ten or twelve years after the events they described, associated Juárez strongly with Álvarez and distanced him significantly from Comonfort. Juárez drew attention to the hatred of Álvarez in Mexico City by both the moderates and the privileged classes. This hatred, it should be stressed, contained a racial element. Although the archbishop celebrated a *Te Deum* on Álvarez's entry into the capital, the *pintos* who accompanied him were despised and feared. Manuel Siliceo, later a minister under Comonfort, described them as a 'collection of shameless degenerates, a hoard of savages', as barbarous and brutal as those of Attila and as ignorant as negroes. Similar language would be used in 1914 to describe Emiliano Zapata's forces when they entered the capital. Comonfort in the mean time promised the archbishop to respect the clergy and Church properties. On 6 December 1855 Doblado, in company with José López Uraga, requested Álvarez to vacate the presidency – a foreshadowing of the later request by deputies in the Congress of 1861 that President Juárez should do likewise. Álvarez had already contemplated the prospect of returning to his home territory and put this into effect on 12 December, when he handed over the presidential office to Comonfort.[16]

. . .

DEEPENING DIVISIONS IN THE LIBERAL PARTY

As promised in the Plan of Ayutla, the Álvarez administration issued on 30 August 1855 a decree of convocation (*convocatoria*) for elections to a constituent Congress, which would formulate a new Constitution to replace that of 1824. It pointedly excluded the clergy from any right of representation. Such a measure demonstrated the Liberal commitment to the establishment of the supremacy of the civil power and the principle of equality before the law. According to Juárez, the intention was not to exclude members of the clergy permanently from the right to exercise the franchise, but to ensure that clerical deputies did not obstruct the process of creating the new political order. Once that had been successfully established, then clerics would be permitted to participate as individual citizens.[17]

The Juárez of 1867 attributed the paralysis of the government of 1856–57 to Comonfort's unwillingness to offend the 'privileged orders', principally the clergy and the military.

In contrast to Ocampo, Juárez had remained in the government. He justified his action on the grounds that he intended to use his position to press forward the reforms. Juárez had not wanted the resignation of Álvarez. He feared the break-up of the Liberal Party through divisions over personalities. Writing in May 1856, his priority was to preserve the unity of the party, maintain its distinct ideological profile, and resist degeneration into personalism. According to the later Juárez, it was the moderates who had tried to force out Álvarez. The latter had left in order to avoid a civil war within the Ayutla camp. The view that Comonfort caused the damaging divisions within the party was also held by Guzmán, writing after Juárez's death. Guzmán saw in the Comonfort administration a sharp departure from radicalism. Comonfort had associated with moderates, and had resisted the new group of progressives, which sought to push the Ayutla coalition in the direction of institutional transformation. According to Guzmán, it rapidly emerged that the staunchest enemy would be the leader of the Liberal Party, Comonfort himself. Guzmán saw Comonfort behind a proposal to forestall the writing of a new constitution by reforming the 1824 Constitution. He had also unsuccessfully attempted to pack the constitutional commission with moderates. As provisional President, Comonfort then witnessed a 'radical' majority in the Congress of 1856–57 draw up a Constitution with which he was in fundamental disagreement.[18]

Comonfort, with the support of the newspapers, *El Siglo XIX* and *El Republicano,* strove to legitimize his regime, which owed its origins to an act of revolutionary force and which was issuing legislation with no Congress actually in session. Ocampo's second abrupt resignation signified the direction in which Comonfort proposed to travel. Moderates controlled the key positions. Lafragua, whose entry into the Álvarez administration Ocampo had blocked, took Interior. Manuel Payno held the Ministry of Finance from 13 December 1855 until 20 May 1856, when succeeded by Lerdo. Juárez remained at Justice. According to Bulnes, Juárez never disagreed with Comonfort on policy, as Ocampo had, and this explained his appointment as governor of Oaxaca for a second time in January 1856. However, by sending Juárez back to Oaxaca, Comonfort removed from the national capital the controversial author of the Juárez Law of November 1855, which had curbed clerical immunity. As in so many other instances, Bulnes's explanations carry little conviction. As governor of Oaxaca, Juárez strongly disagreed with Comonfort's *Estatuto Orgánico Provisional de la República*, issued on 15 May 1856. This measure attempted to give legal shape to the interim regime before the formulation of the constitution. It had been drawn up by Lafragua, considered to be ideologically the closest minister to Comonfort. Lafragua claimed that his principal influences had been the 1824 Constitution and the *Bases Orgánicas* of 1843. Governor Juárez and an array of state officials and local Liberals, who included Manuel Ruiz, Manuel Dublán, Marcos Pérez, Justo Benítez and Félix Romero, called for its suspension on the grounds that it compromised the rights of the states, was essentially 'Centralist', and threatened the principles on which the Revolution of Ayutla had been based.[19]

The 155 deputies in the Constituent Congress of February 1856 to February 1857 were basically Christians, if not actually Catholics. Ramírez, a self-confessed atheist, and Ocampo, who was a sort of eighteenth-century deist, remained by and large the exceptions. Most of them were members of the professions rather than entrepreneurs. It appears that the greater part of the legal profession favoured the Reform, and that a good many of them were of Indian origin like Juárez. They sought to curb the authority of the Church in Mexican life through the use of state power. Contemporary views differed as to their political complexion. Zarco, a committed radical, regarded the majority as 'moderates'. Portilla, who was writing in order to explain the course of action taken by Comonfort, described them as 'the most radical members of the Liberal Party', who pushed forward 'the most advanced theories of the revolutionary school, with disdain for tradition, with fascination for innovations, and behaving all the time with the utmost intolerance and exclusivism'. These *exaltados* organized themselves with the object of undermining the political position of the government. According to Portilla,the 'radicals' had two manias, intolerance and federalism. The breach between Vidaurri and the government over the unilateral merging of the state of Coahuila with Nuevo León in April 1856 made these tensions worse, since Vidaurri appealed to the federal Congress for support against the executive.[20]

This Congress, unlike those which had met under the provisions of the 1824 Constitution, was unicameral. One of the most vocal defenders of unicameralism was Ramírez. Although this body portrayed itself as national and revolutionary, it existed in isolation from the vast majority of the population. Despite its full claims of popular sovereignty, the people, in so far as they existed at all, had certainly not voted it into position. Sierra saw the Constituent Congress as representative only of a minority, which itself was a minority within the totality of the articulate, political classes, which included the military and the clergy. He emphasized the youth of the deputies, and saw the Congress as consisting of a 'group of radical reformers', the residue of federalists of the pre-1853 era, and a 'floating majority that generally voted with the *exaltados*'.[21]

With Ocampo in self-imposed eclipse and Juárez consigned to Oaxaca, the rising star in the administration was Miguel Lerdo. The Lerdos originated from Jalapa. The family had always been close to Santa Anna, though never centralist or conservative in orientation. Lerdo,who had begun his career in the Ministry of Economic Development created by Santa Anna in 1853, held the Finance Ministry from May 1856 until January 1857. From that position he issued, with congressional support,the celebrated Lerdo Law of 25 June 1856, which intended to transform corporate property-ownership into individual possessions. In such a way, Lerdo hoped to encourage the disentailment of both Church and Indian community landownership. We shall examine the ecclesiastical aspects of this measure in Chapter 4. The civil disamortization, however, raised the whole question of popular support for Liberalism. Much of the traditional historical literature emphasizes the urban origins of Liberalism, but recent research has focused more on its potential rural bases. Lerdo's 'privatization' measure cast Liberalism in its more controversial form into the rural arena. Lerdo regarded corporate ownership as an obstacle to economic development. He sought, accordingly, a radical transformation of legal relations on the land. As a result, the Law of June 1856 threatened to have far-reaching social and economic consequences. Although Juárez also subscribed to this 'developmentalist' thesis, it was chiefly associated with Lerdo.[22]

Government attempts to impose the civil disamortization provoked village uprisings in several states, among them Puebla, Michoacán, Querétaro and Veracruz. Armed conflict resulted in a number of districts in Jalisco, as communities resisted attempts by aspiring social groups, such as *rancheros* (smaller landholders) to take advantage of state government enforcement of the new law. In the district of Tepic, Manuel Lozada placed himself at the head of resistance and openly defied the central government until the early 1870s. In the southern belt of sugar-producing districts around Cuernavaca and Cuautla, villagers attacked Spanish-owned haciendas in order to recover lost lands.[23]

In an attempt to understand these movements, John Tutino argues that 'the political forces provoking the escalating agrarian violence in Mexico began to operate on a national scale after 1855'. In other words, he associates the widespread violence with the policies adopted by the regime brought to power by the Revolution of Ayutla. In a variant of this theme, Marcello Carmagnani portrays Juárez, armed with the National Guard, as the leader of a 'white-mestizo project' directed against Indian communities. He puts forward the notion of a 'second Conquest' of the indigenous population, the first by Cortés in the sixteenth century and the second by mid-nineteenth-century Liberalism. This began in Oaxaca with the first governorship of Juárez and continued with greater vigour after the Liberal capture of power at the national level in 1855.[24]

Curiously, it seems to have become fashionable to attribute to Juárez betrayal of his own people. This charge, of course, takes its place alongside all the more traditional allegations levelled against him. Generalizing overviews, however, need to be examined in the light of specific circumstances. Community responses to Liberalism varied over the time-scale of the *Reforma* and Restored Republic. Institutions such as the National Guard, for instance, provided members of communities, as in the case of the northern Puebla sierra, with the possibility of upward mobility and integration into broader national developments. In Oaxaca's central valleys, some Indian communities willingly complied with the provisions of the Lerdo Law with respect to their municipal and confraternity lands. There, however, little urban or *ranchero* demand existed for Indian lands.[25]

Juárez, while anxious to apply the Lerdo Law, sought to clarify procedure and cushion Indian communities from the expenses and disadvantages that might stem from it. On 3 July 1856 Juárez implemented the Lerdo Law in the state. Ten days later, a rebellion broke out in the Tlaxiaco area, also a sugar-producing zone, in the west. The leading producer was Estéban Esperón, brother of one of the principal moderate Liberals in Oaxaca, José Esperón. In September, Esperón requested the state government to authorize the transfer to private ownership of the plantation lands his family had rented for decades from the local Indian community. In order to comply with the law, Juárez instructed the reluctant municipality to do so. The Hacienda de La Concepción, the base of Esperón wealth in the area, became the principal source of rural tension until the Revolution of 1910. Juárez rapidly became worried about the social implications of the Lerdo Law in an Indian state such as Oaxaca. Accordingly, he wrote to President Comonfort on 30 July and again on 14 August to inquire whether communities could distribute available lands among their own members before the lessees, such as Esperón, made their claims effective. The implication would be to uphold peasants' rights to exclude outsiders from securing control of community land. Lerdo replied that his intention had been all along to give priority to existing tenants.[26]

The Lerdo Law proved to be so ambiguous that a continuous series of clarifying decrees had to be issued by the federal government during subsequent decades. Delays, difficulties and changes of regime provided Indian communities with the political space within which to defend themselves wherever they could. Liberal administrations suffered from periodic attacks of bad conscience with regard to the social impact of the law. Comonfort's Resolution of 9 October sought to ease Indian access to individual proprietorship by removing transfer and sales taxes. After he had become President, Juárez issued two measures, on 5 and 7 September 1860, in a similar vein. They assigned lands formerly owned by village religious confraternities to peasant communities for transfer to individual ownership. In his Regulation of 10 December 1862, Juárez recognized that the Lerdo Law had become an instrument for the despoiling of the Indian peasantry, instead of the means of redistributing wealth. In Juárez's judgement, the original aim of the Lerdo Law had been to assist 'those of the indigenous race, so deserving of sympathy and a better lot', to improve their condition. He repeated Comonfort's earlier removal of irksome duties on the transfer of eligible properties and warned municipal governments to return unjustly appropriated lands.[27]

The picture emerges of a Juárez caught in a situation not entirely of his own making and unable to find a way out. He repeatedly sought to mitigate the impact of the law on village society. At the same time, he remained committed to the principle of private property-ownership. Yet the social consequences of the law presented local Conservatives with the opportunity to exploit deeply rooted popular grievances against the Liberal regime. Lerdo believed in pushing forward Reform legislation and using state power to give full effect to the disamortization. He argued that Comonfort's mistake lay in his attempts to conciliate the opposition, instead of destroying the Conservative Party altogether. Lerdo was one of the leading *puros*, and his opponents within the cabinet were Lafragua and Montes. He finally left the government on 3 January 1857 and for a time seriously contemplated challenging Comonfort in the presidential elections due to be held under the terms of the new Constitution.

. . .

NOTES AND REFERENCES

1. Guerra François-Xavier 1985 *Le Mexique: De l'Ancien Régime à la Révolution.* 2 vols, Paris, Publications de la Sorbonne, I, pp. 156, 166–73, 274, 354. Tutino John 1986 *From Insurrection to Revolution in Mexico: Social Bases of Agrarian Violence, 1750–1940.* Princeton University Press, NJ, pp. 258–62. Hart John M 'The 1840s Southwestern Mexico Peasants' War: Conflict in a Transitional Society' in Katz Friedrich (ed.) 1988 *Riot, Rebellion and Revolution: Rural Social Conflict in Mexico.* Princeton University Press, NJ, pp. 249–68.
2. Perry Laurens Ballard 'El modelo liberal y la política práctica en la república restaurada, 1867–76' *Historia Mexicana* XXIII (1973–74), pp. 646–59, 647.
3. Perry Laurens Ballard 1978 *Juárez and Díaz: Machine Politics in Mexico.* DeKalb, Northern Illinois University Press.
4. Castañón Jesús R 'Las mujeres de la Reforma: Margarita Maza de Juárez' *BBSHCP* no. 56 (1 April 1956), pp. 1, 5.

5. Sierra Justo (1905–06) 1948 *Juárez: Su obra y su tiempo.* Mexico City, UNAM, p. 90. Sinkin Richard N 1979 *The Mexican Reform, 1856–1876: A Study in Liberal Nation-Building.* Austin, University of Texas Press, pp. 52–54.
6. 'Juárez y sus amigos cubanos' *BBSHCP* no. 55 (15 March 1956), pp. 3, 7. *BJDOCS* 14, pp. 517, 521–29, 533–39.
7. Berry Charles R 1981 *The Reform in Oaxaca, 1856–76: A Microhistory of the Liberal Revolution.* Lincoln, NB, and London, University of Nebraska Press, pp. 54–56.
8. Quoted in Roeder Ralph 1947 *Juárez and his Mexico: A Biographical History.* 2 vols, New York, Viking Press, I, p. 162.
9. *BJDOCS* 4, pp. 791–805.
10. Berry *Reform in Oaxaca* pp. 53–54, 85.
11. Bushnell Clyde Gilbert 1988 *La carrera política y militar de Juan Alvarez.* Mexico City, Miguel Ángel Porrúa, pp. 213–14. Johnson Richard Abraham 1939 *The Mexican Revolution of Ayutla: An Analysis of the Evolution and Destruction of Santa Anna's Last Dictatorship.* Rock Island, I, Augustana Book Concern, pp. 38–40.
12. *BJDOCS* 2, pp. 10, 13–15.
13. *BJDOCS* 1, p. 199. Hernández Rodríguez Rosaura 1967 *Ignacio Comonfort: Trayectoria política. Documentos.* Mexico City, UNAM, pp. 34–36. González Navarro Moisés 'La Venganza del Sur' *Historia Mexicana* XXI (1971–72), pp. 677–92.
14. De la Portilla Anselmo 1858 *México en 1856 y 1857.* New York, Imprenta de S Hallet, pp. 18, 24–25. Hernández Rodríguez *Comonfort* p. 36.
15. Arnold Linda 'La política de la justicia: los vencedores de Ayutla y la suprema corte mexicana' *Historia Mexicana* XXXIX, ii (octubre–diciembre 1989), pp. 441–73.
16. *BJDOCS* 1, pp. 201–21. Bushnell *Alvarez* pp. 244–46.
17. Bushnell *Alvarez* p. 246.
18. Tamayo Jorge L (ed.) 1957 *Epistolario de Benito Juárez.* Mexico City, pp. 48–49. *BJDOCS* 4, pp. 792–93.
19. Hernández Rodríguez *Comonfort* pp. 49–55, 62. Bulnes Francisco 1967 *Juárez y las Revoluciones de Ayutla y de la Reforma.* Mexico City, pp. 157–58. *BJDOCS* 1, pp. 249, 251.
20. Portilla *México en 1856* pp. 44–55. Bulnes *Juárez y las Revoluciones* pp. 183, 189–93. Sierra *Juárez* pp. 205, 240. Zarco Francisco 1956 *Historia del congreso extraordinario constituyente, 1856–1857.* Mexico City, El Colegio de México, pp. 561–62.
21. Sierra Justo 1948 *Evolución política del pueblo mexicano.* Mexico City, Imprenta Universitaria, pp. 281, 315.
22. Blázquez Carmen 1978 *Miguel Lerdo de Tejada: Un liberal veracruzano en la política nacional.* Mexico City, El Colegio de México, pp. 101–04, 110.

23. See Powell T G 1974 *El Liberalismo y el campesinado en el centro de México (1850 a 1876)*. Mexico City, SepSetentas. Aldana Rendón Mario Alfonso 1983 *Rebelión agraria de Manuel Lozada: 1873*. Mexico City, Sep/80 Fondo de Cultura Económica, pp. 50–51.
24. Tutino *From Insurrection to Revolution*, pp. 258–62. See also Tutino John 'Agrarian Social Change and Peasant Rebellion in Nineteenth Century Mexico: The Example of Chalco' in Katz *Riot, Rebellion and Revolution* pp. 95–140. Carmagnani Marcello 1989 *El regreso de los dioses: El proceso de reconstitución de la identidad étnica en Oaxaca, Siglos XVII y XVIII*. Mexico City, Fondo de Cultura Económica, pp. 158, 233–38.
25. Thomson Guy P C 'Popular Aspects of Liberalism in Mexico 1848–1888' *Bulletin of Latin American Research* 10, iii (1991), pp. 265–92. Berry *Reform in Oaxaca* pp. 143–46, 176–77, 182–89.
26. Berry *Reform in Oaxaca* p. 178. AGEO FJ 7/13750, exp. 18.
27. AGEO FJ 27/13764 Mariano Carrasquesdo to State Secretary, Teposcolula 6 September 1856. Aldana Rendón *Rebelión agraria* p. 57.

Chapter 4

JUÁREZ, THE CONSTITUTION OF 1857, AND THE COLLAPSE OF THE LIBERAL REGIME

The promulgation of the 1857 Constitution marked the victory of the 'radicals' in the conflict that had been going on within the Liberal Party since the overthrow of Santa Anna. The defenders of this Constitution, among them Juárez, saw it as an instrument with which to terminate personalist politics and establish the supremacy of the law. During the Intervention, they employed it as a political weapon with which to defend the legality of their cause. The framers intended to transform the remaining colonial inheritance into a modern society founded upon the principles of equality before the law, sovereignty of the people, the rights of man, and private property-ownership. They were influenced by three earlier examples: the US Federal Constitution of 1787, the Spanish Enlightenment and the Liberal experiments of 1810–14 and 1820–23, and the various phases of the French Revolution.

The Constitution and the accompanying legislation was forced through by a small minority of lawyers and intellectuals, opposed by a President increasingly alarmed at the prospect of counter-revolution, and dependent ultimately upon an army uncommitted to the Liberal experiment. Liberals themselves remained deeply divided over objectives and tactics. The framers of the Constitution identified two overriding problems in Mexico: centralism and executive supremacy. In many respects, exactly the opposite had been the case, but the deputies, with strong regional roots, were reacting against the Bourbon viceregal system and the subsequent attempts by Alamán and various military politicians to create some form of viable central government. This they regarded as a threat to provincial autonomy and control of revenues. Hence, the Constitution should be understood in the light of the perceived experience of the previous seventy-five years.

The Constitution of 1857 provided for a diminished national executive, the supremacy of the legislative power, and a full federal structure of state governments and constitutions. This made Congress powerful and gave the state governors great weight in the political system. The legislature would be unicameral, a marked departure from 1824 and a rejection of the bicameralism of the US Constitution of 1787. There would be no senate to counter-balance an over-mighty lower chamber. Radical Liberals saw in an upper chamber a likely obstacle to their plans for a 'reform of society'. Guzmán, for instance, had urged the Constitutional Commission to create the type of political institutions which would ensure the swift execution of the laws passed by Congress. With that end in view, also, no provision was made for a presidential veto of legislative measures. These two issues would re-emerge after 1867, when Juárez, in the aftermath of the definitive Liberal victory, would seek to diminish the legislative branch. In such a way, no Senate existed in Mexico from the time of Santa Anna's abolition of all the representative bodies of the federal system on 16 December 1853 until President Sebastián Lerdo was able to bring Juárez's work to fruition and re-establish the Senate in 1874.[1]

The Constitution incorporated both the Juárez and Lerdo Laws, and excluded all members of the clergy from sitting as deputies. This same document opened with twenty-nine articles defining the rights of man and outlining individual guarantees. There was a great deal of wishful thinking in article 1: 'The Mexican people recognize that the rights of man are the base and object of social institutions. As a result, it declares that all laws and all authorities in the country shall respect and uphold the guarantees offered in the present Constitution'. Complementing these declarations was article 39: 'National sovereignty resides essentially and originally in the people. All public power derives from the people and is instituted for its benefit. The people have for all time the inalienable right to alter or modify the form of their government'. This sovereign people, the Constitution went on, had voluntarily constituted itself as 'a representative, democratic, federal republic, composed of states, free and sovereign in all respecting their internal government but united in a federation established according the principles contained herein' (article 40). Accordingly, the exercise of popular sovereignty took two forms – in the powers of the Union (where those applied) and in those of the states for internal matters. As in article 40, article 41 was careful to subordinate state sovereignty to the broader interests of the federation. It specified that state Constitutions could in no way contravene what had been laid down in the federal Constitution. Articles 50, 72, 85, 88 and 92 saw in separation of powers the safeguard against executive absolutism.[2]

Although federalism originated from the provinces in 1855–57, as it had done in 1833–34, a good deal of centralism existed within the states themselves. The Constitution of 1857 established the state governors in a strong position. They appointed the district administrators, known as *jefes políticos*, who were to be their executive agents. The Spanish Constitution of 1812 first created this type of official, though the Mexican Constitutions of 1824, 1836 and 1843 had preferred a tier of Prefects and Sub-Prefects beneath the governors. The *jefe político*, who might be described bluntly as 'boss' in the locality, exercised a range of powers, which during the Díaz era (1884–1911) would give him considerable notoriety. He exercised control over the municipalities, decided their disputed elections, drafted to the regular army, and administered unoccupied lands (*tierras baldías*). There were some 300 such officials across the Republic in the latter part of the nineteenth century.[3]

One of the most trenchant critics of the Constitution, Emilio Rabasa, argued that its gravest error was the disequilibrium between the executive and the legislative powers. According to Rabasa, there was no such thing in post-Independent Mexico as the 'people' or the 'nation' in political terms. The Constitution established a system of universal suffrage in what Rabasa described as a population in which the vast majority were ignorant, illiterate and poor, and included the Indians. The federal Constitution of 1824 and the two Centralist Constitutions of 1836 and 1843 'had not committed this inexplicable error'. The explanation for its appearance in 1857 derived from this 'work of an advanced minority', 'work of the populist spirit which prevailed as a result of the revolution and the lack of standing which characterized many of the deputies of the constituent congress'. He argued that the Constitution was flawed at the outset. 'It created a singularly absurd situation: in order to uphold the principle of universal suffrage, it was necessary to violate the Constitution: in order to hold elections, it was necessary to employ electoral fraud'. In the tradition of 1791 and 1812, the Constitution of 1857 adopted a system of indirect election. Electoral districts, representing each segment of 40,000 voters, chose an elector to represent each of its 500 sections. In this way, eighty electors in each district formed an Electoral College which chose deputies to the Congress and the President of the Republic. The essential feature of Mexican republicanism was its commitment to regular elections, but that had always raised the question of how they were to be operated. The 1857 Constitution, with its establishment of universal manhood suffrage, greatly amplified this problem. The outcome of elections, in which different factions or personalities of the same party competed, depended ultimately not on the voice of the people, but on control of the electoral processes by the local administrative and political authorities, most especially the civil authority, the *jefe político*.[4]

On the model of 1787, 1791 and 1812, then, Mexico's two republican Constitutions of 1824 and 1857 defined sovereignty and attributed it to the people or the nation. In the spirit of 1787, but in a marked departure from 1791 and 1812, these two Mexican Constitutions adopted a federal structure, just as their ideological successor would also do in 1917. Federalism opened divisions within the Liberal camp. Disagreement over its extent resulted from the growing scepticism towards federalism which had deepened from the 1830s. The Constitution of 1824 had already become the focus of criticism from within as well as from outside the Liberal camp well before the collapse of the first Federal Republic in 1836. Many moderates were coming to the conclusion that federalism did not automatically guarantee social harmony. Otero had argued for modifications in the 1840s. When the federal system was restored in 1846, both the context and the intent were different from the early 1820s. The 1857 Constitution, then, absorbed two contradictory strains. On the one hand it continued this modification of earlier federalism, while on the other hand it originated from a revolutionary situation in which *cacique* and provincial hostility to the central power in Mexico City had been essential motives for action. The 1824 description, 'Federal Constitution of the United Mexican States', was dropped in favour of 'Political Constitution of the Mexican Republic'. According to Jan Bazant, 'federalism had lost its meaning' by 1857, and Liberals became 'just as centralist as their conservative rivals, although they continued to pay lip service to the federalism with which Liberalism had been identified for so many years'.[5]

. . .

STATE-LEVEL POLITICS

As Bulnes graphically pointed out, Juárez remained absent from Mexico City during this decisive period in the early history of the Reform movement. From 10 January 1856 until 25 October 1857, he was governor of Oaxaca for the second time. Bulnes made that point, in order to demonstrate that Juárez was neither a significant figure in the Liberal Party nor an influence on Reform policy.[6]

Juárez did not remain isolated in Oaxaca: on the contrary, he followed affairs in the capital closely through the medium of his protégé and informant, Matías Romero, a fellow Oaxacan and star graduate of the institute in 1852. This marked the beginning of Romero's long relationship with Juárez that lasted until the latter's death in office. Romero worked at the Ministry of Foreign Relations. He corresponded regularly with Juárez not only on foreign policy matters, such as the rapid deterioration in relations with Spain, but also concerning the political condition of the Comonfort administration. Romero informed him of the Comonfort administration's suspension of the radical newspaper, *El Siglo XIX*, which Juárez regretted. Through Romero, he followed closely the deterioration in relations between the two wings of the party and expressed the wish that the radicals would not provoke a confrontation with the opponents of the Reform. By April 1857 Juárez was anxious that Liberal unity should be preserved at all costs, while by June he had become alarmed at the frequency of ministerial changes, especially since those taking office inspired no confidence at all. On 8 September he confided to Romero his fears of an impending *coup d'état*, one launched, that is, by Comonfort to rid himself of the radical wing of the party and the Constitution it had forced on him, before the new constitutional order actually came into being. However, Juárez seriously doubted that Comonfort would do such a thing.[7]

Four days after resuming the governorship, Juárez reopened the institute and all other educational institutions in the state which had been disbanded by Santa Anna under a law of 19 December 1854. He subsequently founded the Normal School in Tlaxiaco as part of this process. In a public discourse, Juárez denounced the 'enemies of Enlightenment and of all progress' and argued that 'public education is the foundation of social well-being the principle upon which Liberalism is founded and the prosperity of peoples'. In a Manifesto to the People of Oaxaca on 2 February 1856, Juárez reaffirmed his commitment to the completion of the Revolution of Ayutla, the aim of which he described as 'to respect and make respected the constitutional guarantees of man and the citizen'.[8]

In order to have the practical means of doing so, he re-established the Oaxaca National Guard and called for the dissolution of the remnants of the permanent army on the grounds that it would be unlikely to support his administration. In his *Apuntes*, Juárez maintained that, as governor, he had insisted that he, the civil authority, should have been Commander-in-Chief of the armed forces within the state. This was the position he had held in 1847. He believed that state governors never had sufficient forces at their disposal to impose their will. At the same time, he claimed that the Comonfort administration had not dared remove the army commandants-general in the states through fear of alienating the military. He urged the Oaxaca deputies in the federal Congress to press for this. He viewed this as a serious matter, since the state military commander had already attempted to provoke a rebellion in favour of 'Religion and Privileges' and had tried to nullify the Juárez Law. Mejía's quick intervention had been decisive in preserving the Liberal regime in Oaxaca. Within the state, Juárez could count on the militia commanders, Fernández del Campo and Díaz Ordaz, for strong defence of the federal system. The latter would succeed Juárez as governor after Comonfort had summoned him back to Mexico City to become a member of the administration once again. Díaz Ordaz, a 35-year-old landholder and merchant, purchased the Hacienda del Rosario, one of the main estates of the Valley of Oaxaca, under the provisions of the Lerdo Law. The renovated militia was joined by Porfirio Díaz.[9]

At the heart of the liberal, republican system were elections. Any appointed office-holder had to subject himself to public election, when the political circumstances permitted, in order to have his position legitimized. The Constitution of February 1857 established the principle of universal, adult, manhood suffrage, which resulted in a substantial electorate. In order to circumvent the realities of ignorance, suspicion, hostility and distance, the practice of indirect election was adopted. Under the provisions of the Constitution, elections were held in Oaxaca for all political authorities. The state electoral law provided population as the basis for representation and, accordingly, for the election of one deputy for each group of 40,000 individuals. Juárez was elected governor with over 98,000 votes for a four-year term. The remaining candidates secured 12,000 votes combined. Votes cast, then, amounted to around 110,000, or roughly one-fifth of the total population of the state, a relatively substantial proportion. In the elections to the state legislature, only two of the fourteen elected candidates did not belong to the Liberal Party. Díaz Ordaz, Castro, Mejía (and his brother, Manuel), Fernández del Campo, José Esperón, Manuel Dublán and Félix Romero, all leaders of the Oaxaca party, were elected. Governor Juárez addressed the newly installed Congress on 21 June:

> the mission of republican government is to protect mankind in the free development of his moral and physical faculties with the sole limitation being the rights of other men. I shall take scrupulous care to ensure that individual guarantees remain intact and that no one individual, no sectional interest, and no class shall oppress the rest of society. I shall respond with a firm hand to anyone who attempts to undermine the rights of other men.

Juárez promised that the law would protect all persons indiscriminately. He referred to the Constitution as 'sacred', since it contained 'humanitarian principles' and 'civil liberties'. His hope was that it should become deeply rooted in the hearts of the people.[10]

According to Juárez, the Revolution of Ayutla had made possible the enactment of a new Constitution to replace the old one of 1824, torn up in 1853, when the *santanistas* had dissolved the national and state congresses. 'Anarchy and despotism' had followed. With the promulgation of the state constitution of Oaxaca in September 1857, 'legality and order' were restored. Juárez believed that the 1824 Constitution was a dead letter, and that no other recourse existed but to formulate a new one, in order to prevent a return to dictatorship. He vowed, as he took the oath before Congress to uphold the new Constitution, that he would make sure that it would not become a dead letter like its predecessor. 'I shall make use of the power that the people of Oaxaca have bestowed upon me to ensure that their sovereign will shall be complied with, as expressed in the Constitution'.[11]

In this second term of office Governor Juárez put into effect two measures of pressing importance. One of them had long preoccupied him. This was how to stimulate the mining sector and thereby release the potential of the state for silver, gold and copper production. As was well known at the time, Oaxaca had valuable mineral deposits but scant means of exploiting them through shortage of capital and lack of an adequate infrastructure. Along with the small business group in the sierra, several of its members his personal friends, Juárez saw in the mining industry the principal means of reviving the Oaxaca economy to a level comparable to that of the dye-trade boom of the latter part of the eighteenth century. The establishment of a Mint in Oaxaca had been requested since the state first came into existence in 1824, but nothing had been done. Further requests in 1835 and 1840 had finally resulted in a decree in July 1842, but again nothing followed. During his first governorship, Juárez in 1849 again pressed the matter, arguing the urgency of reviving the mining industry in the aftermath of the collapse of the dye sector. Even so, the federal government prevented the state government from going ahead. Permission was finally granted in August 1854, that is thirty years after the initial legislation. The establishment of the Oaxaca Mint contributed to the subsequent revival of mining, the results of which were to be seen after the 1870s. Leading Liberal political figures of the Reform era and the Restored Republic would take part in this process.[12]

The second measure was the reversal of Santa Anna's decree of 11 May 1853, which had separated the Isthmus of Tehuantepec from the state of Oaxaca and constituted it as a separate Territory. Tehuantepec had declared its wish to rejoin Oaxaca shortly after the triumph of the Revolution of

Ayutla, but the federal government had delayed the matter until after the promulgation of the new Constitution. In this regard, Juárez worked closely with the Oaxaca deputies in the federal Congress. This, as in the previous case and with respect also to his close liaison with Romero, belied the idea spread forth by Bulnes that Juárez in Oaxaca remained on the margin of events. Shortly after the reincorporation of Tehuantepec, Juárez went to the Isthmus in person once again in May 1857, in order to deal with local problems on the spot and end the hostility between villages. He appointed Díaz Ordaz to be Governor and Military Commander, and installed new Sub-Prefects in Juchitán and Petapa. His governorship, then, represented a delicate balancing of national and local issues, the state executive always being the nodal point.[13]

. . .

THE BREAKDOWN OF THE CONSTITUTIONAL EXPERIMENT

In the national elections, Juárez had been elected President of the Supreme Court, a position which under the Constitution gave him the presidential succession. As the political situation in Mexico City deteriorated, Comonfort began to search for allies who might help him to salvage his position. On 21 October, he recalled Juárez to the capital as Secretary for Internal Affairs. The President specifically requested Juárez to help him reconcile the warring factions within the Liberal Party at a time of deepening national crisis. The latter accepted this invitation and secured permission from the state Congress to hand over the administration to Díaz Ordaz and proceed to Mexico City.[14] On 27 October 1857 Juárez left Oaxaca, never to return.

In the aftermath of their capture of power, there followed a 'hopeless disarray among the liberal elements' concerning what to do to reform society. This dissension degenerated into sharp hostilities between the various factions of the party. They weakened the federal government and diminished what control it had over national territory. Radicals blamed Comonfort for disarray at the centre and accused him of trying to slow down the pace of change in order not to alienate the moderates and to conciliate the opposition. Miguel Lerdo resigned over such issues in January 1857 and seriously considered challenging Comonfort in the forthcoming presidential election in June.[15]

At the same time, attempts to publish the Constitution led to armed clashes throughout the states of Jalisco and Michoacán, which were centres of popular Catholicism. The enforcement of government policy depended upon the state militia forces, and it rapidly became apparent that ultimately the survival of the regime itself depended upon the attitude of the regular army. Since state governments throughout the centre-north, north and coastal peripheries persisted in taking initiatives of their own with regard to Reform policies without reference to the Liberal administration in Mexico City, the political system, which the Constitution was meant to solidify, seemed to be breaking apart. The Liberal state governors were, in effect, successfully challenging the federal government for leadership of the Reform movement. Their centrifugalism and radicalism presented a double threat to the regular armed forces. Authority in the army centred effectively on Félix Zuloaga, commander of the Mexico City garrison.[16]

Comonfort won the presidential elections with forty votes against one for Lerdo, who had withdrawn in face of the unpopularity of the Lerdo Law in the country, and one for the Conservative candidate. On 17 September the existing cabinet resigned, allegedly to allow Comonfort a free hand in selecting new ministers. According to the outgoing Minister of Development, Manuel Siliceo, however, the explanation was not so innocuous. Siliceo maintained that the ministers were unsympathetic to the Constitution and did not favour the impending transition from executive rule to constitutional government. They recommended, instead, a form of Liberal dictatorship. In this way they sought to impose Reform policies on the country by presidential decree. Siliceo suggested that ministers did not believe that Mexico was at that time capable of constitutional government. Frank Knapp argues that Sebastián Lerdo shared this point of view, since he had no faith in the practicability of the 1857 Constitution.[17]

Right from this early date, then, the issue of the workability of the Constitution divided opinion within the Liberal camp. This issue would continue unresolved through the Restored Republic. The type of argument proposed in 1857 by Siliceo would later provide the moral justification for the construction of a dictatorship by Díaz. The essence of the problem lay in the deliberate weakening of the executive and the central power in favour of a strong legislative power at the centre and strong state governments in the regions. Since the nominees of the state governors controlled the electoral process, the federal deputies tended to reflect overwhelmingly their point of view. Accordingly, they regarded the executive branch as their natural enemy and sought to undermine it at every turn. This problem was correctly identified by Bulnes in his study of the Revolution of Ayutla and the rise of Juárez. Bulnes, in any case, regarded Mexican federalism as nothing but an institutionalized form of provincial *caciquismo.* The ascendancy of the *caciques* – in their new form as state governors – should, of course, come as no surprise. Liberalism depended for its effectiveness as a national movement precisely upon their support. This was the case in 1856–57, just as it had been with respect to the triumph of the Revolution of Ayutla.[18]

One hundred and fifty-five deputies sat in the first Constitutional Congress, which opened on 16 September and lasted until its dissolution on the night of 17 December. Only twenty-one deputies of the Constituent Congress were re-elected. Bulnes saw in that an electoral defeat for the makers of the Constitution. Both radicals and moderates were thrown out, and few of the famous names of 1856 reconvened in the autumn of the following year. Out were Gómez Farías, Zarco, Ramírez, Ocampo, Degollado, Arriaga, Castillo Velasco, Prieto, Vallarta, Montes and Lafragua. In Bulnes's view, Comonfort interpreted these election results as a defeat for the Constitution in a popular election, and accordingly, requested Congress to grant him extraordinary powers – that is the faculty of governing by means of the executive power – in order to reform it. The new deputies reflected the views of the state governors: they were their nominees. In that sense, the elections did not represent a defeat for the Reform movement, still less for the Constitution itself, but for the national leadership of the Liberal Party. The real victors were the radical Liberals of the states, who intended to use this nullification of central power, in order to dispose of the remaining properties of the Church and to secure control of as many federal revenues as they could lay hands on. So far from that representing a defeat for the Constitution, it represented its logical consequence.[19]

The national Liberal leadership would have to be recreated, if political life was again to function at a national level rather than in the form of distinct regional component parts. Mexico in the autumn of 1857 had returned to the centrifugal politics of 1823–24, when state-level assertions of sovereignty had seemed to threaten the territorial integrity of the newly independent state. Comonfort saw his task as precisely the reassertion of national leadership, but in this objective he conspicuously failed. That left the task to the Conservative Party, which Zuloaga's military coup brought to power at the beginning of 1858. The establishment of a Conservative regime in Mexico City, however, gave the states' struggle against the centre an even greater impetus, since they were henceforth fighting against the ideological enemy. They took defence of the Constitution as their rallying cry.

Comonfort's cabinet of 20 October 1857 was predominantly moderate Liberal. Juárez, as Minister of the Interior, was the only member thought to be in any way radical. His position within the cabinet was strong, since he also held the Presidency of the Supreme Court (and with it the presidential succession), and had also persuaded Comonfort to include his Oaxacan protégé, Manuel Ruiz, as Minister of Justice. Apart from Payno at Finance, the other three ministers were of no great distinction. Comonfort's failure to persuade Congress to grant him unlimited powers to suspend individual guarantees and to reform finance and the army placed him in a quandary. Juárez, for his part, sought to prevent himself from being drawn into the vortex. For that reason, he acquired a reputation for circumspection and reserve. When a military rebellion in Cuernavaca frightened Congress into conceding extraordinary powers on 3 November, Comonfort used the opportunity to attempt to reduce the armed forces. That in itself, however, was an extremely provocative action. In the first place, he proposed to discharge 20,000 men from the state-level National Guards, and then to reduce the regular army from 40,000 to 10,000 men. At the time of his legal assumption of the presidency on 1 December, Comonfort pressed Congress to reform the Constitution.[20]

The split in the Liberal Party over the question of reform of the Constitution formed the background to the presidential *coup d'état* under the terms of the Plan of Tacubaya. Comonfort arranged with Zuloaga to dispense with Congress, govern with executive powers, and then convene a new Congress for the purpose of formulating a workable Constitution. The regular army, then, provided the means for the President to dissolve Congress. The coup involved the arrest of the cabinet, among them Juárez. Bulnes presented the view that Juárez knew of Comonfort's intentions but did nothing to prevent them, and, therefore, was implicitly implicated in them. Understandably, there is no evidence for such a view.[21]

As we have seen, Juárez, while still governor of Oaxaca, had been receiving detailed information from Romero and was seriously concerned at rumours of an impending presidential coup. The arrest of Juárez during the night of 17 December 1857 suggests that Comonfort could not trust him in that enterprise and that he was, accordingly, not party to the conspiracy. The crucial role of the military in guaranteeing the coup and then shortly afterwards launching its own coup to remove Comonfort and the Liberal administration altogether went against everything that Juárez had stood for throughout his career. He had ceaselessly warned of the threat to the constitutional order from powerful military commanders. Juárez remained under arrest in Mexico City until 11 January 1858, when Comonfort, deceived by the military and reduced to despair, ordered his release. That enabled Juárez to claim the presidential succession. Juárez fled without delay first to Querétaro and thence to Guanajuato, where on 19 January he endeavoured to re-establish the Liberal regime.[22]

These events, which resulted in the establishment of two rival governments in Mexico, opened the three-year civil war of the Reform. In contrast to the Constitutions of 1824 and 1917, the Constitution of February 1857 had lasted only eleven months. It had, then, an even shorter duration than the previous unicameral system under the Spanish Constitution of March 1812, which had been overthrown in May 1814. In Guanajuato and later Guadalajara and finally in Veracruz, President Juárez found himself in the power of the state governors. He would find it difficult to free himself from their tutelege. That task would become his ultimate objective, no less a task than the defeat of the Conservative regime in Mexico City. Since victory in the civil war depended upon the armed forces of those very governors, this aim would require the utmost political skill. Juárez would not be assisted by the fact that the overthrow of the constitutional system by the Conservative military had made defence of the 1857 Constitution the moral justification of the Liberal cause. While there could be no doubt, judging from his record, that Juárez stood for constitutional government in Mexico, this Constitution became the millstone round his neck. It remained so for the rest of his life.[23]

. . .

NOTES AND REFERENCES

1. Zarco Francisco 1956 *Historia del Congreso Extraordinario Constituyente, 1856–1857.* Mexico City, El Colegio de México, pp. 1,345–61, for the Constitution of 12 February 1857. Paoli Bolio Francisco J (coordinador) 1987 *El Senado Mexicano.* 3 vols, Mexico City, El Senado de la República, II, pp. 44, 50–74.
2. Zarco *Congreso Extraordinario Constituyente.*
3. Mecham J Lloyd 'The Jefe Político in Mexico' *Southwestern Social Science Quarterly* XIII, 4 (March 1933), pp. 333–52.
4. Rabasa Emilio 1912 *La Constitución y la dictadura.* Mexico City, 'Revista de Revotas', pp. 29, 52–55. Cosío Villegas Daniel 1957 *La Constitución de 1857 y sus críticos.* Mexico City, Editorial Hérmes.
5. Hale Charles A 1968 *Mexican Liberalism in the Age of Mora, 1821–1853.* New Haven, CT, Yale University Press, pp. 34, 195–98, 286–87. Bazant Jan 'Mexico from Independence to 1867' in Bethell Leslie (ed.) 1985 *The Cambridge History of Latin America* vol. III, p. 457.
6. Bulnes Francisco (1905) 1967 *Juárez y las Revoluciones de Ayutla y de la reforma.* Mexico City, p. 161.
7. *BJDOCS* 2, pp. 213, 244–55. Tamayo Jorge L (ed.) 1957 *Epistolario de Benito Juárez.* Mexico City, pp. 45–46, 67–68.
8. Sánchez Juan 1972 *Vida literaria de Benito Juárez.* Mexico City, UNAM, pp. 55–56.
9. *BJDOCS* 1, pp. 237–41. Sierra Justo (1905–06) 1948 *Juárez: Su obra y su tiempo.* Mexico City, UNAM, p. 101.
10. *BJDOCS* 2, pp. 249–51. Berry Charles R 1981 *The Reform in Oaxaca, 1856–76: A Microhistory of the Liberal Revolution.* University of Nebraska Press, Lincoln, NB, and London, pp. 37–39, 224 n. 26.
11. *BJDOCS* 2, pp. 256–57.
12. Tamayo *Epistolario* pp. 44–45.
13. *BJDOCS* 2, pp. 238–40, 245–46.
14. Tamayo *Epistolario* pp. 70–71.

15. Knapp Frank Averill 1951 *The Life of Sebastián Lerdo de Tejada: A Study of Influence and Obscurity.* Austin, University of Texas Press, pp. 36–37.
16. Powell T G 1974 *El Liberalismo y el campesinado en el centro de México (1850 a 1876).* Mexico City, SepSetentas.
17. Knapp *Sebastián Lerdo* pp. 43–44.
18. Bulnes *Juárez y las Revoluciones.* pp. 356–57.
19. Zarco *Congreso Extraordinario Constituyente* pp. 21–25. Bulnes *Juárez y las Revoluciones* pp. 194–97, 201, 209.
20. Hernández Rodríguez *Comonfort* p. 63.
21. Bulnes *Juárez y las Revoluciones* pp. 192–93, 202–03. The position of Juárez was made clear by Manuel Payno 1860 *Memoria Sobre la Revolución de Diciembre de 1857 y Enero de 1858.* Mexico City, Imprenta de I. Cumplido, pp. 88, 127.
22. Blázquez *Miguel Lerdo* pp. 119–24. Bulnes *Juárez y las Revoluciones* pp. 212–20.
23. For a general discussion of constitutionalism, see Sayeg Helú Jorge 1992 *El constitucionalismo social mexicano. La integración constitucional de México (1858–1988).* Mexico City, Fondo de Cultura Económica.

Chapter 5

JUÁREZ AND THE CATHOLIC CHURCH

In common with the other Liberal leaders, Juárez was a freemason. Given the masonic origins of Mexican party divisions in the 1820s, this was not surprising. Freemasonry in both Catholic Europe and Latin America had traditionally been the clandestine means of transmitting both the attitudes associated with the Enlightenment and the Liberal critique of the absolute monarchies of the Restoration era. Freemasonry permeated educated circles and even royal families throughout the Catholic world. The Emperor Maximilian, a descendant of Joseph II, was also a mason. François-Xavier Guerra has drawn attention to the linkages provided by masonic lodges in the Mexican Liberal movement of the *Reforma* and Restored Republic. Juárez the mason had been married in the church of St Philip Neri in Oaxaca. He was neither especially Christian nor particularly Catholic, but observed the social customs of his time. While he was neither an atheist nor a deist, he sought to bar the Catholic hierarchy from a political role and to remove the clergy from control of education. He prohibited any clerical participation in the education of his own children. Liberals of the Juárez generation disliked the corporate organization of the Catholic Church in Mexico, which they saw as opposed to the individual liberties which they sought to guarantee by means of written Constitutions. Juárez, whether as state governor, Minister of Justice or President, did not aim to destroy the Catholic Church or obliterate its historic contribution to Mexican culture. He stood instead for the secularization of social and political institutions. Nevertheless, the implications of this position did not emerge overnight: Liberal policy took a long time to evolve, and remained constantly beset by the internal division between moderates and radicals.[1]

. . .

EARLY LIBERALISM AND THE REVIVAL OF THE CHURCH

Church–state relations provided a major source of division. This issue involved not only the balance between the ecclesiastical and the temporal powers, but also the controversial question of religious toleration. The Constitutions of 1812 and 1824 had both upheld the exclusive Catholic establishment, while the latter had maintained ecclesiastical and military privileges (*fueros*). The early generation of Liberals had wanted to attract immigrants, whom they believed would develop the country. At the same time, they were wary, especially after the loss of Texas, of Protestant immigrants from the USA or northern Europe. Mora, for instance, wanted to see the modernization of Mexico but at the same time avoid its transformation into a replica of the USA. This dilemma led, of course, to another, since Liberals were engaged in combating the influence of the Catholic Church, while at the same time not wishing to undermine Mexico's distinct national identity, which owed so much to the Catholicism of the colonial era.

In colonial Mexico, the Catholic Church developed one of its strongest positions in the American continent. Its two chief centres of influence continued to be Mexico City and Puebla, where the ecclesiastical establishment was the most deeply rooted in the Viceroyalty. Evangelization, however, proved to be weakest in the countryside. In areas of heavy pre-Columbian settlement, syncretic cults frequently emerged, as indigenous communities absorbed some of the new and preserved what they could of the old. In the diocese of Oaxaca, where even in 1910 still only 51 per cent of the population spoke Spanish, hybrid forms of Catholicism coexisted with village religious institutions. The city of Oaxaca contained a significant ecclesiastical establishment, though it could not compare with Puebla or Mexico City. Until the mid-eighteenth century, the Dominicans had been far more significant than the secular clergy, but thereafter the Order of Preachers was itself in decline, not least because of the concerted episcopal policy of transferring parishes to members of the secular clergy. By the beginning of the nineteenth century, by far the most Catholic area of Mexico was the zone that stretched across the centre-north-west from Querétaro to Michoacán and Jalisco and from Zacatecas and San Luis Potosí to Guanajuato. There a deeply rooted Catholic popular culture flourished, which was neither Spanish nor Indian. The core, the area from Guadalajara across to Querétaro, was Mexico's most urbanized region, densely populated, intellectually and economically advanced. The struggle for Independence originated precisely there. In that sense, Catholicism and early nationalism were in no way contradictory.[2]

The Church in Mexico, however, experienced a period of relative decline in the century from 1750 to 1850. This coincided with the absorption of the ideas of the Enlightenment, the rupture with Spain, and the creation of an independent sovereign state. This century could be described as the period of the crisis of the Catholic Church in Mexico, even though the full Liberal onslaught would occur later in the twenty years between 1855 and 1875. This crisis had three dimensions, all of them interrelated: intellectual, spiritual and political. It consisted of the decline of vocations, especially to the male religious orders, the Enlightenment critique of scholastic philosophy, the disintegration of Spanish colonial rule, the divisions within the clergy concerning the revolutionary road to Independence, the attempt by the Mexican national state to appropriate to itself royal faculties of nominating bishops, and finally the Liberal extension of Bourbon attempts to subordinate the Church fully to the state. In the immediate aftermath of Independence, it was estimated that vocations had diminished by a quarter between 1808 and 1825, and that ecclesiastical wealth had diminished to one half. The number of priests in Mexico fell from 4,229 in 1810 to 3,283 by 1830 in a Republic of between 6 million and 7 million inhabitants. By that time, most of the bishops, including the Primate, the archbishop of Mexico, had either returned to Spain or died.[3]

The Catholic Church had already begun to recover from the late colonial crisis and the aftermath of Independence by the 1840s. With a reconstituted episcopate, its leaders were ready and able to challenge Liberal measures during the Reform period. The Reform generation inherited the ideas and dilemmas of Mora, Zavala and Gómez Farías. Like this earlier generation, it shared the 'enlightened' perspectives of the Bourbon ministers of the previous century. They differed, however, on the two issues of the relations between Church and state and between debt and disamortization. By the 1850s the question of whether the Church should be subordinated to the state in the Bourbon tradition or separated from it in a secularized society divided the Liberal camp. Mexican Liberalism , given the priority it attached to the 'Church question', could not help but be influenced by the contemporary European idea of a free Church in a free state.[4]

The Catholic hierarchy, most of the clergy and many laymen saw in Liberal policies a threat to the revival of the Church. They saw in the Holy See, itself moving towards a higher political consciousness during the pontificate of Pius IX (1846–78), a protection against nationalism, national churches, and the deification of the state. In Liberalism they saw an attack on the remaining defences that protected the Church – not just a bureaucracy of clerics but the body of believers – from state dominance. In the plurality of beliefs they saw a loss of Mexican identity and the opportunity for the penetration of United States' Protestantism into the country. Pius IX viewed Mexican events after 1855 through Italian eyes, as if they were identical to the circumstances which had led to the creation of the Roman Republic in 1848–49 and Comonfort, Ocampo, Prieto, Lerdo and Juárez were the American equivalent of Mazzini and Garibaldi.[5]

Liberals saw in ecclesiastical defence of corporate privilege not a guarantee of liberty against an all-embracing state, but an anachronistic legacy of the colonial *ancien régime* which they wished to remove. They saw the stance of the Church as an obstacle to both the emancipation of the intellect and the modernization of society. Liberalism countered the charge of amorality with its structure of beliefs. Hobsbawm has perceived in Liberalism 'an attempt both to understand and to change the world, an ideology and a movement, a set of ideas and a set of institutions'. Mexican Liberalism, in effect, created an alternative world to that of Catholicism, which continued to exist alongside it. The foundations of this world lay in republican values, national identity and civic virtue. The function of lay public education was to propagate this alternative morality. The Mexican case certainly lends credence to Owen Chadwick's view that 'we shall not understand liberalism unless we recognize that it was always a moral doctrine'. Fuentes Mares goes as far as to describe the leaders of the Reform as like priests, relentlessly pursuing an idea. Juárez's persistence in dressing in black since his youth served to emphasize this.[6]

The Conservative Party, formed in the late 1840s by Alamán (who also had masonic antecedents), was a secular political agglomeration not necessarily coterminous with the Catholic Church. It sought to exploit religious identification, popular credulity and religiosity in an effort to undermine the Liberal regime brought to power by the Revolution of Ayutla and undo its legislation. In the judgement of one of its leading spokesmen, Luis G Cuevas, the 'war against religion and the Catholic Church' began with the entry of the victors of Ayutla into the capital. In Cuevas's view, the Liberal onslaught struck against the essence of Mexican nationality and 'can be considered a victory in advance for the country's external enemies'. He concluded that the one and only purpose of the Comonfort administration was what it described as 'religious reform'. The party's propagandists strove to rally all those beneficiaries of the existing economic, social and political structures which saw themselves threatened by Liberal measures. Such aims tended to be material and secular rather than spiritual. The divisive and provocative nature of Liberal anticlericalism – particularly at the state government level – proved to be profoundly destabilizing and played into Conservative hands, as the events leading to the *coup d'état* of December 1857 testified.[7]

According to Hale, the principal difference between the Liberalism of Mexico and that of Argentina and Chile was not over philosophical positions but in the predominance of the Church issue in the former. From the time of Mora to the time of Cárdenas, Mexican liberal and revolutionary leaders identified this issue, whether justified in doing so or not, as central to the problems of their country. For that reason they have often been described as 'Jacobins'. Justo Sierra applied that term to Liberals of the Ocampo school. He saw them resorting to the revolutionary process in order to bring about changes in society, turning this process into a system of government, and making extensive use of executive power above the existing legal framework. Although he identified Comonfort as slowing down this process, he argued that Juárez, under the influence of Ocampo, had moved towards the radical wing of Liberalism. Accordingly, Sierra interpreted the Juárez Law of November 1855, which sought to reduce corporate privilege, as a revolutionary act, in the sense that its claim to legitimacy derived solely from the seizure of power by the revolutionaries of Ayutla. In Sierra's judgement, the Juárez Law established the principle of equality before the law, which was the basis of the entire Reform movement.[8]

It is difficult, in the light of the evidence, to see Juárez as a 'Jacobin' at that time. The contrast with Ocampo and Miguel Lerdo was striking. At least until 1858, Juárez remained a moderate on the two central issues of Church–state relations and the appropriation of ecclesiastical properties. He saw the Church issue not so much in terms of state expropriation of clerical wealth, as did radicals such as Lerdo, but in legal terms. On the subject of disamortization, Juárez proved to be conciliatory, if not cool, perhaps as a result of his Oaxaca origins and knowledge of Indian corporate institutions. As state governor in 1847–52, he had sought, as we shall see, a working arrangement with the Oaxacan Church. During the second governorship in 1856–57, which took place in an entirely different national context, Juárez insisted that federal and state legislation should always be complied with by the clergy. In spite of the clergy's continuing corporate identity, Juárez remained adamant that its members should not regard themselves as above the civil law. Governor Juárez was neither looking for confrontation with the Church nor was he a persecutor or confiscator, as were his counterparts in the centre-northern and northern states, above all during the civil war of the Reform.

. . .

GOVERNOR JUÁREZ AND THE CHURCH

The diocese of Oaxaca had remained without a bishop since 1827. When Pope Gregory XVI appointed six new Mexican bishops in 1831, the diocese of Oaxaca was not included. By 1835, seven of the ten episcopal sees still remained vacant and a Primate was not installed until 1839. For seventeen years, then, the Church in Mexico remained without direction, largely as a result of papal refusal to recognize Mexican Independence until 1838 for fear of offending the Spanish crown. In the diocese of Oaxaca, the number of male and female members of the clerical estate fell from 742 in 1777 to 548 in 1828. In 1810 there had been 380 priests for 145 parishes, but by 1847, the total had fallen to 330 for 140 parishes.[9]

The episcopal office was not definitively re-established in Oaxaca until the accession of Dr Antonio Mantecón in July 1844. Presented by Santa Anna, Mantecón belonged to one of the state's principal Hispanic families. The son of a leading colonial merchant, he had trained as a lawyer and had held office on the city council before ordination. Mantecón administered the diocese until his death in February 1852. Juárez, then, was the first state governor to encounter a bishop already established in the diocese, not only a native of the state but also one of its most prominent personalities. Juárez had no ideological quarrel with the Church or religion as such. Even so, two objectives motivated his conduct: the determination to establish the supremacy of the civil power and to remove the clergy from predominance in education. In pursuit of those goals, however, he did not propose to launch himself into direct confrontation with the bishop. On the contrary, he looked to a *modus vivendi.* The possibility of such a working arrangement arose from the fact that the confinement of the clergy within the civil law, while allowing for the continuation of the ecclesiastical courts for internal discipline, implied no necessary breach with the Holy See. It implied no rupture of the apostolic succession and no departure from received dogma.[10]

The sources do not tell us what Bishop Mantecón thought of the Zapotec state governor of masonic affiliation and Liberal inclination. Juárez, for his part, remained suspicious of the military and unsure of the clergy, especially at a time of deteriorating relations in the Isthmus and a continuing US military threat. He was anxious that no conflicts with the Church should jeopardize his position. Nevertheless, he intended to use his office to extend primary education in the main district towns and, where possible, in the Indian areas as well. Oaxaca's Liberals hoped to educate the Indian majority out of what they saw as their inherited superstitions. Liberal intentions encompassed a thorough laicization of society through the full exercise of state power. The only constraint was the perennial weakness of the state. Scant public resources delayed the implementation of Liberal education policies. Here and there, as in Ocotlán and Tehuantepec, private contributions were available. In the former instance, Juárez appealed to the bishop to ensure that funds set aside by a former parish priest of Santa Ana Zegache for the opening of a school were actually released. In July 1848 Juárez reported to the state Congress that 476 schools were functioning throughout the state.[11]

Both the governor and the bishop shared a common concern with the evident abuses among the secular clergy of the parishes and with the frequent unruliness among the city's Dominican friars. Juárez expected the law to be obeyed: Mantecón expected the civil power to reinforce ecclesiastical authority. For a time, a basis existed for mutual understanding on these two points. According to state law, villages were required to contribute to the upkeep of their parish clergy. While the state remained determined to prevent unjust exactions by the clergy, it was equally determined that villagers should pay their contributions. These were not mean sums. Village sustenance of the parish priest implied the transfer of surplus revenue from the community to an authority not technically part of the village corporate structure. Resistance continued to be widespread, though that in itself did not constitute opposition to religion. On the contrary, a substantial part of village income went to maintain the communities' own confraternities through the medium of which the local population expressed its religious beliefs.

Villages were frequently unwilling to sustain a rural priesthood that was often under-educated and at times self-serving, absentee or abusive. In response to repeated complaints by parish priests that dues were not being paid, Juárez instructed all department governors within the state on 24 January 1849 to use their civil authority to reinforce that of the clergy. This was, moreover, the governor's response to a declaration by the bishop recognizing the principles of the Constitution of 1824 and the federal system. The Juárez administration clearly outlined its political principles – as these stood in 1849 – in this instruction:

> the essential basis of a democratic and eminently liberal system such as that which governs us is the strict observance of the law. It takes its characteristic form from neither the capricious behaviour

> of one man nor the interests of any particular class. Guided by a noble and sacred principle, such a system provides the most complete liberty at the same time that it curbs and punishes license … . The punctual compliance with one's duty and the profoundest respect for and observation of the law form the essential characteristics of the true Liberal, of the best republican. For such a reason, it is self-evident that it is never legitimate to commit even the slightest abuse in the name of liberty.[12]

Five days after this circular, Juárez thanked the bishop for his efforts to encourage the parish clergy to cooperate with the civil authorities in ensuring the completion of the projected highways to Tehuantepec and the port of Huatulco. This mutual sustenance indicated the difficulties encountered by both bishop and governor in enforcing their policies in the locality, given the limited resources at their disposal. Open division would have aggravated their problems. In the spirit of the circular of 24 January, Mantecón again appealed to Juárez on 5 September to guarantee payment of dues, this time specifically in the valley town of Zimatlán. This unfortunate Zapotec town had lost its lands to adjacent private estates during the eighteenth century and it was regarded by the state authorities as a perennial source of trouble. Mantecón denounced a 'malicious recalcitrance' in payment of dues there. Juárez instructed the local Prefect to report on the situation in Zimatlán. While the governor sympathized on the moral plane with the often dire straits of peasant communities, he would on no account, on the political plane, countenance disobedience of the law. Juárez would tolerate no deviation from the principle that all the inhabitants of Oaxaca, as citizens of a republic, owed an obligation of loyalty and obedience, regardless of their social and ethnic origin or corporate status. As Juárez saw it, that was the essential meaning of Liberalism.[13]

On deeply sensitive matters, the dormant suspicions between Church and state became active. A dispute arose concerning the deplorable condition of the city's three hospitals at the time of an anticipated outbreak of cholera during the late summer of 1849. Juárez appealed to the bishop to take the lead in repairing them. He offered government assistance in putting them on a sound financial footing. The Hospice of the Poor was supposed to have been funded from capital specifically set aside by a late colonial businessman. After taking office, Mantecón had invested this sum for the assigned purpose for the first time. Juárez was of the opinion, however, that the investment had not been made wisely, and that, as a result, the hospice still did not fulfil its intended purpose. Accordingly, he sent his secretary, Manuel Ruiz, to discuss the matter with the bishop. To his surprise, the bishop refused to allow the subject to be broached. At two subsequent appointments in the episcopal palace, the bishop refused to admit Ruiz to his office. The governor's secretary thereupon informed the bishop's secretary in writing that he had not come on a personal matter but on official business. At the third attempt, the bishop admitted him, along with a deputation from the city council, but reprimanded him for the tone of his letter, on the grounds that no authority was superior to his own. Ruiz rebuked the bishop for his lack of respect for the civil authority. Juárez, challenged in this way, replied in such a manner as to convey to the bishop the precarious nature of his position in relation to the civil power, should the latter decide to challenge it at some stage. Such an exchange, in the relatively peaceful climate of 1849–50, anticipated the more acerbic relations between Church and state in the strained political atmosphere of 1855–57. By that time, Juárez's position had developed strikingly.[14]

The bishop was decidedly reticent on the subject of Church wealth. The state government argued that it needed details in order to compile proper statistics. When Governor Juárez requested the bishop to ensure that parish priests provided department governors with details of the material condition of churches and the value of their contents, Mantecón replied that local clerics were unfamiliar with such a procedure, which might involve seeking expensive, professional advice. In any case, 'the majority of the diocesan parishes are so poor that they possess at most a chalice of minimal value and only rudimentary ornaments'. The bishop warned Juárez that 'the indigenous element', which he described as suspicious by temperament, would never see in such an investigation the innocent motive put forward by the state government but a sinister design directed at themselves. Indian communities would refuse to make any contributions at all to the sustenance of religion. Such a reply implicitly warned the civil authorities that pressure on the corporate position of the Church might conceivably provoke the hostility of villagers who saw their own position threatened as well. It suggested a possible combination of clerical and community opposition to the implementation of Liberal policies.[15]

. . .

THE JUÁREZ LAW

Juárez held the office of Minister of Justice and Ecclesiastical Affairs from 6 October until 9 December 1855. The celebrated Juárez Law concerning the administration of justice was issued by the executive authority of President Álvarez, before the convocation of the promised Congress. Juárez intended to curb exemptions from civil law, though not to abolish corporate privilege outright. Consequently, ecclesiastical and military courts remained intact for the purpose of regulating internal discipline, but the new law excluded them from hearing civil cases. In formulating this law, Juárez acknowledged the assistance of two younger Oaxacans, Manuel Dublán and Ignacio Mariscal. Writing more than a decade later, when himself President, Juárez described his law as 'the spark that produced the conflagration of the Reform'. This uncharacteristically immodest claim derived from the attempt to portray himself at that time as a radical and thereby to dissociate himself from Comonfort.

Yet, even allowing for the radicalization of events between 1855 and 1859, the Juárez Law even at the time of enactment amounted to a moderate, if not conciliatory measure. It formed part of a general Liberal effort not to provoke the clergy into irreconcilable confrontation. Even so, the bishops interpreted the law differently. The archbishop of Mexico condemned it outright on 28 November 1855 as an attack on the Church and clergy. Bishop Clemente de Jesús Munguía of Michoacán argued two days later that the government did not possess any legitimate faculty of restricting the *fuero eclesiástico*. Accordingly, it should apply to the Holy See for formal permission to do so. He urged the government to suspend the law until such agreement had been obtained. Juárez, however, regarded such a view as a challenge to the civil power and to national sovereignty. He replied to Munguía that the government could not discuss with one of its citizens whether a law it had enacted and considered to be in the public interest should be complied with or not. Munguía subsequently argued that the *fuero* was not a 'privilege' but a right possessed by the Church by virtue of its divine constitution.[16]

Bishop Pelagio Antonio de Labastida of Puebla protested to Juárez on 29 November, though not in extreme terms. Juárez replied on 6 December that the President insisted on compliance with the new law. He hoped that the bishop would not sanction disobedience of it. Events in Puebla, however, proved to be beyond the bishop's control. The National Guard put down an attempted rebellion in the city on 12 December 1855. This movement was designed to coincide with the rebellion in Zacapoaxtla, a town in the northern Puebla sierra, led by the parish priest. The rebels, calling for the defence of religion and the re-establishment of the Constitution of 1836, moved down from the mountains and on 23 January 1856 secured control of the state capital, where government forces defected. Antonio Haro, who had originally cooperated with Comonfort in the overthrow of Santa Anna and other Conservative leaders, rallied to the Puebla rebellion. Among them were two of the most renowned Conservative generals in the forthcoming civil war of the Reform, Luis Osollo and Miguel Miramón.[17]

The rebellion dealt a serious blow to the regime brought to power by the Revolution of Ayutla. Rebel leaders called for the appointment of a provisional president above party. During the two months' rebel occupation of the city, Haro sought to construct an alternative regime to the Comonfort administration in Mexico City. This rebellion unnerved the Liberal regime, since it threw into jeopardy its policy of conciliation. Comonfort and the moderate Liberals had been treading an exposed middle path between two armed camps, the Conservatives (with their military supporters) and the Liberal radicals (with the militia forces of the state governors). In 1856 the principal dividing line was the position of the Church in Mexican society. On that issue, most of all, Comonfort had striven to act with circumspection. The Puebla rebellion, however, sent a wave of panic through the administration, and it grossly overreacted.

Comonfort sent 15,000 federal troops to lay siege to the city. Although the Conservatives were forced to capitulate and Miramón was driven into hiding for nine months in the city, the government again overstepped the mark by levying the cost of putting down the rebellion on the diocese of Puebla.

This punitive measure, taken at the end of March 1856, provoked an indignant protest from Bishop Labastida, who had not in any case identified himself with the rebels. For this protest Comonfort banished him from the country. Until that time, Labastida had not been a party man. He had largely been indifferent to politics, though he found himself henceforth caught up in them without possibility of extrication. He proceeded to Rome, where the government still had not managed to place an official spokesman who might try to explain its policies. There he became a powerful enemy of the Reform movement. Labastida's stand on basic principles at a time of extreme government sensitivity made matters worse. This was serious, since both Conservative and Liberal extremists were anxious to exploit the situation for their opposing ends. The Puebla conflict remained alive throughout the year. Miramón seized control of the city and obliged the government to renew its military campaign. After a forty-day siege, the city again fell, on 3 December. In this way, Conservative actions, which foreshadowed those of December 1857 and January 1858, managed to knock the Liberal revolution off course and expose some of its more intolerant aspects.[18]

. . .

DISAMORTIZATION: THE LERDO LAW

On 18 February 1856, the same day that the Constituent Congress opened, the Comonfort administration issued the *Acta de Jacala*, which declared the Juárez Law to be effective in all its parts. Juárez, however, had already returned to Oaxaca as governor for the second time. During his absence from the capital, the administration revived the legislation of the first Liberal regime of 1833–34, removing on 26 April civil legal validity of religious vows. The Lafragua Law for the formation of a Civil Registry followed on 27 June 1857. The most significant measure, however, was the Lerdo Law of 25 June. Both the Juárez and the Lerdo Laws sought to avoid direct confrontation with the Church. Their authors, along with most of the Comonfort administration, still hoped to persuade the ecclesiastical hierarchy to accept the Reform process. They thereby strove to include the Church in the mainstream of the modernizing project, as conceived by the Liberal Party. Both laws veered uneasily between radical objectives and Catholic sensibilities. During the years 1855–57, the moderate element in the party still remained predominant, at least at the federal level. Different situations pertained, however, in the states. The Lerdo Law, moderate in conception, had unforeseen consequences. These served to intensify conflict at all levels.[19]

Envisaging clerical cooperation, Lerdo required the ecclesiastical authorities to assess the value of their own properties and transfer them to private ownership, with the existing tenants given preference. The intention was to convert the annual rent into an interest payment on capital values. The new owners would pay interest on these mortgages to the ecclesiastical body concerned and the state would receive the proceeds of the adjudication and entitlement fees. If, after the lapse of three months, this procedure had not proved successful, then the ecclesiastical authorities were required to put these properties up for sale at public auction.[20]

The ecclesiastical authorities denounced the Lerdo Law as confiscatory. Bishop Munguía argued on 26 July that the properties of the Church were independent of the wishes of governments and that they had been acquired not by a concession of the temporal power but by the nature of the social existence of the Church. He saw the law as an extension of Gómez Farías's attempt of January 1847 to secure money at the expense of the Church. Social and ethnic relations markedly deteriorated after the passage of this law.[21]

Though not made public until later, Pius IX's Allocution of 15 December 1856 denounced the Juárez and Lerdo Laws, the banishment of Bishop Labastida, and the sequestration of Puebla diocesan property. It also condemned the depriving of the clergy of the right to vote in national elections, those articles of the projected Constitution deemed to be contrary to religion, and the procedure of the civil authorities with total disregard for the Holy See and the ecclesiastical authorities. This Allocution became public knowledge during the same month in which the Constitution was put into effect. The government committed a serious error by insisting that all public office-holders should take an oath to uphold it. The archbishop roundly condemned this requirement and used the fullness of episcopal power to counter it. On 15 March 1857 he declared in the cathedral that henceforth he would bind all confessors to request of their penitents whether they had taken the oath or not. If they responded in the confessional that they had, then, if they refused to retract their oath in public and inform the civil authorities, they would be denied absolution. This extreme recourse was deeply compromising for ordinary Catholics and infuriating for Liberals. The archbishop's action compounded the Liberals' own error by escalating the conflict beyond repair.[22]

. . .

GOVERNOR JUÁREZ AND THE BISHOP OF OAXACA

Despite Conservative criticism, Bishop José Agustín Domínguez celebrated a *Te Deum* in Oaxaca Cathedral on 10 January 1856 to welcome Governor Juárez back to the state. Juárez put the federal Constitution into effect in Oaxaca on 23 March 1857. A second *Te Deum* was celebrated by one of the cathedral prebendaries to solemnize the oath to the Constitution at the cost of the public treasury. Bishop Domínguez agreed to comply in spite of his protests to the federal government concerning several articles in the Constitution, which he deemed to contravene canon law. This concession demonstrated the extent to which the bishop was prepared to go, in order to avoid confrontation with the local civil power. A third *Te Deum,* however, to celebrate Juárez's election as Constitutional Governor on 27 June 1857, was not forthcoming. These were normally sung when a state governor took office. This time the cathedral clergy refused to comply. Part of the objection was the *Ley Juárez.* The canons remained determined to close the cathedral doors to Juárez, and thereby oblige the civil government to use force in order to open them, compromising the new administration at the outset.[23]

Juárez refused to be drawn. His tactic was to adhere rigidly to the law as it stood. After an exchange of correspondence with the bishop, which led nowhere, Juárez levied a nominal fine on the clergy, and then simply ignored the closure of the cathedral at the time of his installation. He proceeded to the civil ceremony, which thereafter never again included a religious ceremony.

> Even though I could count on sufficient force to make myself respected ... , I resolved instead to do without insisting on the attendance of the Governor at a *Te Deum,* not through fear of the

> canons, but with the conviction that governors in civil society need not be present in their official capacity at any religious ceremony, although as private individuals they may attend church in order to practice their religion as it so requires.

In Juárez's view, the civil power should adopt no particular religion, since its prime duty was to uphold liberty. The participation of public officials in formal religious ceremonies was, he insisted, a waste of valuable administrative time. They should not govern in the name of the Church, but solely on behalf of the people who had elected them. In this way, Juárez avoided falling into a trap, defused the conflict which had been intended for him, and established a basic principle of republican government.[24]

Governor Juárez further angered the bishop by sponsoring the appointment of Father Bernardino Carvajal, who abandoned the serving ministry, to the civil administration in the same year. Carvajal had been a Oaxaca state senator in 1851 and had rallied to the Revolution of Ayutla. A prominent Liberal, he held the Chair in Jurisprudence at the institute and signed the state Constitution. Shortly afterwards, the Minister of the Interior, Pablo de la Llave, instructed all state governors on 1 April 1857 to dispatch to Mexico City any cleric abusing the pulpit for political goals and thereby threatening public order. Late in June, Juárez ordered the arrest of the parish priest of the sierra mining town of Zoochila and his banishment to the federal capital under the terms of Llave's order. The priest had refused last rites and Christian burial to the late village justice of Tavehua on the grounds that he had not retracted his oath to the Constitution. 'This government cannot view with indifference events that stir up the consciences of its citizens and could lead to a breach of the peace. Determined to ensure that the laws are respected, it will not shrink from taking measures necessary for the public good'.[25]

. . .

THE ESCALATION OF CONFLICT AND THE CIVIL WAR OF THE REFORM

The federal Congress granted Comonfort extraordinary powers on condition that the administration curbed the disobedience of the clergy and put an end to their denial of the sacraments to anyone who had taken the oath to uphold the Constitution. In the mean time, the administration had sent Ezequiel Montes to Rome as its official representative. Ruiz, as Minister of Justice, wrote to him on 1 November 1857 urging him not to agree to any of the Holy See's proposed alterations in the Constitution, which were, in any case, not a spiritual but a temporal matter. The minister was anxious that papal actions should not be allowed to inflame congressional hostility to the clergy any further. Montes was to inform the Holy See of the real danger of schism, as Ruiz put it, should the Mexican Church persist in its current stance. The *coup d'état* of December 1857 brought these issues to a climax. It provided the turning-point in Church–state relations. The coup generated profound anti-Catholic sentiment even among moderate Liberals. Comonfort's disastrous alliance with Zuloaga had, in any case, totally undermined the moral credibility of the moderate Liberal position. It played into the hands of the radicals, who thereafter seized the initiative throughout the states of the centre-north and north, able to do so by the collapse of a Liberal federal government in the capital city.[26]

As a result, Juárez in his first weeks as President found there was little alternative, even if he had wanted to find one, but to let himself be carried along by the radical tide. The civil war increased the revolutionary temper of the Liberal radicals. At some stage, however, Juárez would have to stem the tide. In order to make good his claim to be national leader, Juárez would have to appeal above the heads of the radicals to a wider public opinion. He did not, however, propose to do that by seeking a compromise with the Conservatives, whom he blamed for the civil war. He certainly regarded the bishops as his mortal political enemies and viewed them as devoid of moral worth, since they had used their authority to legitimize a regime which had come to power by force, overthrown the Constitution, and was actively seeking the assistance of Spain. Juárez was determined that, once the war had been won, they should be punished for their actions.

After the coup, Juárez himself initiated no further anticlerical measures. These originated mainly from the state governments themselves. In several states, such as Michoacán, Querétaro and Jalisco, armed Liberal cliques had gained power in traditional Catholic areas. In Michoacán, Governor

Epitacio Huerta stripped the cathedral bare and in five days seized a half-a-million pesos. The journalist, Juan José Baz, later a political opponent of Juárez, founded a radical newspaper in 1858 with the title *La Bandera Roja* (the red flag). The governors of Jalisco, Anastasio Parrodi and Jesús González Ortega, both of them in succession commanders of the Liberal Army, represented the radical wing of the party. In concert with Ignacio Vallarta and Leandro Valle, the latter imposed stringent anticlerical measures on the state. In Coahuila, Vidaurri was the first to legislate the complete nationalization of ecclesiastical properties and make it effective. Both González Ortega and Vidaurri were soon to become bitter opponents of Juárez in the struggle for power in the country in the aftermath of civil war. While in Zacatecas, González Ortega was the first to prohibit religious processions and legalize civil marriage. On 16 July 1859 he imposed the death penalty for any cleric encouraging retraction of the oath to the Constitution or refusing to administer the sacraments to those who had taken it or had purchased disamortized 'national properties'. The state governors were far in advance of the Juárez administration, which had taken up residence in the port of Veracruz. They were determined to use their armed force to extinguish the position of the Church within their domains. Their allies, the Liberal 'reds', attacked not only the traditional role of the clergy in society but also the doctrines of the Catholic Church. Radicals held strong positions in the Liberal Army, and along with the state governors were decidedly cool towards Juárez.[27]

The civil war placed the advocates of revolutionary dictatorship in a formidable position. Within the Liberal administration Miguel Lerdo argued, immediately after his arrival in Guadalajara at the beginning of December 1858, for dictatorship as the method of carrying out Liberal goals. Lerdo proposed the separation of Church and state and the confiscation of ecclesiastical property without compensation. He pressed Juárez to act on measures such as these, which the latter had been putting off. They were, moreover, precisely the measures which the disgraced Comonfort administration had rejected in 1856. After the Juárez regime reached Veracruz, further divisions, this time over the objectives of the disamortization, separated Lerdo from Ocampo. Lerdo considered the negotiation of a loan from the United States' government to be top priority for the Liberal regime, especially in view of evident Conservative intrigues with the Spanish colonial administration in Cuba. Sales of ecclesiastical property should therefore be accelerated. Ocampo, however, was deeply concerned at the state governors' unilateral expropriation of Church property to their own advantage. He favoured close federal government supervision of the disamortization process, once the civil war had been won. The objective, in Ocampo's view, was not simply to raise funds in order to pay for loans, but to create a landholding middle sector which could provide the future social base of the Liberal Party. He saw in Lerdo's policy only the enrichment of the few.[28]

. . .

THE VERACRUZ REFORM LAWS

The period between July 1859 and March 1861 marked a decisive stage in Juárez's attempt to portray himself as a national leader. It began with the issue of the Reform Laws through the months from July to December 1859, encompassed the final victory of the Liberal armies in the civil war and the recovery of the capital, and finished with the death of Miguel Lerdo in March 1861. The radicalization of the Liberal administration produced a body of legislation advanced for any Catholic country of that time and certainly so for Latin America.

Ruiz gave a detailed explanation to Congress, when it resumed sessions once more in 1861, of how the Reform Laws came about. Ministers, with the support of several federal deputies, had originally tried in vain to persuade Comonfort. The latter, however, preferred to postpone controversial matters until better times. Since the coup of December 1857 had led to the dissolution of Congress and the overthrow of Comonfort, the opportunity of securing congressional approval had been lost. The subject was again brought up during President Juárez's brief stay in Guadalajara in February and March 1858, but the Liberal defeat at Salamanca, followed by the events of 13–15 March, in which Juárez and his ministers had been arrested and nearly executed before firing squad in a brief palace coup, aborted any enactment. In Veracruz, which thereafter became the seat of the Liberal government, considerable discussion of the Reform Laws followed. Juárez ordered their formulation in the expectation of a Liberal victory. The defeat at Ahualulco, however, again delayed matters. By the summer of 1859, the initiatives taken in the interior states and the tension within the cabinet over the projected publication of the Reform Laws brought the matter to a head. The dire straits of the Treasury obliged instant action.[29]

Lerdo's pressure on Juárez forced events to a climax. Lerdo wanted a decree for the immediate expropriation of ecclesiastical property, in order that the proceeds of sales could be put towards the guarantee of a loan which he hoped to negotiate in the United States. Juárez appears to have held back on this issue. For that reason, the issue of the Reform Laws was again delayed. Accordingly, on 27 June 1859 an impatient Lerdo tendered his resignation – 'I have had the opportunity on more than one occasion to observe that you and I do not have the same view of things'. Juárez expressed surprise and replied that he was unaware of any differences. Lerdo insisted, claiming that Juárez was 'working against' the ideas of the Reform. For that reason, 'I lack the confidence required to embark on the difficult course which in my judgement should be adopted'. Juárez refused to accept the resignation. Once the law for the nationalization of the Church property had been passed, Lerdo departed immediately for the United States for the purpose of negotiating a loan. To his consternation, he discovered that the United States government had no interest in conceding any loan guaranteed against the sale of Mexican Church property, but, instead, wanted the cession of Lower California to the USA.[30]

The publication of the Reform Laws was preceded by a Manifesto to the Nation issued by Juárez, Ocampo, Ruiz and Lerdo on 7 July 1859. Sierra considered this long and comprehensive document, in which the government set out its principles and goals, to be the moral and ideological turning-point in the civil war. He argued that it gave the Liberals the initiative that they had lost in December 1857. Certainly, through the disastrous months of 1858, in which all the main cities of the centre-north had been lost to the Conservative Army under Miramón, it looked as though the Liberal cause might succumb. In practice, however, the initiative had already been taken, as we have seen, by the state governors.

While the Manifesto was a brave clarification of objectives, the fruit in part of indignation and in part of defiance, much of its opening section, which dealt with the Church issue, had already been put into effect unilaterally in the Liberal zones where the Veracruz administration's authority was little more than nominal.

The Manifesto reaffirmed the principles of 1824 and 1857. It sought to place the clergy under the civil power in all temporal matters, since members of the clergy were to be regarded as ordinary citizens in a republic rather than as possessors of corporate privilege in a supranational entity under the absolute monarchy of the Pope. The Liberal regime intended to deprive the clergy of the economic resources which could make them an independent power capable of challenging the supremacy of the state. The Manifesto looked to the complete separation of Church and state. It proposed the suppression of all religious corporations, the secularization of all priests, the extinction of confraternities, brotherhoods and congregations, and the termination of the female novitiate. This attack on the religious life formed part of the Liberal goal of the secularization of society. At the same time, the Veracruz regime intended 'to declare that all properties at this time administered by the secular and regular clergy under various titles have been and are the property of the Nation'. Thereafter, the clergy would be required to live from the dues which were paid to them by the faithful. Although all civil constraint was removed from their payment, the regime deemed that such funds would be sufficient. It did not envisage a scheme of state payment of the Catholic clergy. On the contrary, the Manifesto strongly affirmed the government's commitment to religious liberty, a marked departure from the conciliatory position of earlier, moderate Liberals. Similarly, the government in Veracruz intended to remove the Catholic clergy from any function in the registry of births, marriages and deaths, and transfer these to a Civil Registry. It saw no reason why the clergy should 'intervene' in the fundamental stages of citizens' lives. The dissemination of free, primary education would be the peacetime goal.[31]

The Manifesto took up both the Ocampo and the Lerdo view of the purposes of disamortization, and sought to reconcile them. On the one hand, government revenues from this process would be assigned to the amortization of public debt, internal and external, and to the regular payment of interest in accordance with recent international conventions regulating the Mexican debt. Purchasers of 'national properties' would be permitted to pay two-fifths in cash and the rest in debt bonds. The cash payments would be stretched over a forty-month period, 'in order to permit even the less well-off to acquire those properties'. Liberalism, conscious of its need to cultivate a popular base, went as far in this Manifesto as to take up the demands of radical social reformers in the Constituent Assembly of 1856 and call for 'the subdivision of landed property' and for the improvement of the situation of the rural, labouring population. There was little opportunity to implement such proclaimed objectives.[32]

The Veracruz Reform Laws, enacted first on 12 July 1859, gave effect to many of the principles set out in the Manifesto. In reality, they reflected the peak of Miguel Lerdo's influence in the government. It should be stressed that they were issued by use of the executive power, since no legislature was in session. In legal terms, they were extraordinary measures. The Law for the Nationalization of Ecclesiastical Property and the Separation of Church and State advanced well beyond the Lerdo Law of 1856 by putting Church properties up for sale at public auction and entering the proceeds into the National Treasury. This measure, however, could be put into immediate effect only in territory under Liberal control. The states with the greatest amounts of religious property remained at that time under Conservative occupation. Nevertheless, the Liberal administration in Veracruz encouraged denunciations of such properties in enemy-held territory, so that effect could be given to them once the war had been won. At the same time, the Juárez regime threatened to punish individuals who had acquired ecclesiastical property and then handed it back to the Church. Nationalization applied, even when the clergy retained the right to use such properties.[33]

This law also separated Church and state, and declared that 'the government will limit itself to protecting with its authority the public celebration of the Catholic religion, in the same way as any other religion'. Ruiz explained the purpose of the law in a circular to the state governors. It had originated from the 'infamy' of the clergy, whose conduct was contrary to the Gospel and unworthy of ministers of Christ. Mexico's best course, he argued, was to adopt the measures taken in Liberal

Spain, where, in his view, the confiscation of ecclesiastical property had contributed to the reform and conservation of the Church. The government aimed to distinguish defence of religion from defence of clerical abuses. He did not believe that the Church, which was a 'perfect association ... sustained and assisted of itself and through the merit of its divine Author', required the protection of the state.[34]

In accordance with the Manifesto's goals, the male religious life was to be brought to an end and the female prevented from recruiting new adherents. On 23 July 1859 another decree established civil marriage. Ruiz justified this law on the grounds that the clergy had been refusing to administer the sacrament of marriage to those who had taken the oath to the Constitution. He portrayed this as a threat to family life, which he saw as the basis of social organization. Some persons had even renounced their oath, in order to have the clergy marry them, only to renew the oath thereafter. The law declared that 'marriage is a civil contract legally and validly entered into before the civil authority'. The contracting parties had the right to apply for a blessing from ministers of their particular religion. On principle, marriage remained indissoluble, though the law provided for legal separation, when the marriage had irretrievably broken down. It listed seven grounds, with adultery in the forefront. This 'divorce' (the term actually employed) did not enable either party to remarry during the lifetime of their estranged partner.[35]

In Juárez's view, popular sovereignty had taken from the clergy their previous monopoly of administering marriage. On 18 August 1859 he wrote to Doblado rejecting Conservative charges that the Liberal Party consisted of 'thieves and heretics', 'dissolutes and libertines'. He denounced the Conservatives as 'the party of retrogression, the enemy of the enlightenment of peoples'. Juárez described the Reform Laws in religious terms as 'these saving laws' and excoriated 'the apostate Comonfort' for not having published them 'at the proper time, when the great Liberal family was dominant throughout the Republic'. He believed that nationalization would 'furnish immense resources with which to develop in full the Liberal idea'. Juárez welcomed the establishment of civil marriage. At the same time, however, he regretted, in a very radical statement for the time, that it had been deemed politic not to provide for the remarriage of divorcees during the lifetime of their former spouses. He suggested that such a development might be enacted subsequently. Thereupon, a series of extraordinary remarks followed: 'you know that I am of one mind with the [French] revolutionaries of '93, whose humanitarian ideas we now have the honour to be implanting in Mexico, in spite of the reactionaries who insist on denying that the indissolubility of marriage is a terrible tyranny'. This rosy view of the Jacobins served not only to illustrate the general Liberal exultation of the France of the 1790s (as opposed to the France of Napoleon III), but also to expose the wide chronological and geographical distance between Veracruz in 1859 and Paris in 1793.[36]

On 28 July 1859 the Civil Registry system was set up in the Liberal zone. Juárez made a point of registering his newly born son at the Veracruz Registry. The intervention of the clergy in burial places and ceremonies was removed on 31 July. The Juárez government on 11 August listed the official celebrations to be observed henceforth: all Sundays, New Year's Day, Holy Thursday and Friday, Corpus Christi Thursday, Independence Day (16 September), All Souls (the Day of the Dead) and All Saints (1 and 2 November), the Feast of the Virgin of Guadalupe (12 December) and Christmas Eve. These combined the basic religious feasts with the required national celebrations, with 12 December neatly combining the two. The law forbade official assistance at religious functions. Religious ceremonies were forbidden outside churches; the use of church bells was made subject to police regulations; clerical dress was forbidden in public, and the clergy were made subject to taxation on the same basis as all other citizens. On 4 December 1860 liberty of religious belief was guaranteed for the first time. Although such measures stunned many Catholics – the bishop of Oaxaca is said to have died of shock – and provided the Conservative regime with a propaganda gift, they were not designed to destroy the Church as such. In that respect, the Juárez government's measures, although legislated in a radical climate in the middle of a civil war, differed from those taken in the states by 'red' governors and their ideological collaborators. There is even the possibility that Juárez himself had had enough of radical measures on the Church issue, especially after the clear establishment of the basic principles of the Liberal regime. He was not prepared to depart from those. Yet, on the other hand, he regarded the Church as an important part of the political balance within the country. At some stage in the future, this balance, overthrown by radical Liberal measures, would have to be rectified. This could not be done, however, until the Conservative Party had first been destroyed.[37]

The Juárez government's Manifesto had blamed the civil war on a part of the clergy determined at all costs to preserve its privileges. It had described the Conservative Party as 'the partisans of obscurantism and abuses'. On 30 August 1859 the bishops' Pastoral Letter from Mexico City defended the conduct of the clergy in relation to the state, and reaffirmed the authority of the Church and the Holy See. Archbishop Garza and the bishops of Michoacán, San Luis Potosí and Linares and the diocesan representative of Puebla condemned the Reform Laws on both economic and moral grounds, and identified Juárez specifically as an enemy of the Catholic Church. The bishops argued that, while they had passively resisted all measures taken against the interests of the Church since 1833, they had never fomented revolutionary movements and never attacked the state as such. As a result, Liberal charges were a calumny, especially since no evidence was given for the charges that they had been in permanent rebellion against the temporal authority and had paid for the civil war out of ecclesiastical revenues. They had been singled out for denunciation and persecution without themselves aligning with the forces which had overthrown the Liberal regime.[38]

. . .

NATIONALISM, SECULARISM AND PLURALISM

The *coup d'état* of Tacubaya and the consequent civil war ended the moderate Liberal attempt to conciliate the Church and build it discreetly (though reformed in legal status) into the new system. The breakdown of the Comonfort administration opened all the latent anticlerical sentiments within the Liberal camp. Since the Veracruz administration itself formed part of this radical tide and found its effective power, in any case, limited more or less to Veracruz, little could be done to bring things under control. Increasingly, two world-views seemed to be in confrontation. Each had its own symbols, ceremonies and belief-systems. Just as the Catholic Church made demands on its adherents, so too did Liberalism. It, too, represented a moral view and required allegiances. Liberals saw themselves as breaking down the religious and legal structures inherited from the colonial era, and they were attempting at the same time to establish alternative allegiances and definitive practices. 'Nation' would supersede Church; 'national' would replace universal. Room existed for religion, but within the new confines. Since these new allegiances were to be enforceable by the state, Liberalism contained aspects of tyranny along with the systems it sought to replace.

The declaration of state protection of religious liberty opened the way for a systematic entry of Protestantism into Mexico. Liberals extended their faith in competition to religion as well. The Reform Laws allowed the formation and development of Protestant groups among the population. Henceforth, Protestantism would be associated with the Liberal project. Its appeal would be to 'certain social groups in transition: mine workers, textile workers, wage-labour in agro-industry, casual labourers, and some small rural proprietors', for all of whom their economic situation was precarious. Typical areas of support tended to be in the northern frontier states and in the Puebla–Tlaxcala sierra and border zones, all of them strongly Liberal during the Reform period. The consequence of Protestant entry was not so much free competition in theological ideas, but an increase in United States' influence. Methodism and Presbyterianism, the two main groups to take root in Mexico, had their principal organizations north of the border. Liberals, as has been stressed, viewed United States' models and influences with enthusiastic approval. In Protestantism they saw the complement to their Reform legislation: no longer simply a Reform but a Reformation as well. Idealists to a man (though less so Juárez), they saw in Protestantism a way out of the dilemma of how to establish a mid-nineteenth-century republic in a post-colonial, multi-ethnic society of corporate allegiances. Juárez saw in Protestantism a means of educating the Indian out of his inherited practices. At the same time, however, the Liberal administration was anxious to retain the support of a section of the Catholic lower clergy and encourage them to break away from the hierarchy and form a schismatic church. However, hopes of a Mexican national church proved to be vain.[39]

Juarista priests, though few, have been compared to the insurgent clerics of the wars of Independence. They both found themselves opposed by the ecclesiastical hierarchy and identified themselves with movements of radical political change. Liberal leaders themselves appealed to the insurgent past. Ignacio Mariscal's commemoration in Veracruz in September 1860 of the Hidalgo rising of 1810 placed the Reform movement in the Hidalgo tradition and its opponents on the moral plane of the Spanish colonial regime. Even so, fifty years had lapsed, and the body of Mariscal's remarks went far beyond the theocratic implications of Hidalgo's movement with its Marian connotations. Mariscal also placed the Mexican Reform alongside England's struggle for parliamentary supremacy in the English civil war, the American colonies' struggle for representative government, and the French Revolution's overthrow of monarchy and Church. Above all, he praised civil and religious liberty, which he argued England had bestowed upon the United States and which had made the latter so powerful in his century.[40]

With the Liberal victory in the civil war and the return of the administration to Mexico City, the Reform Laws became effective at the national level for the first time. Continuing to blame the clergy for the civil war, the government on 3 January 1861 levied a fine of one-third of the tithes and one-fifth of parish dues on them, though with provision for exemption if no damage to the Liberal cause could be shown. One of the first actions of President Juárez was the expulsion of the Apostolic Delegate on 12 January, followed by that of the bishops five days later. Archbishop Garza and his four colleagues were given three days to leave the country. On 20 January 1861 Francisco Zarco, radical Minister of Foreign Relations, blamed the clergy for party spirit and exonerated the Liberals entirely. In his view the Reform Laws had not been enacted in a partisan spirit and showed no hostility whatever to religion as such, especially since he recognized that the majority of the population still continued to profess the Catholic religion. The Reform Laws left the Church free of the state and far from politics. He stressed that the government intended to keep things that way.[41]

The Juárez administration had, in any case, not surrendered the idea of using the sale of nationalized ecclesiastical properties for the purpose of negotiating a loan in the United States. This matter became more and more urgent as the full extent of national financial straits became evident in the aftermath of the civil war. The United States in 1861, however, was in no position to attend to Mexican affairs, with the result that the debt question became an overriding international preoccupation. It rapidly became clear during that year that the Juárez government would be forced to confront the issue of a moratorium on the servicing of its external debt. Measures taken against ecclesiastical property since 1856 had not yielded the desired financial results.[42]

. . .

NOTES AND REFERENCES

1. Hamnett Brian R 1978 *Revolución y contrarrevolución en México y el Perú (Liberalismo, realeza y separatismo 1800–1824.* Mexico City, Fondo de Cultura Económica, pp. 372–78. Guerra François-Xavier 1985 *Le Mexique: De l'Ancien Régime à la Révolution.* 2 vols, Paris, Publications de la Sorbonne, I, pp. 142–56.
2. For the late colonial Church, see Farriss N M 1968 *Crown and Clergy in Colonial Mexico 1759–1821: The Crisis of Ecclesiastical Privilege.* London, Athlone Press.
3. In general terms, the crisis may be explored in Hales E E Y 1960 *Revolution and Papacy 1769–1846.* London, Eyre & Spottiswoode. Heyer Friedrich 1969 *The Catholic Church from 1648 to 1870.* London, Adam & Charles Black. Callahan William J and Higgs David (eds) 1979 *Church and Society in Catholic Europe in the Eighteenth Century.* Cambridge University Press.
4. Hale Charles A 1989 *The Transformation of Liberalism in Nineteenth Century Mexico.* Princeton University Press, NJ, p. 220.
5. See, for instance, Staples Anne 1976 *La Iglesia en la primera república federal mexicana (1824–1835).* Mexico City, SepSetentas; Costeloe Michael P 1978 *Church and State in Independent Mexico: A Study in the Patronage Debate 1821–1857.* London, Royal Historical Society. Hales E E Y 1954 *Pio Nono.* London, Eyre & Spottiswoode.
6. Hobsbawm E J 1962 *The Age of Revolution, 1789–1848.* London, Weidenfeld & Nicolson, p. 82. Chadwick Owen 1975 *The Secularization of the European Mind in the 19th Century.* Cambridge University Press, pp. 25, 45–6, 111–39. Fuentes Mares José 1983 *Juárez: Los Estados Unidos y Europa.* Mexico City, Editorial Grijalbo, p. 152.

7. Cuevas Luis G (1851–57) 1954 *El Porvenir de México.* Mexico City, Editorial Jus, p. 457. Noriega Alfonso 1972 *El pensamiento conservador y el conservadurismo mexicano.* 2 vols, Mexico City, UNAM.
8. Sierra Justo (1905–06) 1948 *Juárez: Su obra y su tiempo.* Mexico City, UNAM, pp. 51–52, 88, 95–98. Hale *Transformation* p. 8.
9. Staples *La Iglesia* pp. 74–93. Berry Charles R 1981 *The Reform in Oaxaca 1856–76: A Microhistory of the Liberal Revolution.* Lincoln, NB, and London, University of Nebraska Press, pp. 23–24.
10. Bravo Ugarte J 1965 *Diócesis y obispos de la Iglesia mexicana (1519–1965).* Mexico City, Editorial Jus, pp. 73–76.
11. *BJDOCS* 1, pp. 533–34, 606–07.
12. Ibid pp. 612–15. AGEO FJ 4/13747 and 5/13478.
13. AGEO FJ 12/13790. Juárez Benito 1852 *Exposición al Congreso del Estado.* Oaxaca, p. 33.
14. *BJDOCS* 1, pp. 655–60.
15. AGEO FJ 4/13747.
16. *BJDOCS* 1, pp. 221–25. Reyes Heroles Jesús 1957–61 *El Liberalismo mexicano.* 3 vols, Mexico City, UNAM, III, pp. 24–25.
17. Bazant Jan, 'La Iglesia, el Estado, y la sublevación de Puebla en 1856', *Historia Mexicana* XXXV; i (julio–septiembre 1985), pp. 93–109.
18. De la Portilla Anselmo 1858 *México en 1856 y 1857.* New York, Imprenta de S Hallet, pp. 4–12, 18–20, 29–37. Fuentes Mares José 1985 *Miramón: El hombre.* Mexico City, Editorial Grijalbo, pp. 18–21.
19. Reyes Heroles *Liberalismo* III, pp. 26, 189–90.
20. Alba Victor 1960 *Las ideas sociales contemporáneas en México.* Mexico City, Fondo de Cultura Económica, pp. 49–50, 83–86.
21. Powell T G 1974 *El Liberalismo y el campesinado en el centro de México(1850–1876).* Mexico City, SepSetentas, p. 27.
22. *BJDOCS* 2, p. 242. Reyes Heroles *Liberalismo* III, pp. 25–26, 211–12. For a challenging defence of the Catholic position, see the articles of J J Pesado in *La Cruz.* 7 vols 1855–58, Mexico City.
23. Tamayo Jorge L (ed.) 1957 *Epistolario de Benito Juárez.* Mexico City, p. 42. *BJDOCS* 2, pp. 227–28, 240–43, 269.
24. *BJDOCS* 1, pp. 259–67.
25. *BJDOCS* 2, pp. 242–43, 248. Taracena Angel 1941 *Efemérides oaxaqueñas.* Oaxaca, pp. 121–22.
26. *BJDOCS* 2, pp. 272–73.
27. Bulnes Francisco 1967 *Juárez y las Revoluciones de Ayutla y de la Reforma.* Mexico City, pp. 261–69. Sierra *Juárez* p. 219.
28. Blázquez Carmen 1978 *Miguel Lerdo de Tejada: un liberal veracruzano en la política nacional.* Mexico City, El Colegio de México, pp. 129–30.
29. *BJDOCS* 2, p. 430.

30. Ibid pp. 471–73, 482.
31. De la Torre Villar Ernesto 1960 *El triunfo de la república liberal, 1857–1860.* Mexico City, Fondo de Cultura Económica, pp. 98–113. Sierra *Juárez* pp. 164–69. Blázquez *Miguel Lerdo* pp. 142–45.
32. Torre Villar *El triunfo* pp. 107, 110–11.
33. Reyes Heroles *Liberalismo* III, pp. 216–23.
34. *BJDOCS* 2, pp. 505–10.
35. Ibid pp. 522–24, Manuel Ruiz, Veracruz, 23 July 1859.
36. Ibid pp. 526–32, Juárez, Veracruz, 23 July 1859; pp. 539–40, Juárez to Doblado, Veracruz, 18 August 1859.
37. Knowlton Robert J 1976 *Church Property and the Mexican Reform, 1856–1910.* DeKalb, Northern Illinois University Press, pp. 78–82. See also Staples Anne 'El Estado y la Iglesia en la República Restaurada', in Staples Anne (ed.) 1989 *El Dominio de las Minorías. República Restaurada y Porfiriato.* Mexico City, El Colegio de Mexico, pp. 15–53, see pp. 18–19, 30.
38. Galindo y Galindo Miguel (1904) 1987 *La gran década nacional o relación histórica de la Guerra de Reforma, interventión extranjera y gobierno del archiduque Maximiliano, 1857–1867.* Mexico City, Fondo de Cultura Económica, I, pp. 304–06.
39. Bastien Jean-Pierre 1989 *Los disidentes: sociedades protestantes y revolución en México, 1872–1911.* Mexico City, El Colegio de México, pp. 11–15, 27–28. Baldwin Deborah J 1990 *Protestants and the Mexican Revolution.* Urbana, IL, and Chicago, Illinois University Press, pp. 3–21.
40. Baldwin *Protestants* pp. 3–7. Torre Villar *El triunfo* pp. 173–83.
41. *BJDOCS* 4, pp. 129, 141, 149–60, 281.
42. Ibid pp. 134. Knowlton *Church Property* p. 88.

Chapter 6

JUÁREZ AND THE STATE GOVERNORS

It could be argued that, even allowing for the Church, the Conservative Party, peasant discontent and foreign intervention, the state governors were Juárez's greatest problem. The changing nature of central government authority in the broader period from the 1770s to the 1870s altered the relationship between the official power and civil society at all levels. Institutional transformation, particularly after Independence, affected the structure of power both in terms of political mobilization within the new constitutional system and in relation to patron–client linkages. The impact of these changes had different consequences according to context. The regional fragmentation that resulted from the wars of Independence and the collapse of the colonial order formed the background to the federal experiments of 1824–36 and 1846–53. There is much to be said for the view that federalism in Mexico institutionalized centrifugalism.

The Liberal government's loss of the capital city between 1858 and 1861 and again from 1863 to 1867 greatly reduced its capacity to influence events in the states. In many respects, the real power within the Liberal Party lay with the political chieftains in the regions. They effectively decided that Juárez should lead the Liberal cause during the civil war of the Reform. They strove to keep him subordinate to their interests: a figurehead, nothing more. They appropriated federal revenues for their own internal purposes. They exploited to the full the diminution of central government authority in the Constitution of 1857. Juárez struggled throughout his presidency to free himself from their tutelage and to bear down upon their defiance. In this endeavour, he pursued every stratagem known to him. An empty Treasury and repeated foreign dangers ensured that Juárez would be working from the worst possible position. Yet in this adversity, Juárez thrived. His strength lay not in the deployment of superior armed force, but in political skills. These he demonstrated to their greatest effect during his moments of greatest weakness and danger. One by one, every opponent was either disarmed or broken completely, from the Conservative generals, Miramón, Mejía and Márquez to the Liberal state governors and political rivals, Miguel Lerdo, Vidaurri, González Ortega, Sebastián Lerdo and Porfirio Díaz. Since all of them were powerful figures and capable national leaders in their own right, the measure of Juárez's achievement in fighting them off and retaining control of power should not be underestimated.

. . .

THE STATE GOVERNORS AND THE CIVIL WAR

Juárez passed through three state capitals, Querétaro, Guanajuato and Guadalajara, in his retreat northwards from the Conservative Army in the spring of 1858. His position depended initially upon the kind mercies of their governors. He had no power base in those regions and was largely unknown in the interior – except as the author of the Juárez Law. Effective power lay with the state governors, elected under the Constitution but risen to prominence through the Revolution of Ayutla. After the Conservatives in Mexico City removed Comonfort from office on 11 January, a coalition of state governors led by Doblado (Guanajuato) and General Anastasio Parrodi (Jalisco), and including those of Colima, Querétaro, Michoacán, Veracruz, Guerrero and Oaxaca, repudiated the coup and denounced Comonfort for breaking his oath to the Constitution. Following constitutional provisions, they pronounced Juárez to be interim President in Comonfort's default. These governors were the principal commanders of Liberal forces and they had at their disposition the National Guard contingents of their respective states. In the civil war they fought, won, lost and paid for the armed conflicts with the Conservative enemy. To all intents and purposes, they, rather than Juárez, inherited the power left by Comonfort. From the vantage point of the state governments, the latter's administration had broken apart over the issue of the reconstruction of the power of the federal executive in relation to that of the states. A great deal of the radical federalism of 1823–24, following the collapse of central authority, recurred in 1858. The existence of an enemy ideology and armed force in control of the federal capital offered a priceless political gift to the state governors. It was their ideal scenario. In fact, they opened the civil war of the Reform with declarations of the reversion of sovereignty to the states.[1]

Juárez owed his presidency, then, to the pronouncement of the governors of the centre-northern tier of states. They themselves owed Juárez nothing. He did not know any of them intimately and came from a different region and another race. The extent to which ethnicity was involved in Juárez's relations with his political allies and opponents (often one and the same) is not easy to determine. It was intangible but implicitly all-pervading. Events demonstrated that the wisest course for Juárez to take would be to trust no one. That course he generally pursued, with the sole exception of his Oaxaca intimates such as Ignacio Mejía, Miguel Castro and Matías Romero, and his Cuban friends.

Doblado had been, in fact, the first to seize the political initiative after the coup of 17 December 1857. Juárez was, in any case, in jail, when Doblado's Guanajuato Proclamation of 25 December warned of the threat of foreign intervention as the country descended into civil war. A moderate Liberal, he had always disliked the Constitution and now made public his belief that it should be reformed. Even so, he admitted that it was the basis of legitimacy for the Liberal cause. Juárez, in Guanajuato, took up precisely that theme on 17 January 1858. He took his stand right from the beginning of the civil war on the idea that law should be the basis of political life, and that Mexico should never again be at the mercy of one man or one faction. The Constitution, he argued, represented the embodiment of the 'general will'. He admitted, however, that Congress could no longer be in session, and that, as a result, 'I shall determine the measures which the circumstances may demand'.[2]

In reality, then, Juárez based his position on the powers of the presidency, while affirming the constitutional origin of his authority. He sought to found his executive action in law, while at the same time creating an alternative source of authority to that represented by the state governors. From Monterrey, Vidaurri, governor of the amalgamated states of Coahuila-Nuevo León, announced his support for Juárez on 31 January. The large number of free municipalities formed out of haciendas and *ranchos* and repeatedly threatened by Indian raids constituted the military base of Vidaurri's power, which rested upon control of the National Guard. The latter claimed to see in Juárez the means of uniting the very divided 'great Liberal Party', but, at the same time, appealed to him not to allow federal troops to operate within the confines of his territory and reminded him that he had opposed Comonfort on that point. Clearly, Vidaurri intended to protect his independent power base in the north-east and concede nothing to the shadow of a federal government that Juárez then represented. The latter found itself largely powerless in face of the appropriation of federal revenues by state governors and by private political chieftains for their own purposes. The Juárez government's diminished area of practical control was evident for all to see.[3]

Juárez, however, had three advantages: the victories of Conservative generals over his Liberal allies; the extraordinary powers he had inherited from Comonfort and which the dissolved Congress had granted on 5 November 1857; and his own ability to play one rival against another. Fuentes Mares, not a *juarista* historian, even argues that 'the Constitution had no importance at all for the constitutional government'. Juárez retained those extraordinary powers until he surrendered them on 9 May 1861 to the Congress elected after the end of the war. In the mean time, the Conservative victory at Salamanca on 11 March 1858 removed Doblado from the war and led to the fall of Guadalajara and the effective elimination of Parrodi. These disasters would have left Juárez dangerously dependent upon Vidaurri, had it not been for the entry of Santos Degollado, governor of Michoacán, into the field. As Minister of War, Degollado took over the supreme command vacated by Parrodi. Degollado, like Doblado, was a native of Guanajuato. A disciple and intimate of Ocampo, he was also the inseparable companion of Benito Gómez Farías, son of Valentín, the Liberal Vice-President of the 1833–34 administration. Unlike Miramón, Osollo, Márquez and Mejía, all professional soldiers, the Liberal commanders were mostly lawyers. This gave the Liberal cause a distinct disadvantage on the field of battle. However, it was outweighed by the fact that Liberals controlled virtually all the maritime and frontier states, with the result that customs receipts, the principal revenue of government, fell into their hands. That did not necessarily benefit the Juárez administration, since these revenues were generally appropriated by the state governors for internal purposes. Vidaurri controlled the US border trade and the revenues of Matamoros; other state governors controlled those of Tampico (Tamaulipas), Guaymas (Sonora) and Mazatlán (Sinaloa), while Álvarez controlled Acapulco and Lozada San Blas.[4]

The carefully nurtured base in Oaxaca could not sustain Juárez in a national leadership. Even so, it did bring skilful political figures on to the national stage, all of them in close alliance with Juárez at least until 1865. Juárez needed support from outside his home state and beyond his personal circle. This he constantly and shiftingly sought to build throughout his presidency. Each of these circles of support represented different stages of the Reform process. Each of the central personalities involved saw in Juárez different things. As he passed through these stages, Juárez was prepared not only to shift ground but also to dispense with individuals. Although President, he often seemed marginalized in his own governments. Two explanations lay at the root. First, his principal ministers tended to be outstanding men who felt themselves to be his intellectual superiors. Second, Juárez from the outset was concerned to cultivate a political base among the mass of ordinary people and beyond the narrow group of intellectuals. While he did not ostensibly have the common touch and decidedly recoiled from charisma, he sought to hold and retain an unassailable moral superiority which distinguished him from all his predecessors and contemporaries. Living that image made Juárez immediately identifiable in the popular mind. It contributed in no small way to his final victories.

This high moral note entered during the first months of the war. As Juárez explained to Santacilia, the two key principles at stake were 'absolute independence of the civil power' and 'religious liberty' – 'for me, these points are the key ones to be gained during this revolution'. After narrowly escaping the firing squad in Guadalajara, Juárez and his ministers, Ocampo, Ruiz, Prieto and Guzmán, defined their principles in a Manifesto directed to the people of the city on 16 March

1858. They described the cause of 'democratic ideas' as a 'holy cause', and as such 'invincible', since 'democracy is the destiny of future humanity'. After darkly hinting that 'persons of great influence in this city' were behind the attempt on the ministers' lives, Juárez's address to the people on the following day referred to democrats as those who worked in the spirit of 1810 for the removal of the privileges that divided man from man. He pointed to the danger that Conservative victories threatened to turn the clock back to 1821, though he remained confident that liberty would prevail over 'aristocracy'. Stressing the constitutional legitimacy of their title, Juárez and his ministers staked out the high moral ground above the governors, chieftains and factions. Juárez stressed the distinction between his 'humble person' and his 'exalted office'. The development of this distinction would form the guiding-line of his presidency.[5]

. . .

THE JUÁREZ REGIME IN VERACRUZ

Juárez and his ministers arrived in Veracruz (by way of Panama) on 4 May 1858. The Gulf port became the seat of the Liberal regime for the duration of the war. The state governor, Manuel Gutiérrez Zamora, was none too pleased to have Juárez on his territory. Son of a Veracruz merchant, he belonged to the 'red' wing of the Liberal Party and was little inclined to bow to the will of a Oaxacan politician who had no immediate claim on the loyalties of Veracruzanos, other than the moral authority he claimed by virtue of the defection of Comonfort. Gutiérrez Zamora's political instincts gravitated more in the direction of Miguel Lerdo, a fellow Veracruzano and radical. Increasingly, Lerdo seemed to many radicals to be more the natural Liberal leader than Juárez. Lerdo, as Minister of Finance and Development from January 1859 until June 1860, occupied the central role in the cabinet. The ideological differences and personal tensions between Lerdo and Ocampo seriously divided the cabinet throughout this period.[6]

From that rivalry Juárez benefited, since he was, thereby, able to strengthen his claim to the leadership. This conflict worsened during the year 1860. Ruiz, who in many respects was Juárez's alter ego, supported Lerdo. Ignacio de la Llave, the Minister of the Interior, was a personal friend of Gutiérrez Zamora and of the Lerdo family. When the year opened, the majority of Juárez's ministers were Veracruzanos with commercial connections, who shared Lerdo's enthusiasm for the USA and his desire for a US loan, even at the cost of territorial concessions, since it could not be guaranteed by the mortgage of nationalized properties. According to Fuentes Mares, Ocampo described Lerdo as despairing of Mexico, believing that only the United States could save it, and wanting to see an 'American and Protestant' republic. Lerdo despaired of Liberal military failures and saw in US armed intervention the only hope of winning the war. Only a US protectorate could destroy the Conservative Party and save Mexico from a return to Spanish colonialism. For that reason, Fuentes Mares condemned the Reform leaders for their 'Poinsettism'.[7]

These rivalries threatened the stability of the Juárez administration in the midst of a civil war, which the Liberal Party was not winning. After the Liberal disaster at Estancia de las Vacas, the Conservatives in October 1859 published the captured correspondence between Ocampo and Degollado concerning Lerdo's attempt to negotiate a loan in the USA. Worse still, however, was the breach between Vidaurri and the Juárez administration. At that time, Juárez was working towards a rapprochement with Doblado, in order to make himself less dependent upon the two principal Liberal commanders, Degollado and Vidaurri. Each wanted supreme command of the army, but Juárez was determined that neither of them should have it, since both had proved themselves no match for Miramón. Accordingly, Juárez in mid-August 1859 transferred the command to Doblado (an even earlier failure), regardless of the offence that the other two would take. Vidaurri's response was the repudiation of the Juárez regime and the declaration of the independence of Nuevo León-Coahuila as a sovereign state on 5 September. Juárez responded by sending his rival, Degollado, then governor of Colima, to reduce Vidaurri to obedience. Degollado declared Vidaurri an outlaw, advanced on his territory, and forced him over the Texas border. In this way, Juárez, while depriving Degollado of the supreme command, had also temporarily removed his most dangerous rival, a task in which the latter was ready to cooperate. By so doing, Juárez strengthened the presidency, made the federal government once more an active factor in Mexican politics, and gave practical effect to his claim to moral superiority over the state governors and party factions.[8]

Within the government itself, nevertheless, Juárez was by no means safe. The threat posed by Lerdo remained. The central issue of contention was Lerdo's proposal of mediation as a means to terminate the civil war. This Juárez resolutely opposed. Lerdo advocated a policy of accommodation with the Conservative regime in Mexico City by means of a negotiated settlement. Ocampo supported Juárez on this issue, since the inevitable precondition would be the abandonment of the 1857 Constitution. Equally seriously, it also involved the abandonment of the Juárez presidency, the election of a new president, the election of a new Congress, which would then form a new Constitution, and finally, the recognition of the measures taken by both the Conservative and Liberal regimes on the same legal footing. These issues led to a complete break between Juárez and Lerdo during March and April 1860. This came to a head when Juárez accepted the latter's resignation on 30 May, after the cabinet refused to concur with his recommendation that Mexico should suspend the payment of its foreign debt, because of the gravity of the country's financial situation. Thereafter, Lerdo was a rival for the presidential office.[9]

Juárez saw in mediation not only an attempt by his rivals to remove him from office but also the sacrifice of the Constitution upon which he had made his claim to legitimacy. From that time onwards, if not before, Juárez trusted no one with the Liberal revolution but himself. He would, accordingly, do his utmost to hold on to the presidential office and fight off all contenders. Juárez's position appeared to worsen, however, in the autumn of 1860, when Santos Degollado, hitherto his tactical ally, joined the camp of those anxious to end the war by mediation. Degollado had been in contact with George Mathews, the British Chargé d'Affaires in Mexico City. From 18 September Mathews had been proposing mediation through the diplomatic corps in the capital – none of whom had recognized the Juárez presidency. The method would be the formation of a junta composed of members of the diplomatic corps and one nominee from each of the state governors. This junta would then appoint a provisional president. Degollado had authorized Mathews to publish this plan. It meant the removal of Juárez, who was considered to be the principal obstacle to peace – as he would be again in 1863–67. Juárez sought to counter this manoeuvre. He wrote directly to Degollado, protesting against 'a course of action as unexpected as it is dangerous for the cause of liberty, the dignity of the nation, and the future of our country'. In his view, the proposal handed over Mexico's future to the representatives of the European powers, all of whom had recognized the regime brought to power by the *coup d'état* of December 1857. Their interest was to see the end of the Liberal revolution by means of a 'transaction in which the Constitution in force would be sacrificed in order that they should not be faced with the inconvenience of having to recognize the present constitutional government'. Juárez refused to lend his support, since 'I cannot renege on my oath to uphold the Constitution, and hand over the tenure of the presidency, along with the custodianship of law and justice'. He regarded Degollado's suggestions as tantamount to surrendering representative government in order to restore peace. Juárez warned Degollado of his total disapproval of his actions, which he would use all his powers to oppose. In effect, he had lost whatever confidence he had had in Degollado. In Juárez's view, Degollado had betrayed the revolution. The desired 'pacification' would be achieved, he wrote to the governor of Chiapas, only with a complete military victory over the Conservative regime.[10]

Degollado's action was also condemned by General Jesús González Ortega, at that time tightening the siege of Guadalajara. González Ortega reaffirmed the idea that the states of the interior were engaged in a military struggle in defence of the Constitution and the Reform Laws. In such a way, Juárez in late October 1860 came into close, tactical alliance with González Ortega, principal Liberal commander and author of the final victory at Calpulalpan on 22 December. No indication existed, however, that the alliance between the two politicians would be anything but short-lived.[11]

The Liberal victory at the end of 1860, which brought the Veracruz administration back to Mexico City, revealed one new significant development. This was the political preponderance of Juárez. That was not, however, to the liking of many in the higher ranks of the Liberal Party. From this time onwards Juárez himself became an issue within the Liberal camp perhaps more so than all the others. Cadenhead gives considerable attention to Juárez's five principal achievements during the Veracruz period. He had kept the cabinet intact; he had promulgated the Reform Laws and begun their application; he had held off US pressures for territorial concessions and transit rights; he had secured US recognition of his administration in 1859 and positive assistance in 1860; he had set the precedents for curbing the powers of the privileged classes. These were powerful achievements – largely attributable to Juárez's skill as coordinator of a cabinet of men with differing viewpoints and objectives. This skill was tested to breaking point during the worst months of the civil war. It enabled him to give sufficient credibility to his regime to merit recognition by the Buchanan administration, which had until then hoped to wheedle concessions out of the Conservatives. The factor of US recognition, with which we shall deal more fully in Chapter 7, proved to be decisive in the outcome of Juárez's struggle to fend off his rivals and forge the Liberal Party into a sufficiently coherent element to overthrow the *golpista* regime.[12]

. . .

JUÁREZ AND CONGRESS

In spite of the professed loyalty to the 1857 Constitution, however, the Juárez regime itself remained, as Sierra made great play of stressing, a virtual dictatorship. After the election of the new Constitutional Congress, Juárez on 9 May 1861 surrendered the extraordinary powers inherited from Comonfort. The regular sessions of Congress nevertheless introduced another dimension into the already deepening (but more traditional) rivalry between personalities. This was the politics of legislative–executive relations, with which the former henceforth became inextricably entangled. The existence of several congressional factions opposed to Juárez provided his pre-existing rivals with powerful allies at the centre of the political system in Mexico City. Juárez, then, found himself fending off both state governors and Congress at the same time. Both accused him of 'presidentialism'. These conflicts left Juárez with a singularly bad impression of the way that the 1857 Constitution worked in practice.

In the presidential elections of March 1861, Juárez faced two opponents, Lerdo and González Ortega, both of whom he easily defeated. Juárez won 5,289 votes, while Lerdo received 1,989 and González Ortega 1,846, mainly from the north-centre tier of states. Lerdo had in any case been eliminated by typhoid on 22 March. Six days earlier, Márquez, operating with Conservative irregular bands, issued a declaration that Juárez and all his committed supporters were traitors, who would, if caught, be summarily executed, with the sole formality of identification. In this way, Ocampo was assassinated on 3 June and Degollado killed in an ambush by Conservative guerrillas on 15 June 1861, the same day that Juárez began his first term as constitutionally elected President. Death also removed Gutiérrez Zamora. This left González Ortega as Juárez's principal rival for the leadership of the victorious Liberal cause. Doblado gave his support to González Ortega. The latter had entered Mexico City at the head of 25,000 men as the victor in the armed struggle and ahead of Juárez. The Zacatecas Division remained in occupation of the national capital for several months. The obvious tension between Juárez and González Ortega over this matter accompanied another concerted attempt to remove the President from office. This time the attempt, which was concerted with the congressional opposition, took place after Juárez's election victory. It therefore represented an opposition attempt indirectly to nullify that result.[13]

The leaders of the anti-Juárez faction in and out of Congress represented the interests of the centre-northern and northern tiers of states. They considered themselves to be the real authors of the Reform. They regarded Juárez as only a secondary figure in the Liberal Party, one who had dragged his feet at every stage of the advances for which they had pressed. The states themselves had taken the radical initiatives, while the Juárez administration had debated what to do about them. In this sense, the conflicts of 1861–63 emerged logically out of the politics of the civil war of the Reform. As such, they represented not merely a replay but the augmentation, if not inflation, of those of 1856–57, which had brought down the Comonfort administration. The essential continuity in Mexican politics was not, as is so often popularly favoured, between Juárez and Porfirio Díaz, but more especially between Juárez and Comonfort. We can appreciate therefore both the precarious nature of Juárez's position and his skill at overriding it. Accordingly, the contrast with Comonfort could not be more striking.

Juárez's skill as a political tactician could be seen from his readiness to work with individuals from all wings of the party. At the same time, he remained unidentified with any one faction. He was never coopted or subsumed into any of them. On the contrary, he distanced himself from both moderates and radicals. The former remained, in his eyes, too closely identified with the coup of December 1857. He suspected them of again wanting to close down Congress and rescind the Constitution. As he explained to Vidaurri in May 1861 – before their rupture – 'the moderates, conservatives, and the ambitious men of Liberalism were working to transform Congress into a Convention with dictatorial faculties. By this means, they would set aside the Constitution and give the Nation a new political structure. However, such a ploy will come to nothing, because Congress itself will prevent it.'[14]

The 'opposition' complained, as it would again after 1867, that Juárez governed through a narrow circle of intimates. Even so, only one other Oaxacan, Manuel Ruiz, held cabinet office at that time. Yet, the opposition in the states and Congress did not constitute an ideologically homogeneous group. They were not uniformly radical or '*rojo*', but spanned the spectrum of Liberalism. They were motivated by the guiding principle of personal dislike of Juárez. A rival personal party formed around González Ortega during August and September 1861. They believed him to be the military man of the moment, as their spiritual heirs in 1867–72 would do with regard to Díaz.[15]

Since the Liberal radicals themselves did not form a solid group, but divided on the issue of who to support, Juárez was able to cream off a sufficient number of their votes. González Ortega had been elected President of the Supreme Court and was at that time Minister of War. With his ally, Doblado, he objected to the radicals in Juárez's cabinet and pressed for their removal. Juárez's cabinet of 1861 was the most radical of his entire presidency. It included Zarco at Internal and External Affairs, Ignacio Ramírez at Justice and Public Instruction, and Prieto at Finance. Juárez could count on the support of radical deputies in Congress and the radical element in the military. This combination proved effective enough to sustain

Juárez in the presidency. With such an array of radical support, Juárez was able to hold off charges that he had halted the Reform process. In such a way, he was able to divide and confuse the opposition to him within his own party. On 15 September, 1861, when fifty-one deputies, who included Mariano Riva Palacio, son-in-law of Guerrero, Manuel Romero Rubio and Ignacio Altamirano requested Juárez to step down in favour of González Ortega, fifty-two deputies voted to sustain him in office. They included Díaz, Manuel Dublán and Ignacio Mariscal, all Oaxacans. Juárez could also count on the support of the state governors of Querétaro, Jalisco and Chihuahua.[16]

The opposition accused Juárez of dithering, of squandering federal Treasury funds, of leaving the country exposed to foreign intervention through the deterioration of relations with Great Britain and France, and of worsening relations between the federal government and the states through attempting to deprive the latter of 20 per cent of their revenues. Above all, these deputies claimed to resent the remoteness, as they put it, of the Juárez circle, which they saw as determined to keep power for itself. Governor Arteaga of Querétaro, however, warned them of the dangers of removing Juárez from office at that time. He made a clear distinction between the Reform movement and all the previous rebellions since Independence, on the grounds that the former was social and national in scale. Its aim was the preservation of the law, not the prevalence of the sword. The current conspiracy to overthrow Juárez threatened to push the country into anarchy, since the President had been only recently elected to office. Arteaga inquired of the deputies, 'What, then, of the Constitution, the electoral law, and the public vote, in a country in which the President is required to step down from the high office to which he has been raised by the national will at the simple behest of a few individuals who request him to do so?' The state of Querétaro had actually voted for González Ortega, but Arteaga emphasized that it conformed entirely to the majority vote in favour of Juárez. The state Congress of Chihuahua condemned the opposition manoeuvre on 21 October 1861 as an attempt to subvert the constitutional order and the democratic system.[17]

In this way, Juárez received powerful support from a broad range of Liberal opinion throughout the Republic, a testimony to the strong position that he had built for himself during the Veracruz period.

The chief issues of the period 1861–63, then, concerned the relation between the legislative and executive branches and between the central government and the states. Once the Liberals regained the capital city, the Constitution of 1857 would be applied to the full extent of national territory. The nature of government according to its precepts soon became clear. The focus fell upon the role of the President within the political system. Similarly, the relationship between official Liberalism – increasingly described as *juarismo* – and the Liberal cadres in the provinces became crucial. For these reasons, this short period is a crucial one, though it has usually been seen as little more than the background to the French Intervention. There was much in those years that foreshadowed the struggle of the last five years of Juárez after 1867. The understandable historiographical preoccupation with the Intervention and the day-to-day struggles of the beleaguered Juárez administration in internal exile has obscured these continuities. Nevertheless, they can be discerned, if we look, beneath all the current issues of those terrible years.

As the holder of the presidential office after January 1858, Juárez portrayed himself as the symbol of Mexican nationhood, the figure upon whom national survival depended. In such a way, he attempted to set the idea of the Republic above the narrower perspectives of the individual states. Juárez's stance was for internal consumption. The identification with Mexican nationalism, however, responded to the deterioration of the country's foreign relations and the real danger of European intervention in the latter part of 1861 to enforce debt-payment. Congress, in session until 31 May 1863, remained preoccupied with its struggle to impose its will on the President. The legislature's efforts to undermine the position of the executive, in the name of defence of the Constitution, continued unabated. This was the case even after European forces had landed in Veracruz in December 1861 and January 1862. Congress interpreted the purpose of the Constitution as the transformation from a presidential to a parliamentary system. Beyond the federal capital, the customary interrelation of personalist and constitutionalist politics operated at all levels.

The allied landings in Veracruz raised relations between

President and Congress to a new pitch of mistrust. Juárez requested investiture with extraordinary faculties, in order to coordinate responses to the foreign threat. Congress saw this as a return to rule by executive decree and a serious threat to its constitutional position. Deputies reluctantly conceded the point on 11 December 1861. Invested with these powers, Juárez issued the law of 25 January 1862 which defined a 'crime against the nation' and established the death penalty for collaboration with Intervention forces. When Napoleon III's designs on Mexico became clear, the British and Spanish contingents of those forces returned home, while the French Army moved to take positions inland. Accordingly, Congress on 3 May 1862 suspended constitutional guarantees until either the meeting of the new session on 16 September or the termination of armed conflict. The French Government hoped to take advantage of the civil war in the United States to establish political control in Mexico.[18]

. . .

THE STRUGGLE WITH VIDAURRI

The most serious challenge to Juárez from a state governor came from Vidaurri. The latter had secured control of three states in the north-east at the time of the Revolution of Ayutla in 1855. He had seized the opportunity of Santa Anna's downfall to consolidate his power base there with the aid of the territorial militia. Since Vidaurri controlled the US border trade and took the revenues of the customs houses, he could keep this personal army regularly paid. In 1856 he had obliged the Comonfort administration to sanction his unilateral merging of the two states of Nuevo León and Coahuila. In order to give some constitutional respectability to his position, Vidaurri sheltered behind the doctrine of defence of states' rights. He saw his relationship to the national government as strictly contingent upon its respect for them. In his dealings with Juárez, Vidaurri behaved as if he were the sovereign of an autonomous territory. He had specifically requested Juárez during the civil war of the Reform not to send federal troops into Nuevo León–Coahuila. Vidaurri protected local business interests and himself controlled large properties. The rise of Monterrey, a border town since 1848, began in this period. He was rabidly anticlerical, a freemason, who admitted Protestant missionaries into his territory. He had arrested and deported the bishop of Linares and then the rest of the clergy in January 1858. By September 1858 Vidaurri, at the height of his power, controlled a force of 7,500 men. His breach with Juárez in that month, however, forced him momentarily across the Texas border.[19]

As events within the USA in 1860–61 moved closer towards civil war, the position of Vidaurri, restored to power in January 1860, became crucial. Vidaurri sought to assert his absolute authority within his territory. The majority of deputies elected to the state Congress, however, opposed this absolutism. The state Congress, accordingly, withdrew from Monterrey and reassembled in Galeana under the protection of General Mariano Escobedo, who had formerly been a protégé of Vidaurri. Escobedo and his fellow officers, Ignacio Zaragoza and Jerónimo Treviño, also from Nuevo León, moved firmly into the Juárez camp. When Escobedo fled into *juarista* territory in July, the President refused to surrender him to Vidaurri, who demanded his trial or expulsion from the army. In this way, the *cacique* of the north-east lost three of his best commanders to Juárez.[20]

After the outbreak of the civil war in the USA, Vidaurri became a key figure in the political calculations of the Confederacy. At about that time a rumour began to circulate that Vidaurri was proposing to set up an independent state to be known as the 'Republic of the Sierra Madre'. This would be composed of Mexico's northern frontier states and the state of Texas. It would be allied to the Confederacy. Vidaurri went to great lengths to deny the rumour. He even wrote to the editor of *Southern Intelligence* in Austin, Texas, on 28 February 1861, which had printed the allegation, that it was a calumny planted by his political enemies. He stressed that, although he had always cultivated good relations with Texas, he remained first and foremost a Mexican patriot who stood for the indissolubility of the Mexican Republic. Nevertheless, he explained to Juárez shortly afterwards that Indian raids across the border prevented the dispatch of any public revenues from his territory to Mexico City, regardless of whether they were legally federal or not. Federal revenue remained so scant in those months that Juárez reduced his own annual salary from 36,000 to 30,000 pesos and imposed further economies in public spending.[21]

Juárez's relations with Vidaurri further deteriorated when Comonfort reappeared in Mexico and was granted asylum in Monterrey. Juárez, still blaming Comonfort for the coup of 1857, ordered his arrest and trial in Mexico City. Vidaurri refused to surrender him. He stood by the right of asylum and argued that Juárez was acting unconstitutionally, especially since Comonfort presented no danger to anyone. Instead of handing him over, Vidaurri in July 1861 appointed Comonfort commander of the Nuevo León militia.[22]

The outbreak of civil war north of the border strengthened Vidaurri's hand considerably. He was actively courted by the Confederates, who depended on Matamoros as the port of entry for war supplies into Texas. Southern cotton passed through the Mexican customs at Piedras Negras and thence to Matamoros, or from Corpus Christi to Tampico. The Confederacy was able thereby to circumvent the Union blockade, and Vidaurri was able to control increasing revenues. In June, Vidaurri received the Confederate agent, José Agustín Quintero, in Monterrey. Sent there by Jefferson Davis in order to secure the border, Quintero brought a letter from the Secretary of State, Robert Toombs, in which the Confederacy renounced any territorial ambitions at Mexico's expense and drew Vidaurri's attention to the initially peaceful struggle of the Confederate States to free themselves from an 'oppressive and discordant alliance'. The Confederate Commander of the Texas Second Cavalry Regiment went as far as to propose joint operations against raiding Indian bands. Vidaurri discreetly declined. Davis also wrote to Governor Luis Terrazas of Chihuahua. Terrazas received Colonel James Reilly of the Texas Cavalry Volunteers early in January 1862. Reilly wanted Terrazas's assurance that no Union troops would be allowed to cross Chihuahua territory. Terrazas took his stand on the sole constitutional right of the federal government to permit or deny the entry of foreign troops. He would permit no violation of Mexican neutrality.[23]

. . .

THE IMPACT OF THE FRENCH INTERVENTION

The Confederates sought to exploit Mexican centrifugalism to their advantage. They encountered, however, two opposing positions, Vidaurri's home brand of secessionism and

Terrazas's ostensible loyalty to the federation. At the same time, the Davis government had still not despaired of winning over the Juárez ministry to the Confederate side. With the landing of the tripartite debt-collection mission in Veracruz, the position of Juárez began to seem hopeless. Once again, the state governors, as in 1858–59, appeared able to seize the initiative from him. With the advance of French Intervention forces towards Mexico City in May 1863, the Juárez government abandoned the national capital and sought refuge in the interior, that is among the state governors. While Confederate diplomacy retained its perennial interest in Vidaurri, attention turned at the national level towards the French and the Empire they were in the process of establishing in Mexico.

From June to December 1863, the Juárez government resided in San Luis Potosí. Moderate Liberals immediately pressed for the removal of Juárez and the formation of a cabinet by Doblado, then virtual chief minister. The latter used his stronger position to undermine the position of Zarco and Zamacona in the cabinet. Juárez protected them and by so doing forced Doblado to resign on 7 September. This cleared the way for the entry of Sebastián Lerdo into the central position in the cabinet. Lerdo, long a sceptic of the Constitution and a well-known moderate Liberal, became Juárez's principal collaborator until their breach over the second re-election issue in 1871. Juárez's alignment with Lerdo neutralized the moderate Liberals and prepared the way for the weakening of the radicals, as the new ministry strove to present itself as the national rallying-point against the foreign invader. The radicalism of the period 1859–63 had clearly come to an end. Lerdo was also a crypto-centralist, as ill-disposed as Juárez to the virtual autonomy of the state governors. Crucially at this stage, Comonfort re-entered the government as Minister of War. The reappearance of a forgiven Comonfort gave the ministry an uncanny resemblance to that of the autumn of 1857. This time Juárez occupied the presidential office, a Juárez who had experienced the independence of the state governors in 1858–59 and the parliamentary aspirations of Congress in 1861–63. Their connivance in September 1861 had posed a serious threat to his position. Increasingly, it would seem that these were his two principal enemies. The scene was already being set for the grim struggles after 1867.[24]

The northward advance of the French Army forced Juárez to seek refuge early in 1864 in Saltillo, which lay within Vidaurri's domain, since it was formerly the state capital of Coahuila. Vidaurri, however, had not organized any forces to oppose the French. Doblado and González Ortega, governors of Guanajuato and Zacatecas respectively, two of Juárez's most bitter enemies, still retained command of Liberal forces. Congress, however, in its last session on 31 May 1863, had conceded to Juárez extraordinary powers for the entire duration of the French occupation, a period that it had been impossible to define. Juárez intended to use these powers to bolster his authority. Again, as in 1860, the issue of Juárez himself became the bone of contention among the leaders of the Liberal camp.

Juárez refused to compromise on the matter of unrelenting resistance to the French, just as in 1860 he had opposed any compromise with the Conservatives. Doblado and Ortega, in company with the governor of Aguascalientes, argued, just as Miguel Lerdo and Degollado had done four years earlier, that the principal obstacle to peace was Juárez. They believed that the political situation would improve considerably, if Juárez were removed from office. Their aim was to open negotiations with the French for an end to the Intervention. This Juárez viewed as treason. He had no intention of being pushed out of office by anyone, especially since he believed that his own removal would lead to the opening of negotiations with an enemy bent on subjecting Mexico to a renewed European tutelage. Representatives of the two generals took a letter to Juárez in Saltillo on 9 January 1864 conveying their views. They also sent another letter to Miramón, offering him the possibility of placing himself at the disposition of moderate opinion. Juárez and Miramón were equally intransigent in their rejection of the proposals. Miramón preferred to place his trust in the Archduke Maximilian, whose arrival was impending. Juárez replied that the French and the Conservatives were not fighting against him personally but against the Mexican Republic. He also reminded his opponents that no guarantee existed that the nation would accept González Ortega in his place.[25]

Governors Patoni of Durango and Terrazas of Chihuahua refused to take part in this manoeuvre against Juárez. Both supported him in his struggle against Vidaurri and in his refusal to come to terms with the Imperialists. Terrazas described the scheme as an 'anti-national pretension'. Vidaurri, however, called for the removal of Juárez.[26]

The years 1862–64 were profitable for Vidaurri and the business interests of Monterrey and Matamoros. The latter was the only exit route for the South's cotton, after the Union blockade of Texas ports. The climax of the conflict between Nuevo León and the federal government came in February 1864. Juárez went in person to Monterrey, but no agreement was reached with Vidaurri. Accordingly, Juárez, upon returning to Saltillo, began the process of destroying his position. On 26 February he decreed the separation of Coahuila and Nuevo León, used rival army officers to force Vidaurri from office and into exile across the Texas border, and established the republican capital in Monterrey on 3 August. Juárez, thereupon, nominated a series of governors of the state loyal to himself. The French advance into the north-east, however, enabled Vidaurri to recover control of Nuevo León, after the flight of the Juárez government, on 7 September 1864. In order to consolidate his position, Vidaurri repudiated the republican cause and rallied to the empire at the invitation of Marshall Bazaine, who had been making overtures to him since February. In return for this support, Maximilian appointed him to the Imperial Council and for a time Vidaurri held the Ministry of Finance. Juárez believed that he was in league with the Confederates to fulfil Napoleon III's designs in northern Mexico. To Romero in Washington he expressed the hope that the Lincoln Administration would invoke the Monroe Doctrine, in order to counter them.[27]

. . .

JUÁREZ IN CHIHUAHUA

From October 1864 the Liberal position was desperate. The Juárez government, such as it was, found itself confined to the state of Chihuahua from 12 October 1864 until 10 December 1866. In fact, from 14 August to 13 November 1865 and again from 18 December 1865 until 10 June 1866 Juárez was obliged to take up residence in the border town of Paso del Norte (now Ciudad Juárez) on the south bank of the Río Grande opposite El Paso, Texas. According to the US Consul in Chihuahua, Rubén Creel, only Juárez's strong character kept him from despair. The situation within the state of Chihuahua did not appear in any way favourable to Juárez. Governor Terrazas had already put the product of the sale of nationalized ecclesiastical property towards the administrative costs of his state, in order to pay off debts contracted during the civil war. This contravened the federal law of 5 February 1861, which excluded state governors from any intervention in the disposal of such property. Terrazas, moreover, found himself by February 1864 in no position either to release funds to the federal government or to send military support, in view of continued Indian threats. This position initially prejudiced Juárez against him and a series of misjudged actions on the President's part thereupon followed.

The Terrazas family were already in the process of constructing a powerful economic and political position within Chihuahua. Although it did not turn out to be the case initially, Juárez came to depend upon this strong position for his survival as a national political figure during the gravest moments of his presidency. Terrazas's father had been a prominent member of the city council of Chihuahua City, owned a shop, a soap factory, rural property, livestock and slaughter-houses. After Luis Terrazas abandoned all idea of a priestly vocation by 1849, he began to accumulate further landed properties and livestock. By 1884, the family owned 5.6 million hectares of the best land in the state. Initially a *santanista*, he rallied to the Revolution of Ayutla in September 1855, along with other Chihuahua notables, only after its triumph. Several members of the family, which was related to the Zuloagas, who had settled in the state since the 1780s, took the Conservative side during the civil war of the Reform. By 1859, Luis Terrazas was *jefe político* of the capital city, and in the following year colonel of the National Guard. Pressure by his armed supporters took him to the interim governorship in September 1860 and supreme authority. Elected Constitutional Governor for the term October 1861 to October 1865, he was technically barred by the state Constitution from taking office, because he was under 35 years of age. After having taken office, he issued a decree altering that provision to 25 years of age. Terrazas pursued a strong anticlerical policy and rigorously enforced the Reform Laws.[28]

Relations between Juárez and Terrazas, however, began badly, especially since the precedent in Juárez's dealings with northern state governors was Vidaurri. Governor Terrazas ignored federal government instructions with regard to sales of nationalized ecclesiastical property and disposal of federal revenues. The proceeds of both went to local needs, even though the Ministry of Finance Circular of 13 May 1862 had specifically prohibited that. In such a way, the hard-pressed federal government lost control of the northern frontier customs' revenues. When Terrazas claimed to be unable to supply funds and reinforcements, Juárez decided to remove him from office, in order to prevent a repetition of the case of Nuevo León. He placed Chihuahua under a state of siege on 6 April 1864, in face of the protestation of the local Congress, which refused to publish the decree and begged an implacable Juárez to desist. These actions were arbitrary, since they went against an election result, albeit one surrounded by constitutional irregularities. Employing his usual technique of setting one state governor against another, Juárez ordered Patoni, whom he appointed Military Commander of both Durango and Chihuahua, to proceed to Chihuahua and enforce the removal of Terrazas.[29]

In many respects, however, Terrazas's position was stronger than that of Juárez within his home state. He stepped aside, as he could afford to do, in order to let matters take their course. Juárez discovered that he could not undermine Terrazas's position by supporting his political enemies there. Terrazas had won strong support through a policy of land grants from ecclesiastical and especially 'unoccupied' lands, the *tierras baldías* of Juárez's own San Luis Potosí decree of 22 July 1863. This decree ordered the occupation and alienation of all such lands not already put to public or private purposes up to a limit of 2,500 hectares per individual. In such a way, Terrazas gained loyal friends in the state legislature. Juárez's nominee for the governorship, J. J. Casavantes, had no base there. Patoni, thereupon, appointed General Angel Trías to be state governor (June 1864 to July 1865). Accordingly, northern customs revenues for the first time reverted to the federal government. Although a rival of Terrazas, Trías was old and ill, and could not be a satisfactory replacement, especially since Terrazas still controlled the legislature. In any case, Juárez in April 1865, hoping to clear the atmosphere, called for elections in the state, which Terrazas won in June. This second term of office would expire in October 1869.

However, since Chihuahua remained under a state of siege, he could not take office at all. This situation placed Juárez in a quandary, which he resolved by a reconciliation with Terrazas, since only by such an action could he expect to survive as a political counter in the state. Accordingly, Juárez restored Terrazas to the governorship and military command on 7 November 1865, in order to safeguard his own position in the north. Until that time, Terrazas, though governor since 1861, had lent no positive support to the republican cause, despite his constitutional obligation to do so.[30]

. . .

THE DECREES OF 8 NOVEMBER 1865: JUÁREZ'S *COUP D'ÉTAT*?

In November 1865 Juárez's constitutional term as President was due to come to an end. This raised the issue of the succession. The Constitution did not exclude re-election, but no elections could take place during the civil war. Some formula would have to be devised to provide for the succession without any election. Since Juárez's main political enemy was González Ortega, elected President of the Supreme Court in 1861, an office which gave, as it had to Juárez in 1858, the presidential succession, the issue remained full of danger. Juárez identified him as the intended beneficiary of the intrigues of September 1861 and January 1864. He believed that if the succession were handed over to González Ortega or any of his allies, a compromise would be sought with the French and an accommodation with the empire. Working in close concert with Lerdo, Juárez was determined to block González Ortega's claim to the presidency, initiated in November 1864, and, if possible, to break him in the process. Juárez and Lerdo, who was a master of constitutional subtleties, set out to expose the spuriousness of Ortega's claim by arguing that he had never in fact exercised the presidency of the Supreme Court, which had ceased to function in May 1863. Ortega was also governor of Zacatecas, but article 118 of the Constitution forbade the holding of two elective offices at the same time and imposed a choice between them.[31]

Juárez's conduct in 1865 constituted his political reply to the intrigue of 1864. So far from violating his own principles, Juárez's stance in 1865 was consistent with his position on mediation in 1860. González Ortega had obtained Juárez's permission to proceed to the USA in December 1864 and re-enter Mexico in order to rejoin republican forces. Instead, he proceeded to New York, where he was detained by a law suit. His activities in the USA were monitored by Juárez's agents, Romero and Santacilia. Juárez maintained that González Ortega did not have official permission to remain outside Mexico indefinitely, since he was a serving army officer. Accordingly, Lerdo instructed the state governors on 28 October 1865 that persons who had remained abroad for more than four months or without permission were to be arrested and tried as absentees. Out of this context came Juárez's two decrees of 8 November.[32]

Using his extraordinary powers and founding his actions on articles 78–82 of the Constitution concerning the absence of presidential authority, Juárez extended the presidential term for the duration of the war and the term of President of the Supreme Court for the same period. At the same time, he proposed to nominate a substitute to exercise that office, since Ortega had deserted his post. The latter protested that Juárez's actions were unconstitutional, dictatorial and a usurpation. The political reality, however, was that Juárez could count on the support of the state governors of Chihuahua, Sonora, Sinaloa, Durango, Tamaulipas, Coahuila and Zacatecas, a cross-section of Liberal armed power in the north, and of the four Military Commanders of the Armies of the South (Álvarez), East (Díaz), North (Mariano Escobedo) and West (Ramón Corona). Faced with that galaxy of strength, Ortega remained ineffective. Nevertheless, Juárez's *realpolitik* had cost him the support of two cabinet ministers, Ruiz and Prieto, and made irreconcilable enemies of Ortega and his close ally Miguel Negrete. Romero worked with the US Secretary of State, William H Seward, to frustrate Ortega's attempts to organize support and return to Mexico. When, in company with Patoni, who supported his claims, he arrived in Zacatecas in January 1867, Governor Auza, a *juarista*, ordered the arrest of the two men. They remained in custody until 18 July 1868.[33]

The decrees of 8 November did not under any circumstances constitute a presidential *coup d'état.* The contrast between November 1865 and December 1857 was striking. In the first place, Juárez's intention had not been to overthrow the Constitution, still less, in association with the armed forces, as Comonfort had done, but to preserve the continuity of the executive power at a time of national emergency, when all other branches of government had lapsed. While in San Luis Potosí, Juárez had attempted to convene Congress, in order to demonstrate that the loss of the national capital did not signify the destruction of republican institutions. The Supreme Court did, in fact, convene there on 26 June 1863. When, however, the Permanent Deputation summoned Congress, only thirty-seven deputies appeared early in September 1865. A total of sixty-four had arrived by mid-November, but they were still not quorate. By the end of the month, Juárez was obliged to give up the attempt. Even so, the Permanent Deputation issued a Manifesto to the Nation on 27 November 1865, signed by all the deputies in San Luis Potosí, explaining the original intention. After the government abandoned San Luis, the Supreme Court disintegrated, and its president, González Ortega, who was also commander of the republican army, gave up the struggle.[34]

The close relations that developed between Terrazas and Juárez in 1865–66 enabled Juárez to maintain his authority in the north, combat Vidaurri, and ultimately push back French military power. Since French power reached its maximum extent in Mexico by the spring of 1865, Juárez's experience in Chihuahua proved to be the decisive phase not only in the struggle for national survival against Intervention forces but also in his own career. He could count on the loyalty of younger commanders, such as Escobedo and Treviño, who opposed Vidaurri's course of action. Escobedo began the reorganization of the Army of the North from March 1865, and Juárez appointed him governor of Nuevo León. Over the next twelve months the struggle for control of the state began in earnest. Escobedo recovered Monterrey in March 1866. Along with Díaz, who recovered Oaxaca in October 1866, he became the architect of the Liberal victory over the Empire. Díaz's forces seized Vidaurri and executed him as a traitor on 8 July 1867.[35]

Juárez worked with the state governors as well as against them. He took advantage of tactical alliances of limited duration, in order to bring independent political figures to rein and to neutralize opponents. Within the Liberal zone, the 1857 Constitution, at least technically, remained in force: it had not, in fact, been suspended for the duration of the war.

Elections were held, where possible, as in Chihuahua in 1865. Juárez, armed with extraordinary powers, operated in practice both within the Constitution and above it. These powers were of congressional origin and in that sense his possession of them was constitutional. The uses to which he put them, however, were primarily political. In the circumstances of 1858–60 or 1863–67, he had little leeway. As a result, his assertion of the presidential office and at the same time of his own person, clothed as they were in the rhetoric of moralism and the symbolism of republican virtue, was a remarkable achievement. Above all, we need to take into account the intangible factor of Juárez's relationship with ordinary people, who were the victims, participants and bystanders in the conflicts of 1857–67. The ethnic and social origins of this self-created paragon of republican moralism would not have been lost on the mestizo-Indian majority, regardless of the side communities happened to be taking at any particular time. Juárez's ability to humble his opponents, often of a superior station to himself, might well have induced a sense of jubilation that in the end served to bolster his authority among this majority and foster at the same time the already deepening Juárez myth. Much literature at the time and since has been expended on Juárez's supposed violations of the Constitution and his dictatorial tendencies. This has obscured the real significance of 8 November 1865. Those decrees represented Juárez's determination to see the fight with Maximilian's empire through to the finish.

He was determined to go through to the end, no matter the cost to himself. This cost, in family terms, was exceedingly high. His wife lived in difficult circumstances in New York. Already in November 1863, Juárez was telling Santacilia that he was desperate to hear news of his family. From Nazas, Juárez wrote to Margarita in late September 1864, telling her not to worry about him, but adding that he was distraught at not knowing how she and the family were faring. Then, in February 1865, his cherished son, José ('Pepe') – 'my joy, my pride, and my hope' – died in infancy, while he, grieving in silence, could not leave Mexican soil, lest the enemy should claim a propaganda victory. Juárez had also heard of the death of his father-in-law, and hoped that his wife would not become ill, because of the double blow.[36]

The ruthlessness that Juárez showed to those who crossed

him was matched only by that which he meted out to himself. Juárez intended at all costs to bring down the empire, turn the Intervention into an irremediable disaster, humiliate the Europeans beyond recall, vindicate the Republic, and force Mexicans to fight for the independence of their country. This humiliation of the Europeans Juárez intended to be at the hands of the mestizo-Indian majority of a non-European country in an epoch in which European notions of racial supremacy were predominant. What Mexicans did with their country thereafter was their affair, but, at least, they would do it without the political tutelage of European empires. Juárez saw this as the issue in 1863–67, and resolved to cede power to no one. Although ostensibly he stood for Law and Constitution, Republic and Independence, all nebulous concepts that belied a soft exterior, he was inside, as his tenacity, obduracy and self-denial revealed, undeniably a politician made of pure steel.

. . .

NOTES AND REFERENCES

1. Cadenhead Ivie E (1973) 1975 *Benito Juárez y su época.* Mexico City, El Colegio de México, p. 56.
2. De la Torre Villar Ernesto 1960 *El triunfo de la república liberal, 1857–1860.* Mexico City, Fondo de Cultura Económica, pp. 28–30.
3. *BJDOCS* 2, pp. 293–94, 300–02.
4. Bulnes Francisco 1967 *Juárez y las Revoluciones de Ayutla y de la Reforma.* Mexico City, pp. 305–13. Fuentes Mares José 1983 *Juárez: Los Estados Unidos y Europa.* Mexico City, Editorial Grijalbo, p. 150. Torre Villar *El triunfo* pp. 36–41.
5. *Archivo Privado de D. Benito Juárez y D. Pedro Santacilia* (hereafter cited as *APBJPS*) (prologue by J M Puig Casauranc) 1928 Mexico City, I, p. 11. *BJDOCS* 2, pp. 321–37. Torre Villar *El triunfo* pp. 45–50.
6. Blázquez Carmen 1978 *Miguel Lerdo de Tejada. Un liberal veracruzano en la política nacional.* Mexico City, El Colegio de México, pp. 132–33, 154–55. See also Blázquez Carmen 1986 *Veracruz liberal 1858–1860.*
7. Knapp Frank A 1951 *Sebastián Lerdo de Tejada.* Austin, University of Texas Press, pp. 51–3. Fuentes Mares *Juárez* pp. 151, 156–57. Joel Poinsett, a close associate of Zavala in the *Yorkino* masonic rite, was the first US Minister to Mexico, 1825–27.
8. *BJDOCS* 2, pp. 539–40. Blázquez *Miguel Lerdo* pp. 154–56.

9. Blázquez *Miguel Lerdo* pp. 154–61, 168. Tamayo Jorge L (ed.) 1957 *Epistolario de Benito Juárez.* Mexico City, pp. 118–20.
10. Tamayo *Epistolario* pp. 100–01, 113–17.
11. Cadenhead Ivie E 'González Ortega and the Presidency of Mexico' *HAHR* 32, 3 (August 1952), pp. 331–46.
12. Cadenhead *Benito Juárez* pp. 69, 78.
13. Sierra Justo (1905–06) 1948 *Juárez: Su obra y su tiempo.* Mexico City, UNAM, pp. 242, 255–57, 272, 295.
14. Tamayo *Epistolario* pp. 134–36.
15. Sierra *Juárez* p. 303. Knapp *Lerdo* p. 69.
16. *BJDOCS* 5, pp. 13–17. Quiriarte Martín 1973 *Relaciones entre Juárez y el Congreso.* Mexico City, Cámara de Diputados, p. CI.
17. *BJDOCS* 5, pp. 35–38, 40–45.
18. Scholes Walter V 1957 *Mexican Politics during the Juárez Régime, 1855–1872.* Columbia, University of Missouri Press, p. 89. Quiriarte *Juárez y el Congreso*, pp. CXVII–CXVIII.
19. Tyler Ronnie C 1973 *Santiago Vidaurri and the Southern Confederacy.* Austin, Texas State Historical Association, pp. 15–32, 35–36.
20. Tyler *Vidaurri* pp. 37–38.
21. *BJDOCS* 4, pp. 282–83, 287–90.
22. Ibid pp. 300–01, 306–07. Tyler *Vidaurri* p. 59. See also Broussard Ray F 'Vidaurri, Juárez, and Comonfort's Return from Exile' *HAHR* 49, 2 (May 1969), pp. 268–80.
23. *BJDOCS* 4, pp. 613–21.
24. *BJDOCS* 8, pp. 75–76, 81, 85, 94–95. Cadenhead *Benito Juárez* pp. 92–94.
25. *BJDOCS* 8, pp. 501–06. Fuentes Mares José 1985 *Miramón: El Hombre.* Mexico City, Editorial Grijalbo, p. 135.
26. Tamayo Jorge L 1970 *Juárez en Chihuahua.* Mexico City, Fondo de Cultura Económica, pp. 30, 129–51, 166–69.
27. *BJDOCS* 8, pp. 639–70. Tyler *Vidaurri* pp. 136–53. Vidaurri's son-in-law, Patricio Milmo, was a business partner of Evaristo Madero, governor of Coahuila (1880–83), and grandfather of Francisco I Madero, initial leader of the Revolution of 1910.
28. Almada Francisco R 1958 *Juárez y Terrazas: Aclaraciones históricas.* Mexico City, pp. 11–12, 29, 45–51, 66, 74–83, 317–34. Sims Harold D 'Espejo de caciques: los Terrazas de Chihuahua' *Historia Mexicana* XVIII (1968–69), pp. 379–99. Wasserman Mark 1984 *Capitalists, Caciques, and Revolution: The Native Elite and Foreign Enterprise in Chihuahua, Mexico, 1854–1911.* Chapel Hill, University of North Carolina Press, p. 44.
29. Tamayo *Juárez en Chihuahua* pp. 29–30, 127–28, 167–69. Wasserman *Capitalists, Caciques, and Revolution* p. 44.
30. Tamayo *J en Chihuahua* pp. 306–08, 323–32. Almada *Juárez y Terrazas* pp. 83, 263, 286.

31. Cadenhead *Benito Juárez* pp. 101–05. Cadenhead 'González Ortega' pp. 331–46.
32. Archivo Juárez MS-J S-63 and S-91. *BJDOCS* 9, pp. 800–01, 807–09.
33. *BJDOCS* 8, pp. 310–12, 389–90.
34. Almada *Juárez y Terrazas* pp. 244–51.
35. Dabbs Jack Autrey 1963 *The French Army in Mexico, 1861–1867: A Study in Military Government.* The Hague, Mouton & Co, pp. 267–73.
36. Archivo Juárez MS-J S-39, S-136 and S-150. *BJDOCS* 8, p. 410. *APBJPS* I, pp. 35–39.

Chapter 7

JUÁREZ AND THE UNITED STATES

Mexico is both a Latin American country and a part of the North American continent. For that reason, the career of Juárez forms not only part of Latin American history but also part of North American as well. The outcome of the struggles of 1857–67 affected both the balance of power in North America and the relationship of the European Powers to the American continent as a whole. The civil war in the United States between 1861 and 1865 further reinforced the importance of Mexican events in that period. These issues were clearly perceived at the time in Washington, Richmond (Virginia), Paris, Madrid and London, as the diplomatic sources abundantly testify.[1] Mexico's relations with the United States remained uneasy in the aftermath of the War of 1846–47 and the Treaty of Guadalupe Hidalgo of 1848. Deep suspicion of US designs prevented any working understanding between the two countries. The continued supremacy of the Democratic Party, with its strong southern connection, ensured that US pressure for further territorial cessions and for transit rights across Mexican territory would not cease. Mexican governments saw southern expansionists behind the War of 1846 and the pressures that followed.

. . .

TERRITORIAL CESSION AND TRANSIT RIGHTS

Several irksome issues dominated Mexican relations with the USA between the 1840s and the 1870s. Following the incorporation of Texas in 1846, the USA harboured designs of further annexations or territorial concessions. Mexico's defeat in the War of 1846–47 increased these pressures, especially since the Californian border south of San Diego still remained undefined. The projected dismemberment of Mexico took several forms, one of which included the incorporation of the entire country or even the whole of Meso-America as far as the Isthmus of Panama and including Spanish Cuba. Another took the form of the establishment of a Texas-style independent republic out of the four northern Mexican states first mooted in 1848 and to be called, as we have seen in Chapter 6, the 'Republic of the Sierra Madre'. President James Polk (1845–49) favoured the annexation of Yucatán and the purchase of Cuba, the latter enthusiastically supported by Senator Jefferson Davis in 1848, on the grounds that it would substantially increase the pro-slavery interest within the Union. The Zachary Taylor administration (1849–53), anxious to bring California and New Mexico into the Union as free states, categorically opposed the southern annexationist tendency.[2]

The acquisition of half of Mexico's territory by the United States at the Treaty of Guadalupe Hidalgo in 1848 altered the balance of power on the North American continent. It also exacerbated the question of political hegemony within the United States between the southern slave states and the growing number of free states. That, in turn, increased southern pressures on Mexico. At the same time, the condition of Mexicans in the newly occupied territories north of the Río Grande caused friction between the two governments.

The US government remained anxious throughout the 1850s to acquire transit rights across the Isthmus of Tehuantepec, the greater part of which was located in Juárez's home state. US acquisition of Mexico's former province of Upper California made it imperative to secure rapid routes of communication between one part of the country and another. Mexico, however, stood geographically in the midst of this projected route. The object was to construct a railway, road or canal. The original Mexican concession of 1842 had come to nothing, and US interests sought to negotiate its transfer to themselves. The US State Department assured Mexico that the USA did not want sovereignty over Mexican territory but only the mutual guarantee of persons and properties. Under the convention of 22 June 1850 for the construction of a railway by a US company, the Mexican government established that US assistance in such protection depended on a prior Mexican request. The moderate Liberal Herrera administration (1848–51) resisted any grant of territory.[3]

Pressures for concessions were renewed during the presidency of Franklin Pierce (1853–57), heavily under southern influence. The Mexican government agreed to recognize the concession to the Sloo Company on 5 February 1853 for the construction of the Tehuantepec railway. As it turned out, nothing concrete ever materialized from this contract. In the mean time, US–Mexican relations between 1848 and 1853 hovered on the brink of war. The Pierce administration favoured the construction of another railway, this time from New Orleans to San Diego and passing across part of northern Mexico. When the governor of New Mexico threatened to annex this strip by force, the Santa Anna regime (1853–55) was obliged to talk, in order to avoid war. Accordingly, the US administration appointed James Gadsden, a railway entrepreneur, as its chief negotiator in Mexico City in July 1853. The US agreed to pay 10 million dollars for the La Mesilla strip across northern Sonora and Chihuahua in the so-called Gadsden Purchase of 30 December 1853. The Mesilla Treaty also authorized rail or road transit across the Isthmus of Tehuantepec, including troops and munitions, without payment of tax or need for passports. This provision remained in force until finally abrogated in 1937. The Gadsden Purchase raised hopes of further cessions during the administration of James Buchanan (1857–61).[4]

Even though the Plan of Ayutla declared national territory to be inalienable, the US Minister in Mexico, John Forsyth (from Alabama), pressed the Comonfort government for a free trade agreement, territorial cessions, and the possibility of railway construction across Mexican territory. Since rumour spread that the government was proposing to negotiate a loan in the USA guaranteed against the mortgage of national territory, Comonfort found it expedient to deny any such aims on 5 March 1857. Shortly afterwards, the US Secretary of State, Lewis Cass, began to devise a scheme whereby Mexico might be persuaded to surrender Baja California and further segments of Sonora and Chihuahua, in return for the sum of 15 million dollars at the most. At the same time, the US interest in constructing a railway across the Isthmus was to be stressed. The Comonfort administration, through the Secretary of Foreign Relations, Sebastián Lerdo de Tejada, from this early time a defender of national sovereignty, refused any concessions on 12 September 1857. In the following month, Comonfort nullified the Sloo contract of 1853.[5]

After the Conservative seizure of power at the beginning of 1858, the US government recognized the Zuloaga regime along with the rest of the diplomatic corps, on the grounds that the latter controlled the capital city. Forsyth continued to urge concessions in the form of perpetual transit rights and rectification of borders, but with the same lack of success. The United States broke off diplomatic relations with the Conservative regime in protest at the imposition of a 1 per cent property tax on all residents including foreigners, and Forsyth left Mexico City on 20 October 1858. Accordingly, once the Juárez cabinet had finally taken up residence in Veracruz on 4 May 1858, it became clear that, despite impressive Conservative victories, two rival regimes existed within Mexican national territory.

. . .

THE ISSUE OF RECOGNITION

A key factor in Mexican politics from the 1850s to the 1940s was US recognition or abstention from it. This could determine the internal survival and international credibility of regimes. A price would usually be exacted for recognition. That factor became apparent for the first time during the civil war of the Reform. Throughout the year 1858, no Power, not even the United States, recognized the wandering Juárez administration as the legitimate government of Mexico. In April 1858 Juárez's agent in the United States, José María Mata, failed to secure either a loan or recognition. Mata had been empowered to negotiate a loan of 25 million dollars in return for the mortgage of ecclesiastical properties, which the Liberal regime intended to nationalize. The Finance Minister, Prieto, outlined for Mata's benefit the views of Juárez on the subject of Mexico's relations with the USA. The United States would be the nucleus around which future humanity would gravitate. Identity of ideology and institutions would prevent future rivalries and suspicion between Mexico and the United States. This would remove for good the issue of whether Mexico would become another star on the US flag. Juárez saw the wealthy United States giving a helping hand to 'a lesser and unfortunate sister, which desires to raise itself from prostration and make amends for its errors'.[6]

The US government, however, remained sceptical of the capacity of the Juárez regime for survival and, in any case, wanted to see what advantages could be gained from Mexico's internal conflict. Juárez, however, attached prime importance to US recognition. He saw it as the guarantee of the maritime security of Veracruz, the only effective means of removing the Spanish threat from Cuba, and the counter-stroke to Conservative attempts to involve the European Powers in the internal affairs of Mexico. Conservatives saw in the USA a mounting threat to Mexican survival and identity. Juárez regarded the USA as a powerful reinforcement of the Liberal cause within Mexico. The problem with that view, however, continued to be the expansionist tendencies of the southern interests which predominated in the Democratic Party. This clearly emerged when Mata discussed the matter of a loan of 2 million dollars with Buchanan early in July 1858. The latter raised the subject of the Isthmus and the projected railway from west Texas across Chihuahua and Sonora to the Gulf of California. He wanted the ports at either end of the transit routes to be free ports. Mata reiterated the Mexican opposition to any territorial cessions. He was aware that, should this opposition be removed, then a US loan at a low 5 per cent interest would be immediately forthcoming.[7]

The central task of Juárez and his ministers during 1859 was how to exploit the US government's rupture with the Conservative regime and obtain the desired recognition. The course of action determined proved to be politically very dangerous. Miramón's threat to secure Spanish assistance in a siege of Veracruz made it essential for Juárez to obtain US support. The only way that this could be secured, however, would be by making it appear as though a desperate Mexican regime were prepared to offer territorial concessions and transit rights to the USA. Since these had not been obtained from the Conservatives, the Buchanan administration seriously considered recognition of the Juárez regime.

Juárez and his Foreign Minister, Ocampo, were playing for time, in the expectation of the disintegration of the Democratic Party on the eve of the presidential elections in 1860 and the capture of power by the Republicans. Several prominent Republicans, Abraham Lincoln among them, had opposed the Mexican War of 1846 and rejected the expansionist policies of the southern states. Buchanan's special envoy, William Churchwell, received the impression from Lerdo and Ocampo that concessions might be forthcoming, since neither had denied that they would not be, should recognition be given. (Nor had they specifically stated that there would be.) As a result, Buchanan, hoping for a political triumph at the eleventh hour, sent the Maryland Senator, Robert McLane, to Veracruz with full authority to decide the question and, having done so, to conduct negotiations concerning the regulation of new frontiers – with a proposed payment of 10 million dollars for Lower California – and the definition of transit rights. Feeling the situation to be favourable, McLane officially recognized the Juárez regime on 6 April 1859. Mata, received formally by Buchanan, affirmed his belief that the futures of Mexico and the United States were irrevocably bound together. He warned, though, that desire for further territorial acquisitions at Mexico's expense had reached a point of mania in Washington.[8]

Juárez hoped that recognition would strengthen the moral position of the Liberal cause and increase the possibilities of raising a loan in the United States with which to ensure the military victory. Accordingly, Lerdo, following the issue of the Reform Laws, left for the USA, as we have seen, in order to negotiate such a loan. McLane, however, opposed the idea of a Mexican loan guaranteed against nationalized ecclesiastical property, since this would remove the possibility of territorial concessions and transit rights. Securing these remained the basis of US policy towards Mexico. Juárez was determined to avoid the surrender of Lower California to the United States, an action which he thought would bring down upon his administration the same opprobrium that had fallen upon Santa Anna after the Mesilla Treaty.

A major motive for US recognition, however, was the increasing tendency of European Powers to involve themselves more closely in the affairs of Mexico. Spain's naval demonstration off Tampico was followed by an Anglo-French demonstration off Veracruz in January 1859, designed to warn the Juárez regime not to default on debt arrears. The debt question defined European relations with Mexico. European pressures alarmed the US government, which began to redefine its Mexican policy in broader terms than borders and concessions. The Juárez regime was anxious and able to exploit these preoccupations in Washington. The McLane–Ocampo Treaty, about which much, mostly polemic, has been written, should be understood in that context. The US government wanted the cession of Baja California as its price for recognition. Juárez needed US support desperately during Miramón's first siege of Veracruz in June and July 1859. A protracted series of negotiations followed, which resulted in the so-called treaty. It never came into effect, since neither the US Senate nor the Mexican government ratified it. Juárez formally rejected it in November 1860, when the Conservative danger had virtually passed.[9]

The treaty was conceived as an offensive and defensive alliance between the United States and Mexico. Juárez, Ocampo and Degollado (Minister of War) were those most intimately involved in the negotiations. McLane attempted to make the Mexican government accept the principle of no financial assistance without territorial and transit concessions. The Mexican position was to avoid commitment but to prolong negotiations. Having gained nothing, McLane returned to the United States on vacation and did not return until the end of November. In view of Juárez's firm opposition to any cession of national territory, McLane withdrew pressure on that issue and confined himself instead to the question of transit rights. This was also a serious matter for Mexico, but a good deal less menacing than requests for the cession of strips of northern territory and for the entire Baja California peninsula. Faced with the gathering threat to Veracruz by Miramón, the Juárez government opted for concession on the transit question across the Isthmus and from Arizona and Texas to the Pacific (at Guaymas and Mazatlán). Accordingly, the treaty was signed on 14 December 1859. The concession of transit rights across the Isthmus resembled the treaty signed by Colombia and the United States in 1846, which had permitted passage across the Isthmus of Panama, in return for a US guarantee of the neutrality of the transit route. It had recognized Colombian sovereignty over the territory. The McLane–Ocampo Treaty permitted US intervention to protect transit, but only at the specific request of the Mexican government. By making such concessions, Juárez and Ocampo sought to stave off direct US intervention in Mexican affairs, prevent loss of territory, maintain US recognition, and perhaps secure financial assistance. The treaty contained no provision for the cession of Lower California, Sonora or Chihuahua to the USA. The ultimate objective was the survival of the Liberal regime, both internally and internationally, and therefore of the republican form of government in Mexico, the Constitution of 1857, and the Reform Laws. Concessions on transit were the price the Liberals were prepared to pay. The sense of an impending European intervention and the reintroduction of monarchy in Mexico encouraged Juárez to pay that price.[10]

The immediate benefits of the treaty proved remarkable. Miramón's military successes in November 1859 demonstrated that the Liberal regime could not win the civil war on its own. When Miramón tightened the siege of Veracruz, its days appeared to be numbered. At that decisive moment, Juárez secured the intervention of the US Navy in April 1860 in preventing Spanish ships contracted in Havana by Miramón's regime from investing Veracruz by sea in conjunction with the second Conservative land siege. This became known as the Antón Lizardo Incident. In the longer term, the likelihood of a political change in Washington made it improbable that the treaty would ever take effect. In the US Senate during 1860 the treaty became a political football between slave and anti-slavery states. The treaty damaged political reputations more than national sovereignty. It ruined Ocampo, whose reputation was salvaged only by the brutal manner of his death in 1861. It provided at least fifty years of allegations against Juárez as a traitor to his country. These formed a powerful part of the corpus of strictures that were employed to destroy his reputation, and which Bulnes amply exploited. Finally, it provided the Conservatives with a propaganda weapon with which to mask their own intrigues with European Powers. It enabled clericals to brand Juárez, the destroyer of religion, as the traitor who handed over Mexico to the Protestant enemy north of the border.[11]

. . .

MEXICO AND THE AMERICAN CIVIL WAR (1861–65)

Juárez's intimate, Matías Romero, acted as Mexican Minister in Washington from 1860 until 1868. A talented and perceptive Oaxacan graduate of the Institute of Sciences and Arts, he consistently supported the Republican Party and the Union cause. The selection of Romero attested to Juárez's ability to choose the right man for the place and time. Romero reported closely on internal politics, exerted a powerful intellectual influence wherever he could, in order to bring home to US government and public opinion the dangers of renewed European activity on the North American continent, and sought to turn US politicians in a direction favourable to the Juárez administration. He expected a Republican victory in the presidential elections of November 1860, especially in view of the irrevocable split in the Democratic Party. That removed the immediate danger of expansion at Mexico's expense or the annexation of Cuba. The Republican Party had grown with the rapid development of the western states. However, Romero explained to Juárez that both US parties were divided by the slavery issue. He saw the secession of South Carolina and a war between the fifteen slave and eighteen free states as a great calamity for the republican system throughout North America. Yet, at the same time, both powers would solicit Mexican support, and the formation of the Confederacy would restore the balance of power on the continent and end the threat of the total absorption of Mexico into the USA. He believed that Mexico could count on the sympathies of the Republicans, but that it would have to learn how to exploit these advantages carefully. A Republican government from March 1861 under Abraham Lincoln would provide 'the safest guarantee of the inviolability of our rights and of the faculties required in making them effective'.[12]

The effective head of the Republican Party was Senator William H Seward, whom Romero regarded as 'a man of great wisdom', but who at the same time remained highly susceptible to the influence of European diplomatic representatives. Romero advised Juárez that Seward would be Lincoln's Secretary of State and the political director of the administration. He felt it urgent to impress upon Seward the real nature of events in Mexico and to guard against the prejudices of the Europeans against the Liberal regime. Seward, as it turned out, would show a marked tendency not to offend the European Powers. Romero favoured collective action by the Republics of the Americas to counter the European threat. Seward, however, informed the other American representatives in Washington in March 1865 that the United States wished to avoid any complications with the European Powers and especially war with France.[13]

Juárez decided to appeal directly to Lincoln. He stressed the identity of constitutional principles shared by Mexico and the United States. The Mexican people were unanimously opposed to slavery. He saw in shared ideas the basis for lasting and intimate friendship between the two countries. No practical benefits came from this appeal. Initially, Romero was convinced that the USA would not permit the disembarkation of Spanish forces on Mexican soil without just cause. Throughout 1861, however, it became abundantly clear that the US government sought to avoid any complications with the European Powers and stood by George Washington's basic principle of avoiding foreign alliances or involvements. Juárez still continued to hope for a loan from US sources, this time for half-a-million dollars. European pressures on Mexico for a settlement of claims and payment of outstanding debts, however, made the US government wary. The outbreak of civil war between the states in April 1861 thwarted altogether Mexican hopes for support. In dire straits, Juárez ordered the suspension of payments on the foreign debt on 17 July 1861. This brought the Mexican debt question to a head. It formed the context for the tripartite debt-collecting intervention by Great Britain, France and Spain under the terms of the Convention of London of 31 October. The imminence of intervention encouraged the Juárez government to seek an accord with Great Britain, the largest creditor. However, when Congress unanimously repudiated the treaty arranged on 21 November between Zamacona, then Foreign Minister, and Sir Charles Wyke, British Minister in Mexico, the Juárez government found itself politically isolated. Seward refused to believe that the European Powers would actually land troops on Mexican soil. Romero's disillusionment was complete.[14]

At the same time, the repudiation of the Wyke–Zamacona Treaty ensured that the US government would abruptly terminate any discussion of a loan to Mexico. Romero again warned the Juárez government of Seward's 'reserve and coldness' on the matter of the European threat, and came to the conclusion that as long as he remained Secretary of State, the United States would involve itself in Mexican affairs not in good faith but only in order to draw from them advantages to themselves. While Seward rejected any US participation in the tripartite debt-collection, the US government, nevertheless, fully recognized the right of the European Powers to intervene in that way or to make war on Mexico. It could not countenance any European acquisition of territory at Mexico's expense, and declared its intention to send a naval force into the Gulf of Mexico, in order to protect American interests. Ten days later, Seward showed a renewed US interest in reviving the original Isthmus transit contract of 1842, but placing it in northern rather than southern hands. By the end of the year, Juárez, bitterly disillusioned, had come to the reluctant conclusion that no support of any kind would come from the US government. Since Mexico possessed no navy, Veracruz lay open to the European fleets.[15]

After the Allied landings at Veracruz, Mexico found itself caught between European forces on its Gulf flank and a potentially expansionist power on its northern frontier. Mexico was the only foreign state that bordered on the Confederacy. The government of Jefferson Davis in Richmond (Virginia) was concerned, however, to win over Mexican cooperation – if not of the Juárez administration, then, at least, of the northern state governors.

Early in 1862, Lincoln considered Corwin's draft proposal of a 10 million dollar loan to Mexico towards payment of the European claims. If agreed, the United States would then receive the mortgage on all public lands, mineral deposits, and national properties throughout Baja California, Sonora, Sinaloa and Chihuahua. A joint US–Mexican commission would then administer the mortgaged properties. Since the plan did not stipulate how the Juárez government was to spend the 10 million dollars, the problem arose that it could be used for military purposes against the Allied Powers. That, in effect, would have threatened to make the US government an accessory to an act of war with European states. For that reason, first the Committee on Foreign Relations and then the Senate opposed the loan entirely.[16]

Confederate diplomacy intensified during 1862 and the first months of 1863. The French defeat at Puebla on 5 May 1862 helped to explain this, since Intervention forces were pushed back to the Gulf hinterland and their advance was not resumed for another year. The Juárez government, reprieved, as it were, sought to purchase arms in the United States. Lincoln, however, forbade the export of arms on 2 November

1862, thereby reducing drastically the possibility of successful resistance once the French advance was resumed. Juárez, nevertheless, remained resolutely opposed not only to arrangements with Confederate agents but also to the Confederacy itself. Yet his consistent maxim was Mexican neutrality in the war between the states. This did not prevent Mexican exploitation of the booming cotton trade through Matamoros and Brownsville. Union forces made a show of strength in the area in November 1863, when they seized Brownsville from the Confederates, in order to stem the arms trade. This diverted the lucrative Confederate trade further up-river to Piedras Negras and Nuevo Laredo, until Seward pressed for a Union withdrawal, in order to remove possible causes of armed conflict with the French.[17]

When the French finally advanced towards the Valley of Mexico, the Juárez administration sought refuge in San Luis Potosí. Lincoln, who had always opposed the Intervention and the monarchist design which was its central purpose, ordered Corwin to return to the USA. Seward, nevertheless, informed the British Minister in Washington on 10 September 1863 that the USA would not seek to block the Archduke Maximilian's acceptance of the Mexican crown. The latter reported Seward's alarm at the pro-Mexican sympathies of his countrymen and his consequent determination to prohibit the export of arms, which could be used to challenge the French occupation. Seward ordered US representatives abroad to maintain neutrality with regard to the French Intervention, under Napoleon III's assurances that there would be no alteration in the government of Mexico.[18]

The Confederacy began to court the French in earnest, hoping to exchange recognition of the Mexican Empire for recognition of the Confederacy by Napoleon III. The latter, through fear of further antagonizing the US government, never recognized the Confederacy. The itinerant Juárez administration, nevertheless, was left without a resident US minister for seventeen long months. That raised once again the issue of recognition. The principle in 1858 which determined recognition by the Powers had been occupation of the capital city. All the European Powers recognized the empire after the arrival of Maximilian in June 1864. Since no US minister appeared in the Juárez camp, it seemed as though recognition had been withdrawn. Romero, accordingly, became involved in domestic political struggles in Washington. He lent discreet support to various attempts to oust Seward from office and generally cooperated with the Radical Republicans, who were working to defeat Lincoln in the presidential elections of 1864. A skilful lobbyist, he sought to influence appointments to the Foreign Relations Committees of Congress during 1866 and to awaken public opinion to the dangers posed by the French Intervention in Mexico. Throughout the grim period of defeat, Juárez could not count on visible diplomatic support from the US government.[19]

In view of the itinerant nature of the Juárez cabinet, this was perhaps understandable. During the Intervention, Juárez from late in 1864 sent his official letters to Romero by means of the Mexican consul in Franklin, New Mexico, situated near El Paso, which lay on the northern bank of the Río Grande. He sent his private correspondence to Santacilia, who had taken charge of the Juárez family in New York, via Romero in Washington. Through these precarious channels Juárez maintained contact with the outside world. The situation for the republican cause remained truly desperate during the Chihuahua exile. Even so, Juárez consistently looked to a northern victory in the civil war as the only effective counterbalance to the French in Mexico. Despite the overbearing strength that a reconstituted USA would represent, Juárez believed that the military defeat of the Confederacy would be the principal guarantee of the survival of Mexico as an independent, sovereign state. He remained fully aware, however, that the USA would lend no direct support to the Mexican republicans. Their ultimate victory would have to depend upon their own efforts and derive from their own meagre resources.[20]

During the three-year period of the wandering cabinet, from January 1864 until December 1866, the principal influence in Mexican foreign policy became that of Juárez's close political ally, Sebastián Lerdo. The latter opposed humiliating arrangements with foreign powers, and had earlier been the central figure in the congressional rejection of the Wyke–Zamacona agreement. Lerdo, strongly nationalist, remained determined to avoid any further McLane–Ocampo treaties. Accordingly, he warned Romero late in 1864 to enter into no agreement with the United States, once the civil war had finished, that might compromise national dignity and territorial integrity. Nevertheless, Romero was quite at liberty to secure US help through threats, protests, financial aid, arms supplies or even auxiliary forces integrated into the Mexican Army.[21]

Juárez applauded Lincoln's 'inflexibility' in ensuring the full defeat of the South. Long delayed as that victory was, he saw it working to Mexico's benefit, rather than an earlier compromise peace. He welcomed the destruction of slavery, and the Lincoln administration's refusal to recognize the Empire of Maximilian. That dealt a serious blow to Napoleon III's Mexican policy. Mexico would continue to fight on alone against the French. 'Our aim', Juárez told Santacilia on 6 April 1865, 'is to wear down the French and oblige them to abandon their iniquitous attempt to subjugate us'. Three days later, the American civil war came to an end with the final collapse of the Confederacy.[22]

. . .

THE VICTORY OF THE *JUARISTAS*

Until the end of the civil war the Monroe Doctrine appears to have been largely inoperative, in spite of Mexican appeals for its invocation. Juárez welcomed the accession of Andrew Johnson, following the assassination of Lincoln, on the grounds that he was believed to be a strong partisan of the Monroe Doctrine. The survival of the Confederacy would have seriously compromised the policy of 1823, especially if it had enabled the parallel survival of the Mexican Empire. French defeats in Coahuila and Nuevo León encouraged Juárez to believe, even before the fall of Richmond and the surrender of Robert E Lee, that the days of the empire were numbered. Shortly afterwards, however, Juárez was forced back to the border and remained in El Paso del Norte from 14 August until 13 November 1865. He politely declined the offer to take up residence across the border in New Mexico.[23]

Maximilian's regime contemplated offering a haven to defeated Confederates. The Colonization Law of 5 September 1865 affirmed the principle that 'once persons of colour placed their feet on Mexican soil, they were automatically free men'. At the same time, it permitted immigrants to bring with them 'workmen in considerable numbers, of whatever race they might be'. They would contract with their 'patron' for the provision of foodstuffs, clothing, lodging, wages and help in sickness. The latter also would undertake to maintain the children of his employees. Workmen would carry a booklet with details of their employer and place of employment and a certificate of good conduct. Any change of employer would have to receive the consent of the existing employer, which would be written down in the booklet. A deceased owner's heirs inherited his workmen. Romero made successful political capital out of this apparent attempt on the part of Maximilian to import southern slavery into Mexico by disguising its name.[24]

The United States finally appointed a Minister to Republican Mexico in October 1865. To French offers to withdraw all troops from Mexico in return for US recognition of the empire, Seward replied that the USA would recognize no regime opposed to that of Juárez. This appointment was more for French consumption than effective implementation, since Juárez still remained in Paso del Norte. The Union Army and radicals in Congress, however, were pressing the Johnson administration to finish off Confederate resistance. They argued, however, that this could not be accomplished without first bringing down the empire of Maximilian. Instead, the administration set about reducing the armed forces. The danger of war between the USA and France receded. Napoleon III, however, his Mexican policy in ruins, his position challenged both in North America and Europe, ordered the phased withdrawal of French troops in January 1866. Juárez saw this as an inevitable step in the final Liberal victory, which would be accomplished without either the assistance of foreign forces or any need to make transactions with the Conservative 'traitors'. Even after the end of the American civil war, Seward continued to put obstacles in the way of purchases of arms for Mexico, especially since in the summer of 1866 the price of armaments was rising, because of the deterioration of the situation in Europe. Significantly, however, the US Congress closed its sessions at the end of August 1866 without recognizing González Ortega as legitimate President of Mexico, in spite of his repudiation of Juárez's unilateral extension of his own term of office in November 1865.[25]

Imperialist propaganda made great play of Liberal sympathies for the United States and posited a European alliance as a counter-balance. The official imperial press presented the expansionism of the USA in the Americas as an equal danger to that of the Russian Empire in Europe and Asia: in such a way, the French Intervention in Mexico complemented the joint European intervention in the Crimea in 1854–56; since the USA wanted hegemony from the Bering Straits to the Isthmus of Panama, its post-civil war triumphalism threatened not only the Mexican Empire but also the British position in Canada and the Spanish in Cuba. The imperial press condemned radical Liberal efforts to bring about US intervention in the Mexican conflict and denounced them as false defenders of national independence, as the McLane–Ocampo Treaty demonstrated. Imperialists, just as Conservatives had done in 1858–61, argued that the real threat to Mexico came from the United States, and the proofs were the defeat of 1847 and the Mesilla Treaty of 1853: Mexicans who were resident in the US-acquired territories of California, New Mexico and Texas were being subjected to degrading treatment. Imperial propagandists seized on the issue of Juárez's prorogation of the presidential term of office. They argued that the US government had recognized a government whose leaders had violated the principles of their own Constitution, as the defection of Manuel Ruiz illustrated: why, then, did the USA insist on recognizing a usurper and not the *de facto* government of Mexico?; if, as the US government claimed, the Mexican Empire lacked popular support, with whom did Juárez actually consult in November 1865?[26]

Since Juárez saw the whole of Mexican history since 1821 as a struggle between privilege and liberty, the issue of extension in 1865 fell into place as one, temporary expedient in the long campaign to eradicate the former. As Juárez explained in an interview published in the *New York Herald* on 16 December 1866, the object of Liberal politics was to take government out of the hands of one class, in which the predominant elements were the ecclesiastical hierarchy and army officers. The 1824 Constitution had begun the challenge, which the 1857 Constitution and the Reform Laws brought to a climax. The long-term object of Liberalism was, in Juárez's view, the education of the people, which would provide the lasting basis for a democratic form of government. He saw the 1857 Constitution as the dominant symbol of a new era of national consciousness.[27] After the restoration of the Republic in 1867,

Juárez wrote to a German liberal sympathizer in March 1868, that democracy would be the future course of humanity: 'each day I grow even more confident that the republican institutions of the American world will be extended to the unfortunate peoples of Europe, where to their detriment monarchies and aristocracies still persist'.[28]

Despite Juárez's identification of the republican cause of Mexico with the principles upon which the USA had been founded, little else but moral aid came during the period of the Intervention. Zarco, writing to Juárez from New York in September 1866, argued that even that came too late and with many vacillations. In his view, it would be completely untrue to attribute to the USA the downfall of the empire in Mexico. 'We were saved by the resistance of our own people and by your tenacity, and we owe no thanks at all to the United States'.[29] In effect, purchases of arms were allowed on any systematic basis only after the French had begun their process of withdrawal. This was in accordance with Seward's policy of not antagonizing Napoleon III.[30] For that reason, the struggle of a fellow American liberal republic was left in abeyance, even after the end of the American civil war.

Similar views were expressed in equally strident terms by Fernando Iglesias Calderón, the son of Juárez's minister, Iglesias, and by Hilarión Frías y Soto, writing in 1905 and 1907 respectively. Frías argued that the USA had not been neutral at all during the Intervention, but, on the contrary, had implicitly favoured imperial France. Such conduct he attributed to fear in Washington of French recognition of the Confederacy, which Napoleon III (along with Great Britain) had already recognized as a 'belligerent'. At the same time, Frías defended Juárez from any charge of readiness to concede territory to the USA in return for aid. That idea, he sought to demonstrate, had originated with Romero and Doblado in October 1864, who were preparing a dupe to induce Washington to provide support. In any case, Frías pointed out, the territories mentioned, Baja California and Sonora, had at that time been under French rather than republican control, with the result that the Juárez government had not been in a position to cede them anyway. The French had withdrawn from Mexico not because of US pressure, which had only been on the level of diplomacy, but because of the logistical impossibility of sustaining their military position, and the combination of opposition at home and mounting dangers in Europe.[31] Iglesias, for his part, objected to Seward's plea in the name of civilization for the life of Maximilian in 1867, and denounced 'the audacious and arrogant pretensions of the State Department'.[32]

Although professions of dislike for European monarchies and systems of alliance proliferated in the United States during the period of the French Intervention in Mexico, in reality the USA conducted itself as a factor in European balance of power diplomacy, rather than as the foremost representative of republicanism and democracy in the Americas. The relationship with France had been given priority over that with Mexico. Romero had rapidly lost any early illusions concerning Seward's policy. Juárez, while not losing faith in the ultimate capacity of the United States for high-minded conduct, saw his hopes shattered in the short term. Accordingly, relations between the two governments continued to be uneasy thereafter. Mexican suspicions of US designs remained unabated, though latent rather than virulent for the rest of the century. They revived actively, however, as a result of the Spanish–American War of 1898–99, when Cuba and Puerto Rico fell under United States' control. A forward US policy in the Caribbean and Central America stimulated fears that the powerful industrial state of the 1900s would revive the Manifest Destiny politics of 1846.

In the aftermath of the French Intervention, however, the Juárez government still saw the European Powers as the natural enemy of Mexico. As Romero explained in Washington in July 1868, when vacating office, 'Mexico has been regarded and treated up to now as a semi-barbarous state by the European nations, and will always recall with pleasure that the United States was the first powerful nation to begin the wise policy of treating Mexico as an equal to all the other civilized nations'.[33] Such a view did not necessarily accord with the facts. There is much to suggest that the United States government regarded Mexico as distinctly inferior, if not for racial considerations, then at least for economic and political. Mexican sensitivity, and above all the recognition that Mexico for much of the nineteenth century was in decline, while the USA was rising to hegemony throughout the continent, smarted under such treatment. Not even the wishful thinking of Juárez or the hyperboles of Romero could alter any of that. Mexico's relationship with the USA would continue to be prickly, especially since US governments never seemed prepared to work out a policy towards the southern neighbour capable of producing an amicable working relationship on both sides. This was precisely the promise to which Juárez had looked, but which never materialized during his lifetime. Yet, at the same time, Mexico and the United States remained inextricably bound to one another. No other Latin American country had such a relationship. In fact, Mexico had no particularly significant relationships with any other country of Latin America. This intimacy with the USA remained the bugbear of its existence. It clouded Mexican visions of everything inescapably. Juárez had been one of the first to recognize and accept this. He had attempted, without a great deal of success, to make it work in Mexico's favour. Nevertheless, he looked to the future. He argued that the principles on which both the United States and the Mexican Republic had been founded were identical: those of constitutional democracy. He envisaged a future in which Mexico's perceived backwardness would be overcome by means of Liberal republican institutions. He saw the United States assisting in such a process. In that way, the two North American republics, which had successfully fought for their independence against the European monarchies – in Mexico's case twice – would become an example to all peoples struggling to be free.

. . .

NOTES AND REFERENCES

1. Basic literature includes Rippy J Fred 1931 *The United States and Mexico.* New York, A A Knopf. Cline Howard 1968 *The United States and Mexico.* 4th edition, New York, Atheneum. Zorrilla Luis G 1965 *Historia de la relaciones entre México y los Estados Unidos.* Mexico City, Biblioteca Porrua. Romero Matías (ed.) 1870–92 *Correspondencia de la legación mexicana durante la intervención extranjera, 1860–1868.* 10 vols, Mexico City, José M Sandoval provides a basic source.
2. Vázquez Josefina Z and Meyer Lorenzo 1982 *México frente a Estados Unidos: Un ensayo histórico, 1776–1980.* Mexico City, El Colegio de México, pp. 55–60. Moyano Pahissa Angela 1987 *México y Estados Unidos: Orígenes de una relación 1819–1861.* Mexico City, Diamante, pp. 264–65.
3. Vázquez and Meyer *México frente a Estados Unidos* pp.62–63.

4. Moyano Pahissa *México y Estados Unidos* pp. 270, 274.
5. Ibid p. 279. Tamayo Jorge L 'El Tratado McLane–Ocampo' *Historia Mexicana* XXIV (1974–75), pp. 573–613.
6. *BJDOCS* 2, pp. 342–89.
7. Ibid pp. 385–89.
8. Ibid pp. 398–402. *APBJPS* I, p. 9. Tamayo 'Tratado McLane–Ocampo' pp. 592–93. *BJDOCS* 3 deals virtually entirely with the McLane–Ocampo Treaty, and *BJDOCS* 4 with its fate in the US Senate.
9. *BJDOCS* 2, p. 482. Blázquez Carmen 1978 *Miguel Lerdo de Tejada: Un liberal veracruzano en la política nacional*. Mexico City, El Colegio de México, pp. 126, 147–48. Roeder Ralph 1947 *Juárez and his Mexico: A Biographical History*. 2 vols, New York, Viking Press, I, p. 241.
10. Moyano Pahissa *México y Estados Unidos* pp. 271–72, 289.
11. *BJDOCS* 3, pp. 751–66. *BJDOCS* 4, pp. 17–95. Sierra Justo (1905–06) 1948 *Juárez: Su obra y su tiempo*. Mexico City, UNAM, pp. 143, 192–99. Iglesia Calderón Fernando (1907) 1972 *Las supuestas traíciones de Juárez*. Mexico City, Fondo de Cultura Económica, pp. 260, 267, 504–05. Roeder *Juárez and his Mexico* I, pp. 212–28.
12. *BJDOCS* 3, pp. 11–13, 64–66.
13. *BJDOCS* 5, pp. 175–58.
14. *BJDOCS* 2, p. 604. *BJDOCS* 3, p. 92. *BJDOCS* 5, pp. 161–63, 211–226. Schoonover T D 1986 *Mexican Lobby: Matías Romero in Washington, 1861–1867*. Lexington, University of Kentucky Press, pp. xiii, xiv, 52–53.
15. *BJDOCS* 3, p. 92. *BJDOCS* 5, pp. 294–96, 312–15, 399–400, 482–85.
16. *Parliamentary Papers* 1862 LXIV, f279 no. 14; f315 no. 57.
17. Bulnes Francisco (1904) 1965 *El verdadero Juárez y la verdad sobre la intervención y el imperio*. Mexico City, Murguía, p. 135. Hanna Alfred Jackson and Hanna Katherine Abbey (1971) 1973 *Napoleon III y Mexico*. Mexico City, Fondo de Cultura Económica, pp. 135–44.
18. *BJDOCS* 8, pp. 152–54. No correspondence between Juárez and Lincoln has ever been discovered in the archives: see Gordon L 'Lincoln and Juárez: A Brief Reassessment of their Relationship' *HAHR* 48, i (Feb. 1968), pp. 75–80.
19. Archivo Juárez MSJ 10–131.
20. *BJDOCS* 9, pp. 541–42.
21. Ibid pp. 450–52. *APBJPS* I, pp. 18–19. Tamayo Jorge L 1970 *Juárez en Chihuahua*. Mexico City, Fondo de Cultura Económica, pp. 266–71, 287–89.
22. Archivo Juárez MSJ S-47.
23. Ibid MSJ S-59. Tamayo *Juárez en Chihuahua* pp. 297–300.

24. *BJDOCS* 10, pp. 15–21, 223–25, 283–85.
25. *BJDOCS* 11, pp. 265–67. Archivo Juárez MSJ 10–1370, MSJ 12-1820. Tamayo Jorge L (ed.) 1957 *Epistolario de Benito Juárez.* Mexico City, pp. 275, 373–77. Hanna and Hanna, *Napoleon III*, pp. 223–30.
26. *Boletiín Oficial: Periódico Bisemanal de la Prefectura Superior de Oaxaca* I, nos 89, 95, 96.
27. *BJDOCS* 11, p. 636.
28. Tamayo *Epistolario* pp. 452–53.
29. *BJDOCS* 11, pp. 479–80.
30. Ibid pp. 475–77.
31. Frías y Soto Hilarión 1905 *Juárez glorificado y la Intervención y el Imperio ante la verdad histórica.* Mexico City, pp. 209–16, 338–43, 378.
32. Iglesias Calderón *Supuestas traíciones* p. 192.
33. *BJDOCS* 13, pp. 411–12.

Chapter 8

JUÁREZ AND THE EUROPEAN POWERS

Juárez never believed much good could come from the European monarchies. The experience of the French Intervention appeared amply to confirm such a view. Juárez saw the old monarchies as a permanent threat to the American republics that had come into existence during the period from 1776 to 1826. His negative views on 'aristocracy', the 'privileged classes' and hereditary right made him ill-disposed to the political systems that still prevailed throughout most of Europe. Juárez, as we have seen, regarded the United States as the natural ally of Mexico and the logical defender of republicanism throughout the continent, in spite of its frequent unwillingness to perform such a role. Nevertheless, Juárez saw Mexico's position in the mid-nineteenth-century world as closely tied to the outcome of events in both Europe and the United States. He was generally well briefed on European affairs. In May 1859, for instance, during the Liberal regime's exile in Veracruz (closer, of course, to the sources of news from Europe), Juárez argued that the outbreak of war in Italy would draw the Powers' attention away from Mexico and thereby benefit the Liberal cause. In August 1866, after five and a half years of opposing outright the ambiguous policies of Napoleon III, a considerably more jaded Juárez welcomed news of the outbreak of war between Prussia and Austria. In his view, Bismarck 'has succeeded in throwing into alarm and activity all the other wolves of Europe. May God keep him in his determination, so that the fire does not go out until it devours the last oppressor in that part of the world'.[1]

. . .

THE DEBT QUESTION AND THE ALLIED INTERVENTION OF 1861–62

Three European Powers, Spain, Great Britain and France, each with widely differing foreign policy perspectives, exerted pressure on Mexico during the late 1850s concerning the debt question. They combined together under the Convention of London of 31 October 1861 to send armed forces to seize control of the port of Veracruz, in order to enforce the payment of debt. This external debt had first accrued after the two London stock market loans of 1824. From 1827, Mexico had been unable to service the debt. Consequently, foreign bond-holders and investors lost confidence in the Republic. In that sense, the new Mexican state had grown up with the external debt question, which had worsened as the country descended further into turmoil and defeat. Since the debt rescheduling agreement of 4 December 1851, however, the Mexican government had had a relatively good record of debt-servicing and had resumed interest payments for the first time since 1827. In 1852 the total debt stood at 98,186,029 pesos, of which as much as 52,744,496 pesos represented the British debt. The debt rose to 109,598,887 pesos by the end of 1856. Mexico had honoured its external obligations until 4 December 1860. The impact of the civil war of the Reform, however, had reduced the Treasury to a critical position during the first months of 1861. As much as 77 per cent of the customs revenues of Veracruz, the principal source of national income, had already been set aside for foreign creditors, half of them British. Ocampo had already warned back in October 1859 that Liberal estimates of Church wealth were grossly exaggerated and that the disamortization and nationalization policies would not yield sufficient revenues to rescue the bankrupt state. No loans had materialized from US sources, but the cabinet had balked at Lerdo's proposal in May 1860 for the suspension of payment of the foreign debt.[2]

Despite these difficulties, the Juárez administration managed to pay off 24 million pesos of debt. Even so, the total still reached 81,632,561 pesos in 1862, of which 64,266,354 pesos represented the British debt. The immediate cause of the European Intervention was the decision of the Juárez government on 17 July 1861 to suspend payment of debt for a two-year period. The object was to give priority to internal reconstruction in the aftermath of civil war. Great Britain's motives for participating were financial rather than political. The debt question explained the difference between Britain's opposition to a European counter-revolutionary intervention in the Americas in 1823 on behalf of Bourbon Spain and its participation in 1861. The withdrawal of the United States as an effective counter in North American politics helped to account for the timing. Britain had previously cooperated with France in the naval blockade of Buenos Aires in 1845–47 over tariff and navigation questions, and in the naval demonstration off Veracruz in January 1859, which had been designed as a warning to the Juárez regime to honour the debt convention. Mexico's first foreign war had been with France, in 1838, a diversion which had prevented the recovery of Texas. Bourbon Spain, between 1856 and 1866, was engaged in a process of reasserting its power in North Africa and the Americas, following decades of convulsion over issues similar to those of the Mexican Reform era. In 1861, for instance, Spain recovered control of the Dominican Republic. The temptation still existed to attempt to place a Bourbon prince on the Mexican throne, vacant since 1823, in cooperation with the Mexican Conservatives.[3]

Such a view appealed to the Captain-General of Cuba, Serrano, with whom Miramón had close contact. The latter saw the Spanish connection as a counter-balance to the US influence which Juárez and the Liberals were anxious to cultivate. Miramón, however, had also introduced a further factor into the Mexican debt question by contracting the notorious Jecker bonds on 29 October 1859. Under that arrangement, credits of 15 million pesos were assigned to cover an immediate loan of little more than 500,000 pesos, half in cash and the other half in war material and uniforms. Since Napoleon III's influential half-brother, the Duc de Morny, was an investor in the Jecker Bank, the Juárez government's total repudiation of Miramón's new debt became an issue between France and Mexico. The French Minister in Mexico from 1860 to 1863, Alphonse Dubois de Saligny, effectively the mouth-piece of Morny, intrigued with Conservatives and pressed the Jecker claims. Miramón went into exile after the collapse of his regime, first to Havana, and then to Paris in April 1861, where he first became aware of separate French designs in Mexico, though he himself was never party to them.[4]

The appointment of General Juan Prim, a sympathizer with the Mexican Liberal cause, to the command of the Spanish Expeditionary Force late in 1861 greatly angered Serrano, and indicated that the O'Donnell government in Madrid had abandoned any idea of altering the political regime within Mexico. O'Donnell went out of his way to reassure the Palmerston government that Spain had never been party to any design on the part of the French government to intervene in Mexican internal affairs on behalf of the rumoured candidacy of the Archduke Ferdinand Maximilian of Habsburg to the imperial throne. Juárez, however, still regarded Spain as the principal enemy of Mexican independence in his Manifesto of 18 December 1861. Napoleon III, since at least October, had begun to conceive of such a scheme, partly at the suggestion of a handful of Mexican monarchist exiles who had no influence at all at home, but who had apparently gained the ear of the Empress Eugenie, herself of Spanish noble descent. Miramón, in Paris again late in August, had already warned Napoleon that no monarchist party existed in Mexico. This was repeated later by Prim and then by Marshal Bazaine, who would become the French military commander in Mexico, on 25 October 1863.[5]

Right from the beginning, Napoleon III had been warned of the dangers of intervening in Mexico. He had chosen to take no notice. The Mexican consul in Paris, Armand de Montluc, who had had close relations with Mexico for some thirty years, was a supporter of Juárez and had contacts with the French republican opposition. Montluc warned Napoleon of the high military costs of intervention and drew his attention to the difficulties encountered by the United States when it had invaded Mexico in 1846–47. The French were contemplating the dispatch of between 25,000 and 30,000 men, whereas the Americans had been obliged to send between 40,000 and 50,000 men and lost half of them. Montluc praised the qualities of Juárez as an eminent jurist who had emerged as the victor in the civil war of the Reform.[6] The French emperor viewed the Mexican situation, in so far as he ever examined it in depth, from the vantage point of France's expanding global interests in the 1850s and early

1860s. Mexico, in that way, became an object of policy, much as Algeria and Indo-China continued to be. Napoleon intended to distinguish his regime from that of his uncle by complementing revision of the Vienna Settlement of 1814–15 with a reassertion of France's imperial position largely undermined a hundred years previously. In this enterprise, he needed British support or acquiescence. An integral part of the transatlantic design was to be the construction of a canal and railway across the Isthmus of Tehuantepec, which was part of the Mexican Republic. This American canal would complement the Suez Canal on the routes to the East. This aspect of Bonapartist policy was highlighted in the Mexican Liberal press in Oaxaca: 'the great goal of Napoleon in bringing about the invasion of the Republic has been first and foremost the Isthmus'. This would be the source of a large expansion of French power, especially since the design provided for the settlement of colonists there. The paper commented in August 1864 that all the Powers had their eyes on the Isthmus, which Mexicans, in their inimitable manner, had managed successfully to keep as an underdeveloped wilderness. Maximilian perfectly understood the priority of the Isthmus. In August 1866 he wrote to Napoleon expressing a preference for French construction of the Tehuantepec Canal and railway, with colonists, in preference to US companies. In Maximilian's view, it should be a European enterprise.[7]

France had a long history of interest in Spanish America, going back at least to Louis XIV's designs on the Spanish succession. Within two and a half years of Louis Napoleon Bonaparte's assumption of the imperial title, the Mexican scheme was formulated. The secession of South Carolina in December 1860, the formation of the Confederacy, and the outbreak of the American civil war in April 1861 provided unparalleled opportunities for its realization. Yet at no time did it appear that Napoleon III examined at any stage the career and significance of Juárez in Mexican politics. He would have benefited from so doing. Juárez certainly revealed an extraordinary ability to survive in the intractable and inscrutable world of Mexican politics. He perfectly understood its tergiversations. He had learned how to spot a quicksand as much by instinct as by touch. When Mexican Conservatives, appalled at the policies of Maximilian, began to look in despair at the exiled administration of Chihuahua, Juárez commented caustically:

> This is the way the world is – and the Mexican world, in particular, which is capable of startling Louis Napoleon himself, should he ever trouble himself to come and live here for a few days. The Mexicans are quite unique: anyone who does not know them and is at the same time conceited, allowing their praises and adulations to intoxicate him, will be cast aside by them and ruined. Anyone who is weak, disheartened by their insults and malicious remarks, will similarly be cast aside and ruined.[8]

Once French objectives became clear, the British and Spanish withdrew from Veracruz, and left the French to their own devices. The French Intervention opened with a military disaster, the defeat of Lorencez's force at Puebla on 5 May 1862. This victory by a non-European army over a Power believed at the time to be supreme on the European continent had profound repercussions not only throughout the Americas but also in Europe, since it exposed the political and military weaknesses of Napoleon III's grand design. The victory at Puebla enabled the Juárez government to retain control of the central valleys for one more year. It thereby delayed the French advance into the interior and put back, with long-term damaging results, the establishment of the empire. General Forey did not enter Mexico City until 10 June 1863. This meant that Maximilian did not ascend the throne until well after Union Forces had taken Vicksburg and won the battle of Gettysburg in July 1863, which made it unlikely that the Confederacy would survive for long as an independent state. Napoleon III had gambled on its survival. Juárez's analysis was primordially based on the demise of the Confederacy. At many stages, it seemed as though the survival of the Mexican Empire had been predicated upon that of the Confederacy, though neither recognized the other.

. . .

THE ESTABLISHMENT OF THE MEXICAN EMPIRE

Forey transferred sovereignty to the Regency Council, consisting of former President Mariano Salas, the Conservative politician Juan Nepomuceno Almonte and Archbishop Labastida. They expected the immediate withdrawal of the

Reform Laws and the repudiation of all Liberal measures. This brought them into repeated conflict with the French military command, which followed Napoleon III's Secret Instructions given in Fontainebleau on 3 July 1862. These provided for both the protection of the Catholic Church and the seemingly contradictory policy of leaving purchasers of nationalized properties unmolested. The Instructions made it clear that the objective of the Intervention was not to support the Conservatives, even though they had helped to bring it about. The real aim was to establish a popularly-based, liberal form of government, which could give shape to the French foreign policy objective of containing the United States in Mexico, Central America, and in the route between the Atlantic and Pacific Oceans, and keeping markets open. The Mexican Empire was designed to give expression to Napoleon III's political ideas, though on the other side of the Atlantic. There existed, then, a fundamental incompatibility of aims between the architects of the empire and those in the Conservative Party who had initially seen in European intervention their own deliverance.[9]

With 27,000 French troops under his command, a remarkably small number for such a huge country, Forey convened an Assembly of Notables (some 250 individuals) early in July 1863, which invited the Archduke Maximilian to assume the vacant Mexican throne. Napoleon III persisted throughout the enterprise in the mistaken belief that the empire could be lastingly established on the basis of a free public vote, once Maximilian had arrived. This delusion was shared by Maximilian himself almost to the end. The reality, however, was that presidential elections had already been held in 1861 and they had overwhelmingly returned Juárez, whose constitutional term of office the foreign intervention had interrupted. Maximilian formally accepted the offer of the crown on 10 April 1864, nearly two and a half years after the original French military campaign in Mexico had been launched. Pope Pius IX and the Mexican episcopate, the leading figures of which would arrive in Mexico with Maximilian, expected the emperor single-mindedly to pursue a policy of dismantling the Juárez inheritance. Napoleon, however, had recommended Maximilian on 2 October 1863 to establish a strong power 'which would proclaim the great principles of modern civilization, such as equality before the law, civil and religious liberty, probity in government, and the impartial administration of justice'. For that reason, he concluded, 'what Mexico needs is a liberal dictatorship'. Maximilian envisaged a constitutional monarchy.[10]

In accordance with the Treaty of Miramar of 12 March 1864, Napoleon undertook to maintain an army initially consisting of 38,000 French troops (but progressively reducing to 20,000) in Mexico until 1867 and the Foreign Legion (8,000 men) until 1873. The Mexican government (that is Maximilian's regime) would bear the entire cost of the Intervention, estimated at 270 million francs (or 55 million pesos) from Mexican resources, as well as cover past debts. By such a means, Napoleon hoped to dispel the hostility already mounting within France towards the Intervention. The treaty, nevertheless, presented Maximilian with an intolerable political burden. It clearly established the principle that the French military presence in Mexico would be only temporary. That amounted in effect to Napoleon III's escape clause. Maximilian, however, far from being alarmed, was anxious to emancipate himself from dependency on the French military, in the hope of forming an independent political base in the country. This Maximilian and Carlota sought to do, almost immediately after arrival in Mexico City on 12 June 1864. To the outrage of Conservatives, Maximilian's first cabinet included moderate liberals, such as Siliceo, who had been a minister in the Comonfort administration. To the despair of Bazaine, who had replaced Forey as supreme commander on 17 July 1863, the majority of ministers seemed to be anti-French and anxious to distance themselves from the Intervention. Teodosio Lares, a moderate and former minister of Santa Anna, sat on the Council of State newly appointed on 4 December 1864.[11]

In the period from June 1864 until December 1866, which corresponded to the high point of French military success and to the lowest point of the *juarista* cause, Maximilian sought to attract moderate and moderate-liberal opinion to the empire. The object was to present his regime as one of national consensus, especially in view of Imperialist control of most of the major cities and ports. The *juaristas* were regarded as little better than bandit groups beyond the law. This moderate profile, however, while it had limited success in attracting intellectuals such as José Fernando Ramírez and Manuel

Orozco y Berra, to the empire, led not to unity but to sharp internal conflict. Maximilian's dislike of the Conservatives lay at the root of this. His suspicion of the two principal Conservative generals, Miramón and Márquez, led to the dispatch of the former to Berlin in November 1864 to study artillery techniques and the latter to Constantinople as Minister Plenipotentiary to the Porte at the end of the year. By January 1865, then, the Mexican Conservatives found themselves without the two military commanders who had led them in the civil war of the Reform. This left Maximilian dependent upon the French, in spite of the arrival of several thousand Belgian and Austrian troops in October 1864 loyal to himself.[12]

For two years, Maximilian's regime was beset by deepening conflict with the ecclesiastical hierarchy over the refusal to rescind the Reform Laws. The Papal Nuncio, who arrived on 7 December 1864, brought a personal letter from the Pope complaining of the delay in suspending the Liberal measures. The Nuncio's request for the sole Catholic establishment, the restoration of the religious orders, ecclesiastical supervision of education, and the re-establishment of the right of property-ownership, all contradicted the policy aims of Napoleon III. Maximilian, similarly, had no intention of giving way on any of those points, since he favoured religious toleration and the abandonment of the Church's claim to nationalized properties. He sought to base his empire on broader support than that of the clergy and the Conservatives, and regarded the imperial authority, in the Habsburg tradition, as the heir of the Spanish royal patronage over the Church. His ultimate aim was turn the clergy into a useful department of state by paying them a state salary, and thereby eliminating the need for ecclesiastical dues and tithes. Late in the same month, Maximilian rebuked the archbishops of Mexico and Michoacán and the bishops of Oaxaca, Querétaro and Tulancingo, who had taken the side of the Nuncio, for interference in politics. Two Imperial Decrees, on 28 December 1864 and 26 February 1865, confirmed purchasers' possession of *bienes nacionales* and renewed sales of ecclesiastical property, though with the provision that they were to be divided before sale and sold only to those with no land.[13]

For Mexico the French Intervention and the formation of a European empire in the territorial heartlands of the republic was a serious matter. This has not been sufficiently recognized by European historians. For a time, between 1861 and 1865, the Mexican scheme was a priority of French foreign policy, and at that time France was perceived to be continental Europe's leading Power. Several of France's most experienced commanders, above all Bazaine, were responsible for implementing policy in Mexico. From the summer of 1863 until the spring of 1866 this army performed credibly against what eventually appeared as overwhelming odds. The struggle which Juárez engaged in was very real. Emilio Castelar, the Spanish Liberal, compared Mexico's struggle against Napoleon III to Spain's against Napoleon I. For Castelar, it showed the vitality of 'democracy' and republicanism: 'we hope that Mexico will be the Spain of Napoleon the Less'. *La Victoria*'s editorial of 28 January 1864 linked the Intervention – a foreign army extinguishing a liberal republic – with the repression of the 1848 revolutions by the European monarchies. It compared the Mexican republicans to Garibaldi's forces in Italy. Juárez and Lincoln were identified as defenders of American Independence.[14] The struggle ended with three catastrophes for the invaders: the abandonment of Maximilian by Napoleon III, the execution of Maximilian by firing squad and the collapse of the French Second Empire in 1870–71. Juárez's tenacious resistance throughout contributed greatly to the French military humiliation in Mexico. That, in turn, exposed the myth of French prowess, undermined the credibility of the Napoleonic system and prepared the way for the disaster of 1870.

. . .

JUÁREZ'S POLICY OF UNCOMPROMISING RESISTANCE

Juárez responded with characteristic firmness to the reality of European Intervention. He secured the concession of extraordinary faculties from a reluctant Congress on 11 December 1861, for the purpose of prosecuting the struggle against Intervention forces. His decree of 17 December closed the port of Veracruz and declared anyone cooperating with Spanish forces to be traitors. The law of 25 January 1862 declared the allies to be outlaws and established the death penalty for collaboration with them. Collaboration was also the subject of the decree of 20 October 1862, which applied the penalties for treason to it. These decrees explained Juárez's policy towards the Intervention right through to his insistence upon the death sentence for Maximilian. By this means, Juárez armed his government with the legal authority to pass the death penalty on traitors, should it see fit to do so. Those laws were not meant as a daily instrument of terror. They were a warning, designed above all to be a deterrent to passive acceptance of conquest, followed by willing or unwilling collaboration with the occupying power and the regime that it intended to impose. They were intended to form the basis of punishment for those who actively sought to destroy the Republic, the Constitution and the Reform Laws. The San Luis Potosí decree of 16 August 1863 defined traitors as all public functionaries of the Intervention and its defenders in writing, and established graded penalties for such persons.[15]

In Chihuahua in March 1865, Juárez explained that those exercising authority under the empire all fell under the scope of the law of 25 January 1862. In a revealing letter to Escobedo, Juárez insisted that the decree certainly applied to the wealthy Sánchez Navarro landowning family of Coahuila. The family, which had begun its accumulation of property in 1765, had been Conservatives during the civil war of the Reform and bitter enemies of Vidaurri. They controlled seventeen haciendas and over 16.5 million acres of land between the Sabinas River and the Zacatecas state border. Carlos Sánchez Navarro became a close friend of Maximilian, who appointed him Grand Chamberlain of the imperial court. Juárez was determined that confiscation of property would be the penalty for collaboration. According to Juárez,

> now is the chance to destroy the monopoly those men have over immense tracts of land with prejudice to agriculture and to the towns of the state. Those properties will be sold at reasonable prices and their product will be used to pay for the upkeep of our forces, or be given in lots to our chieftains, who with such constancy uphold the national cause.

The process of confiscating the Sánchez Navarro *latifundio* began in earnest with the state governor's decree of 22 November 1865 and continued throughout the following year as the republicans pushed back imperialist forces. In reality, however, the confiscation was undertaken less by the authorities than by republican forces on the spot. Juárez's hostility towards the Sánchez Navarros of Coahuila, who were effectively ruined as major landowners in the last years of the empire, was political rather than economic. Accordingly, it did not prevent close cooperation with another rising *latifundista*, Luis Terrazas of Chihuahua, whose family would come to dominate their home state until the Revolution of 1910–11.[16]

Marshal Bazaine disliked the Mexican Conservatives – and Miramón in particular – as much as Maximilian did. He delayed the formation of a separate imperial army, upon which Maximilian hoped to rely in order to emancipate himself from the French. Juárez, who had nothing but contempt for Napoleon III and Maximilian, never underestimated Bazaine. The French commander represented the most effective challenge to the continued survival of the Republic. Juárez's insistence on countering that threat reflected his perception of his own historical role at that time. Juárez believed the survival of the sovereign state created in 1824 to be at stake, and that no other political figure but himself understood the real nature of the struggle or could be trusted to fight through to the end. Bazaine combined a policy of forward military advance with competition for the political middle-ground behind the lines. The object was to deprive Juárez of his natural clientele. The latter roundly condemned the 'so-called moderate liberals, cowards, and men without shame and dignity', who collaborated with Maximilian and the French. He regarded 'those pitiable creatures' as of no political worth; they would desert as soon as the empire foundered – 'but then repentance will fall on sterile ground, because the Nation will know how to call them to account for the blood they have spilt'.[17]

The chief obstacle to the realization of the goal of a liberal empire remained Juárez himself. In the fullness of his political naïvety, Maximilian even conceived of inviting Juárez to an interview with the object of discussing the future shape of the country. Maximilian's ideal solution would have been to see Juárez as Prime Minister at the head of a moderate liberal imperial administration. To Juárez, such a notion would have been laughable, had it not resembled Satan's temptation of Christ in the wilderness. Any suggestion of accommodation with the empire involved the nullification of his own election in 1861, the abolition of the 1857 Constitution, the recognition of the moral right of foreign Intervention forces to be in Mexico and to alter the form of government in the country as they saw fit. It meant wilfully allowing the subjection of Mexico once more to a foreign dynasty and a European metropolis. Such propositions conflicted with everything Juárez stood for throughout his career: they sharply conflicted with the moral basis of his own position. Juárez saw himself not as one man, but as the Republic itself. In that sense, he took upon himself the wounds inflicted on the Republic, in order to save it not only from its enemies but also from itself. The black coach, which bore Juárez deeper and deeper into retreat, became the tabernacle of the Republic.[18]

At no stage did Juárez ever cease to regard himself as President of the Republic. He never left national soil and never once intimated any political recognition at all of the presence of the French high command, the Regency Council and the empire within national territory. This position was praised by Juárez's political opponent, Altamirano, who contrasted his conduct after 1863 with that of national leaders in 1847. Instead of organizing resistance and then disputing territory inch by inch, as Juárez did, they had made peace with the enemy. Altamirano believed the situation in 1863 was infinitely more dangerous than in 1847, since the foreign invaders could rely on the support of the Mexican Conservatives: 'again these privileged and aristocratic castes' were allied to a foreign power, just as in 1810, when they had collaborated with Spain in order to oppose Independence; 'the same conflict but a new aspect'.[19]

Juárez closely watched French military strengths and weaknesses. He accurately assessed the fundamental flaw in French strategy, which lay in the inability to hold down all national territory in a speedy conquest. That ensured that the military penetration of Chihuahua would be incomplete, when for French political objectives, its full occupation was essential. The French were obliged to leave garrison forces in the Pacific port of Mazatlán and across the state of Coahuila. The French government was also under pressure at home from opposition leaders such as Jules Favre and in the European political sphere. Juárez's continued presence ensured that the national government would continue to function, in spite of French campaigns in Chihuahua. The French advance obliged him, however, to transfer the seat of government to Paso del Norte on 14 August 1865. Despite this retreat, Juárez believed that the French would gain nothing, since they had already failed to destroy his government and their own interior lines remained exposed and under constant attack from irregular forces. 'If the enemy advances as far as this town, they will be doing us a favour, since the more they extend their line of communication, the weaker they become'. He also watched Maximilian's political difficulties with the clergy and the Conservatives, and noted the implications of his removal of Miramón and Márquez. Juárez noted with pleasure the political isolation of 'the Austrian' and savoured rumours of a possible clerico-Conservative rising against the Empire.[20]

Since neither side recognized the other as belligerents, no official interchanges could take place between them. This meant that military commanders in the provinces dealt with their counterparts on an *ad hoc* basis. The question of treatment of prisoners of war, therefore, became largely a matter of individual temperament or response to the heat of the moment. Escobedo became notorious for summary execution of French prisoners, whereas Vicente Riva Palacio, operating in Michoacán, earned a reputation for generous handling. These *ad hoc* arrangements became virtually institutionalized during the last months of the French evacuation. Bazaine and other commanders had private understandings with Díaz and other Mexican generals that their forces would not be molested during the withdrawal. That left the republicans free to deal with the ill-equipped and inadequate imperial forces henceforth required to fight on their own. This was the harsh reality behind Napoleon's policy of 'Mexicanizing' the war. The period from December 1866 to June 1867 became a replay of the last months of the civil war of the Reform, with the difference that an Austrian archduke found himself caught in the middle.

Juárez remained constantly aware of the weakness of the Liberal 'Army' in the face of French advances northwards in 1864. He understood perfectly well how unreliable as military commanders his own Mexican generals were. Before and during the Intervention he was engaged in a complex power struggle with them, whether as individuals or as allies one with another. The defections from the *juarista* camp were always spectacular, because they took place at the highest levels: Vidaurri, González Ortega, Doblado, López Uraga, Ruiz and Dublán. The weak link in the *juarista* geo-political position was, as it had been in 1858–59, across the north-central tier of states: Michoacán, Jalisco and Zacatecas. The north-east, controlled by Vidaurri, was a special case. Juárez, however, could count for the most part on the support of the remaining northern states: Sonora, Sinaloa, Durango and Chihuahua. These formed the rear base of *juarismo* in the lean years of 1865 and 1866. For that reason *juarismo*, which had emerged in the late 1840s in the southern state of Oaxaca, increasingly acquired a profoundly northern character. This would continue in the decades after Juárez's death as an ideology centred on the appeal to liberal republican principles, and would re-emerge during the 1900s in the form of a political challenge to the repeated re-elections of Porfirio Díaz and to central government interference with municipal autonomy. One explanation for the deep roots that *juarismo* acquired in the north was the fact that Juárez was the first President who spent a significant length of time there, above all at a decisive stage in his own struggle for survival. The political alliance with Terrazas, moreover, lasted right through the period of the Restored Republic after 1867. Juárez could also count on the loyalty of Mariano Escobedo, enemy of Vidaurri. Escobedo later became a close political ally of Sebastián Lerdo throughout the 1870s. In April 1865 Juárez appointed him General-in-Chief of republican forces in Coahuila and Nuevo León and Governor and Military Commander in the latter state, from which he originated. He also advised Escobedo that a reliable benefactor of the republican cause was Jesús Carranza, a resident in Cuatro Ciénegas (Coahuila). Carranza was shortly afterwards appointed *jefe político* of Monclova.[21]

Juárez did not view his politically unreliable and militarily undistinguished generals as indispensable. He knew their limitations and was, in any case, a shrewd judge of men. He had never felt at ease with them, in view of their independent political base and distinct outlook. They frequently threw fits of pique, when they felt themselves not given sufficient attention or credit for their achievements. Even Riva Palacio refused to cooperate, when he felt that Juárez had slighted him. The generals, in turn, resented Juárez's reliance on Ignacio Mejía, benefactor of the Juárez family during the Conservative occupation of Oaxaca in the civil war of the Reform. Juárez did not trust his rival Liberal politicians to wage war unrelentingly against the French and the empire, regardless of the personal consequence for themselves. Instead, he saw them opting for compromise arrangements, designed allegedly to bring the war to an end, but in reality to salvage their own positions and remove him from office. Juárez's determination to remain in power responded not primarily to lust for power or a sense of indispensability but remained founded in his deep distrust of his own Mexican Liberal generals and politicians. In July 1866 Juárez made a list of loyal generals and state governors: Escobedo, Terrazas, Pesqueira, Viesca, Corona, Régules, Álvarez, Díaz and García. These, by and large, would be the architects of victory in June 1867. As the case of Díaz would show, their loyalty could not necessarily be taken for granted.[22]

Since the republican army was unable to prevent the French advance north, other means than pitched battles were used to slow them down. Juárez strongly believed in the effectiveness of guerrilla warfare. Irregular bands operated throughout the lowlands of Veracruz, harrassing French lines of communication inland from the Gulf. There a counter-guerrilla force was organized under the notorious Colonel Dupin. These units wore special, informal 'uniforms' to distinguish them from regular forces, but operated under the command of serving army officers. Further north, in the Huasteca, guerrilla bands led by Desiderio Pavón operated against imperialist positions in the higher altitude zones. In Guerrero, which never fell under French control, the tactical alliance between the Álvarez and Jiménez clientele upheld the *juarista* cause. Their relief of Chilapa, besieged by 5,000 imperialists, on 10 November 1864, presented Juárez with a republican victory during the darkest days. By mid-March 1865 Juárez was able to report to Santacilia that Guerrero was entirely free of the French. Juárez used his executive authority to sustain Diego Álvarez in office in the state. The latter's constitutional term expired in 1866, but the continuation of the war made it unlikely that elections could be held in December, when they were due. Accordingly, Juárez on 27 August 1866 declared Guerrero to be in a state of siege and appointed Álvarez Governor and Military Commander.[23] The perpetuation of the Álvarez hegemony in Guerrero led to the break-up of the alliance with Jiménez, and to a protracted power struggle in the state, which we shall examine in Chapter 9.

. . .

MARSHAL BAZAINE AND THE FRENCH RESPONSE

Juárez had in Bazaine a worthy opponent. Bazaine was the real central figure in the Intervention from the time of his accession to the supreme command in July 1863 until his departure with the last French troops in February 1867. Never given credit for his work in Mexico (understandably not by Mexican historians), Bazaine fell victim first to Napoleon's embarrassment with the whole Mexican problem and second to the mismanagement of the Franco-Prussian War, which obliged him to surrender Metz in 1870. In France, Bazaine's reputation was broken; in Mexico, he can never be admitted to the pantheon of heroes. Bazaine's connections with the Hispanic and Maghrebian worlds ran deep. From 1832, he had served in the Foreign Legion in Algeria, operating against Abd-el-Kader, and later in the decade in Spain on the side of the Regent María Cristina in the First Carlist War. He learned Spanish and studied Spanish politics closely. His first wife was Spanish and his second was Mexican. In Algeria he learned Arabic and acquired the techniques of absorbing and unscrambling contradictory information from a host of dubious sources, while remaining himself inscrutable. These techniques and his intimate knowledge of irregular warfare would serve him well in Mexico. He became head of the Bureau Arabe in Tlemcen in 1842 and of the Département des Affaires Arabes for the Province of Oran in 1850. The Mexican campaign followed service in the Crimea and Italy. Bazaine took to Mexico several contingents of the special North African forces that he had helped form in Algeria, the Zouaves and the Spahis. A number of Egyptian forces accompanied them. Bazaine believed that Algerian-style warfare was best suited to Mexico. Once on campaign in Mexico, the hunt for Juárez repeated the earlier search for Abd-el-Kader.[24]

On 10 April 1864 Bazaine instructed all military commanders to treat the *juarista* bands as bandits, irrespective of any military or administrative rank that their members might possess. They were, accordingly, to be subject to martial law. The imperial decree of 3 October 1865, which Maximilian attributed to Bazaine, represented the response to the war of the guerrilla bands. It may well have originated in Conservative pressure for retaliation against Juárez's decree of 20 October 1862. This draconian law established a new courts martial system staffed by Mexican imperial officers, in which sentences would be carried out within twenty-four hours. The death penalty was assigned for all members of unauthorized bands, whether ostensibly political or not. A graded series of penalties was then established for all those who in any way assisted such bands with cash, material aid, information or lodgings, by spreading false alarm, or by failing to report their activities. The decree also sought to mobilize self-defence units in the villages and on the private estates, with penalties for non-cooperation. Bazaine's confidential circular to military commanders on 11 October 1865 specified the methods to be used in the war against the *juarista* bands. He singled out the examples of the seizure of Uruapan by bands operating in Michoacán under the command of the former governor of Querétaro, Arteaga, on 18 June, in which the Prefect and a notable citizen had been executed, and the attack on the Veracruz railway at Arroyo de Piedra, in which nine officers and men had been killed. Bazaine instructed his commanders to take reprisals under the terms of the decree of 3 October 1865. No prisoners were to be taken: everyone found with arms in his hand was to be immediately shot. There were to be no further exchanges of prisoners, in order to impress upon imperial soldiers the futility of surrendering to the enemy. 'This is a war to the death, a war without quarter, which is engaged today between barbarism and civilization. It is necessary for both sides to kill or be killed'. Bazaine, as a European, assumed that civilization was on the side of the French. Juárez held Maximilian directly responsible for the decree of 3 October and for the measures taken in accordance with it. On 21 October, for instance, Arteaga and three other republican commanders were executed in Uruapan. Juárez remained determined to bring Maximilian to account for the bloodshed that resulted from the decree. That measure formed a central part of the accusations against the fallen emperor during his court martial in June 1867.[25]

Juárez, for his part, insisted that no exchange of prisoners could take place unless the French military command formally recognized the republicans as 'belligerents' and ceased to treat them as 'bandits'. He explained to Governor Viesca of Coahuila in June 1866 that the former term should apply without distinction to both regular troops and guerrillas, reserving all their rights under international law. Only then could prisoners be exchanged. However, the exchange applied only to foreign troops. It did not apply to the Mexican imperial forces, who were subject to the legitimate Mexican government, against which they had committed acts of treason. Juárez stipulated that they would be pardoned or punished, in accordance with the law. He would not allow any foreign commander or authority to intervene in such cases.[26]

The French returned to Chihuahua in December 1865, and the Juárez government arrived back in Paso del Norte on 19 December. Even so, it had already become evident that the French were rethinking their strategy as a result of the end of the American civil war. Bazaine decided to concentrate French forces in Durango and San Luis Potosí away from the border. Juárez attributed that to the US government's final decision not to recognize the empire and to Bazaine's fear that any small border incident might lead to war between France and the USA. For that reason, Bazaine was sending Mexican and Austrian troops to the north and the Foreign Legion to Monterrey. The French withdrawal from Chihuahua in the spring of 1866 Juárez believed to be definitive, motivated precisely by the fear of war with the USA. Napoleon III had by then publicly committed himself to military withdrawal from Mexico, a situation which had thrown the Imperialists into panic. Accordingly, Juárez proposed to move south to the state capital in the company of Terrazas's forces.[27]

. . .

THE COLLAPSE OF THE EMPIRE

The end of the American civil war made it imperative to set in motion the final evacuation, even though no real danger existed of war between the two countries. The central plank of Seward's foreign policy had always been to avoid precisely that. By the end of 1865, withdrawal had become the overriding issue. Napoleon pressed for an evacuation date, and early in January 1866 insisted on the beginning of the following year as the final stage. This made it all the more urgent for Maximilian's government to organize the Mexican Imperial Army as a capable defence force. At the same time, it raised the issue of whether Maximilian should remain in Mexico or leave with the French. Bazaine believed that the empire had no popular support, that the evacuation of the north was essential, and that Maximilian should cut his losses and return to Europe. Napoleon III was anxious somehow to preserve what he perceived to be the French achievement in Mexico (while at the same time withdrawing French forces), lest the Intervention should be regarded a failure. During the spring of 1866, *juarista* forces began to advance across the north; by 14 August they had taken Hermosillo, the Sonora state capital. In that same month, Napoleon wrote to Maximilian, shortly after receiving the distraught Carlota, that henceforth it would be impossible for France to 'aid Mexico' either with men or money. All French troops would have to be out in 1867. He inquired whether Maximilian could sustain himself with his own forces. He stressed that no one should have any illusions that, as far as France was concerned, the Mexican question was finished.[28]

The last stages of the evacuation began in September 1866. By December, Bazaine was urging speed, anxious at the same time to dissociate himself from the Conservatives who had inevitably regained control of government with the defection of the moderates in the wake of the French withdrawal. Maximilian, in any case, had always disliked Bazaine, whom since October 1866 he had been pressing Napoleon to recall. Carlota in Paris made accusations against him at the French court, in the hope of undermining his position. Maximilian, though he would soon be forced into self-reliance, declined to make use of Bazaine's expert knowledge of the Mexican situation, and took advice instead from his own household retinue. Between the emperor and Bazaine 'suspicion and private recrimination had reached the point where frankness was impossible'.[29]

Late in October 1866, Maximilian arrived in Orizaba, on the road to Veracruz, in the company of Austrian volunteers, with the purpose of meditating the question of abdication, while at the same time adding to his collection of butterflies. His personal possessions had already been put into crates ready for shipment to Europe. He spent five weeks in virtual seclusion. Conservative pressures and above all the influence of Fr Fischer, his German Jesuit confessor, persuaded Maximilian to stay. This decision was communicated to the public on 30 November. At that stage, Miramón returned from exile in Europe to take command of the imperial army and attempt a last stand of the Conservative cause. Maximilian, who still dreamed of a national assembly and a liberal regime, found himself the prisoner of the Mexican Conservatives, whose policies he had obstructed for so long. On 14 January 1867 a junta in Mexico City decided by one vote to sustain the empire, despite Bazaine's grave reservations concerning the military situation. From that time, Bazaine washed his hands of the empire and preferred instead to deal directly with *juarista* generals in order to ease the process of evacuation. In spite of Bazaine's order for the immediate evacuation of Mexico City on 5 February 1867, Maximilian again refused to leave.[30]

Late in January 1867, the Juárez government moved as far south as Zacatecas. There, however, it was nearly cut off by Miramón's rapid thrust against the city. Juárez, Lerdo and Iglesias abandoned the black coach and fled on horseback, only narrowly escaping capture. When Juárez and his ministers returned to Zacatecas, they discovered there Maximilian's order of 5 February 1867 for their own execution. This discovery may well have influenced them to press for the execution of Maximilian and the Conservative generals. In the short term, Escobedo, stunned by Miramón's boldness, avenged the attack on Zacatecas by routing his forces at San Jacinto on 1 February, and forcing him back in the direction of Querétaro. In the aftermath of the near capture of the republican leadership, Escobedo ordered the execution of all foreign volunteers taken with arms in their hand, sparing only the wounded. In this way, a total of 139 prisoners were executed in one day, followed two days later by the execution of Miramón's brother, Colonel Joaquín Miramón.[31]

The encirclement of Mexico City and the remaining imperialist positions followed rapidly. On 14 January 1867 Corona's Army of the West had entered Guadalajara; Tomás Mejía abandoned San Luis Potosí for Querétaro on 25 January; also on 25 January, Guanajuato fell to the republicans, followed by Morelia on 18 February. About that time, Diego Álvarez entered Cuernavaca, to the south of the capital. The Juárez administration left Zacatecas on 17 February and four days later took up residence in San Luis Potosí. In the mean time, Maximilian had taken the decision on 10 February to proceed to Querétaro, in order to deal with unauthorized military actions by Miramón. Three days later, he left the capital, leaving most of his cabinet behind him. He entrusted José María Lacunza, President of the Council of Ministers, with his abdication, should he be taken prisoner. From Querétaro, Maximilian on 20 February 1867 appointed a Regency Council, consisting of Lares, Lacunza and Márquez, to replace him, if killed. In any event, their commission was to summon a Congress for the reconstitution of national affairs at the end of the war. This fanciful proposition illustrated the extent of Maximilian's self-delusion and his still inadequate grasp of the nature of the forces he had journeyed to Querétaro to oppose. From late February, Maximilian and the Conservative generals with some 10,000 men began the fortification of Querétaro, a city regarded by Juárez as hostile to the republican cause. By the second week of March, the bulk of the Imperial Army was in the city. On 8 March 1867 Corona's forces arrived in the vicinity of Querétaro; from 14 March, Escobedo, with more than 25,000 men, began the process of investing the city. Since this was not completed until ten days later, Maximilian was able to order Márquez and Vidaurri to take a cavalry force of 1,200 men through the open southern route and bring back reinforcements from Mexico City.[32]

Márquez's movements around Mexico City encouraged Porfirio Díaz in the south to advance with the Army of the East across the Valley of Puebla. On 2–4 April 1867 Díaz took Puebla and the Forts of Loreto and Guadalupe, forcing Márquez back towards the capital. Díaz's objective was the investment of Mexico City. By this time, the besieging forces around Querétaro included most of the principal republican generals, with Escobedo in command and Corona his second-in-command. Treviño, Rocha, Alatorre, Vicente Riva Palacio, Aureliano Rivera, Juan N Méndez, Florencio Antillón, Francisco O Arce and Vicente Jiménez, all of them were there, and all of them were to play a major political role during the period of the Restored Republic after July 1867.[33]

Maximilian and the Imperial Army were trapped in Querétaro. A siege of more than seventy days followed: it would not end until 15 May 1867, when the emperor, Miramón and Mejía were betrayed and captured in an assault on their headquarters on the Hill of the Bells and formally surrendered. The prospect of the capture of Maximilian and the imperial generals in the aftermath of San Jacinto sent a shock wave through the chancelleries of the Great Powers. From April onwards, mounting fears were expressed for the life of Maximilian. Romero communicated from Washington Seward's concern that prisoners taken at Querétaro should not be slaughtered. Romero pithily added the comment that Seward had never expressed any similar concern for the life of Juárez, should he have fallen into the hands of the French. The Austrian Minister in Washington, Count von Wydenbruck, asked the US government, at the request of the Emperor Francis Joseph, to intercede with Juárez for the safety of Maximilian. Seward passed this message on to Lewis D Campbell, who had been appointed US Minister to Mexico in October 1866 but was still in New Orleans. Campbell wrote to Lerdo that severity would bring all republics into disrepute. The USA, furthermore, sympathized with the Mexican Republic, but, he warned, any repetitions of the shootings after San Jacinto would jeopardize that. Seward was anxious to press Juárez for assurances that Maximilian and his followers would be, as he put it, accorded the treatment of civilized nations towards prisoners of war.[34]

Juárez, throughout the months of the siege, corresponded with Escobedo virtually three times a week. Escobedo, who had earlier referred to Maximilian as a 'pirate', received general instructions from Juárez on 23 April 1867, concerning the treatment of all prisoners of war. He agreed with Escobedo that ordinary soldiers should not be shot, when taken prisoner, 'but this should not apply to the leading figures and commanding officers'. Special circumstances applied in their case, and they would be subjected to the full vigour of the law. Similar instructions had earlier been sent to Díaz. Lerdo, at this time, replied to Campbell, whom he tartly reminded that he had not presented his credentials, that Maximilian had been free to leave with the French. Instead, he had taken the decision to spill yet more Mexican blood in a futile last stand, which ensured the continuation of the civil war. 'In the case that persons upon whom such responsibility weighs should be captured, it is inconceivable that they shall be considered mere prisoners of war, since such responsibilities are defined by the law of Nations and the laws of the Republic'.[35]

In this way, Juárez, already under international pressure which he was determined to ignore, had begun to set up the legal framework for the execution of Maximilian and the Conservative generals before they had even been captured.

. . .

THE EXECUTION OF MAXIMILIAN

By the middle of May, imperial forces in Querétaro had shrunk to 5,000 men, while those of the besiegers increased to 30,000. Miramón and Mejía, greatly incensed at Márquez's failure to relieve them, advised the emperor on 14 May 1867 to attack and attempt a break-out, since they did not trust the clemency of the republicans – 'a savage enemy without faith and without honour'. On the following day, a republican assault resulted in their capture and that of Maximilian. Juárez, upon receipt of news of the capitulations of 15 May, instructed Escobedo to convene a court martial for the trial of the three prisoners, on the grounds that they were 'criminals' under the terms of the law of 25 June 1862. He explained that the military authorities could have executed them on the spot, in accordance with that law, after the mere formality of identifying them. The government, however, proposed to go through the legal procedure of a trial in which charges would be made public and a defence prepared. In such a way, Juárez believed that 'all imputations of rancour and hastiness, which bad faith may want to attribute to the government, can be removed'.[36]

The Minister of War informed Escobedo on 21 May 1867 that the government intended to try the three prisoners by court martial under the law of 1862. Such a procedure virtually guaranteed a sentence of death. In the government's view, the archduke had allowed himself to be the principal instrument of an attempt by the 'corrupt classes' to put their interests before those of the nation, with a civil war of five years' duration and untold calamities as the consequence. Maximilian was described as the instrument of a war of foreign intervention and filibusterism. Accordingly Escobedo appointed his aide-de-camp, who was a qualified lawyer, to act as prosecutor. Maximilian chose as his defence counsel two prominent Liberal figures, Mariano Riva Palacio (father of Vicente) and Lic. Rafael Martínez de la Torre, both resident in Mexico City and well-disposed to the emperor but loyal to the republican cause. Their political credentials were impeccable. They were deeply shocked, however, by Juárez's insistence that the prisoners should be tried by court martial, rather than in a civil court, and under the punitive law of 1862.[37]

The prosecutor interrogated Maximilian from 24 to 27 May. The archduke refused to answer the questions on the grounds that a court martial was incompetent in political matters. He argued that only Congress could try him, though none had been in session since 1863. Maximilian requested a personal interview with Juárez. Miramón argued that the Álvarez regime had been illegitimate and that the nation had rejected the 1857 Constitution in the coup of Tacubaya. Mejía pointed out that, unlike Escobedo, he had never shot prisoners of war. Miramón stated that he had never supported the French Intervention but had recognized the legitimacy of the junta of notables' invitation to Maximilian to take the throne. All of those replies ran deeply counter to the Juárez government's current intentions and to its claims to legitimacy. On 31 May 1867 Escobedo rejected Maximilian's claim that the 1862 law did not apply.[38]

With a safe conduct from Díaz, the defence counsel left the besieged capital for Querétaro in the company of the Prussian minister, Baron Anton von Magnus, and the Belgian Chargé d'Affaires, M. Hooricks. They discussed matters first with Escobedo and then interviewed Maximilian himself on 5 June. In Querétaro, the defence counsel became aware that the Juárez government intended to allow them only twenty-four hours to prepare their case, before the trial and then immediate execution of sentence. This unseemly haste increased their indignation at the entire proceedings. They strongly objected to the government's insistence on the law of 1862 as the basis of its case. Juárez informed Santacilia that the trial would probably be over in eight days.[39]

In Querétaro, Maximilian's two defence lawyers, Lic. José María Vázquez and Lic. Eulalio Ortega, repeated on 6 June 1867 the view that the court martial was incompetent to try the cases in question. They pointed out that Jefferson Davis had not been tried by extraordinary tribunals or executed after capture in 1865. Riva Palacio, for his part, considered the law of 1862 to be 'cruel and bloody' and 'in conflict with the philanthropic principles of the Constitution'. The defence counsel requested a free and open trial before the normal federal courts, a procedure which would add distinction to the Republic. They remained convinced, however, that nothing would stop the government in its determination to have the three prisoners executed. At their request, Juárez granted three more days for the preparation of the case for the defence, an extension they regarded as derisory, since they had hoped for a full month. On 8 June, they arrived in San Luis Potosí, in order to present their arguments to ministers in person. The defence was anxious to save Maximilian's life, but Lerdo, after a three-hour discussion, insisted that the procedure should be in accordance with the law of 1862. Juárez received Riva Palacio and Martínez de la Torre as two old friends, but repeated what Lerdo had said. He claimed to have no personal enmity towards Maximilian, but took his stand on the law, which in this case was the law of 1862. Faced with this 'terrible' law and the 'intransigent resolution' of Juárez, the defence counsel fully comprehended the probability that Maximilian and his generals would be required to die.[40]

Even so, they still sought to press the government to change its position. They argued that the law of 1862 belonged to the period of confrontation and not to the era of reconciliation. Lerdo, however, countered that the Archduke Maximilian had been well aware of that law when he set foot on Mexican soil. The defence then argued that the law dealt with specific cases at a particular time, and could not possibly apply to a government of three years' duration, which had been recognized by all the European Powers and the Brazilian Empire as well. In any case, no one could pretend that Maximilian had come to Mexico with the intention of causing premeditated harm. On the contrary, he had hesitated for a year after his appointment by the junta of notables, and had come only when finally convinced that it was the popular will that he should take office. He had constantly sought to free himself from the tutelege of the French military commanders and to 'Mexicanize' his government. For those reasons, the defence argued that the death penalty would be unjust. Article 23 of the Constitution had, in any case, specifically prohibited the use of the death penalty for political offences. When they reminded ministers of that, the latter replied that the Constitution had been in suspense for the duration of the war. Since the war still continued, the extraordinary powers granted to Juárez remained in force. The defence wanted to know why discretionary powers should not conform to constitutional provisions. What a reflection on five years' struggle to uphold constitutional principles, followed now by victory, they commented, only to be told that the Constitution was not in force and that the law consisted of the law of 1862.[41]

Unable to dissuade the Juárez government, the defence appealed for clemency on 12 June 1867. Two days later, a specially appointed court martial passed the death sentence for 'crimes against the Nation, the right of peoples, order, and public peace'. The prosecutor had listed a series of charges, virtually all of which were strictly political in character. Those which were not, such as passage and enforcement of the decree of 2 October 1865, were consequences of the political situation in which Maximilian had found himself. The Prussian minister appealed for a pardon. Lerdo rejected the appeal on the grounds that, if allowed to live, Maximilian might return to Mexico at the behest of the European Powers. The government intended to make republican institutions respected in Europe and did not propose to rush into a hasty pardon.

Riva Palacio and Martínez de la Torre then went to see Juárez on 15 June 1867 and repeated the request for a pardon. Was it not sufficient to sentence Maximilian to death, they argued, but was it necessary to execute that sentence? All the legal and political arguments of the defence had fallen on stony ground. They were now reduced to the moral case, their last hope. They warned that the execution of Maximilian would lead to the isolation of Mexico. Juárez replied that the final decision whether to confirm the death sentence now lay with Escobedo. The government would then decide whether to pardon Maximilian or not. On 16 June, the defence went to see Juárez once more, pleading for Maximilian's life and appealing to the President as leader of the Liberal cause and as a family man. Lerdo read them the telegram that he had sent to Escobedo, telling him that a pardon had been requested but that the government had seen fit to deny it. The executions had been scheduled for that same day, immediately after Escobedo's confirmation of sentence. The government decided to postpone the execution of sentence until the morning of 19 June, in order to give the prisoners time to put their affairs in order. Ortega and Vázquez, however, reported from Querétaro that the three prisoners had already made their last confessions and communicated, and had been ready to face death. Postponement of sentence meant that they would now die twice.[42]

Maximilian telegraphed Juárez on 18 June to request not his own life, but those of Miramón and Mejía. The government remained inflexible. Miramón's wife arrived in San Luis Potosí with a supporting entourage of weeping ladies, but Juárez refused to receive her. Riva Palacio and Martínez de la Torre spoke to Juárez about her plea for her husband's life in the name of their children, but Juárez replied that, if he admitted her, she would only suffer more pain, since he would have to tell her that the decision of the court martial was irrevocable. Martínez begged Juárez to prevent any further bloodshed and warned that the three impending executions would cloud Mexico's future. Instead, Juárez thanked the defence counsel for their work, and noted that 'they had suffered greatly through the inflexibility of the government. Today you are unable to understand the necessity for that and the justice which reinforces it. Time will assist you to appreciate it. The law and the sentence are at this moment inexorable, because public welfare requires them to be'.[43]

Maximilian, who believed that Carlota was already dead, thanked the defence counsel for their efforts. Just before his execution, he wrote to Juárez expressing his readiness to lay down his life, if it would mean the end of civil war. He asked Juárez to ensure that the impending sacrifice would be the last bloodshed and appealed to him to bring about lasting peace and reconciliation. At 7.05 a.m. on 19 June 1867, Maximilian, Miramón and Mejía were executed together by firing squad on the Cerro de las Campanas to the west of the city.[44]

Although executed on 19 June, Maximilian was not buried until 18 January 1868, because Juárez refused to hand over the body. The Austrian minister, followed by Magnus, had first requested it the day after the execution, in order to fulfil Maximilian's instructions for the embalming of his corpse. The Austrian envoy, Vice-Admiral Tegetthoff, who arrived in Mexico City on 1 September 1867, also failed to secure it. The government itself undertook the embalming, instructing that it should be done by Mexicans and under close guard, lest the body should be visited for veneration. After its transfer from Querétaro to Mexico City and before the body was robed,

Juárez and Lerdo incognito went by carriage to the church where it lay naked on a table, in order to inspect it. That was the first time Juárez had seen Maximilian. He studied the body and commented to a silent Lerdo, 'He was tall that man, but he didn't have a good body. His legs were too long and disproportionate. He had no talent: because, although he had a high forehead, it was due to receding hair'. Juárez made no other comment. After half an hour in front of the body, they left. The following day the body was robed and photographs permitted.[45]

In the weeks following the execution, news arrived in Mexico of the appeals for the life of Maximilian from European celebrities, such as Garibaldi and Victor Hugo, both great admirers of Juárez and supporters of the Mexican republican cause. On the other hand, several Liberal politicians praised the Juárez government for its 'indomitable energy' in insisting upon the execution. Juan José Baz, whom Díaz had made *jefe político* of the Federal District just before the fall of the capital on 21 June, argued that Maximilian had to be 'sacrificed', as he put it, in order to kill the principle that he represented. 'This example will ensure that in Europe we are respected and will remove any desire on the part of any other adventurers to come here'.[46]

Juárez himself published a Manifesto justifying his conduct, in which he argued that Maximilian had been condemned for the crime of attempting to assassinate the Anáhuac nation. Juárez intended to contrast the villainy of European absolute monarchies with the American republics' resolute defence of democracy. He unequivocally stated that the death of Maximilian was 'just, necessary, urgent, and inevitable'. The use of the Aztec name, Anáhuac, to describe Mexico hinted that the earlier, successful conquest in the name of an ancestor of Maximilian, the Emperor Charles V, had now been avenged. 'We inherit the indigenous nationality of the Aztecs, and in full enjoyment of it, we recognize no foreign sovereigns, no judges, and no arbiters'. This was a curious statement for a Zapotec to make, but it indicated the extent to which Juárez had absorbed the intellectual construct of Mexico City-based nationalism. He condemned the false morality of the European colonial states – strictly pagan when it came to political conduct – in India and North Africa, denounced their wilful preservation of the Ottoman Empire ('the scandal of the Christian world'), and drew attention to barbarities committed by the Christian kings of

Europe such as had never been witnessed in Latin America. Clearly, Juárez took his stand on the rights of peoples and nations to resist colonialism and to challenge great empires. He presented Mexico as an exemplary case. He regarded Maximilian as a filibusterer and chief in a war of bandits. His death was an 'expiatory sacrifice'.[47]

The Juárez government took the decision to have no diplomatic relations with European Powers which had supported the empire. The British Mission closed, although consuls remained in position outside the capital. Diplomatic relations were not restored until 1884. With the collapse of the Bourbon monarchy in Spain in 1868, Prim hoped to see a renewal of relations, but this was not achieved until June 1871. Relations with France were restored after the collapse of the Second Empire in 1871.[48]

The conduct of Juárez during and after the capture, trial and execution of Maximilian, Miramón and Mejía was quite extraordinary. The haste, which he claimed he wished to avoid, was self-evident. More still was the premeditation with which the legal circle around the prisoners closed. The insistence on the law of 1862, while technically credible in view of the suspension of constitutional guarantees for the duration of the war, remained highly dubious in legal and moral terms. Ultimately, the object of the execution of Maximilian was political, a lesson to the European monarchies. The life of the archduke remained in human terms beyond consideration. The frequent use of the term 'sacrifice' had a certain resonance at a time when Juárez was recalling the continuity between the Mexican Republic and the Aztec state. Juárez believed that clemency constituted weakness. The government intended to accomplish its aims before anyone really understood what was happening, and to present the European Powers with a *fait accompli.* Juárez and his ministers exploited the telegraph system, inadequate though it still was, to their fullest advantage, in order to make for speedy execution of their orders.

. . .

NOTES AND REFERENCES

1. *BJDOCS* 11, pp. 395–96. *APBJPS* I, p. 10.
2. *BJDOCS* 4, pp. 311–12. Sierra Justo (1905–06) 1948 *Juárez: Su obra y su tiempo.* Mexico City, UNAM, p. 624.

3. *BJDOCS* 5, pp. 245–49. McCaleb Walter Flavius 1921 *The Public Finances of Mexico.* New York, Harper & Brothers, pp. 44, 50, 53, 77. Bazant Jan 1968 *Historia de la deuda exterior de México(1823, 1823–1946).* Mexico City, El Colegio de México, pp. 86–87. Barker Nancy N 1978 *The French Experience in Mexico, 1821–1861: A History of Constant Misunderstanding.* Chapel Hill, University of North Carolina Press.
4. Montluc Léon de 1905 *Correspondencia de Juárez y Montluc.* Mexico City, pp. 35–36. Bazant *Historia de la deuda,* pp. 88–91. Fuentes Mares José 1985 *Miramón: El Hombre.* Mexico City, Editorial Grijalbo, pp. 109–12.
5. *BJDOCS* 5, pp. 414–15, 457–58. *Parliamentary Papers* 1862 LXIV, no. 4, pp. 272–73; no. 6, pp. 273–74; no. 8, pp. 276–77. Miquel i Vergés (1949) 1987 *Prim en Mexico: General de una causa justa.* Mexico City, Pangea Editores.
6. Montluc *Correspondencia* pp. 100–09, 131–38, 207.
7. *BJDOCS* 11, pp. 337–38. *La Victoria* (Hemeroteca Pública de Oaxaca) IV no. 15, 5 July 1864; V, no. 26, 1 August 1864. Simpson F A (1909) 1968 *The Rise of Louis Napoleon.* London, Frank Cass, pp. 261–63.
8. *BJDOCS* 9, pp. 807–09.
9. *BJDOCS* 8, p. 165.
10. Ibid pp. 40–42, 191–211.
11. Ibid pp. 799–804. Fuentes Mares José 1982 *Juárez: El Imperio y la República.* Mexico City, Editorial Grijalbo, pp. 30–37, 54–55.
12. Fuentes Mares *Miramón* pp. 60–61.
13. Ibid p. 71.
14. *La Victoria* IV no. 56, 14 January 1864; no. 60, 26 January 1864; V, nos 22, 28, 29, 35, 48.
15. *BJDOCS* 5, pp. 452–53.
16. *BJDOCS* 9, pp. 728–32. Harris Charles H 1975 *A Mexican Family Empire: The Latifundio of the Sánchez Navarro Family, 1765–1867.* Austin, University of Texas Press, pp. 301–02.
17. *BJDOCS* 9, pp. 728–32.
18. See for instance Kératry Comte E de 1867 *L'Elévation et la Chute de L'Empéreur Maximilien: L'Intervention française au Mexique.* Paris, Revue Contemporaine, pp. 90–91.
19. Altamirano Ignacio 1986 *Obras completas* II, pp. 75–76.
20. *BJDOCS* 9, pp. 715–17. *APBJPS* I, pp. 31–34. Archivo Juárez MSJ Supl-131, f 4v.
21. *BJDOCS* 9, pp. 795–97. Jesús Carranza was the father of Venustiano Carranza, First Chief of the Constitutionalist Revolution (1913–17) and President (1917–20).
22. *BJDOCS* 11, pp. 198–200.

23. *BJDOCS* 8, pp. 70–71; *BJDOCS* 9, pp. 715–17; *BJDOCS* 11, p. 206. Kératry Comte E de 1869 *La Contre-Guérilla française au Mexique, Souvenirs de la Terre Chaude.* Paris, Librairie Internationale.
24. Guedalla Phillip 1948 *Two Marshals, Bazaine and Pétain.* London, Hodder & Stoughton.
25. *BJDOCS* 8, p. 765; *BJDOCS* 10, pp. 242–47.
26. Archivo Juárez MSJ Supl. 131, f 10; f 12.
27. Ibid f 6; f 7v.
28. *BJDOCS* 11, pp. 338–39.
29. Dabbs Jack Autrey 1963 *The French Army in Mexico, 1861–1867.* The Hague, Mouton & Co, p. 187.
30. Kératry *Empéreur Maximilien* pp. 227–8.
31. *BJDOCS* 11, pp. 709–11, 718, 726, 729–31.
32. Ibid pp. 762–63, 802–03, 808–09.
33. Ibid pp. 875–76.
34. Ibid pp. 891–94.
35. Ibid pp. 721–23, 883, 894–96, 905.
36. Ibid pp. 919–20, 943–46, 948–50.
37. *BJDOCS* 12, pp. 12–14, 53. Archivo Juárez MSJ S-191.
38. *BJDOCS* 12, pp. 79–88, 105–08. Riva Palacio Mariano and Martínez de la Torre Rafael 1867 *Memorandum sobre el proceso del Archiduque Fernando Maximiliano de Austria.* Mexico City, F. Díaz de León y S White, should be studied closely.
39. *BJDOCS* 12, pp. 45–47. See also Weber Frank G 'Bismarck's Man in Mexico: Anton von Magnus and the End of Maximilian's Empire' *HAHR* 46; i (Feb. 1966), pp. 53–65.
40. Riva Palacio *Memorandum* pp. 20–24.
41. Ibid pp. 26–30, 40–42, 48–49. *BJDOCS* 12, pp. 66–68.
42. *BJDOCS* 12, pp. 132–39. Riva Palacio *Memorandum* pp. 55–65, 67–70.
43. Ibid pp. 71–74. Archivo Juárez MSJ S-193.
44. *BJDOCS* 12, p. 156.
45. Ibid pp. 160, 162–65, 280, 288.
46. Ibid pp. 173–77.
47. Archivo Juárez MSJ 15-2279.
48. *BJDOCS* 13, pp. 929–31; *BJDOCS* 14, pp. 627–29; *BJDOCS* 15, p. 106.

Chapter 9

THE LAST PERIOD OF JUÁREZ: PARTY, CONSTITUTION AND POWER

The last years still remain unclear. Most of the literature skirts over them, as though the career of Juárez effectively terminated in 1867. There continues to be a tendency to view the five years after 1867 as an appendage or aberration. Yet the period is complex: it deserves to be examined in its own right. First and foremost, we need to see this early phase of the Restored Republic within a context of repeated conflict from the rebellions of the 1840 until the consolidation of the Porfirian regime in the second half of the 1880s. The scale of disruption throughout the Republic has generally not been sufficiently appreciated. Furthermore, the restored Liberal regime remained circumscribed by its weak tax base, which resulted from inadequate statistics and widespread resistance to payment. Throughout the last years of Juárez, deteriorating relations between national government and federal Congress prevented cooperation on tax policy. Nevertheless, Romero, a very capable Finance Minister, produced the first budget surplus of independent Mexico in 1867–68.[1] Even so, he remained deeply pessimistic about long-term trends: for the following year he estimated a deficit of nearly 5 million pesos. The worsening situation in several states, Puebla and Guerrero in particular, diverted funds away from the task of national reconstruction. Romero warned the state governors on 17 January 1868 that the resolution of national tax problems lay in the states themselves. He appealed against the long tradition of resistance to payment of adequate contributions to the central administration. Such revenues kept the states viable but the national government diminished.[2]

. . .

THE LATER JUÁREZ

During the last years of Juárez, constitutional and political issues already apparent in 1856–57 and 1861–63 rose to a climax. The civil wars of the Reform and Intervention had concealed an underlying continuity of outstanding problems. Not the least of these were the social and constitutional questions. The mobilization of lower socio-ethnic groups responded to the renewed expansion of private properties and the fiscal pressures of the central administration. The relationship of these movements to the main currents of Liberal politics remained ill-defined. It may be that 'moderate' criticism of the alleged excesses of the 1857 Constitution derived from fears of lower-class influence in the electoral process. Juárez had moved in the direction of the moderates, though primarily for constitutional rather than social reasons. Although he had scrupulously distanced himself from Comonfort in 1858, Juárez found himself in 1867 the latter's heir in the advocacy of reform of the Constitution.

From mid-1863 until early 1871, the principal political ally of Juárez was Sebastián Lerdo, who along with Siliceo (later a minister under Maximilian) had expressed scepticism towards the Constitution right from the first instance. In mid-1863, as we saw, Juárez abandoned his earlier cooperation with the radical Liberals. In a desperate attempt to stave off the French advance, he had attempted in vain to construct a national consensus. Moderate opinion, however, had already divided between a diminishing loyalty to *juarismo*, increasingly marginalized in terms of territory, and a belief that the empire might bring the desired peace and order to Mexico. From 1864 until December 1866 Maximilian had hoped to construct the consensus which had eluded Juárez. Defeat and internal disorganization doomed these efforts. The return of the Conservatives to power in December 1866 for the first time since December 1860, and the crucial position of their three generals, Miramón, Mejía and Márquez, in the final months of the imperial regime, threw moderate opinion back into the *juarista* camp. This development opened the way for the reconstitution of a Juárez administration, purged of radicalism, at the national level. When Juárez returned to power in Mexico City in July

1867, his platform was very different from what it had been in 1861–63 or 1859. Essentially, it combined the moderate Liberal position of Comonfort and Sebastián Lerdo with the centralist, consensus strategy of the empire.

The end of the Intervention enabled a resumption of earlier and ongoing conflicts at the local and provincial levels. The intensifying struggle for control in the key southern state of Guerrero was a case in point. The hostility between General Vicente Jiménez, with his local bases of support in the Tixtla zone, and Diego Álvarez, heir to the Álvarez *cacicazgo*, with his core of support along the Acapulco coastal zone and hinterland, destabilized the state. This conflict threatened to spill over into national politics. Although the historiographical focus has chiefly been on national level politics, state politics were often more significant – in that they tended to determine the outcome of national events. The central government frequently seemed a shadow. At best, it appeared to be engaging in a vain effort to coordinate its support in the provinces and then attempt to govern through these local poles of loyalty. Federal government superimposition of authority rarely proved feasible.

Furthermore, the Liberal Party could not provide an element of unity: it could not provide the executive with an instrument through which to spread its authority outwards and downwards through national territory. On the contrary, party proved, as much as the Constitution itself, to be a bugbear of the late Juárez period. The collapse of Conservatism left the Liberal ideology triumphant. Support it or not, all those who could not isolate themselves from contact with contemporary politics would have to live with it somehow. The Liberal Party, though supreme after 1867, remained divided within itself over personalities, over the nature of the Constitution, the pace of reform, the purpose of the Reform movement, the relationship between the executive and the legislative branches, and between the central power and the rights of the states. The removal of foreign troops had raised to the forefront once again the issue of the nature of the Liberal Party itself, whether it was to be an instrument of state-formation and national integration, or whether it was to be the sum total of all those local, provincial and popular elements – multi-ethnic and multi-class – which constituted its base of support.

Juárez's principal achievement in the years 1867–72 lay in his ability to remain in office at a time of continual unrest in the country. Mexico, as a national polity, was not unstable during these last years of Juárez: there was no instability within the administration itself; there was no possibility that the Republic itself would cease to cohere and break up into its component parts. The instability lay within these component territories. The whole remained viable, but the parts were in a constant state of adjustment. Juárez rode out the storm over his proposals for constitutional reform – a further testament to his political skill. He survived the opposition to his two re-elections in 1867 and 1871. Through the alliances that he constructed, he broke the armed challenge to his authority by Porfirio Díaz in the Rebellion of La Noria in 1871–72. Many within the Liberal camp blamed Juárez himself for the endemic turmoil in the country. They argued that his work had been completed with the downfall of the empire. Díaz, who had broken Márquez's last ditch attempt to hold on to Puebla and Mexico City in June 1867, felt himself to be the real victor in the struggle against the Intervention, not Juárez. He wanted the presidential succession without further delay. The radical Liberals wanted revenge for their abandonment after 1863. The supporters of González Ortega wanted to reverse Juárez's successful attempts in 1865 to cheat their candidate of the presidency. The political opposition came, then, not so much from the cowed Conservatives but from within the Liberal camp. This opposition called Juárez the betrayer of the Constitution. They portrayed his administration as a creeping dictatorship – centralist, presidentialist and dedicated solely to the principle of self-preservation. Provincial Liberal cadres, such as those in the northern highlands of Puebla, went starkly into opposition to the attempts by the national leadership to assert control over the entire breadth of national territory. This confrontation obliged the administration to destabilize rival leaders in the sub-regions and create alternative poles of allegiance. Constant executive interference became the charge from the provinces and from the 'left' of the party.

. . .

THE *CONVOCATORIA* OF AUGUST 1867 AND THE CONTROVERSY OVER CONSTITUTIONAL REFORM

Juárez returned to the national political centre still invested with the extraordinary powers granted to him by the last sitting

Congress in 1863. Anxious to forestall a recurrence of the legislative predominance of the autumn of 1857 and the 'parliamentary experiment' of 1861–63, he decided to appeal directly to the electorate as a whole, that is to what he described as 'the sovereign people', over the heads of party and intelligentsia, for a series of fundamental reforms in the Constitution. The convocation to elections on that basis, issued on 14 August 1867, originated from the extraordinary powers before the technical restoration of constitutional government. An immediate outcry followed, with accusations of betrayal of the most sacred tenets of Liberalism, and defections from the *juarista* camp multiplied. Juárez was accused not only of halting the Liberal Revolution in its tracks but also of perverting its course in the direction of 'presidentialism' or sheer personalism. The administration, which affected to appear taken aback, attempted to justify itself on the grounds that the Veracruz Reform Laws of 1859 had also been issued by executive decree. These were now regarded as part of the fundamental law, adjuncts to the Constitution, and the purist wing of Liberalism had not uttered one word of protest at their unconstitutionality. The *convocatoria* called for a plebiscite or referendum to ratify five reforms of the Constitution. Of these, the principal proposal was for a return to the type of bicameralism that had been established in accordance with the Constitution of 1824 and which had functioned in the United States since the ratification of the Constitution of 1787. Juárez and Lerdo associated unicameralism with a weak central power and congressional predominance. These they identified as the root causes of the disintegration of Comonfort's presidency in September–December 1857. Juárez, then, saw himself in 1867 in a similar situation to Comonfort ten years earlier, frustrated by a Constitution which he intended to reform. This Constitution had, in any case, been formulated in a different epoch, and it sought to respond to the problems that its Liberal framers identified with the post-Independence decades. The proposed reforms sought to respond to the post-Intervention era.[3]

The *convocatoria* outraged the political class. It did not split the Liberal Party: the party was already divided into warring factions, dating from at least the first days of the Reform. Later issues, such as Juárez's unilateral extension of the presidential term by his decree of November 1865 and his breach with González Ortega, inflamed these differences. The *convocatoria* reawakened them and presented them in a dramatic new light. When the governors of Puebla, General Juan N Méndez, and of Guanajuato, León Guzmán, refused to publish it, Juárez used his extraordinary powers to remove them from office. The new appointees thereupon used their positions to change all the *jefes políticos* within their states before the forthcoming elections. Guzmán, a lawyer and constitutional purist, argued that the majority of the population were too ignorant to understand what the issues really were.[4] The opposition to Juárez after 1867 inherited and extended the opposition that had existed since his elevation to the executive office in January 1858. More especially, it resembled the appeal by Liberal deputies in 1861 for him to step down. There had, then, always been hostility to Juárez within the Liberal camp. The conflicts after 1867 confirmed an underlying trend, a long and concerted attempt to break his power and to remove him from political life. The *convocatoria* provided this opposition with a valuable new weapon. These attempts, however, conspicuously failed. Yet they sought to deprive Juárez of the high moral ground – defence of the constitutional principles of 1856–57 – on which he had taken his stand during the wars of the Reform and the Intervention. Juárez replied to these attacks not by impassivity or imperious disdain, but by *realpolitik*. In spite of continued defence of the civil power and the superiority of the law, Juárez had, in fact, shifted his ground after August 1867 from defence of the Constitution to reform of it. He intended to persist.

Although Juárez opposed on principle all non-legal and non-civil sources of political power, he recognized the reality before him, and not only tacked skilfully between rival *caciques* and factions, but also worked through whichever was able at any given time to promote the broader policies for which he stood. It is not a question, then, of juxtaposing constitutionalism and *caciquismo* but of understanding their intimate interrelation: how they worked in concert. In this respect, Juárez, the man of principle, was ready to seize any opportunity that presented itself.

. . .

THE GROWTH OF OPPOSITION

Contrary to opposition claims, Juárez in the period from 1867 until his death in 1872 was not working to construct a personal dictatorship, nor even a reforming Liberal dictatorship, but searching for some means to make the constitutional system work – in spite of the Constitution. He readily delegated power, frequently to army officers, such as Escobedo, Ignacio Alatorre and Sóstenes Rocha, each of whom dealt effectively at different times with provincial or local rebellions. In that sense, Juárez responded to the provincial bases of opposition by using federal authority to set up rival poles of power in the provinces. The state of Puebla was a case in point. Two governors, first General Rafael J García (1867–69) and then the lawyer, Ignacio Romero Vargas (1869–76), strove to hold back the autonomous power of the sierra chieftains, Juan Méndez and Juan Francisco Lucas, who controlled the locally raised National Guard contingents. In Guerrero, he interposed General Francisco Arce, who originated from Jalisco, between the two armed factions of Álvarez and Jiménez. In Oaxaca, where the *juaristas* lost control of the state to Félix Díaz in the elections of 1867, the latter's adherence to his brother's Rebellion of Noria led to his downfall and violent death early in 1872. Rebellion in Oaxaca enabled Juárez, in concert with Alatorre, who had been his principal ally against the Puebla *serrano caciques*, to re-establish political control over his home state. There the deciding factor was the intervention on his behalf of the *caciques* of the Oaxaca sierra, with Castro, the Meijueiros and Hernández in the forefront. Castro duly returned to the state governorship in 1872.[5]

Although Juárez emerged strengthened and largely successful in the outcome of these conflicts, the events of the years 1867–72 demonstrated, nevertheless, the extent to which he had lost control of his party. The Liberal Party, in any case, drew much of its support from defence of the legislative power and the sovereignty of the states, precisely the two elements that Juárez and Lerdo had identified as the specific weaknesses of the Constitution. If he could not retain control of the party, Juárez was determined to keep control of the federal bureaucracy, the state governments – where not overwhelmingly resisted – and the *jefes políticos* within the states, especially since these agencies supervised the electoral process. Under the Constitution, the state Congresses elected the President of the Republic. Above all, he assiduously ensured that he retained control of the army – or, at least, the majority of the senior command, in order to counter plans and *pronunciamientos* by dissident officers. A central issue became the employment of federal forces in the conflicts between factions within the states. Since the opposition in the federal Congress was often to be found allying with anti-administration factions in the states and exploiting renewed conflict in the provinces as a political weapon with which to discredit the national government, Juárez found himself, often against his will, drawn into these struggles. The congressional response was the charge of centralism and abuse of executive authority.

The key figure in the administration was not so much Sebastián Lerdo, as is usually thought to be the case, but Ignacio Mejía, Minister of War from 1867 until 1874. Mejía, as we have seen, was a fellow Oaxacan, absolutely loyal to Juárez throughout the period 1847–72. Mejía broke with Lerdo in 1874 over the presidential succession question and, following Díaz's seizure of power in 1876, went into voluntary exile for several years, before finally returning to Oaxaca to pursue his extensive business activities. As Minister of War it was Mejía's job to keep the bulk of the army loyal to Juárez. This was assisted by the mutual rivalry of the principal commanders, Escobedo, Díaz and Corona. Mejía presided over the administration's projected reduction of the army from 60,000 men at the restoration of peace to 20,000 by 1870. This had serious repercussions at all levels, not least since the army share of the federal budget in 1868 still reached 45 per cent and the total number of troops stood as high as 47,000. In Romero's budget estimates for the financial year 1869–70, revenues reached more or less the normal level of 15,536,363 pesos, whereas expenditure was put at 18,324,472 pesos, of which just under 7 million pesos constituted the army estimate. The rebellions that escalated after 1868 delayed the reductions and kept the army share high, with disastrous results for government policy objectives in all other spheres. This was a continuing problem that outlived Juárez himself. The budget estimates for 1872–73, for instance, provided for a deficit of 7,218,882 pesos. Out of a total expenditure estimated at just over 23 million pesos, the army share was over 10 million for a force of just under 32,000 men.[6]

At the same time Juárez was discreetly offering the Catholic Church a *modus vivendi.* Under the electoral law of 4 August 1864, issued by the itinerant republican government, the clergy, as citizens, were permitted to vote and to hold elected office. This provision was reaffirmed in the *convocatoria* of 1867. In this way, Juárez, who was attempting to tap the popular, electoral base of Liberalism, put out feelers in the direction of the Catholic clergy, whom he hoped to incorporate into his political clientele as a counter-balance to the radical wing of the party. Nevertheless, he emphasized that the government itself held no specific view on religion and intended to maintain freedom of worship in the country. An amnesty allowed Archbishop Labastida to return from exile. Late in June 1868, Pius IX designated six new bishops to fill vacant sees in Mexico.[7]

Juárez stood for the supremacy of the law in a society in which law remained subordinate to personal, factional or corporate interests. The national government possessed neither the fiscal resources nor the infrastructure to impose the law. As a result, much depended upon symbols of authority and on the mundane ability to deal with men. Juárez excelled at tacking a way through seemingly endless and insoluble problems. As governor of Oaxaca, he had learnt that lesson the hard way, by trial and error, largely the latter, as the experience of the Isthmus had shown. The executive could not command and expect to be obeyed. Instead, the authority of the republican state had to be given effect through tact, guile, cajolery, moral blackmail and the threat of force. This threat Juárez rarely shrank from transferring into reality, when the situation required, through the medium of one or other of the loyal generals. Juárez did not see his life's work completed with the defeat of the Intervention. On the contrary, the civil wars of the Reform and Intervention had delayed the application at the national level of the principles for which he had stood when governor of Oaxaca in 1847–52 and 1856–57. The victory of 1867, then, marked the delayed starting-point of Juárez's national political career – as he himself saw things. His central aims were to ensure that constitutionalism took root and that the Liberal Party transformed itself into a responsible party of government. These aims conditioned his decision to stand for re-election in 1867 and again in 1871. Facing opposition from many quarters within his own party and plagued, as he saw it, by repeated rebellions, he developed a heightened consciousness that time was running out.

In the period 1867–71 Juárez appeared to be losing part of his vital base of support at the popular level. This was particularly serious in view of Porfirio Díaz's self-portrayal as spokesman for popular Liberalism. The *convocatoria* of 1867 should be seen within that context: it was a response to the *porfirista* challenge, an attempt to pre-empt its populist appeal. It sought to do so by appealing directly to the people above the heads of politicians. The objective was to separate the popular base of the Liberal Party from the anti-*juarista* politicians of the 'left'. At the opening of the newly elected Congress on 8 December 1867, Juárez surrendered the extraordinary powers. At the same time, he tacitly accepted defeat on the question of the plebiscite. He had been re-elected President, but had been defeated within his own party on the question of a direct appeal to the electorate. This failure exposed all the more the weakness of the executive in the constitutional system created in 1857. Nevertheless, he set about thereafter submitting each one of the five proposals of August 1867 to congressional vote as individual pieces of legislation.[8]

From the collapse of the empire until his death, the principal opponent of Juárez was his fellow Oaxacan, Porfirio Díaz. Around this impatient and aggrieved soldier, one of the heroes of the Liberal victory, all those who resented the continued predominance of the civilian Paso del Norte group congregated. Those radicals and constitutional purists, such as Ignacio Ramírez and Ignacio Altamirano, who mistrusted Juárez's intentions and saw in Díaz, at that time still Commander of the Army of the East (a force of 20,000 men), the champion of the principles of 1857, also rallied to the *porfirista* cause. Díaz's presidential ambitions brought about the breach with Juárez after the Liberal recovery of Mexico City. He believed that the work of Juárez had been completed, since national independence had been saved. He looked back to the exclusion of González Ortega in 1865 and portrayed Juárez as intending to construct a life presidency. Díaz maintained that he had paid back in military victories, such as the recapture of Puebla in 1867, all the favours that Juárez had shown both himself and his brother. Díaz subsequently justified his opposition stance by claiming that Juárez had slighted him in the aftermath of victory. Díaz founded his position in military resentment at the proposed reduction of the armed forces from 60,000 to 20,000 men and in rejection of the *convocatoria*. His intimate counsellor was another Oaxacan, Justo Benítez, a companion of his youth, and his allies, Juan José Baz, and Manuel Zamacona, editor of *El Globo*, and the two army commanders, Vicente Riva Palacio and Luis Mier y Terán. Although few of the rebellions against the Juárez administration were in fact *porfirista*, many of their leaders ultimately aligned with the Díaz camp.[9]

Rebellions and repeated unrest seriously undermined Juárez's aim to establish the supremacy of the civil law. They tarnished his reputation and exhausted him physically. His efforts to deal with them appeared to give credence to opposition allegations that he intended to perpetuate his own personal rule.

We should now examine more closely the provincial milieu and its relationship to the national level of politics. The federal system institutionalized the typical factional struggles – over family or personal rivalries and ideological conflicts – that characterized state-level political life. Frequently, these provincial struggles had national consequences, especially in cases when military-led rebellions, such as those in Puebla in 1869 and Zacatecas and San Luis Potosí in 1870, corresponded to mounting opposition to the national government in the federal Congress. Despite such ideological linkages, however, no opposition movement, not even the Rebellion of La Noria, which represented the culmination of this entire process, ever presented a coordinated threat at the national level. For that reason, Juárez was able to eliminate or neutralize one storm centre after another.

. . .

LIBERAL DIVISIONS IN PUEBLA

The situation in Puebla, located perilously close to Mexico City, remained completely unresolved, in spite of Juárez's efforts to neutralize the *serrano* National Guard commanders. Ex-Governor Méndez of Puebla had taken some 7,000 rifles with him into the sierra and maintained a hostile stance to the new *juarista* state governor, Rafael García. The latter could count on little support there beyond that of General Rafael Cravioto in Huauchinango, which acted as the watching station for developments in the sierra. Puebla itself was full of redundant army officers expecting the state Treasury to pay their salaries. García's aim was to win over Méndez's fellow commander, Lucas, by sending a confidential agent to speak to him and by asking Juárez to write a personal letter requesting him to adhere to the government. This Juárez did on 19 February 1868, urging him to counter subversion in the sierra, and again on 15 June, warning him that to take up arms would only bring about his own ruin. The administration viewed the Puebla situation with concern, since it appeared likely that the local sierra chieftains would ally themselves with General Miguel Negrete, a former supporter of González Ortega and perennial enemy of Juárez. The restored Liberal regime's efforts to reimpose the ecclesiastical disamortization had already provoked a disturbance in Cuetzalan. The restlessness in the Puebla sierra was not an isolated instance, but formed part of a broad pattern of popular discontent that ranged as far as Tlaxcala and Hidalgo. The attitude of Lucas was, therefore, crucial. Even so, Juárez received warnings that he could not be relied upon and that Negrete was behind the widespread unrest, acting in league with local armed bands. Mejía, for his part, made a point of reminding all state governors in May 1868 of Negrete's Conservative and imperialist past.[10]

Ready and able to give effect to his warnings to the sierra chieftains, Juárez appointed General Ignacio Alatorre chief of operations in the rebel districts of Puebla. The intention was to challenge them to take up arms or else concede political defeat. This type of brinkmanship was designed to avoid bloodshed. Alatorre took up position in the heart of the sierra at Zacapoaxtla, but confirmed the deep hostility there to García, who was regarded as an executive imposition in contravention of the Constitution. Alatorre also pointed out the connections already established between the sierra chieftains and the neighbouring territories of Veracruz as far as the Gulf coast. Although Alatorre had been able to occupy three of the main sierra towns without a fight, Cravioto was prevented from taking Zacatlán by an enemy force of 1,000 men. Although Negrete was trying hard to exploit the situation, in order to bring down Juárez, Alatorre succeeded in persuading Lucas not to join the rebellion.[11]

With Juárez's support, Alatorre pressed for the establishment of a local force in the sierra paid for by the state government, rather than sections of the federal army. At the beginning of 1869, Cravioto urged Juárez to secure tight control over Zacapoaxtla and Zacatlán, the key positions, in order to prevent the situation in Puebla and Veracruz from deteriorating further. In his view the overriding objective should be to disarm the sierra towns where the former revolutionary chieftains had their headquarters. Governor García had made the position worse, in Cravioto's judgement, by insisting on compliance with the law of 1863 for the adjudication of unoccupied lands, a measure which had thrown virtually the entire district of Huauchinango into outright rebellion, since many such lands actually belonged to the villages. He appealed to Juárez to write to García instructing him to suspend the measure, at least until sufficient forces were in place in those two key towns.[12]

The difficulty of García's position was revealed even in the state capital itself, since on 3 February 1869 Negrete, who had been concealed there by supporters of Méndez, suddenly made his presence public and issued a call to insurrection against the Juárez administration. Negrete denounced Juárez's supposed *coup d'état* of 1865 and called for an end to the 'presidential dictatorships', which, he alleged, had been the rule since Mexican Independence. He condemned the 'illegal *convocatoria*'. He maintained that Juárez had corrupted local authorities, bribed Congress and overthrown the ballot box. The Negrete plan stood for rigorous observation of the Constitution of 1857, the calling of fresh elections and the replacement of all existing authorities. In these respects, it foreshadowed Díaz's later Plan of La Noria.

Negrete's ostentatious appearance in the city underlined the full extent of collaboration between him and the sierra chieftains, and, in turn, connected the opposition of 1869 to that of 1865. Negrete, however, failed to win over Félix Díaz in Oaxaca, who, while tacitly concurring with much of the anti-*juarista* rhetoric, had other intentions than to align with a cause that could well expect defeat. Díaz's caution was astute, since Alatorre routed Negrete's forces at Tepejí, though the rebel leader himself escaped with 200 followers. The rebellion, therefore, continued, and in mid-November Lucas rose in his stronghold of Xochiapulco, and took Zacapoaxtla. When Juárez ordered Alatorre and Cravioto to proceed against the rebels, his two loyal generals were obliged to point out that the state government had no funds to pay for a military campaign in the sierra, and the federal government itself would have to pay. In such a way, the rebels, without ever succeeding in toppling the Juárez administration, were able to undermine its support by obliging it to divert funds from its principal objective of national reconstruction into repression. Rebellion throughout the Puebla sierra, moreover, provided the state Congress, centre of opposition to the federal executive, with the opportunity to undermine the position of Governor García, and to conduct a constant, debilitating battle against his successor, Romero Vargas. The two state governors of the period from 1867 to 1872 had no base of support in the state, in contrast to the *serrano* chieftains. In effect, they depended on federal assistance to prevent domination of the whole state by these *caciques* who had risen with the Reform movement. This situation considerably modified in practice Juárez's proclaimed ideal that the executive had no specific preference in elections to the state governorships, sought to maintain a discreet neutrality, and intended to uphold the will of the majority as a 'sacred duty', so that democratic and republican principles would not become a farce in Mexico.[13]

The Puebla problem continued throughout 1870 and merged into the more serious, nation-wide movement formed by Porfirio Díaz around the Plan of La Noria. On 21 November 1871, for instance, Lucas once again rose in rebellion in Xochiapulco. The state remained in turmoil into the spring of 1872. The widespread unpopularity of Romero Vargas prevented any recovery of support by the federal government. Accordingly, despairing of a civil solution to the problem, Juárez placed the state of Puebla under siege on 5 March 1872, and thereby removed at a stroke Vargas's civil authority. He requested the governor to place himself at the disposal of Alatorre, who became Military Commander and Governor of Puebla after the collapse of the Rebellion of La Noria.[14]

. . .

THE CIVIL WAR IN GUERRERO

In Guerrero, Juárez found himself caught in the middle of the power struggle between the Álvarez clientele and the supporters of Vicente Jiménez. The latter were *porfiristas* and, in league with the opposition in the federal Congress, blamed

Juárez for condoning the Álvarez family's continued domination of the state. Diego Álvarez, however, had inherited few of his father's political talents. Unable to retain the support of a large part of the popular base which Juan Álvarez had built up over decades, Diego Álvarez preferred to withdraw to his estate, the Hacienda La Providencia, surrounded by his armed men, and appeal to Juárez to deal with the *jimenistas.* The latter could count on the sympathy of one of Mexico's most notable literary figures, Ignacio Altamirano, who like Jiménez and Vicente Guerrero before him was a native of Tixtla, then the state capital. Altamirano portrayed the Álvarez clientele as 'feudal powers' which should be made to conform to the republican system. Álvarez, for his part, accused Altamirano of stirring up anarchy. In the elections of 1867, each armed faction had secured control of its own local territory. When Jiménez refused Juárez's request to desist, the latter called in General Francisco Arce, an outsider, to impose peace in Guerrero.

Arce's function as mediator, however, placed Álvarez in a compromising position. While Juárez disclaimed any interventionist intent, Álvarez felt himself slighted. Juárez attempted to resolve the problem by writing to Álvarez on 22 April 1868 in an attempt to persuade him voluntarily to step down from the state governorship under special federal licence and to proceed to Mexico City. He explained that this was not an executive order but a personal suggestion, though he recommended Álvarez to take it seriously. Arce at the same time ordered Álvarez to disband his private forces. Juárez argued that a comparable arrangement had been worked out in the case of Yucatán, where the governor and Congress had been locked in conflict. Álvarez, however, felt that to abandon office would seem to put him in the wrong. Accordingly, he refused to budge. Juárez called upon him to make a sacrifice, in order to defuse the situation. Although Juárez managed to persuade Jiménez to proceed to Mexico City, Álvarez maintained that if he ventured out of La Providencia, where he kept his stocks of arms, the *jimenistas* would kill him.[15]

Arce complained of Álvarez's entrenched position on the Pacific coast. There the inhabitants regarded him virtually as a divinity and did only what he commanded. Álvarez protested to Juárez that Arce had garrisoned Acapulco and Tlapa with one hundred men in each. In Acapulco, his intention was clearly to deprive the state government of control of the customs revenues, which legally pertained to the Federation.

For his part, Álvarez, in a not very veiled threat, advised Juárez that he could make mincemeat out of Arce's forces, should he choose to do so. At the same time, he complained that the cabinet had shown nothing but enmity towards him. He excluded Juárez from that charge, and referred to his complaint as one 'between friends'. Juárez, however, attached prime importance to the role of Arce, who, conversely, began 'cultivating' Álvarez, in order to counterbalance the jimenistas and their allies in the federal Congress. Arce called for an effective military presence in Tixtla, which remained under jimenista control. The latter, however, had already in the first months of 1870 subverted the National Guard both in Tixtla and in Chilapa. Arce needed federal military support to sustain his position. The Guerrero state Congress, in the mean time, concentrated on ways to bring him down. Successfully branding Arce as a violator of the Constitution, Congress forced him out of office and by June 1870 the state government in Tixtla lay in jimenista hands. This turn of events obliged Juárez in October to appeal directly to Álvarez to put himself at the head of federal forces and attempt to salvage Arce's position. Such a request indicated the debt that juarismo owed in Guerrero to the Álvarez network.

Juárez considered the legislature's action as an affront to the authority of an acting governor and thereby to the federal government, which had appointed him as mediator. In Juárez's view, federal intervention in no way compromised the national government's complete neutrality in the factional fighting within the state. Jiménez countered by writing to the editors of *El Siglo XIX* alleging calumny on the part of his opponents. The federal government, however, always short of funds, was obliged to authorize the transfer of the Acapulco customs revenues to Álvarez, in order to pay for his three battalions from the coast, and promised further federal funds. Arce regained control of Tixtla. The apparent collapse of Jiménez's forces, however, did not end the turmoil in the state, because opposition continued to simmer and, as in the case of Puebla, merged into the *porfirista* opposition to Juárez's projected second re-election in 1871. During the Rebellion of La Noria, Jiménez organized *porfirista* forces along the coasts of Guerrero and Oaxaca and inland as far as Putla, with the object of joining up with Félix Díaz.[16]

. . .

SOCIAL MOVEMENTS AND THE AGRARIAN QUESTION

The collapse of the empire meant that many Indian peasant communities lost all hope of government recognition of corporate properties. Maximilian's Imperial Decree of 26 June 1866 had not reversed Liberal privatization policies. On the other hand, it had vested landownership in the village community and recognized corporate proprietorship once more. In that sense, the decree marked a significant departure from the Lerdo Law of 1856. The decree had forbidden sales of common pasture lands, woodland and water resources. Maximilian's regime had also established a Junta for the Protection of the Impoverished Classes, which functioned between 1865 and 1867. The records of this junta recall Spanish colonial government efforts to stave off peasant land loss and the erosion of customary rights. These procedures were dismantled, once the Liberals returned to power in Mexico City.[17]

In the aftermath of the collapse of the empire in central Mexico, a series of peasant rebellions broke out in opposition to the reimposition of the Liberal order. The Juárez administration managed to persuade Congress to suspend constitutional guarantees on 18 December 1867, in order to deal with each instance in turn. The renewal of hacienda pressures in the eastern sector of the Valley of Mexico, a major cereal-producing zone, and the construction of the Mexico City to Veracruz railway in the late 1860s, which pushed up land values, placed enormous pressures on the free villages. A wave of unrest swept across this central area, its focus on Chalco. Several of the villages involved had received redress at the hands of the imperial government, whether from the emperor in person or by way of the Junta of Protection. The most important of these movements was led by Julio Chávez López in 1868. Chávez López had been an hacienda tenant farmer and a soldier in the Liberal armies. Originally hoping that the Liberal state would mediate between peasants and landowners, he came rapidly to realize that the Juárez government intended to use the federal army to put down any peasant resistance to disamortization policies in the central zone, in which it could operate in relative proximity to the national capital. For that reason, Liberal measures defended the position of the estate-owners, among whom was the Riva Palacio family, against peasant demands for redress. Chávez López had come under the influence of anarchist ideas from Mexico City, though it seems unlikely that the restored Liberal regime felt especially threatened by them at this early stage. The federal army put down the peasant rebellions in succession, and on 7 July 1868 Chávez López was executed. Further waves of rebellion swept Morelos, parts of Puebla and Tlaxcala, the Mezquital, north of Mexico City, and into Hidalgo in the following year, but federal troops had extinguished them by January 1870. Army intervention also checked further unrest across the centre-north-west during the same years.[18]

After July 1867, the new elite of Liberal politicians, army officers and entrepreneurs began to consolidate its position in the central zones of the Republic. This process reached its climax during the years of the Díaz dictatorship from 1884 to 1911. Peasant resistance, which was intense during the period of the Restored Republic (1867–76), diminished as the dictatorship strengthened its hold on the country. Uprisings, such as those of 1868–70, did not reverse Liberal policies. Yet they delayed them and frustrated those who sought to implement them. Since the government was also preoccupied at the same time with rebellions by opposition political figures, full attention could not be given to what Liberals increasingly identified as the 'peasant problem'. Accordingly, the implications of Liberal policy would not be worked out until the Díaz era. In the economic conditions of the immediate post-Intervention period, several landowners were forced to sell up because of mounting debts. Mariano Riva Palacio, governor of the state of Mexico, sold in 1870 the properties owned in Chalco from the 1830s.[19]

On 8 May 1868 the Juárez government obtained from Congress further extraordinary powers by securing the re-enactment of the punitive law of 25 January 1862. The administration intended to use it for the summary trial and execution of rebels taken in the insurrection of General Trinidad García de la Cadena. Cadena's personal political base lay in the state of Zacatecas. This state had since the late 1820s frequently found itself in opposition to central government because of its radical and federalist stance. Support there for González Ortega served to confirm this hostility to Mexico City politicians. Cadena had been politically associated with Negrete from the mid-1860s and would remain so until their joint defeat by Díaz in 1886, which led to Cadena's capture and execution when federal forces invaded Zacatecas. Both Cadena and Negrete had a reputation for supporting urban social and agrarian causes, though this was always complicated by their association with the old González Ortega cause and the regionalism of Zacatecas. The federal army's defeat of Cadena's rebellion in 1868 served merely to postpone further conflicts.[20]

Cadena protected the nascent factory worker movement from his stronghold in Zacatecas. The first major textile workers' strike, which occurred in Mexico City in July 1868, brought home to the Juárez administration the changing nature of labour organization in the urban areas. This process had begun with the gradual mechanization of the processes of production during the 1840s, and it would culminate in the early 1900s, when Mexico became virtually self-sufficient in textile manufacture. Although the supersession of artisans by factory workers proved to be a slow and irregular process, the relatively open political life of the Restored Republic enabled a first attempt to consolidate worker organization to take place. Anarchist influence led in September 1870 to the formation of the *Gran Círculo de Obreros de México*, which in the following year opened branches in Toluca and San Luis Potosí. Pro-administration Liberals, seeing the danger of radical control of the incipient labour movement, began penetrating the organization during 1872 and were able to take control. Their attempts to prevent radicals from continuing the politicization of factory workers came to nothing. Díaz's hostility aborted the movement, however, in the later 1870s, and radical leaders fled to Zacatecas.[21]

. . .

NAYARIT AND THE AGRARIAN MOVEMENT OF MANUEL LOZADA

In the case of Lozada a different criterion applied, at least during the lifetime of Juárez. The impact of Liberal measures upon the peasant population differed widely according to time and place. In Nayarit, on the Pacific seaboard of Jalisco,

Indian resistance to private encroachments antedated the Reform period. Distant from the centre of regional power in Guadalajara, this was a geographically compact area with ethnic groups ready and able to defend entrenched traditions. Nayarit shared these characteristics with other zones which continued to present obstacles to the Juárez regime, such as the southern Isthmus in Oaxaca and the Sierra Gorda of Querétaro. The impact of Liberal privatization policies accelerated popular mobilization, especially in the district of Tepic, where powerful business interests operating from the rising city of Guadalajara wanted to extend their control. Originally an hacienda *peón*, Manuel Lozada, a violent mestizo with criminal tendencies, put himself at the head of resistance in Tepic. Between 1856 and his execution in 1873, Lozada led a full-scale confrontation with the state government of Jalisco. Supported by foreign contrabandists, such as Eustace Barron, in the port of San Blas, Lozada controlled virtually the entire trade of Nayarit. For that reason, he earned from an early date the bitter enmity of Ramón Corona, later to become one of Juárez's principal generals, who worked in a rival firm. Corona first took up arms against Lozada in 1858. It was his intensifying ambition to see Lozada in his grave.[22]

Strong defence of community rights in opposition to Liberal disamortization measures led Lozada first into the Conservative camp in 1858–61 and subsequently to support the empire in 1865–66. Apart from Corona, his other personal enemy was the Liberal governor of Jalisco, Pedro Ogazón, who had been one of the main beneficiaries of the Lerdo Law in Guadalajara. Although the French General Douay awarded Lozada a cash subsidy in return for supplying 3,000 fighting men for the Imperial Army, he defected in December 1866, when the disintegration of the empire became apparent. Accordingly, Lozada rallied to Juárez, who, for his part, detested everything that Lozada represented. This expedient attachment to the Liberal cause brought Lozada paradoxically into alliance with Corona and Ogazón, his two worst enemies. Clearly, such a situation could not last.

In July 1867, following the restoration of the Republic, Juárez accepted Lozada's public recognition of his government. This involved a significant transaction. Juárez authorized the separation of the district of Tepic from the state of Jalisco and reconstituted it as the military district of

Nayarit under the direct jurisdiction of the federal government. In such a way, Juárez implicitly placed Lozada under his protection by depriving Ogazón and Corona of the opportunity to strike at him in the aftermath of the collapse of the empire. Lozada reciprocated by issuing a circular to the villages of Tepic in which he appealed to them to uphold the laws and expel bandits from their territories. The tacit understanding with Juárez, however, enabled Lozada to consolidate his position in Nayarit during the following years. He used this period to reinforce community defence of landholding. The circular of 12 April 1869 provided for village direct action in defence of land rights. As long as Juárez lived, nothing could be done, whether from Guadalajara or Mexico City, to eliminate Lozada, in spite of pressure to do so. Six months after Juárez's death in July 1872, the new Lerdo administration authorized Corona to begin the final campaign. This provoked Lozada's ill-judged invasion of central Jalisco with 10,000–12,000 men. He was defeated, betrayed to his enemies, and executed on 19 July 1873.[23]

. . .

NOTES AND REFERENCES

1. Cadenhead Ivie E (1973) 1975 *Benito Juárez y su época.* Mexico City, El Colegio de México, pp. 123, 125–26.
2. *BJDOCS* 13, pp. 99–100, 379, 382.
3. *BJDOCS* 12, pp. 319–22, 332–42, 407–14, 525–30. Scholes Walter V 1957 *Mexican Politics during the Juárez Regime, 1855–1872.* Columbia, University of Missouri Press, pp. 118–22.
4. *BJDOCS* 12, pp. 430–31. Perry Laurens Ballard 'El modelo liberal y la política práctica en la república restaurada, 1867–76' *Historia Mexicana* XXIII (1973–74), pp. 678–79.
5. *BJDOCS* 15 for details.
6. McCaleb Walter Flavius 1921 *The Public Finances of Mexico.* New York, Harper & Brothers, pp. 129–30, 134–45.
7. *BJDOCS* 12, pp. 424–25; *BJDOCS* 13, p. 604. Schmitt Karl 'Catholic Adjustments to the Secular State: The Case of Mexico, 1877–1911' *Catholic Historical Review* 48 (July 1962), pp. 182–204. Knowlton Robert J 'Clerical Responses to the Mexican Reform, 1855–1875' *Catholic Historical Review* 50 (January 1965), pp. 509–28.
8. *BJDOCS* 12, p. 345; *BJDOCS* 14, pp. 403–04. Cosío Villegas Daniel 1971 *Historia Moderna de México: La República Restaurada: Vida Política.* Mexico City, Editorial Hérmes, p. 143.

9. *BJDOCS* 13, pp. 224–26. Altamirano Ignacio 1986 *Obras Completas*, II, p. 96. López Portillo y Rojas, José (1921) 1975. *Elevación y caída de Porfirio Díaz.* Mexico City, Editorial Porrua, pp. 63–73.
10. *BJDOCS* 12, pp. 559–61; *BJDOCS* 13, pp. 151, 168–69, 394–96.
11. *BJDOCS* 13, pp. 440–43, 561.
12. Ibid pp. 797–98.
13. *BJDOCS* 13, pp. 274–77, 812–13; *BJDOCS* 14, pp. 181–84.
14. *BJDOCS* 15, pp. 530, 819–22, 831.
15. *BJDOCS* 12, pp. 197–200, 397–400; *BJDOCS* 13, pp. 147–48, 288–300.
16. *BJDOCS* 13, pp. 651, 661–63, 720–21, 813–18, 895–904, 978–80; *BJDOCS* 14, pp. 75–76, 450, 456–57, 685–90; *BJDOCS* 15, pp. 378–79, 691–97, 708.
17. *BJDOCS* 11, pp. 72–76. Archivo General de la Nación (Mexico City) Junta Protectora de las Clases Menesterosas, 5 vols, for particular instances. See also Hart John M 1978 *Anarchism and the Mexican Working Class, 1860–1931.* Austin, TX, and London, University of Texas Press, pp. 32–37. Hart John M 1987 *Revolutionary Mexico: The Coming and Process of the Mexican Revolution.* Berkeley, CA, Los Angeles and London, University of California Press, pp. 38–44.
18. Reina Leticia 1980 *Las rebeliones campesinas en México (1819–1906).* Mexico City, Siglo XXI, pp. 64–82. Tutino John 1989 'Agrarian Social Change and Peasant Rebellion in Nineteenth Century Mexico: The Example of Chalco', in Katz Friedrich (ed.) *Riot, Rebellion and Revolution: Rural Social Conflict in Mexico.* Princeton University Press, NJ, pp. 95–140, see pp. 129–34.
19. Tutino 'Agrarian Social Charge' pp. 135–37.
20. Hart *Revolutionary Mexico* pp. 56–58. See also Hart John M 'Miguel Negrete: La epopeya de un revolucionario' *Historia Mexicana* XXIV, i (julio–sept. 1974), pp. 70–93.
21. Hart *Anarchism* pp. 37–40.
22. Olveda Jaime (et al) 1981 *Historia de Jalisco.* 4 vols, Guadalajara, Gobierno de Jalisco, III, pp. 348–57.
23. Aldana Rendón Mario Alfonso 1983 *Rebelión agraria de Manuel Lozada: 1873.* Mexico City, Sep/80 Fondo de Cultura Económica, pp. 94–178. Meyer Jean 'El ocaso de Manuel Lozada' *Historia Mexicana* XVIII, iii (1969), pp. 535–68.

Chapter 10

JUÁREZ, THE DÍAZ BROTHERS AND THE REBELLION OF LA NORIA

Few issues concentrated Latin American minds more than presidential re-elections. Traditionally, they had always seemed to be the starting-point for self-perpetuation in office, the basis for personal dictatorship. In Mexico, neither the 1824 nor the 1857 Constitution had specifically prohibited re-election. Porfirio Díaz, however, subsequently modified constitutional practice after 1884, his first re-election – after the intervening term of Manuel González (1880–84), in order to allow for six further re-elections before he was finally overthrown in the Revolution of 1910–11. Significantly, the initial revolutionary slogan was 'Effective Suffrage: No Re-election'. The Constitution of 1917 stipulated in article 83 that there should be no presidential re-election. It did not state, however, that there could never be any re-election. Accordingly, ex-President Álvaro Obregón (1920–24) interpreted this to signify that re-election was allowed but after the expiration of a successor's term of office. The government of President Plutarco Elías Calles (1924–28) early in 1927 secured a constitutional reform enabling one sole re-election at some undefined date. Obregón stood for re-election on 1 July 1928, and was elected in spite of opposition within the revolutionary camp, but assassinated on 17 July. The assassination of the President-elect plunged Mexico into a political crisis that resolved itself with the formation of the official revolutionary party, the Partido Nacional Revolucionario in 1929. The outcome was that Mexico adopted a system whereby any form of presidential re-election was avoided. The official party, however, permanently continued in office.[1]

The potency of the re-election issue in Mexican politics

should not be underestimated. To contemporaries, Juárez's two re-elections in 1867 and 1871 must have seemed particularly striking phenomena. Furthermore, Juárez died in office. Before him, the problem had not exactly been re-election but completion of the elected – or even un-elected – term. Only two presidents, Guadalupe Victoria in 1829 and José Joaquín Herrera in 1851, completed their elected term of office during the period from 1825 to 1867. Leaving aside Díaz's transfer to González in 1880 and seven subsequent re-elections, there had been only one peaceful transfer of office in the entire nineteenth century, that of Herrera to Mariano Arista in 1851. The explanation lay in contested legitimacy, the absence of any consensus or agreed method of transferring power during the decades following the collapse of the Spanish Bourbon monarchy in 1821. Juárez sought to address exactly that problem. He saw it as the central legal and constitutional issue of his time. He decided upon re-election in 1867 and 1871, because he felt that his work had scarcely even begun, after its interruption by the civil wars of the Reform and Intervention. His objective was to establish a lasting basis for a new form of political legitimacy founded upon respect for constitutional legality. Imperfect as the 1857 Constitution was, Juárez took his stand on its principles. For that reason, he sought to reform it, in order to make its political provisions more practicable. Constitutionalism had been tried before in Mexico – in 1812, 1824 (and again in 1846), 1836 and 1843 – and each experiment had ultimately failed. Mexico shared that failure with most of Hispanic America and also with Spain itself.

The charge of 're-electionism' went back to Juárez's unilateral extension of the presidential term in 1865, and, accordingly, it originated from the González Ortega camp. After 1867, with the five projected constitutional reforms and the first re-election, these charges multiplied. They became stock allegations in the opposition camp. They entered the political vocabulary of the *porfiristas.* For a time, the *lerdista* Liberals in 1870–71 reiterated them, until forced into silence by the reality of Díaz's Rebellion of La Noria.

This rebellion, while unwelcome for financial as well as political reasons, did have one hidden advantage. It presented Juárez with the opportunity to strike at entrenched opposition groups within the states. During the repression of the rebellion, Juárez with the aid of loyal federal commanders was able to neutralize most of the dissident military groups which had felt themselves strong enough to challenge – and seek to undermine – his administration from the security of their regional bases. Always ready and able to exploit the divisions of his opponents, Juárez, although physically worn out, passed through the spring of 1872 in the knowledge that the most serious threats to his position had been destroyed. One of the gravest of these dangers emerged in his own home state of Oaxaca in the aftermath of the collapse of the empire.

. . .

FÉLIX DÍAZ IN CONTROL OF OAXACA (1867–71)

Juárez lost control of his home state from November 1867 until the fall of Félix Díaz in November 1871. A combination of the military fame of Porfirio Díaz in recovering the city of Oaxaca from the Imperialists in December 1866 and the electoral skills of his younger brother cost the *juaristas* control of Oaxaca in the gubernatorial elections of 10 November 1867. Although the brothers were not at that time close, and considerable rivalry divided them, the *porfirista* vote fell behind Félix Díaz, commonly known as 'El Chato', in opposition to Miguel Castro, the *juarista* stalwart. Intense competition for control of the electoral procedure in the municipalities and villages characterized the elections. This proved to be strikingly so in the case of the committees of five which determined who was eligible to vote and counted the final tally in each of the electoral districts. Félix Díaz successfully courted the *jefes políticos,* the key officials involved in securing the delivery of votes in the districts. Out of a total of 124,892 votes cast, 95,361 went to Díaz and 22,770 to Castro, although the latter did well in his stronghold in the sierra.[2] The political situation in Oaxaca was very different from that in Puebla, where the strength of opposition to Juárez lay precisely among the Liberal militia of the sierra. In Oaxaca, Díaz could not count on the personal loyalty of the sierra militia, which remained under the control of Francisco Meijueiro and Fidencio Hernández, primarily loyal to Castro and Juárez. The mining interests opposed, furthermore, the increasing involvement of Díaz in the industry in the Ixtlán district. At the same time, Ignacio Mejía, the Minister of War, strongly suspected the motives of the Díaz brothers.[3]

Díaz consolidated his hold on Oaxaca successfully during the following years. In 1868 he replaced the editor of the official Liberal newspaper, *La Victoria*, who was a partisan of Castro, with one of his own supporters. The newspaper became the medium for a government-sponsored campaign of vituperation against the clergy. Díaz's anticlericalism led to the prohibition of the ringing of church bells throughout the state. Such measures, combined with high-handedness and a readiness to offend, lost El Chato popular support, and, as we shall see, ultimately cost him his life.[4]

Apart from Castro, Juárez could count on a number of informants in Oaxaca, who reported to him the current activities of the Díaz brothers. One of these was his relative, the sometimes unreliable Joaquín Mauleón, a deputy in the state Congress, who in March of that year informed him that the *juarista* party still remained intact. Mauleón reported in October 1869 that the Díaz brothers had effected a dramatic reconciliation at the baptism of Félix's son. One of the godparents was the businessman, Roberto Maqueo, recently entrusted with the sale of Juárez's house in the city, who had one foot in the *juarista* camp and the other in the Díaz camp. Félix Romero was another informant, a central figure in *juarista* politics in the state. Juárez's strategy had been for Romero to secure election as President of the State Supreme Court, which would give him the constitutional right of succession to the governorship in the event of Díaz's demise. Not only was this achieved, but also Romero from 7 January 1870 acted as the governor's secretary, that is Juárez's spy at the heart of the Díaz administration.[5]

Díaz constructed his own political machine in the state through selective administrative appointments, particularly the *jefes políticos.* He was, thereby, able to secure a majority in the congressional elections of 6 November 1869 and ensure the election of supporters as federal deputies and state magistrates. This demonstrated graphically that the federal government exercised no effective authority within the state of Oaxaca. The state government, rather than the federation, controlled the electoral machinery in Oaxaca. Díaz based his predominance in the state on the reconstruction of the National Guard, begun after his election in 1867. By 1871, El Chato had at his disposal a well-equipped force of some 3,000 men, paid for from the proceeds of the capitation tax. The

National Guard had represented in the Liberal camp the bolster of the federal system. Juárez had seen it as such from the first moments of his governorship in 1847–52. What had not been anticipated was the use of the National Guard by dissident Liberal chieftains to bolster themselves against a Liberal central government. Féliz Díaz's stance in Oaxaca after 1867 came as an unpleasant shock to Juárez and Mejía. In many respects, Díaz's position in the home state resembled that of Vidaurri in the north-east in 1855–64. It constituted both an embarrassment and a threat.

Díaz was re-elected in the state elections of 25 June 1871 and secured a legislature which contained a majority of supporters either for himself or his brother. He remained firmly in control during the presidential elections of July 1871, when the state rejected Juárez, who was seeking a second re-election, in favour of Porfirio Díaz. All sixteen electoral districts in Oaxaca voted for Díaz.[6]

Díaz used the National Guard to deal with Juchitán. The Isthmus proved to be the ultimate cause of his undoing, an irony since it had also destabilized Juárez's earlier governorship. *Juchitecto* resistance to political control and taxation imposed from the Valley of Oaxaca reached a climax in 1870, when Albino Jiménez attacked a state militia corps and then extended resistance to the neighbouring districts of Ixtaltepec and Petapa. This threatened a rebellion in the southern Isthmus on the scale of 1847–52. Díaz, accordingly, decided to make an example of the *juchitecos* by sending the Guerrero National Guard Battalion to deal with them, but it failed to do so. After Congress sessions had ended on 15 December, Díaz went in person to the Isthmus with further troops. He encountered strong resistance on 27–29 December, and, after an incident which led to the burning of many thatched houses, Díaz ordered a bayonet attack on Juchitán, which resulted in many casualties. The *juchitecos* were ruthlessly pursued into neighbouring villages and nearby woods, and many were done to death. Díaz had the parish priest shot in the main square on the grounds that he had instigated rebellion. To add insult to injury, Díaz's forces broke into the church where the image of St Vincent Ferrer, patron of the town, was venerated, and removed it from the town amid despair and outrage. Díaz thereupon ordered the image to be taken to the city of Oaxaca but, in order to make its transportation easier, he instructed that its feet should first be cut off. In Oaxaca, the image was dragged through the streets, its head cut off, and then burned by order of El Chato. For such a crime, the *juchitecos* seethed with vengeance. When the atrocities in Juchitán became known in Oaxaca, the city turned against Díaz, though fear prevented any action. State forces remained in occupation of Juchitán for more than a year.[7] For these reasons, the position of Féliz Díaz was less strong than it appeared to be on the surface during the months in which Juárez was preparing for his second re-election.

. . .

THE REBELLION OF LA NORIA AND THE DESTRUCTION OF PORFIRIO DÍAZ (1871–72)

At that time, Porfirio Díaz began preparations to challenge Juárez for a second time in the presidential elections of July 1871. The Hacienda of La Noria, on the outskirts of the city of Oaxaca, which had been given to him in recognition of his services during the War of the Intervention, became the centre of intense political intrigue. Furthermore, Sebastián Lerdo, who aspired to be Juárez's successor, went into opposition, once it became clear that the President intended to seek re-election. Accordingly, the *lerdistas* in Congress formed a tactical alliance with the *porfiristas* against the Juárez administration. The election results, however, showed that Juárez with 5,837 electoral votes had again won, though this time without an overall majority, since Díaz secured 3,555 votes and Lerdo 2,874. Juárez's current term of office was due to end on 30 November.

When the federal Congress, acting on 12 October 1871 in its constitutional capacity as an electoral college, declared Juárez to be constitutionally elected President, Díaz abandoned any further hope of winning by legal means. Instead, he launched a military rebellion known as the Rebellion of La Noria. Since El Chato had won the gubernatorial elections, the state of Oaxaca became the base for the rebellion to overthrow Juárez. Accordingly, the state government published the Plan of La Noria on 8 November. In the first place, the state government withdrew its recognition of the federal government and resumed its sovereignty, taking as its precedent Governor Díaz Ordaz's action at the end of 1857 in opposition to the *coup d'état* of Tacubaya. This placed Oaxaca in outright rebellion against the Juárez administration.

The Plan argued that Juárez's 'indefinite, imposed, and outrageous re-election' undermined republican institutions. The federal Congress and Supreme Court of Justice had been reduced to impotence, because they were packed with *juarista* supporters. Juárez had used his executive authority to intervene with federal forces in the several states, and thereby deprived them of their sovereign rights. The Plan of La Noria attributed to the army the task of restoring constitutional legality. The army was described as 'the glorious personification of the principles conquered between the Revolution of Ayutla and the surrender of Mexico City in 1867 which the Government should observe and respect'. Instead, the Juárez administration had used the army as its 'instrument of loathsome violations of the freedom of popular suffrage', and therefore debased it. The Juárez administration had become a closed group, remote from the earlier aspirations of the Revolution of Ayutla. Recent rebellions in Tamaulipas, San Luis Potosí and Zacatecas testified to the depth of discontent within the Liberal Party. Many of the charges contained in the Plan were wild and ill-considered. Although Díaz had been contemplating an armed uprising for most of that year, no clear political philosophy emerged in the Plan. That, in itself, revealed the personal nature of the uprising. Many *porfiristas* in Congress and outside it found themselves unable to support this ill-considered rebellion. Díaz claimed that he stood for the Constitution of 1857 and electoral freedom. He proposed, however, to depart from the Constitution, upon the triumph of the rebellion, by establishing a convention consisting of three representatives of each state, who would 'provide a programme of constitutional regeneration and nominate a provisional President of the Republic.' After the experience of congressional election of Juárez, Díaz proposed direct election to the presidency. He promised to guarantee municipal autonomy and to abolish oppressive taxation.[8]

Díaz's rebellion fell into a context. It should be seen in relation to the northern rebellions against the Juárez administration, which had begun in February 1871 in Nuevo León, Zacatecas and Durango. Although politically connected, in the sense that they claimed that Juárez had betrayed the high hopes of the victors of 1867, they were not militarily coordinated and could be dealt with one by one. Juárez could rely on the loyalty of the remaining northern governors and his principal military commanders, Escobedo and Rocha. Díaz hoped to attach his movement in Oaxaca to those in the north, and thereby transform the rebellion into a national movement. He used General Manuel González, a former Conservative, subsequently personally loyal to him, as intermediary with the northern generals and the chieftains of the Puebla sierra, Méndez and Bonilla, who, as we have seen, equally stood out in opposition to Juárez. González, as governor of the National Palace, was Díaz's spy in the Juárez camp.

The Hacienda de la Noria, in the mean time, became an arsenal, as did the Convent of Santo Domingo in the city of Oaxaca. Díaz's allies, however, were restless to strike at Juárez and anxious to precipitate him into action. Rocha put down an abortive uprising by the Tampico garrison in May–June 1871, an indication of the effectiveness of Juárez's military support. Similarly, another abortive uprising, this time by the Mexico City Citadel, found no support and collapsed. These failures did not augur well for the success of a Díaz rebellion in the south. However, the rebellion of General Gerónimo Treviño, governor of Nuevo León, on 29 September 1871, promised to keep the administration occupied. Treviño condemned 'acts of immorality and corruption' by the Juárez government, which had betrayed the hopes of 1867. The rising was to re-establish 'constitutional legality' and to remove the 'despotic and capricious' Juárez administration from power. Treviño proclaimed himself General-in-Chief of the Army of the North. The state of Nuevo León severed its connection with the federation and resumed its sovereignty. Juárez, in the mean time, could rely on Corona in Guadalajara to neutralize the rebellion of Cadena in Zacatecas. Corona warned that General Donato Guerra, popular among the Durango opposition and with contacts in Sinaloa, particularly among the merchants of Mazatlán, had already gone over to the Cadena rebellion.[9]

In many respects, the *porfirista* movement of 1871 recruited from the former González Ortega clientele. Similar charges of violating the Constitution and subverting freedom of suffrage were levelled against Juárez in 1871, just as they had been since 1865. Díaz had been waiting for the opening of Congress in September and the decision of the deputies concerning the final outcome of the election. The Rebellion of La Noria was the consequence of the congressional majority decision to sustain Juárez's second re-election. In that sense, the rebellion played into Juárez's hands, because it was directed not only against the President personally but also against a majority decision of the Congress. Juárez was successfully able to portray Díaz as a military adventurer in the tradition of Santa Anna. The Plan of La Noria, thereby, became the negation of the principles of Ayutla and the Reform. Once they had taken the fateful decision to rebel, the Díaz brothers, without initially realizing it, soon found themselves ensnared in a carefully prepared trap. The location lay in the home state of Oaxaca. In the first place, Ixtlán and the sierra remained loyal to Castro in the elections of July 1871 and opposed to the Díaz brothers' schemes. The other edge of the pincer was Juchitán, which was still biding its time for a strike against El Chato, and declared its loyalty to Juárez. Then there was Romero, already installed as Governor Díaz's prospective successor. Over the Puebla border, General Alatorre, in command of federal forces, awaited Juárez's instructions.[10]

El Chato's fear of the Ixtlán *caciques* and their sierra militia led him to commit troops to a preventive assault on their positions, which Porfirio Díaz sought hurriedly to neutralize, in order to prevent a catastrophe before the rebellion had actually begun. The latter, who had been *jefe político* of Ixtlán in 1855, came to an arrangement with Fidencio Hernández, whereby the militia remained inactive at least until the outcome of the rebellion became clear. Once the rebellion had been launched, however, Romero left Oaxaca secretly for Ixtlán and proclaimed himself acting governor of Oaxaca, under the protection of Castro and Hernández, on 9 November. There he awaited the arrival of Alatorre. On the day before the publication of the Plan of La Noria in Oaxaca, Juárez had ordered Alatorre to advance on Oaxaca. Díaz erroneously believed that federal forces would defect. Since they did not, Díaz, who had lost time by delaying, left Oaxaca, in order to rally support across central Mexico, arriving finally in the stronghold of Méndez and Bonilla in the Puebla sierra. There also, in Xochiapulco, Juan Francisco Lucás pronounced in favour of the rebellion on 26 November.[11]

In his address to Congress on 1 December 1871, President Juárez condemned the Rebellion of La Noria as yet another sterile rebellion such as those which had plagued the country since Independence. Accordingly, Díaz sought to impose political change by armed force, since he had failed in an election. Juárez reminded Congress that at no time since he had taken office in 1858 had legal government ceased to exist in Mexico. He saw this as the great achievement of his age. Díaz's rebellion, he argued, put that achievement in jeopardy: he falsely appealed to the Constitution, but in reality sacrificed the laws to his own ambition. At the same time, Juárez requested Congress to grant him extraordinary powers, in order to deal effectively with the rebellion. Until the outbreak of Díaz's rebellion, Juárez had been faced with a largely hostile Congress in which the *lerdistas* and the *porfiristas* had combined forces. This tactical alliance dated from the time that a second re-election had been mooted at the end of 1870. Díaz's recourse to armed force, however, split that alliance asunder, and threw the *lerdistas* back into the arms of Juárez. The opposition newspaper *El Siglo XIX* described the Plan of La Noria as infinitely worse than Juárez's *convocatoria* of 1867. As a result, Congress approved the suspension of constitutional guarantees by eighty votes to forty-five. *Porfiristas* such as Zamacona found themselves in a difficult position. Zamacona opposed the grant of extraordinary powers, but declared that he could no more support a Díaz dictatorship than that of Juárez.[12]

Alatorre's swift advance led to the defeat of Díaz's commander, Mier y Terán, in a bloody night attack at San Mateo Xindihuí, near Nochixtlán in the Mixteca Alta, on 22 December. This enabled Alatorre to move against the state capital, in the vicinity of which he found 2,000 sierra militiamen under Hernández and Meijueiro waiting to join forces with him. Felix Díaz fled southwards in the first days of January 1872, but part of his escort deserted on the road to Ocotlán. Virtually defenceless, Díaz missed the ship that was supposed to take him into safety from the tiny port of Puerto Ángel. Moving inland to Pochutla, he hid in the nearby woods, but his presence was reported to the band of *juchitecos* under Albino Jiménez and Benigno Cartas which had come looking for him. Díaz was seized on 22 January 1872 by the *juchitecos*, who cut off the soles of his feet and made him walk amid jeering and insults to his place of execution. At

Chacalapa, El Chato Díaz was bayoneted to death and then horribly mutilated.[13]

After the disaster at Xindihuí, Porfirio Díaz fled in disguise to Veracruz, where his close friend, the merchant Teodoro Dehesa, secured his passage to New York on 1 February. Díaz crossed the USA by rail, and left San Francisco for Manzanillo, and thence Tepic, where he hoped to recruit the support of Lozada. The latter, however, refused to be drawn and declared his indifference to both bands in the Liberal Party. He argued that the Juárez government was illegitimate not for the reasons suggested by Díaz, but because it owed its origins to the armed insurrection begun under the Plan of Ayutla in 1854. Lozada saw nothing but a struggle between personalities in the conflict, which he believed could lead only to US intervention, if it continued, and the final incorporation of Mexico into the USA. No benefit would come to the people from the struggles within the Liberal Party.[14]

Juárez began the reorganization of government in Oaxaca. The collapse of the rebellion in the state had destroyed the power of the Díaz brothers and restored Oaxaca to *juarista* control. Juárez expressed the wish that Castro should resume the governorship and appealed to the *juchitecos* to work with him. In the mean time, Alatorre had removed Romero from the acting governorship on 8 January 1872 and taken over full military and political control himself, apparently at Juárez's instruction. Both Castro and the other leaders of the *borlado* (moderate Liberal) group, which had been removed from power by Díaz in 1863, were determined to block Romero, whom they accused of complicity with the conspirators. Alatorre nominated Castro provisional governor, again presumably under Juárez's instructions, since federal appointment followed on 16 January. Juárez urged Castro to call fresh congressional elections in the state, in order to remove Díaz's supporters from domination of the legislature. The new Congress met in June 1872, and Juárez congratulated Castro for their satisfactory outcome. At the same time, Castro was to ensure that no conflicts between Tehuantepec and Juchitán disturbed the Isthmus. Juárez attributed the militancy of the *juchitecos* to their provocation by Félix Díaz, and did not believe that their grievances were against his own government in Mexico City. Even so, their pressure for separation from the state of Oaxaca, an enterprise in which they could count on the support of Tehuantepec, and the creation of a Territory of the Isthmus, greatly preoccupied him, as it had in the early 1850s. Juárez continued to attach priority to the prospective inter-oceanic route across the Isthmus, which an alteration in the political order threatened to jeopardize. The *juchitecos*, by contrast, urged the federal government to finance a new image of St Vincent from Díaz's estate to replace the one that he had destroyed.[15]

The conflict in the north continued to drag on. Treviño threatened San Luis Potosí and the Bajío with 8,000 men during January 1872, but on 29 February, Rocha took Aguascalientes, and three days later routed the Zacatecas rebels. Díaz continued his peregrination in search for support, and on 3 April, at Ameca in Jalisco, modified the Plan of La Noria, in a vain attempt to attract *lerdista* support. The new version appeared to allow Lerdo, then President of the Supreme Court, the immediate right of succession, once Juárez was removed from office. It did not win further support and the generals who were loyal to Juárez did not defect. Finally, on 9 July, Rocha entered Monterrey and terminated the rebellion of Treviño. To all intents and purposes, the rebellion which the Díaz brothers had begun on 8 November was over. It had been badly conceived in both political and military terms right from the start. Díaz had been skilfully outmanoeuvred at every level by Juárez. Although the second re-election had been bitterly opposed by the *lerdistas*, Díaz's rebellion drove them back into the Juárez camp, terminated their temporarily successful alliance with the *porfiristas* in Congress, and provided Juárez with a propaganda weapon with which to brand him as a latter-day Santa Anna. Many who were not *juaristas* were not prepared to back a rebellion that seemed to jeopardize the survival of the Constitution of 1857, however tenuous that might be. Once again, as in so many previous crises, Juárez could count on the loyalty of crucially placed state governors in Jalisco, San Luis Potosí, Guanajuato, Coahuila, Chihuahua and Sonora, and of an array of effective military commanders, such as Alatorre, Rocha and Escobedo. Within Oaxaca, Castro and the sierra militia remained loyal, and the spontaneous intervention of the *juchitecos* brought about the ruin of Félix Díaz.[16]

. . .

CONSTITUTIONAL REFORM REVIVED

With the disintegration of the Rebellion of La Noria and the humiliation of Díaz, Juárez again proposed reform of the Constitution. The revival of this policy in April 1872, particularly the establishment of a Senate, reveals the essential motive for Juárez's determination to secure a second re-election in the previous year. He had come to believe that only by substantial reform of the Constitution could the system constructed in 1857 take root. While defence of the Constitution had been his platform in 1858, reform of it became his programme after 1867. Congressional opposition, party hostility, repeated rebellions often in the name of defence of constitutional purity, and finally the long-lasting Rebellion of La Noria had delayed the realization of Juárez's political aims. These intense frustrations made Juárez all the more determined to press upon Congress the need for reform, as he saw it. Congress, which saw itself diminished by the adoption of bicameralism, had at that time no interest whatever in cooperating with Juárez in the creation of a Senate. During the opening session of 1 April 1872, Juárez attempted in vain to persuade Congress that constitutional reform would help to avoid clashes between the federal power and the state governments, and mediate in disputes between the powers at the state level, since no authority actually existed for such a purpose. The function of the Senate, he explained, would be to 'moderate and perfect the actions of the legislature' and act at the same time as the grand tribunal for the trial of offences by state officials.[17]

In reply, the President of Congress avoided mention of the issue of constitutional reform. Although he emphasized the importance of making the institutions created in 1857 viable, he stressed the material achievements of recent months, such as the establishment of a telegraph network linking Mexico to the USA and the rest of the world and the construction of the highway from Mexico City to Veracruz. Leaving the matter of a Senate to one side, he pressed upon the administration the need for balanced budgets, the suppression of banditry, and European immigration. Accordingly, when closing the two-month session on 31 May, Juárez regretted that Congress had not discussed constitutional reform, and expressed the hope that it might do so in the forthcoming session. He also took the opportunity to remind deputies of the importance of opening the inter-oceanic route across the Isthmus of Tehuantepec.[18]

The defeat of Díaz had not brought peace. Rebel bands still operated in Sinaloa and along the northern frontier. The Puebla sierra remained largely out of government control, and new disturbances had broken out in Yucatán. Bandit groups and marauders had taken advantage of the general disruption that resulted from the rebellion in order to promote their own specific interests. The problem of public security became a matter of priority during this fourth Juárez presidency. Accordingly, Juárez requested Congress on 1 April for an extension of the extraordinary faculties granted to him on 1 December 1871 during the Rebellion of La Noria. These involved the suspension of constitutional guarantees and the power to impose a state of siege where required. Juárez informed Congress that he had declared a state of siege in only a few states, and in several instances at the request of the citizens themselves. In Aguascalientes, he had terminated it promptly. He argued that the object was not to levy extraordinary taxes or impose forced loans, but to bring about a return to peace as soon as possible. Nevertheless, the administration proposed to raise new revenues through tariff changes. Although clearly exposing himself to the charge of substituting executive rule for constitutional reform, Juárez managed to persuade Congress to agree to his request, and in a vote of ninety-five in favour and thirty-seven against, he secured the extension of the extraordinary powers on 17 May. He stressed that they would be used to combat the banditry and robberies that were rife in the country.[19]

. . .

THE DEATH OF JUÁREZ – JULY 1872

The presidential term begun in 1871 was due to end on 30 November 1875. Juárez would then have held the presidency for seventeen years, if that term had been completed. His original intention, then, must have been to give himself eight years (after the first re-election in 1867) within which to implement reform of the Constitution and supervise the solidification of national institutions. He would in 1875 have been 69 years of age, a reasonable time for retirement. The course of events moved differently. Margarita, his wife, had been frequently unwell from 1868, probably from the strain of exile on limited resources and above all from the loss of two young sons while in New York. A more serious illness developed during 1870. Juárez himself fell gravely ill in October 1870, though he recovered completely. In December, however, Margarita's illness became terminal and on 2 January 1871, she died at the age of 44. The citizens of Guelatao sent Juárez a letter of condolence. José Fuentes, the bishop of Durango, who had been a fellow student at the Oaxaca Seminary in the mid-1820s and had remained a friend ever since, also wrote to him. The strain of fifteen years' intense political struggle eventually told on Juárez, and his health broke down during the spring and early summer of 1872. He had thrown himself into the re-election campaign of 1871, following the death of Margarita, and then worn down the rebels of La Noria, but his body could no longer sustain the pace of politics. On 20 March 1872 he suffered a heart attack, followed by another on 8 July, and a further one during the night of 17 July. He died of angina at 11.30 p.m. on 18 July. The news was communicated to his constitutional successor, Sebastián Lerdo, President of the Supreme Court, by Mejía, and a formal notification of Lerdo's accession to the presidency came from Lafragua, the Minister of Foreign Relations. Lerdo inherited the unresolved problems of the late Juárez era. The death of Juárez removed the pretext for the Díaz rebellion. On 17 November 1872 Díaz arrived in Mexico City and was granted an amnesty by President Lerdo.[20]

Juárez was the father of twelve children, two of them before his marriage to Margarita and ten by her. Five of them died in early childhood, but five survived. Manuela married Santacilia, and Benito Juárez Maza became governor of Oaxaca in 1911–12 during the early stage of the Revolution.

. . .

NOTES AND REFERENCES

1. Garrido Luis Javier 1982 *El partido de la revolución institucionalizada: la formación del nuevo estado en México (1928–1945)*. Mexico City, Siglo XXI, pp. 36–37, 55–59.

2. *BJDOCS* 13, p. 203; *BJDOCS* 14, pp. 64, 69–70. Falcone Frank S 1974 'Federal–State Relations during Mexico's Restored Republic: Oaxaca, A Case Study 1867–1872' PhD dissertation University of Massachusetts, pp. 141–42.
3. Falcone 'Case Study' pp. 156–57.
4. Ibid p. 150.
5. *BJDOCS* 13, p. 203; *BJDOCS* 14, pp. 64, 69–70.
6. Falcone 'Case Study' pp. 146–47, 153–60.
7. Berry Charles R 1981 *The Reform in Oaxaca, 1856–76.* Lincoln, NB, and London, University of Nebraska Press, pp. 126–27.
8. *BJDOCS* 15, pp. 501–07, for the Plan of La Noria. See Cosío Villegas Daniel 1953 *Porfirio Díaz en la Revuelta de La Noria.* Mexico City, Editorial Hérmes.
9. *BJDOCS* 15, pp. 383–87, 411–13, 461.
10. Ibid pp. 224–28, 413–16.
11. Ibid p. 496.
12. Ibid pp. 324–35, 567–74.
13. Ibid pp. 615, 631, 643, 646, 651.
14. Ibid pp. 907–15.
15. Ibid pp. 632–35, 646–47, 654–55, 690, 716–26, 952–53. Governor Castro appointed Benigno Cartas *jefe político* of Tehuantepec.
16. Ibid pp. 730–32.
17. Ibid pp. 923–26.
18. Ibid pp. 929–30.
19. Ibid pp. 923–26, 929–30. Scholes Walter V 1957 *Mexican Politics during the Juárez Regime, 1855–1872.* Columbia, University of Missouri Press, p. 165.
20. *BJDOCS* 14, pp. 771–848; *BJDOCS* 15, pp. 1,010–17.

CONCLUSION

Tenacity and obduracy remained the two most striking characteristics of Juárez throughout his career. Yet, beneath the intransigence, lay another Juárez, the pragmatist, the tactician, the ruthless exploiter of political opportunities and of opponents' weaknesses. On the other hand, contemporary Mexico has made of him the impassive 'man of bronze', the symbol of dark-skinned Mexican nationality. The myth of Juárez dates back to his own lifetime, since Juárez himself was a politician acutely conscious of image. For popular consumption he transformed himself into the Republic incarnate, unyielding and incorruptible. Four times arrested, once banished from the country, and twice nearly executed, Juárez the person became subsumed into a god-like imagery. He was the embodiment of the Constitution and the Law. Expelled like Quetzalcóatl, he would inevitably return vindicated to recover his inheritance and punish the evildoers.

Through the study of Juárez and his time we can gain an insight into the complex world of Latin American political and social life in the aftermath of the collapse of Iberian colonial rule. We can appreciate the search for a new legitimacy and a fresh symbolism to supersede those of the Bourbon monarchy. We can deepen our understanding of the process of constructing the nineteenth-century state, particularly where the ideology of Liberalism was applied to it. Mexico, in spite of its specific historical circumstances, shared a common contemporaneous experience with other societies throughout the Atlantic world from Buenos Aires to Berlin. Constitutional politicians in Mexico, as elsewhere, were attempting to regulate political life through a new legitimacy founded upon a written Constitution. At the same time, as an emergent American state, Mexico had passed through a long period of revolutionary struggle and civil war after 1810. The implications and consequences had still not been fully worked out by the time that Juárez assumed the presidency in 1858.

Though of Zapotec origin, Juárez represented neither Indian revindication nor any specific peasant culture characteristic of Oaxaca. On the contrary, he identified with mid-nineteenth-century republican Liberalism and its rejection of the Spanish colonial inheritance. In his defence of national sovereignty and his implacable resistance to the monarchy of Maximilian, Juárez developed the nationalism of progenitors such as Miguel Hidalgo, José María Morelos and Vicente Guerrero in the 1810s and 1820s. He placed himself in that tradition. The years 1846–67 were perhaps the most decisive in the history of the independent Mexican state. Mexico was not only defending its very existence without the assistance of foreign allies, but at the same time struggling to discover its own identity. During the 1860s, nationalism was Juárez's keynote. As the opponent first of Spanish neo-colonial designs and then of Napoleon III's imperial ambitions, Juárez was a forerunner of nationalist leaders in the mid-twentieth century in their struggles against the European colonial empires.

Juárez had clear antecedents within the Liberal camp from the late 1820s. This Liberal adherence was nowhere more clearly defined than in his association through three decades (1827–57) with the Institute of Science and Art of the State of Oaxaca, execrated by local conservatives and clericals. The Liberalism of Juárez was not acquired in middle age during the New Orleans exile of 1853–55 under the influence of superior intellects, as traditional historiography intimates.

At the national level in the period from the 1810s to the 1880s, no class, occupational or regional hegemony could be discerned in the political processes. That gives the period a fluidity and openness which contrasted with what came before and after. Three Centralist experiments in 1836–46, 1853–55 and 1863–67 failed to re-create a neo-Bourbon state and reconstitute a form of hegemony based upon an uneasy alliance of land, business, army and Church. Regional opposition and resistance by middle and lower social groups effectively scuppered these experiments. Yet, these opposition elements remained insufficiently coherent to establish a viable national government on a lasting basis. The Liberal Party itself could not provide the necessary framework within which they could coalesce, except for only brief periods of time. The party consisted more of disunited factions and warring personalities (with their armed clientele) than of a disciplined party in the modern sense. Juárez was as much a victim of this factious movement as a beneficiary. For these reasons the problem of state-formation in nineteenth-century Mexico and much of Latin America proved to be arduous and deeply frustrating.

Mexico, once the jewel of the Spanish Empire, had fallen on lean times during the period from the 1800s to the 1870s. The often perceived 'decline of Mexico' accompanied the rise of the United States. Mexico had contributed to Spain's recovery during the eighteenth century. In 1821 the Mexican Empire had stretched from Oregon to the Isthmus of Panama. The crisis of the mining sector, the inadequacy of agriculture, the collapse of government finances, the disintegration of late colonial commercial and investment linkages, the shortage of capital, and educational and technological backwardness had all combined to undermine the search for a viable form of government. The loss of Texas in 1836 and the catastrophe of 1846–48 further compounded the sense of national humiliation. It fell to Juárez to govern Mexico at its most abject, at the most dangerous moment in its history.

Juárez was the first Mexican national leader fully to appreciate the advantage of a close working relationship with Washington. This marked an especially painful departure for Mexico in the aftermath of the loss of half the national territory. The country still reeled from the defeat of 1848 during the Juárez era, especially since it marked a dramatic and irreversible shift in the balance of power on the North American continent. In spite of the pre-Columbian civilizations which Mexico shared with the rest of Meso-America and the Andean zones, in spite of the viceregal past that it shared with Peru, and in spite of the profound impact of Liberalism which it shared with Colombia, Mexico remained first and foremost part of the North American continent. Mexico's nineteenth-century history demonstrated that the essential relationship would be with the USA, rather than with the rest of Latin America, with which Mexicans had little contact and not an overwhelming interest. For the USA, conversely, the relationship with Mexico was also vital, especially during the era of Juárez.

The southern states of the USA were anxious to exploit internal divisions in Mexico during the civil war of the Reform (1858–61). Juárez regarded their aspirations and those of the Confederacy after 1861 as a serious threat to territorial integrity. Mexican Liberals sympathized with Abraham Lincoln's administration and the Union cause in the civil war of 1861–65 in the USA. Juárez sought to repair the damage done to Mexican – US relations in the three decades following the secession of Texas through his capable minister in Washington, Matías Romero, during the years of the French Intervention. At the same time, Juárez in concert with his Foreign Minister, Sebastián Lerdo de Tejada, staved off further US pressures for territorial concessions and transit rights. After the collapse of Maximilian's empire in 1867, Mexico's principal external relations were with the new states of the nineteenth century: the USA, the North German Confederation and the Kingdom of Italy. Yet, if Mexico were to enter the type of intimate association with the USA favoured by Juárez, what would be the consequences? What would be the advantages for the USA, the more powerful state? The risks for Mexico could be diplomatic subordination to the USA in the international order, permanent US involvement in Mexican domestic affairs, special trade relations on the basis of most favoured nation or a free trade area in which Mexico became the supplier of cheap labour. For Mexico the risk could be permanent subordination and perpetual cultural humiliation. Such issues are alive at the beginning of the 1990s with the discussion of a projected North American Free Trade Area, consisting of Canada, the USA and Mexico. For Mexicans, suspicion of the great predator of the north mingled with admiration for its technological achievements. Yet as Juárez foresaw, the USA would be the predominant factor in Mexico's external relations (and frequently internal as well) from his time onwards.

Juárez's position on issues changed as his career progressed, though certain underlying principles obtained throughout – supremacy of the civil power, respect for the law, and the depersonalization of political life. Juárez had differing perceptions at different times in response to the prevailing questions of his day. His tactical alignments within the Liberal Party demonstrated this clearly. As governor in Oaxaca in 1847–52, Juárez scrupulously avoided direct confrontation with either the bishop or the social elite, in view of the precarious nature of his own position. As a minister under Álvarez, his *Ley Juárez* of November 1855, though conceived as moderate, was perceived as radical within and without the Liberal camp. Aligned with Álvarez, Juárez was regarded as a radical, especially in view of his ethno-social origins. Comonfort, anxious to construct a cabinet of moderates, sent him back to Oaxaca, where his policies in 1856–57 further reinforced the radical reputation. Yet at no stage was Juárez a 'Jacobin', to employ Justo Sierra's use of the term to describe those in favour of a Liberal dictatorship through which to enforce the reform policies. Still less did he concur with those radicals who in 1861 advocated the formation of a Committee of Public Safety for that purpose. Even a radical, such as the unicameralist León Guzmán, balked at that. Juárez, however, was not a moderate, either. The moderate faction, grouped around Comonfort in 1855–57 and some of them around Maximilian in 1864–67, were constitutionalists who favoured a limited form of representation. In 1857 this group joined with Comonfort in advocating a reform of the Constitution promulgated in February of that year. They saw it as too popular and too federalist, and hoped to avoid a confrontation with the Church and an open breach with the army. Fresh from his gubernatorial experience in Oaxaca, Juárez remained sceptical of the loyalty of federal military commanders to any form of constitutionalism or federalism. He had placed his trust in the national militias, organized by the state governments, to counter-balance them. Mindful of the career of Santa Anna in the period from 1828 to 1855, Juárez had no confidence in a reform of the Constitution that depended upon the dissolution of the elected Congress with the support of the army. Although brought back to the cabinet by Comonfort in October 1857, Juárez was quick to dissociate himself from the moderates, once the full implications of the *coup d'état* of Tacubaya on 17 December had become clear. Thereafter and for the following five and a half years, from January 1858 until June 1863, Juárez remained aligned with the Liberal radicals. The loss of the capital city, first to the Conservatives and subsequently to the

French, placed him in close proximity to the state governors, who were by no means his supporters or admirers. Though not a committed radical (and certainly not one of the party's leading ideologists), Juárez depended upon radical support, even though many radicals in the senior levels of the party opposed him in favour of González Ortega, whose power base lay in the radical state of Zacatecas. Liberal radicals were never a homogeneous group. Their two principal representatives in the cabinet, Miguel Lerdo de Tejada and Melchor Ocampo, remained political rivals: Juárez frequently had to act as mediator and pacifier within his own cabinet during the Veracruz years, 1859 and 1860. The alliance between Juárez and the radicals came to its climax in 1859–60 with the publication of the Reform Laws, which sought to diminish the position of the Church in Mexico and promote the institutions of a secularized society.

The alliance with the radicals broke apart in the late spring of 1863. The experience of two and a half years of obstruction by Congress from January 1861 to the end of May 1863, in spite of financial crisis, default on external debt payment, and foreign threat, exasperated Juárez, who had always sought to recover what dignity and authority he could for the office of the presidency. By June 1863 Juárez had broken with the radicals and realigned with their *bête noire*, Sebastián Lerdo. He was to cooperate with Lerdo until their rupture of the projected second re-election of Juárez late in 1870. The Liberals' loss of Mexico City and the principal cities left the task of reconstruction to the regency (1863–64) and empire (1864–67). Moderate opinion gravitated in that direction, even though the most outstanding moderate, Lerdo, was Juárez's closest associate in the itinerant republican administration. The foreign connection and the constant pressure of the clerico-conservatives frustrated Maximilian's efforts to construct a moderate consensus at the political centre. He sought to uphold at one and the same time both the Catholic establishment and the Reform policies, to align with business and land, but at the same time to put right peasant grievances, to found his regime on national elections while imposing rigorous counter-insurgency measures on armed dissent. Such measures undermined the imperial regime's claims to legitimacy. The collapse of imperial finances and the failure to organize an effective Mexican army sealed the fate of the empire by May 1867.

Juárez played on Maximilian's lack of political skill. He ably exploited the ambiguous position of Maximilian as a Habsburg within the political development of Mexico. The anti-Habsburg struggle in the 1860s had a strong anti-colonialist flavour. The War of the Intervention became the second War of Independence. Juárez, determined that Maximilian should pay with his life, portrayed the execution of the Habsburg emperor as the reversal of the Spanish Conquest in 1521, the revindication of Moctezuma and Cuauhtémoc. The execution of Maximilian signified the end of any further European attempts to establish tutelage over Latin American countries. On the other hand, the removal of the European factor (except, perhaps, in the case of Argentina) left Latin America dangerously exposed in relation to the United States.

For Mexico, it meant the end of the Conservative Party as a serious contestant for power. Liberalism became the official ideology of the Mexican state after 1867, but the factious Liberal Party could not provide stable and coherent government. It could not transform itself into an effective and lasting monopoly party. As a result, the way lay open for a recrudescence of personalism and extra-constitutional action. Juárez's attempts to forestall such a turn of events were frequently interrupted by rebellions, generally from within the Liberal camp, or congressional obstruction in the years from the restoration of the Republic in June 1867 until his death in July 1872. Juárez's alignment with the moderates threw aggrieved radicals into the arms of the military politicians in the regions.

The euphoria of national victory in 1867 obscured the deeply rooted and long-lasting problems of the country. Not the least of these was the tradition of armed networks of private power. Rivals for the provincial and national leadership remained disposed to resort to armed force in order to attain their objective, regardless of the principles of the Constitution. Frequently, defence of the Constitution was their pretext for rebellion. The constitutional system of 1857 was the work of a generation imbued with the abstract ideas of popular sovereignty and the rights of man, though without any real experience of how government operated in practice. Juárez, in contrast, had direct experience of government in Oaxaca, through participation at several levels before reaching the governorship in 1847. His attempts to introduce legality and stability in government broke his health by the summer of 1872. Even so, he thwarted his most dangerous rival, Porfirio Díaz, who, by an act of violence disguised as defence of the Constitution, precipitated the Rebellion of La Noria in 1871–72. Juárez demonstrated in sickness and old age the political mastery that had brought him to the highest position of state and kept him there longer than anyone else before him.

Politics was the air he breathed. Yet the cult of Juárez transformed the tactician into symbol. Again like Quetzalcóatl, Juárez became transformed from flesh and blood into immutable stone. Devoid of humanity, he could be revered in the new official pantheon along with Hidalgo, Morelos and Guerrero. Together they displaced the Christian Trinity, the Virgin Mary and the saints. Juárez took his place in the Liberal religion of the state.

BIBLIOGRAPHICAL ESSAY

Although several attempts were made in the aftermath of the death of Juárez to assess his career, notably by Gustavo Baz, *Vida de Benito Juárez* (Mexico 1874), the principal impetus came around the year 1906 with the approach of the centenary of his birth. This fell in the middle of the decade of deepening political controversy concerning the succession to Porfirio Díaz, who had taken power in 1876. Not only the duration but also the entire nature of the Díaz regime had by that time become a subject of concern. As a result, the assessment of Juárez's role in Mexican politics was bound to give rise to radically varying interpretations, several of which have already been discussed in the text. One of the first works to appear, Juan Sánchez, *Vida literaria de Benito Juárez* (Oaxaca 1902), exalted Juárez's constitutionalism and respect for legality. Sánchez, an Oaxaca lawyer, belonged to the Liberal opposition to Díaz, and sought to revive Oaxacan *juarismo*, which the *porfiristas* had displaced. This little-known work was reprinted in a facsimile edition in 1972 at the initiative of Miguel León-Portilla to coincide with the centenary of Juárez's death.

The publication which aroused the fiercest controversy was Francisco Bulnes, *Juárez y las revoluciones de Ayutla y de la Reforma* (Mexico City 1905). Bulnes, not a historian but by training an engineer, who had become a Liberal politician in the Díaz era, possessed a remarkable talent with words and imagery. On occasions his political insights were incisive, though a passion for effect frequently led him to dispense with evidence. Bulnes portrayed Juárez as an insignificant provincial lawyer with no clear ideology until he met Ocampo in New

Orleans during their common exile. Juárez, according to Bulnes, was pushed into the main Liberal reforms: he was not in the vanguard of Liberalism, and was consistently overshadowed by the real leaders, who were the state governors and *caciques.* Such a view was indignantly rebutted by Genaro García, *Refutación a D. Francisco Bulnes* (Mexico City 1904). Bulnes, *El verdadero Juárez* (Mexico City 1905), argued that Juárez's negligence opened the way for the Intervention, that his wartime leadership was deficient, and that he owed his victory to US indirect intervention. In the judgement of Bulnes, the principal enemy of Mexican democracy after 1867 was Juárez himself, since he sought nothing less than the perpetuation of his own position. In that sense, Juárez prepared the ground for the Díaz regime, which governed according to similar principles. This portrayal was hotly disputed by Hilarion Frías y Soto, *Juárez glorificado y la Intervención y el Imperio ante la verdad histórica* (Mexico City 1905), who argued that Juárez had not depended upon the USA for the Liberal victory in the wars of the Reform and Intervention and was an effective wartime leader. A further positive interpretation of Juárez appeared in Justo Sierra, *Juárez: Su obra y su tiempo* (Mexico City 1905–06), which stressed his early commitment to Liberalism and portrayed a radical, if not Jacobin Juárez, with other reformers at his side. Sierra saw Juárez as the key figure in the *Reforma* constellation, but regarded his supreme accomplishment as the defeat of the Intervention and the preservation of national independence. He regarded Juárez as instrumental in the downfall of Napoleon III and in the rise of a new German-led political order in continental Europe after 1871. In this way, Sierra dramatically placed Mexican events within the wider geo-politics of the Atlantic world. He stressed the importance of the struggle in Mexico between 1857 and 1867 in determining the balance of power on the North American continent. Sierra accordingly placed little emphasis on Juárez's early career and little on the neglected last years, 1867–72.

For Miguel Galindo y Galindo, *La gran década nacional o relación histórica de la Guerra de Reforma, intervención extranjera y gobierno del archiduque Maximiliano, 1857–1867* (Mexico City 1904, 3 vols 1987), those ten years were the decisive period, with Juárez at the centre point, presiding over the preservation of national sovereignty and the formation of the modern

Mexican state, purged of the influence of the Catholic Church. Galindo, who originated from the northern Puebla sierra, provided much local detail of the military struggle in the Puebla–Tlaxcala zone. Fernando Iglesias Calderón, *Las supuestas traíciones de Juárez* (Mexico City 1906), argued against the revival by Bulnes of earlier Conservative claims that Juárez had depended on the USA for Liberal successes. Iglesias reasserted Liberal claims that the real traitors were the Conservatives themselves. Frías declared that Bulnes, *El Verdadero Juárez*, could have been written by the earlier Conservative historian, Lucas Alamán, who had argued for a type of neo-Bourbon state and for a European monarchy in Mexico. For Frías, that book was a 'historical libel'. Bulnes had failed to examine the origins of the Intervention, which lay not in France but in Mexico in 1840 with conservative and clerical arguments for monarchy. Juárez was not an 'impassive Indian, a spineless coward', as Bulnes had called him, but 'energetic and active' in regrouping the Liberal Party after the coup of 1857 and in opposing the designs of Napoleon III.

Contemporaneous with this exploration of Juárez in fact and myth was the re-examination of the 1857 Constitution, especially in the light of Díaz's abuse of re-election. This process began with Ricardo García Granados, *La Constitución de 1857 y las leyes de la Reforma en México: Estudio histórico-sociológico* (Mexico City 1906), who regarded it as unrelated to Mexico's political culture. This process continued with Emilio Rabasa, *La Constitución y la dictadura* (Mexico City 1912), which argued that the Constitution had been unrealistic, since it did not conform to Mexican realities. First, manipulated election and executive interference, and then finally dictatorship had been the result of the Liberal experiment in Mexico. These arguments have been reviewed in Daniel Cosío Villegas, *La Constitución de 1857 y sus críticos* (Mexico City 1957), who criticized Rabasa for ignoring entirely the period 1867–76, when political life in Mexico was free and open. Rabasa's view was that good men, such as Comonfort, Juárez, Lerdo and Díaz, were converted into dictators by the inadequacy of the Constitution. Cosío Villegas argued that, to the best of his knowledge, neither Juárez nor Lerdo had ever declared that it was impossible to govern in accordance with the provisions of the Constitution. Díaz, however, who faced no national emergencies, as

Juárez had, took the decision to govern without recourse to constitutional provisions.

Jesús Reyes Heroles, *El Liberalismo mexicano* (Mexico City 1957–61, 3 vols), examined the earlier roots of Liberalism in the generation prior to the Reform, stressing its anticlericalism, while at the same time highlighting the debate concerning the nature of economic development. Reyes Heroles in this way placed the ideology of Liberals of the Reform era into its historical context. This work had a profound impact on Mexican and North American scholarship. Even so, it reinforced the already existing emphasis on studies of Liberalism. Several of Juárez's discourses during the civil war of the Reform, in which he sought to define the position of the Liberal Party, appeared in Ernesto de la Torre Villar, *El triunfo de la República liberal, 1857–1860* (Mexico City 1960). A position not especially sympathetic to Juárez appeared in José Fuentes Mares, *Juárez: Los Estados Unidos y Europa* (Mexico City 1960–61, 1962, 1964, 1971; reprinted in one volume in 1983) and *Juárez: El Imperio y la República* (Mexico City 1963, 1965, 1973, 1975; reprinted in one volume in 1982), although the author's sympathies began in the course of these two works to drift more towards a *juarista* position. Fuentes Mares drew attention to Mexican Liberals' sympathies towards the United States. He described Juárez as 'far more dangerous with a law or decree than with a brace of pistols'. Fuentes Mares, *Miramón: El hombre* (Mexico City 1974, 1975, 1978, 1985), brought about the historical recreation of the Conservative General and President, stressing his aloofness from Napoleon III's designs and Maximilian's coolness towards him (until the end at Querétaro). A fellow historian from Chihuahua, Francisco Almada, *Juárez y Terrazas: Aclaraciones históricas* (Mexico City 1958), argued that Terrazas was a bogus Liberal, and essentially an opportunist, who sought only to strengthen his political and economic position in the home state. Juárez's eventual cooperation with Terrazas enabled the formation of the vast family domain in Chihuahua, which contributed in no small way to the revolutionary explosion there in 1910–11. The Chihuahua experience was taken up by Jorge L. Tamayo, *Juárez en Chihuahua* (Mexico City 1970), which clarified Juárez's political difficulties with Terrazas over federal revenues, and then assessed the President's position in the politics of northern Mexico in the mid-1860s.

The myth and symbol of Juárez continue to be potent elements in Mexican politics. In a recent television address to the Mexican people concerning the proposed North American Free Trade Area (NAFTA), President Carlos Salinas de Gortari (1988–94) spoke against the background of a huge portrait of Juárez. The Indian from Guelatao stands at the central point of Mexican nationalism. That, in turn, has consisted of rejection of the colonial inheritance, commitment to the secularization of society and the development of the economy, independence from foreign powers, and distrust of the foreign business. To the anger of the nationalist Left, this virtually sacrosanct creed has been transgressed stage by stage during the past decade. Relations with the Holy See, broken off by Juárez in 1867, were restored by Salinas in September 1992. To whom, then, does Juárez belong?

At every stage, the pressing question of the role of the United States has reappeared. Much of the historical and polemical literature favourable to Juárez has been concerned to exonerate him from the Conservative charge (later taken up and developed by the Left) that Juárez was subservient to the United States, and was prepared to hand over Mexican interests to that power in order to win support for the Liberal cause. In this polemic, much has hinged upon the interpretation of the McLane–Ocampo Treaty of 1859. This subject was re-examined by Agustín Cue Canovas, *El Tratado McLane-Ocampo* (Mexico City 1956). Jorge Tamayo, *Benito Juárez: Documentos, discursos y correspondencia* (Mexico City 1964–72, 15 vols) devoted virtually one entire volume to the treaty (III, pp. 111–846). The object was to refute claims that Juárez handed over Mexican interests to the USA, and was therefore qualitatively little different from Santa Anna. Tamayo's 'El Tratado McLane–Ocampo' *Historia Mexicana* XXIV (1974–75), pp. 573–613, carefully argued against such views in succinct form. The documentary compilation, anticipated by Jorge Tamayo, *Epistolario de Benito Juárez* (Mexico City 1957), originated as a government-sponsored project during the presidency of Adolfo López Mateos (1958–64) and was concluded in 1972, the centenary of Juárez's death, during the presidency of Luis Echeverría Alvarez (1970–76). Both presidents were strong nationalists, conscious of the role of Juárez as the link between Independence in 1810 and the Revolution in 1910. Echeverría portrayed Juárez as an earlier instance of

'Third World' resistance to neo-colonialism. In many respects, the PRI (Partido Revolucionario Institucional) regime, which they represented, formed the twentieth-century continuation of the Liberalism which had culminated in the era of Porfirio Díaz. While the symbolism of Juárez stood intact, the constitutionalism at the centre of his political stance still remained to be worked out. Tamayo's documents formed a belated rebuttal of Bulnes as well, a demonstration that 1972 would not be marred by the type of controversy which had tarnished 1906. This collection was a decidedly Liberal affair, concerned to refute hostile comment and unconcerned with the contemporary Conservative point of view. The controversial execution of Maximilian was given scant treatment. The subject of Mexican–United States relations has always been fraught with difficulties. They are a constant issue, no less so than during the NAFTA negotiations of 1990–92. Bearing in mind the debate concerning Juárez's position in the 1850s and 1860s, it would be interesting to explore the thematic linkage between the 'old' Liberalism of the 1850s and 1860s and the 'neo-liberalism' of the 1980s and 1990s.

Tamayo's collection is vital as a printed primary source in view of its range of archival evidence. The last four volumes, dealing with 1867–72, form a primary alternative to Daniel Cosío Villegas, *La República Restaurada: Vida Política* (Mexico City 1955, 1959), which has frequently been used as a basic source itself. This formed technically the first part of *Historia General de México* (Mexico City 1955–72, 10 vols), which Cosío Villegas coordinated and authored in part. The objective was to demonstrate that the origins of modern Mexico lay not specifically with the Revolution of 1910, but with the *Reforma* and, indeed, with the economic modernization associated with the Díaz era. Daniel Cosío Villegas, *Porfirio Díaz en la revuelta de La Noria* (Mexico City 1953) dealt with the first armed insurrection of Díaz and its disintegration.

Much of the English-language literature has focused on the Reform period as a whole, rather than on what has often appeared to be the inscrutable personality of Juárez himself. Three studies, however, have made significant steps towards understanding the position of Juárez within the context of nineteenth-century political life. Ralph Roeder, *Juárez and his Mexico: A Biographical Essay* (New York 1947, 2 vols), dealt very much with power politics and diplomacy, but had little to say concerning Juárez's early career and, consequently, failed to explain adequately how he rose to occupy the central position in national Liberal politics after 1857. Walter V Scholes, *Mexican Politics during the Juárez Régime, 1855–1872* (Columbia, MO 1957), was a stark and perhaps overly succinct survey, which did attempt to draw attention to the last years. Ivie E Cadenhead, *Benito Juárez* (New York 1973), provided a very helpful study of the overall career, placing stress on Juárez's considerable achievement in the seemingly hopeless position of head of the beleaguered Liberal regime in Veracruz in 1859 and 1860.

Between 1968 and 1983 a number of studies appeared in English which examined early Liberalism and the conflicts of the Reform era. This cycle began with Charles A Hale, *Mexican Politics in the Age of Mora (1821–1853)* (Yale, CT 1968), which discussed both the European intellectual roots of Mexican Liberalism and the impact of the United States' model of development. Jan Bazant, *Alienation of Church Wealth in Mexico: Social and Economic Aspects of the Liberal Revolution, 1856–1875* (Cambridge 1971), and Robert J Knowlton, *Church Property and the Mexican Reform, 1856–1910* (DeKalb, IL 1976), examined the Liberal disamortization process from different methodological perspectives. Laurens Ballard Perry, *Juárez and Díaz: Machine Politics in Mexico* (DeKalb, IL 1978), stressed the electoral management practised during the Restored Republic and the quantity of insurrections directed against it. Richard N Sinkin, *The Mexican Reform, 1855–1876: A Study in Liberal Nation-Building* (Austin, TX 1979), drew attention to the relatively homogeneous composition of the Constituent Congress of 1856–57 and to the Liberal preoccupation with law and order during the Reform era. Charles R Berry, *The Reform in Oaxaca: A Microhistory of the Central District, 1856–1876,* (Lincoln, NB 1983), dealt with the provincial dimension of the Liberal measures in Juárez's home state.

J M Puig Casauranc (ed.), *Archivo privado de D. Benito Juárez y D. Pedro Santacilia* (Mexico City 1928), revealed the intimacy of the Cuban connection and the influence of the son-in-law as the link between Juárez and his family during the period of separation. The role of Juárez's wife was studied in Jesús B Castañón, 'Las mujeres de la Reforma: Margarita Maza de Juárez', *Boletín bibliográfico de la Secretaría de Hacienda y Crédito Público* (1 April 1956), Angeles Mendieta Alatorre, *Margarita*

Maza de Juárez: Antología, iconografía y efemérides (Mexico City 1972), and Carlos Velasco Pérez, *Margarita Maza de Juárez: Primera dama de la nación* (Oaxaca 1986). Two recent studies have set Juárez within the context of his contemporaries: Carmen Blázquez Mantecón, *Veracruz liberal, 1858–1860* (Mexico City 1986), and Jorge Fernández Ruiz, *Juárez y sus contemporáneos* (Mexico City 1986).

Jacqueline Covo, 'L'image de Juárez dans la presse française á l'époque de l'intervention au Mexique (1862–1867)', *Bulletin Hispanique* lxxiii, nos 3–4 (July–Dec. 1971), pp. 371–95, examined the negative portrayals of Juárez in the Napoleonic press. In contrast, Noël Salomon, *Juárez en la conciencia francesa, 1861–1867* (Mexico City 1975), showed that most of the French resident community in Mexico sympathized with Juárez. In France, the principal Juárez supporter was Jules Favre, who with his fellow republicans in the Chamber of Deputies condemned the Intervention, and on 2 December 1867 declared that Juárez's victory over 'Napoleon the Less' would contribute to the downfall of the Second Empire.

Charles A Weeks, *The Juárez Myth in Mexico* (Tuscaloosa, Alabama 1987), explored the origin and development of the myth from the Reform era to the present. Weeks showed how the Díaz regime, from the late 1880s, sought to exploit the Juárez myth to its own advantage. The object was to demonstrate that Juárez was the precursor of Díaz. Opponents of the dictatorship intervened to portray Juárez as the defender of constitutional government and national independence, and Díaz as the friend of foreign companies and the perpetrator of arbitrary rule. Weeks drew attention to the presence of Juárez the symbol in the revolutionary mural paintings of Diego Rivera, José Clemente Orozco and David Siqueiros. This symbolic presence of Juárez recurs in the painting of Francisco Toledo, who also originated from Oaxaca.

CHRONOLOGY

1806	Birth of Juárez at Guelatao, Oaxaca, 21 March
1810–21	Mexican War of Independence
1812	Cádiz Constitution published in Spain, 18 March
1818	Juárez arrives in Oaxaca City
1821	Final stage of the Independence movement opens with the Plan of Iguala, 24 February
Jul 1822 – Mar 1823	FIRST EMPIRE
1824	Federal Constitution published in Mexico, 12 October
1824–36	FIRST FEDERAL REPUBLIC
1829	Vicente Guerrero, President, January – December
1830–32	Proto-Conservative administration of Anastasio Bustamante
1833–34	Liberal administration of Vice-President Valentín Gómez Farías (1781–1858)
1833	Juárez elected to the Oaxaca State Congress
1836	Secession of Texas

1836–46	CENTRALIST REPUBLIC
1841–44	Santa Anna in power
1841–45	Antonio de León, Governor of Oaxaca
1843	Juárez marries Margarita Maza (1826–71), 31 July
1846–47	Mexico at war with the United States
1846	Restoration of federalism, 6 August
1846–53	SECOND FEDERAL REPUBLIC
29 Oct 1847 – 12 Aug 1852	*Juárez Governor of Oaxaca*
1848	Treaty of Guadalupe Hidalgo ends war with USA, 2 February
Apr 1853 – Aug 1855	Santa Anna's last regime
1853–55	Juárez and other Liberal leaders in exile in New Orleans
1854	Revolution of Ayutla begins, 1 March
1855	Fall of Santa Anna, 8 August
1855–76	REFORM PERIOD
1855	Álvarez President, 4 October – 10 December Juárez Minister of Justice and Ecclesiastical Affairs, 6 October – 9 December *Ley Juárez*: Law for the Administration of Justice, 23 November
Dec 1855 – 21 Jan 1858	Comonfort President
10 Jan 1856 – 25 Oct 1857	*Juárez Governor of Oaxaca*
1856	Constituent Congress convenes in Mexico City, 18 February *Ley Lerdo*: Law for the Disamortization of Corporately owned Properties, 25 June

	Pope Pius IX condemns Juárez and Lerdo Laws, 15 December
1857	Publication of the federal Constitution, 5 February
	Constitutional Congress convenes, 16 September
	Juárez President of the Supreme Court
	Juárez leaves Oaxaca never to return, 27 October
	Grant of extraordinary powers to Comonfort, 5 November; inherited by Juárez in January 1858; surrendered to Congress in 1861
	Coup d'état of Tacubaya; arrest of Juárez, 17 December
Jan 1858 – Dec 1860	*Civil War of the Reform*
1858	Mexico City Garrison under Félix Zuloaga removes Comonfort, 11 January; release of Juárez by Comonfort before his fall; Conservative regime in Mexico City; Juárez flees to Querétaro
	Conservative generals Miramón and Osollo rout Parrodi at Salamanca, 10 March; capitulation of Doblado
	Juárez and his ministers nearly executed in Guadalajara, 13–15 March
	Conservatives take Zacatecas, 12 April
	Juárez administration reconstituted in Veracruz, 4 May
	Miramón defeats Santos Degollado at Atenquique, 2 July
	Miramón defeats Liberal forces at Ahualulco, 29 September
1859	Miramón replaces Zuloaga as Conservative President, 31 January
	Buchanan administration recognizes the Juárez regime in Veracruz, 6 April
	Miramón's first siege of Veracruz fails, June–July

Reform Laws issued by executive decree, 12 July
Law on Civil Marriage, 23 July
Civil Registry established in Veracruz, 28 July
Santiago Vidaurri declares Nuevo León-Coahuila to be an independent state, 5 September
Miramón contracts the Jecker Bonds, 29 October
Conservative victory at Estancia de las Vacas, 12 November
McLane–Ocampo Treaty, 14 December

1860 Miramón's second siege of Veracruz fails, 3–21 March
US Senate rejects the McLane–Ocampo Treaty, 31 May
Miramón defeated at Silao by González Ortega, 10 August
Ignacio Zaragoza, Liberal commander, takes Guadalajara, 30 October
Juárez rejects McLane–Ocampo Treaty, November
Law for the Liberty of Religious Worship, 4 December
González Ortega defeats Miramón at Calpulapan, 22 December
Liberal forces recover Mexico City, 25 December

1861 Juárez administration returns to Mexico City, 11 January
Juárez expels the Apostolic Delegate and five bishops, 12 January
Juárez wins presidential elections, March
Márquez declares Juárez and his supporters to be traitors subject to summary execution, 16 March
Miguel Lerdo dies of typhoid, 22 March
Civil war begins in the USA, April
Federal Congress in session, 9 May (until 31 May 1863)

	Melchor Ocampo killed, 3 June
	Santos Degollado ambushed and killed, 15 June
	Mexican government suspends payment on foreign debt for two years, 17 July
	Convention of London for tripartite intervention in Mexico, 31 October
	Wyke–Zamacona Agreement, 21 November; repudiated by Congress, 22–23 November
	Congress grants Juárez extraordinary powers, 11 December
1862–67	*The French Intervention*
1862	Allied fleets land in Veracruz, 7 January
	Juárez's Law for the Punishment of Collaboration, 25 January
	Allied meeting in Orizaba (Veracruz) terminates Tripartite Intervention, 9 April
	Lorencez defeated at Puebla by Zaragoza, 5 May
	French retreat to Orizaba, 13 June
	Napoleon III's Fontainebleau Instructions to Forey, 3 July
	Congress ratifies grant of extraordinary powers to Juárez, 27 October
1863	French besiege and take Puebla, 16–19 May
	Congress ratifies grant of extraordinary powers to Juárez, 27 May
	Forey enters Mexico City, 10 June
	Regency Council (Almonte, Labastida, Salas), 18 June
	Juárez government in San Luis Potosí, 9 June – 22 December
	Maximilian at Miramar agrees to accept the throne, 3 October
	French take Guanajuato, 8 December
1864	French take Guadalajara, 5 January
	Juárez in Saltillo, 9 January: opposed by Vidaurri

	Juárez in Monterrey, 12–14 February; interview with Vidaurri
	Juárez back in Saltillo, 14 February – 2 April
	Juárez deposes Vidaurri and separates Nuevo León and Coahuila, 26 February
	Juárez returns to Monterrey, 2 April – 15 August
	Juárez places the State of Chihuahua under siege, 6 April
	Maximilian formally accepts the Mexican crown, 10 April
	Maximilian and Carlota arrive in Veracruz, 28 May
	Maximilian and Carlota in Mexico City, 12 June
	French take Durango, 4 July
	French take Saltillo, 20 August
	French in Monterrey, 26 August
	Vidaurri returns to Monterrey, 7 September; defects to the empire
12 Oct 1864 – 10 Dec 1866	Juárez in the state of Chihuahua
12 Oct 1864 – 5 Aug 1865	Juárez in Chihuahua City
1865	Bazaine takes Oaxaca and captures Porfirio Díaz, 8 February
	French take Guaymas, 29 March
	Juárez in Paso del Norte, 14 August – 13 November
	Maximilian's Colonization Law, 5 September
	US government appoints a minister to Juárez's Mexico, October
	Maximilian's Imperial Decree establishes courts martial for insurgent bands, 3 October
	Juárez extends his presidential term and excludes González Ortega, 8 November

18 Dec 1865 – 10 June 1866	Juárez once more in Paso del Norte
1866	Napoleon III orders phased withdrawal of French troops, January Juárez in Chihuahua City, 17 June – 10 December Imperial Decree reaffirms corporate ownership of land, 26 June Republicans recover Hermosillo, 14 August Juárez declares the state of Guerrero under siege, 27 August; Diego Alvarez, Governor Last stage of French withdrawal begins, September Maximilian in Orizaba to consider abdication, October Maximilian decides to remain in Mexico, 30 November Lozada defects to Juárez camp, December
26 Dec 1866 – 14 Jan 1867	Juárez in Durango
1867	Mexico City junta sustains the empire by one vote, 14 January Ramón Corona recovers Guadalajara, 14 January Tomás Mejía's Imperial forces abandon San Luis Potosí for Querétaro, 25 January Bazaine orders the evacuation of Mexico City, 5 February Republican forces take Morelia, 18 February Juárez administration in San Luis Potosí, 21 February Bazaine and last French troops leave Veracruz, 12 March Escobedo begins the siege of Querétaro, 14 March Díaz takes Puebla, 2–4 April Querétaro taken; capture of Maximilian,

	Miramón and Mejía, 15 May
	Execution of Maximilian, Miramón and Mejía, 19 June
	Díaz enters Mexico City, 21 June
1867–76	*The Restored Republic*
1867	Juárez in Mexico City, 15 July
	Convocatoria and five projected reforms of the Constitution, 14 August
	Juárez wins presidential elections, October
	Félix Díaz elected governor of Oaxaca, November
	Juárez surrenders extraordinary powers to the new Congress, 8 December
	Juárez persuades Congress to suspend constitutional guarantees, 18 December; peasant rebellions in central Mexico
1868	Negrete active in the Puebla sierra, February – June
	Juárez obtains further extraordinary powers from Congress, 8 May; re-enactment of law of 25 January 1862
	Pius IX designates six new Mexican bishops, June
	Mexico City textile workers' strike, July
	Execution of Chávez López, leader of Chalco rebellion, 7 July
1869	Negrete's sudden appearance in Puebla, 3 February
	Lozada's Circular for the defence of village lands, 12 April
	Agrarian rebellions across central and western Mexico, 1869–70
1870	In Guerrero *jimenistas* seize control of Tixtla, June
	Gran Círculo de Obreros de México formed, September
1871	Death of Margarita Maza de Juárez, 2 January

	Anti-*juarista* rebellions in Nuevo León, Zacatecas and Durango, February
	General Sóstenes Rocha puts down anti-Juárez rising in Tampico, May – June
	Félix Díaz wins election again in Oaxaca, 25 June
	July, Presidential elections; second re-election of Juárez; congressional decision (12 October 1871)
	State of Nuevo León resumes its sovereignty, 29 September
	Díaz issues the Plan of La Noria in Oaxaca, 8 November; state of Oaxaca resumes its sovereignty
	Lucas rising northern Puebla sierra, 21 November
	Juárez's new presidential term begins, 1 December; grant of extraordinary powers; suspension of constitutional guarantees
	Defeat of Mier y Terán at Xindihuí (Oaxaca), 22 December
1872	Félix Díaz killed by *juchitecos*, 22 January
	Rocha takes Aguascalientes, 29 February
	Rocha routs Zacatecas rebels, 2 March
	Puebla under state of siege, 5 March
	Alatorre Governor and Military-Commander of Puebla, 8 March
	Juárez again proposes constitutional reform, 1 April
	Congress extends extraordinary powers, 17 May
	Rocha takes Monterrey, 9 July; end of rebellion in Nuevo León; Juárez surrenders extraordinary powers to Congress
	Death of Juárez, 9 July; accession of Sebastián Lerdo, 18 July

GLOSSARY

amortization	The process of extinction of national debt.
audiencia	Supreme judicial and administrative body within the Spanish American territories, it acted also as the viceroy's consultative committee and provided senior officials for the fiscal bureaucracy.
Bases Orgánicas	Sanctioned on 12 June 1843 by Santa Anna, these bases for a constitution represented a high point of centralism. Departments were placed strictly under executive authority. High income qualifications restricted the franchise.
bienes nacionales	Nationalized ecclesiastical properties under the Reform Laws of 1859.
borlados	The moderate faction of the Liberal Party in the late 1850s and 1860s.
cacicazgo	The domain of a *cacique,* it included patron–client linkages and networks of command frequently, though not always, connected to landed proprietorship.
cacique	A local notable with an armed following who exercised influence and commanded obedience by virtue of landownership and patronage. Caciques often acted as brokers between local interests and the outside power or provided political leadership at the sub-regional or provincial levels. State-level or even national politicians who operated in the style of such figures were often themselves described as *caciques.*

caciquismo — Prevalence of networks of private power at the head of which were *caciques.*

caudillo — Generally a military figure, such as Santa Anna or Paredes y Arrillaga, acting in a political capacity at the national level in the competition for influence and power. He could command substantial sections of the official armed forces as well as his own network of personal loyalties. Civilian politicians regularly appealed to such figures, while at the same time deploring their existence.

convocatoria — Presidential decree calling for national and state-level elections, whether to a Constituent Congress or to ordinary sessions of the legislature.

Cortes — Originally a royal council and court, the Castilian Cortes included the three estates of the nobility, clergy, and commons during the High Middle Ages. The Cortes withered away under absolutism. The Cádiz Cortes (1810–13) was a representative assembly that claimed the right to exercise sovereignty in the absence of the monarch.

disamortization — The use of state power (usually by Liberal administrations) to release property hitherto inalienable on to the market. Ecclesiastical properties held in mortmain fell into this category. In mid-nineteenth century Mexico Liberal policy, notably the Lerdo Law of 1856, sought to release property from corporate-ownership by the Church or Indian peasant communities and transform it into private units of ownership.

escoceses — Members of masonic lodges that followed the Scottish Rite. In Mexico in the 1820s, they followed a moderate constitutionalist position, but later moved to a more conservative and centralist stance.

exaltados — Term frequently applied to radical Liberals.

fueros — The term derived from medieval Castilian legal history and signified corporate privilege or exemption. In Mexico the *fuero eclesiástico* guaranteed ecclesiastical immunity from civil prosecution. The *fuero militar* (1768) provided similar immunity for members of the newly formed colonial militia.

golpista — A regime coming to power as a result of a *coup d'état* (Sp. *golpe de estado*).

hacienda — A private estate, which could be large or small in size, depending upon the purpose it served. Topography and ecology usually determined its function. It was generally market-oriented and, while specialising in cereals, livestock-raising or sugar-planting, cultivated a range of products, which normally included maize for the consumption of its own workers. A wide range of labour practices tended to co-exist.

Jacobins — A term given to radical Liberals who were prepared to use state power in order to impose a revolutionary programme which involved reducing the role of the Church in society.

jefe político — The term originated in the Spanish Constitution of 1812. In accordance with the Mexican Constitution of 1857, this official became a district administrator appointed by the state governors. He exercised special supervision over the municipalities and the electoral process.

jimenistas — Followers of General Vicente Jiménez in the state of Guerrero in opposition to Juárez after 1867. They were supporters of Porfirio Díaz and enemies of the Álvarez clan.

juaristas — Supporters of Juárez, notably after 1867, when the term gained currency in political circles. After 1872, it was used to describe those who adhered to Juárez's brand of constitutionalism (*juarismo*), generally differentiating them thereby from *porfirismo*.

juchitecos Inhabitants of the southern Isthmus town of Juchitán (Oaxaca) frequently in opposition to state and federal government.

latifundio An accumulation of landed properties, generally consisting of haciendas. The possessor would be described as a *latifundista.*

lerdistas Supporters of Sebastián Lerdo. The term came into use in 1870–71, when Lerdo aspired to succeed Juárez, when the latter's term of office expired in 1871. A distinct faction within Liberalism from the *juaristas* and *porfiristas.* During the 1870s, they increasingly represented the technocratic wing of the Party.

mestizos Technically mixed race (Indian and Hispanic), but more especially the term applied to those who lived within Hispanic society, spoke Spanish, and had adopted European ways.

peones Resident workers on haciendas, who received a wage but also a regular maize ration to supplement it. They were usually guaranteed housing, a subsistence plot, and a measure of protection by their landlord. Conditions varied across the country.

pintos Racially mixed militia soldiery of Juan Álvarez in the 1850s, mainly mulattos from the Pacific coast.

polkos Pro-clerical rebels in Mexico City opposed to Liberal measures in 1847.

porfiristas Adherents of Porfirio Díaz and opponents of Juárez after 1867.

pronunciamiento Military rebellion, usually led by a caudillo, against either civilian administration or that of a rival military figure. Sometimes accompanied by a political declaration, generally known in Mexico as a Plan.

pueblo The term signified more than simply 'village'. It generally referred in the pre-*Reforma* era to a legally constituted Indian community with the right of corporate land-

	ownership. Land frequently had a religious as well as economic significance, and possession of it defined the identity of a community.
puros	Radical, anticlerical Liberals, anxious to push forward the Reform programme.
rancheros	Smaller landowners, often located either on poorer lands adjacent to haciendas or on lands of higher altitude. Some *pueblos* rented out *ranchos* to Hispanic cultivators or planters or as livestock ranges.
Reforma	Usually dated from 1855 to 1876, this was the movement for the restructuring of Mexican social, legal, and political institutions in accordance with the doctrines espoused by the Liberal Party.
rojos	Radical Liberals anxious to strip the Church of its properties, revenues, and influence in Mexican society during the early Reform period, 1856–61.
santanistas	Adherents of General Antonio López de Santa Anna (1795–1876) or members of his personal clientele, particularly in the state of Veracruz.
serranos	Those who originated from highland zones (sierras), such as Juárez, Méndez, Pérez, and Castro, in Oaxaca. The political chieftains of the northern Puebla or Oaxaca sierras were referred to as the *caciques serranos.*
Siete Leyes	The 'Seven Laws' represented the centralist response in 1836 to the federal Constitution of 1824, abolished in that year. The franchise was restricted by property qualifications.
tierras baldías	Lands legally defined under the Reform Laws as 'unoccupied' and, therefore, eligible for sale to private individuals. Juárez's Law of 22 July 1863, issued from San Luis Potosí, provided for the alienation of all such lands, not already put to public use, up to the limit of 2,500 hectares per person.

unicameralism — The 1857 Constitution provided for a one-chamber assembly (with no upper chamber), a departure from the bicameralism of the 1824 Constitution, in accordance with which Congress had been divided into two chambers, a lower chamber and a senate. The Spanish Constitution of 1812 had been unicameral, rejecting an upper house with representatives of the nobility and clergy.

yorkinos — Members of the masonic Yorkist Rite, generally associated in the late 1820s with the radical and popular wing of Liberalism.

DRAMATIS PERSONAE

Alamán, Lucas (1792–1853) Founder of the Conservative Party in 1848. Born in Guanajuato into a silver-mining family. Witnessed Hidalgo's entry into the city in September 1810. Foreign minister, 1823–25, 1830–32, 20 April – 1 June 1853. Sponsored the Bank of Development (*Banco de Avío*) 1830–42 and invested in the textile factory at Cocolapam (Orizaba, Veracruz). Published *Historia de México* 1849–53, in which he criticized the leaders of the Independence movement and praised the achievements of the colonial era.

Almonte, Juan Nepomuceno (1803–69) Son of Morelos, moderate but Conservative from 1850. Born in Michoacán. In the USA for most of the period 1815–24. Second-in-command to Santa Anna in Texas in 1836; Minister of War, 1839–41, 5 January – 26 February 1846; Minister to the USA, 1842–46 and 1853. Subsequently appointed Minister to Great Britain and France in 1856. Presidential candidate in 1845, 1849, 1856. Signed the Mon-Almonte Treaty with the Spanish Minister in Mexico City on 27 April 1859, offering reparations for damage to life and property in the civil war. Fled to France in 1861; intrigued with Napoleon III for a monarchy in Mexico. Returned to Mexico in March 1862. President of the Regency Council, 1863–64. Maximilian's special envoy to Paris in 1866, and remained there after 1867.

Altamirano, Ignacio (1834–93) Radical Liberal novelist, poet, and journalist, critic of the later Juárez. Born in Tixtla (Guerrero), son of illiterate, Nahuatl-speaking parents. Pupil of Ignacio Ramírez at the Toluca Literary Institute, took his law degree in Mexico City in 1857. Represented Guerrero in Congress in 1861. Became the first Secretary of the Mexican Geographical and Statistical Society, 1871–74. Leading figure in the literary revival of the later nineteenth century.

Álvarez, Diego (1812–99) Son of the Guerrero *cacique* Juan Álvarez. Born in Coyuca (Guerrero). Soldier from 1829, colonel in 1846. Ally of Juárez as state governor from 1867.

Álvarez, Juan (1790–1867) Insurgent chieftain, President 4 October – 10 December 1855. Born in Atoyac (Guerrero) into a family of means. Studied in Mexico City but withdrew on parents' death. Joined Morelos's revolutionary movement in 1810. Supported the Plan of Iguala in 1821. Political heir of Vicente Guerrero and initiator of the Revolution of Ayutla in March 1854. Liaison officer between the Juárez government and Liberal forces in the field from 1862.

Arista, Mariano (1802–55) Moderate, President 15 January 1851 – 5 January 1853. Born in San Luis Potosí. Joined Royalist Army as a cadet in 1813; Military Commandant General in Tamaulipas in 1839; Division General in 1841; Commander of the Army of the North in 1846.

Arriaga, Ponciano (1811–65) Radical Liberal. Born in San Luis Potosí. Exiled in New Orleans with Juárez and Melchor Ocampo. Minister of the Interior under Álvarez in 1855. Member of the Constituent Assembly of 1856–57.

Baz, Juan José (1820–87) Radical Liberal. Born in Guadalajara (Jalisco). Partisan of Valentín Gómez Farías after 1838 and especially in 1846–47, when he argued against the corporate privilege and properties of the Church and for religious toleration. Governor of the Federal District, 1846–47, 1861–63, and after 1867. Edited *La Bandera Roja* in Morelia during the civil war of the Reform. Partisan of Porfirio Díaz after 1867 and critic of the later Juárez. Minister of the Interior, 27 September – 20 November 1876.

Bazaine, Achille (1811–88) Marshal of France, 1864; Commander-in-Chief of the French Expeditionary Force in Mexico 1863–67. Born in Versailles. Rose from private soldier in Algeria in 1831 to Brigade General in the Crimean War in 1855. Fought with Marshal Forey in the Crimea and in the Italian campaign of 1859. Fluent in Spanish and Arabic. Brought North African troops to Mexico. Distrusted Miguel Miramón and the Conservatives and opposed the objectives of the Catholic hierarchy. Court-martialled in 1873, as a result of the surrender of Metz to the Prussians in the Franco-Prussian War (1870–71). Escaped from prison in 1874 and died in Madrid.

Benítez, Justo (1839–1900) Liberal politician and close associate of Porfirio Díaz. Born in Ejutla (Oaxaca). Educated at the Oaxaca Institute and took his law degree in 1857. Opponent of the later Juárez and supporter of Díaz in the Rebellions of La Noria (1871) and Tuxtepec (1876). Minister of Finance, 29 November 1876 – 14 February 1877. Broke with Díaz over the presidential succession in 1880.

Bravo, Nicolas (1786–1854) Insurgent commander. Born in Chilpancingo (Guerrero). Part of a leading creole family which rallied to Morelos in 1811. Supported the Plan of Iguala. Member of the Supreme Executive Power after the fall of the First Empire in March 1823. Vice-President from 1825 and head of the Scottish Rite masons. Became a bitter opponent of Guerrero after 1827. Interim-President in 1824.

Bulnes, Francisco (1847–1924) Qualified engineer but more known as a political journalist and historical commentator. Born in Mexico City. Attacked the reputation of Juárez in 1904–05 (see Bibliographical Essay).

Bustamante, Anastasio (1780–1853) Royalist commander and Conservative politician. Born in Jiquilpan (Michoacán) of Spanish parentage. Studied medicine in Mexico City with Valentín Gómez Farías, but preferred a military career, which effectively began in the Royalist Army under General Félix Calleja in 1810. Rallied to the Plan of Iguala in 1821. Vice-President in 1829 but rebelled against Guerrero in the Plan of Jalapa. Acting Executive, 1 January 1830 – 14 August 1832, close collaborator of Alamán. In exile in Europe 1833–34. Fought in the Texas War. President, 19 April 1837 – 22 September 1841. Second exile in Europe 1841–44. President of Congress in 1846.

Bustamante, Carlos María (1774–1848) Insurgent propagandist, historian and political figure. Born in Oaxaca, educated in Oaxaca and Mexico City. In 1805 co-founder of *Diario de México.* Joined Morelos's insurgent forces in the Pacific zone in 1812 and edited *El Correo del Sur* in insurgent-held Oaxaca. Represented the province of Mexico in the Congress of Chilpancingo in 1813. Requested amnesty, 8 March 1817. Royalist prisoner until 1821. Deputy in First and Second Constitutent Congresses, 1822–23 and 1823–24, but opposed federalism. One of the five members of the *Supremo Poder Conservador,* 21 November 1837–41.

Comonfort, Ignacio (1812–63) Born in Puebla, son of a sub-lieutenant of the Izúcar Batallion in the Royalist Army. Entered the army as an ensign in 1822; captain in the Puebla National Guard; Prefect of Tlapa, 1838; Deputy for Puebla in the Constituent Congress of 1841–42. Author of the Plan of Acapulco which modified the Plan of Ayutla. President, 8 December 1855–21 January 1858. To exile in USA, disgraced by the presidential *coup d'état* of Tacubaya, 17 December 1857. Minister of War under Juárez, 2 September – 13 November 1863, until killed by bandits in an ambush near Celaya (Guanajuato).

Degollado, Santos (1811–61) Liberal commander. Born in Guanajuato. Brought up by a cleric in Michoacán and worked for twenty years in the Cathedral of Morelia. Federalist in 1836. Political career began when elected to Michoacán Congress in 1845. Close associate of Melchor Ocampo, whom he replaced as Governor, 27 March – 6 July 1848. Rallied to the Revolution of Ayutla. Governor and Military Commander of Jalisco under Comonfort. From late 1859, advocated a truce with the Conservatives in the civil war of the Reform. Opposed by Juárez, who removed him from office. Killed on campaign against Conservative guerrillas on 15 June 1861.

Díaz, Félix (1833–71) Ill-fated younger brother of Porfirio Díaz. Governor of Oaxaca 1867–71.

Díaz, Porfirio (1830–1915) Re-elected President seven times, until forced to resign on 25 May 1911 by the Mexican Revolution. Born in Oaxaca of mixed Hispanic and Mixtec descent. Popular and successful Liberal commander in the civil war of the Reform and above all during the Intervention. Federal deputy in 1861 and supporter of Juárez. Usually associated with the radical wing of Liberalism until 1880, and principal opponent of Juárez, 1867–72.

Doblado, Manuel (1818–65) Liberal politician (moderate). Born in San Pedro Piedragorda (Guanajuato). Professor of Geography and Public Law in the Guanajuato State College in 1844. Deputy in the Querétaro Congress during the war with the USA in 1847, and opposed the peace treaty. Supported the Plan of Ayutla in 1854. Juárez's Minister of Foreign Relations, 11 December 1861 – 5 April 1862, 12 April – 13 August 1862, 2–7 September 1863; and Minister of the Interior, 10 December 1861 – 6 April 1862, 13 April – 13 August 1862, 22 August – 12 September 1863. Governor and Military Commander in Jalisco, November 1862. Escorted Juárez from Saltillo to Monterrey in April 1864. Retired to New York on health grounds.

Dublán, Manuel (1830–91) Moderate Liberal. Born in Oaxaca. Educated at the Oaxaca Institute, the son of a wealthy Frenchman and a Oaxacan. Deputy in the Oaxaca Congress in 1851. Law degree in 1852, Magistrate of the State Supreme Court. Secretary to the state governor in 1858. Accompanied Juárez to Veracruz, and supported in the Congress of 1861. Magistrate of the federal Supreme Court. Broke with Juárez in November 1865 and rallied to the empire. After rehabilitation, became a deputy in the federal Congress during the Restored Republic. Supported Díaz after 1876. Minister of Finance, 1 December 1884 – 31 May 1891.

Dubois de Saligny, Alphonse (1812–88) French Minister in Mexico from 1 April 1860 until recalled in disgrace by Napoleon III at the end of 1863. Promoted the Intervention.

Gómez Farías, Valentín (1781–1858) Liberal leader in the 1830s and 1840s. Born in Guadalajara. Practised medicine from 1807 and entered politics in Aguascalientes as city councillor and deputy to the Spanish Cortes. Deputy in the First Mexican Constituent Congress, 1822–23; Minister of Foreign Relations, 2 February – 31 March 1833; Vice-President, 3 June

1833 – 24 April 1834, 26 December 1846 – 21 March 1847. Close associate of José María Luis Mora. Favoured radical social and political reforms. In exile 1834–38, 1840–45. Opposed the peace treaty of 1848. Briefly returned to prominence with the Revolution of Ayutla. Deputy for Jalisco in the Constituent Congress of 1856–67.

Guerrero, Vicente (1783–1831) Insurgent commander. Born in Tixtla (Guerrero). Joined Morelos in 1810 and played the leading role in sustaining insurgency in the south after 1815. Came to a tactical accord with Colonel Agustín de Iturbide, Royalist commander in the south, on the issue of Independence, and collaborated in the implementation of the Plan of Iguala, 24 February 1821, for that purpose. Breach with Nicolas Bravo in 1828 led to the latter's possible collaboration in the betrayal of Guerrero in 1830–31. President 1 April – 16 December 1829. Judicial murder, 14 February 1831.

Guzmán, León (1821–84) Radical Liberal. Born in Tenango del Valle (Mexico). Jurist. Rallied to the Revolution of Ayutla, and sat in the Constituent Congress of 1856–57. Minister of the Interior, 10 May – 17 June 1861; Foreign Relations, 17 May – 17 June 1861; Interim-Governor of Guanajuato 10 February – 17 September 1867. Removed by Juárez for opposing the *convocatoria.*

Hidalgo y Costilla, Miguel (1753–1811) Initial insurgent leader, parish priest of Dolores (Guanajuato) from 1803. Born near Pénjamo (Guanajuato). Taught at San Nicolás Obispo College, Valladolid (now Morelia) (Michoacán), 1776–92. Executed 30 July 1811.

Iglesias, José María (1823–91) Moderate Liberal. Born in Mexico City. Law degree 1845. Mexico City councillor in 1846. Opposed the peace treaty of 1848. Chief editor of *El Siglo XIX* in the early 1850s. Worked in the Ministry of Finance, 1855–57. As Minister of Justice, issued the law of 11 April 1857 on parish dues. Minister of Finance, May – 16 September 1857; magistrate of the Supreme Court until the coup of December 1857; senior official in the Ministry of Finance from January 1861. Accompanied Juárez into the interior in 1863. Minister of Justice, 11 September 1863 – 21 July 1867 and 22 July 1869 – 10 March

1871; Minister of Finance, 10 January 1864 – 16 January 1868; federal deputy and magistrate of the Supreme Court in 1868, then Minister of the Interior 18 September 1868 – 28 October 1869; President of the Supreme Court under Sebastián Lerdo. Opposed Lerdo's re-election in 1876 and established his own 'legal' government in Salamanca (Guanajauato) 28 October 1876 – 17 January 1877 with the support of the Governors of Guanajuato, Querétaro, San Luis Potosí, Aguascalientes, and Jalisco. In exile in the USA until October 1877.

Iturbide, Agustín de (1773–1824) Royalist commander. Born in Valladolid (Michoacán). Formed the Plan of Iguala with Guerrero. Led the 'Army of the Three Guarantees' into Mexico City, 27 September 1821. First Emperor of Mexico 20 May 1822 – 20 March 1823. Executed upon return from exile, 19 July 1824.

Lacunza, José María (1809–69) Poet, lawyer, Imperialist politician. Born in Mexico City. Minister of Foreign Relations, 10 May 1848 – 15 January 1851; Minister of Finance, 11 May – 26 July 1866; President of the Council of Ministers, 13 June 1864 – 6 October 1866. Went into exile in Cuba after 1867.

Lafragua, José María (1813–75) Moderate Liberal politician and writer. Born in Puebla and educated at the Caroline College. Qualified in law in 1835 and became a Puebla deputy in Mexico City in 1837. Minister of the Interior under Comonfort, 13 December 1855 – 31 January 1857, and author of the *Estatuto Orgánico Provisional* of 1856. Mexican diplomatic representative in Madrid, 1857–60. First director of the National Library and principal author of the Civil and Penal Codes.

Lerdo de Tejada, Miguel (1812–61) Radical Liberal. Born in Veracruz. City councillor in Mexico City from 1849. Took charge of the Ministry of Development 15 August – 11 December 1855. Minister of Finance, 20 May 1856 – 3 January 1757. Author of the *Ley Lerdo* of 26 June 1856. Took refuge in the US Legation in Mexico City after the coup of December 1857, until he joined Juárez in Veracruz. Finance Minister, 18 May 1858 – 16 July 1859, 18 December 1859 – 31 May 1860.

Lerdo de Tejada, Sebastián (1823–89) Moderate Liberal. Born in Jalapa. Studied at the Palafox Seminary in Puebla 1836–41 and took minor orders, but abandoned an ecclesiastical career in favour of jurisprudence, in which he graduated in 1851. Rector of the College of San Ildefonso, Mexico City, 1852–63. Minister of Foreign Relations, 15 June – 16 September 1857. Out of politics from September 1857. Deputy in the Congress of 1861–63. Accompanied Juárez and Iglesias in internal exile, 1863–67, as Minister of Justice, Relations, and the Interior. Author of the decrees of 8 November 1865 and the *convocatoria* of 14 August 1867. Minister of External Relations, 21 July 1867 – 10 June 1868, 10 September 1867 – 15 July 1871; Minister of the Interior, 21 July 1867 – 24 March 1868; Interim-President from 12 July 1872; Constitutional President, 1 December 1872 – 20 November 1876. In exile in the USA after Díaz's seizure of power.

Mariscal, Ignacio (1829–1910) Liberal politician. Born in Oaxaca. Studied in the Conciliar Seminary in Oaxaca and then took a law degree in Mexico City in 1849. Returned to Oaxaca to become Financial Attorney in the Juárez government. Opponent of Santa Anna. Deputy in the Constituent Congress, 1856–57. With Juárez in Veracruz, 1858–60. Legal Assessor of the federal government in 1861: supervised the enforcement of the laws of disamortization. Federal deputy in 1862; magistrate of the Supreme Court in 1863. In Washington as First Secretary and Legal Counsellor to the Mexican Legation during the Intervention. Federal deputy and magistrate of the Supreme Court in 1867; Minister of Justice, 16 June 1868 – 20 July 1869 and 20 December 1879 – 30 November 1880; Minister of Foreign Relations, 1 December 1880 – 1 December 1883 and 19 January 1885 – 16 April 1910.

Márquez, Leonardo (1820–1913) Controversial conservative General, who long outlived Miramón and Mejía. Born in Mexico City, took part in the Texas War (1836) and in the War against the United States (1846–47). Opposed the Revolution of Ayutla and defended Puebla, for which he was exiled. In 1858 became Conservative *jefe político* of Acámbaro (Guanajuato) and Governor-Military Commander of Jalisco in 1859. Won the Battle of Tacubaya, 11 April 1859, at the time of Miramón's first siege of Veracruz. Blamed for the execution of captured Liberals and known as the 'Tiger of Tacubaya'; blamed also for the murders of Melchor Ocampo and Leandro Valle in 1861. At the end of the Civil War of the Reform, took refuge in the Sierra Gorda of Querétaro, still recognizing Zuloaga as President. In May 1862, joined French Intervention forces under Lorencez in Veracruz, though he had not been party to initial French designs. Maximilian virtually exiled him to Constantinople in 1864, but returned in 1866 to take part in the attempt to save the Empire. At Querétaro with Maximilian, who commissioned him late in March 1867 to break out of the siege and bring back reinforcements. Instead, attempted to relieve Puebla, but was defeated and returned to Mexico City, where he was trapped by the Liberal victory. In disguise there until his escape to Havana later in the year. In exile in Cuba until granted permission to return to Mexico in 1895, but his unpopularity obliged him to return to Havana, where he died.

Maximilian (1832–67) Emperor of Mexico (1864–67), Archduke Ferdinand Maximilian of Habsburg. Born in Schonbrunn (Vienna), brother of the Emperor Francis Joseph (1848–1916). Widely travelled, including to Brazil, by the end of 1859. Became Governor of Austrian Lombardy-Venetia, 1857–59. In 1857 married Charlotte (Carlota), daughter of Leopold I of the Belgians, who had earlier declined an offer of the Mexican throne. Built Miramar on the Gulf of Trieste, where he accepted the offer of the Mexican crown on 10 April 1864, a proposal first mooted in 1861. Agreed to the Treaty of Miramar with Napoleon III on 12 March 1864. Arrived in Mexico City on 12 June 1864, and until November 1866 attempted to form a moderate liberal regime which at the same time provided for the Catholic establishment, though with the Church effectively under imperial control and the Reform Laws largely maintained intact. Executed with Miramón and Mejía at Querétaro on 19 June 1867. Carlota was childless; Maximilian had several illegitimate children, including in Mexico.

Mejía, Ignacio (1814–1906) Moderate Liberal. Born in Zimatlán (Oaxaca). Governor of Oaxaca 1852–53. Intimate associate of Juárez. Minister of War, 30 November 1865 – 30

August 1876. Went into exile until 1884 after Diaz's seizure of power. Property-owner and businessman in Oaxaca.

Mejía, Tomás (1820–1867) Conservative General of Otomí origin. Born in Pinal de Amoles (Querétaro), his military career began in the local militia as an ensign in 1841. His father was Prefect of Jalpan (Que) under the centralist regime. Advanced to the rank of squadron commander by 1849 and to Lieutenant-Colonel in 1854. Became famous for his terrifying cavalry charges, which possibly he learned from early experience in the Apache wars. Fought against the US invaders in Neuvo León and Coahuila in 1846–47. Military Commander in the Sierra Gorda of Querétaro from September 1848, entrusted with the pacification of the rebellion led by Eleuterio Quiroz, which he completed by September 1849, for which he was promoted two months later to Lieutenant-Colonel; Prefect of Jalpan from 1853; Brigade General 1854. Jointly proclaimed the Plan of Sierra Gorda on 2 December 1855 in opposition to the Liberal regime, in defence of religion, independence, and the 1824 Constitution. Always defended the idea of a Catholic Mexico and saw the military struggle against the Liberals as a crusade. Fought at Salamanca and Ahualulco in the Civil War of the Reform. Recognized and fought for the Empire in 1864, but was captured and executed at Querétaro on 19 June 1867 with Miramón and Maximilian.

Miramón, Miguel (1831–1867) Conservative General and President. Born in Mexico City, combined military skill with political miscalculation. As a cadet, fought US invasion forces at Chapultepec in 1847; Captain 1853; opposed the Revolution of Ayutla; fought in Puebla against the Comonfort Administration in 1856. Principal Conservative commander in Civil War of the Reform, but two attempts to take Veracruz failed. President from 15 April – 24 December 1860. Exile in Cuba and then Europe. Not a party to French Intervention plans, finally returned to Mexico City on 28 July 1863, but experienced deteriorating relations with Bazaine. Disliked by Maximilian, who sent him to Berlin in November 1864, allegedly to study artillery techniques. Returned two years later, in the belief that he could save the Empire. Nearly captured Juárez in Zacatecas in January 1867. Executed with Maximilian and Mejía and Querétaro on 19 June 1867.

Mora, Dr José María Luis (1794–1850) Early Liberal ideologist. Born in Chunacuero (Guanajuato). Family ruined by the Insurgency. Deputy in the State of Mexico Congress in 1823. Law degree in 1827. Leading member of the Scottish Rite Lodge. Edited the moderate Liberal, *El Observador.* Close collaborator of Gómez Farías in 1833–34. In exile in Paris after April 1834, where he published his principal works.

Morelos y Pavón, José María (1765–1815) Successor to Hidalgo as principal commander in the Insurgency. Born in Valladolid. Ordained 1799. Parish priest of Carácuaro in 1810. Executed 22 December 1815.

Ocampo, Melchor (1814–61) Radical Liberal, strongly anticlerical. Born in Michoacán, the son of hacienda workers. Patronized by the hacienda-owner's wife, but squandered his inheritance, and went to Europe in 1840. From early legal studies after 1831, he went into politics on his return. State deputy. Governor of Michoacán, September 1846 – March 1848, June 1852 – January 1853. Senator and Minister of Finance under President Mariano Arista. Conflict with the clergy over parish dues. Initiated education reforms. Forced into exile by Santa Anna; with Juárez in New Orleans. Minister of Foreign Relations for 15 days under Álvarez, and again under Juárez, 21 January 1858 – 15 August 1859, 1 December 1859 – 22 January 1860, 27 September 1860 – 17 January 1861; Minister of War, 19 January – 15 March 1858; Minister of the Interior, 21 January – 2 February 1858, 21 May 1858 – 17 July 1859. Promoter of the Reform Laws concerning civil matrimony and separation of Church and State. Killed by Conservative guerrillas on 3 June 1861.

Payno, Manuel (1810–94) Liberal politician (moderate) and writer. Born in Mexico City. Minister of Finance, 4 July 1850 – 13 January 1851, 14 December 1855 – 5 May 1856. Contributed to Comonfort's *coup d'état* of 17 December 1857. Several times federal deputy after 1867. Senator, 1882 and 1892. Diplomatic positions in Spain, 1886–92, where he wrote *Los Bandidos de Río Frío* (1888–91).

Poinsett, Joel Roberts (1779–1851) US politician and diplomat. Born in Charleston (South Carolina). President James Madison's Special Agent in Chile, 1811–15; President James Monroe's agent in Mexico in 1822 to report on Iturbide's empire. President John Quincy Adams appointed him US Envoy Extraordinary and Minister Plenipotentiary in Mexico, 1825. Opposed British influence, involved in politics, and assisted in the foundation of the *yorkino* masonic lodge. Intimate of Zavala and Guerrero. Asked to leave Mexico in July 1829. Supported Texas secession and then annexation to the USA, 1836–37.

Prieto, Guillermo (1818–97) Liberal politician, poet, dramatist and journalist. Born in Mexico City. Protégé of Andrés Quintana Roo (Independence leader and Liberal minister, 1833–34). Minister of Finance, 14 September 1852 – 5 January 1853, 6 October – 6 December 1855, 19 January – 17 May 1858, 16 July – 18 December 1859, 20 January – 5 April 1861. Supported the Plan of Ayutla. Deputy in the Constitutent Congress, 1856–57. Out of government from April 1861 until November 1876. Minister of the Interior, 1 November 1876 – January 1877.

Prim y Prats, Juan (1814–70) Conde de Reus (1844), Spanish general and Liberal politician. Captain General of Puerto Rico in 1844. Fought in North Africa in 1860. Led the Spanish expeditionary force to Mexico, which landed in Veracruz on 9 January 1862, but withdrew after the Orizaba meeting with Doblado.

Ramírez, Ignacio (1818–79) Liberal politician (radical) and journalist (pseudonym 'El Nigromante'). Born in San Miguel Allende (Guanajuato), studied law in Mexico City and taught at the Toluca Literary Institute. Deputy in the Constituent Congress, 1856–57. Supported the candidacy of Miguel Lerdo in 1861. Juárez's Minister of Justice, 21 January – 9 May 1861 and Minister of Development, 18 March – 3 April 1861. Opposed Juárez's re-election in 1867. Magistrate of the Supreme Court of Justice after 1867. Rejected the Christian idea of the Creation. Minister of Justice, 29 November 1876 – 7 May 1877.

Santa Anna, General Antonio López de (1794–1876) Born

in Jalapa (Veracruz), entered the Royalist army as a cadet in 1810 and fought against the insurgents until 1821, when he adhered to Iturbide's Plan of Iguala. Rose against Iturbide on 2 December 1822 and ultimately contributed to the downfall of the First Empire in March 1823. Pronounced in favour of federalism in June 1823, while Military Commander in San Luis Potosí. Transferred to Military Commander of Yucatán, 1824–25. Pronounced in favour of the candidature of Guerrero in 1828. Repulsed the Spanish invasion force of 1829; contributed to the removal of Bustamante in 1832 and to the restoration of Gómez Pedraza in 1833. Elected President of the Republic in March 1833, but left the administration to Vice-President Gómez Farias. After the latter's removal in April 1834, Santa Anna was associated with centralism until 1846. Presidency interrupted by the Texas War of 1836 and his capture at San Jacinto. Returned to become President, 1841–44; recalled after exile to take command of the army in the War with the USA 1846–47; in exile 1847–53, but restored following a military rebellion. Last regime 1853–55. Overthrown definitively in August 1855, with the triumph of the Revolution of Ayutla. Schemed to return to Mexico and to power on several occasions thereafter, including during the Empire. Died in Mexico City in June 1876.

Vallarta, Ignacio (1830–93) Radical Liberal politician who also engaged in journalistic and literary work. Born in Guadalajara. Law degree from University of Guadalajara. Private secretary to Santos Degollado, State Governor, in 1855; deputy for Jalisco in the Constituent Congress, 1856–57. Secretary to Pedro Ogazón, State Governor, in 1858. In the USA during the French Intervention, but joined Juárez in Zacatecas in 1867. Federal deputy for Jalisco in 1868. Minister of the Interior, 24 March – 18 September 1868; governor of Jalisco, 1871–75 (promoted education); Minister of Foreign Relations, 29 November 1876 – 20 June 1878 (negotiated US recognition of the Díaz regime). Defender of the 1857 Constitution; President of the Supreme Court until 1882.

Zamacona y Murphy, Manuel María (1826–1904) Liberal politician (radical) and journalist. Born in Puebla. Studied at the Palafox Seminary; practised law. Directed *El Siglo XIX* (founded in 1852) in Mexico City. Juárez's Minister of Foreign

Relations, 13 July – 26 November 1861, when resigned after congressional rejection of the Wyke–Zamacona Treaty. Leading figure in the opposition to Juárez later in the 1860s. Aspired to succeed Díaz in 1892.

Zarco, Francisco (1829–69) Liberal politician (radical) and journalist. Born in Durango. Edited *El Democrata* in 1850 and *La Ilustracion Mexicana,* 1851–55. Directed *El Siglo XIX* from 1855. Represented Durango in the Constitutent Congress (1856–57). Under arrest in 1858 and 1860 in Mexico City under the Conservative regime. Juárez's Minister of Foreign Relations, 20 January – 11 May 1861 and Minister of the Interior, 6 April – 10 May 1861. Federal deputy from 1867.

Zavala, Lorenzo de (1788–1836) Liberal politician (radical). Born in Conkal (Yucatán). Studied at the Conciliar Seminary of San Ildefonso (Mérida) until 1807. Protagonist of Mexican Independence and founder of the first newspaper in Yucatán. Confined in San Juan de Ulua fortress prison, 1814–17. Deputy in the Spanish Cortes, 1820–22. Deputy in the First Mexican Constituent Congress 1822. Strongly federalist. Signatory of the Constitution of 1824. Senator for Yucatán from 1825. Leading member of the *yorkino* rite masonic lodge and instigator of the 'Revolution of the Acordada' in December 1828, which resulted in Guerrero's capture of power. Minister of Finance, 1829 and 1833–34. Compromised by participation in the secession of Texas in 1836.

Zuloaga, Félix María (1813–98) Conservative President and army officer. Born in Álamos (Sonora). Grew up in Chihuahua and joined the State Civic Militia in 1834. Joined the Permanent Army as an engineer in 1838. Opposed the Plan of Ayutla, but won over by Comonfort in 1855. Brigade Commander in Mexico City in 1857 and military arm behind Comonfort's *coup d'état* of 17 December. Conservative Interim President, 22 January 1858 – 24 January 1859, when replaced by Miramón. Remained in Cuba during the Intervention.

MAPS

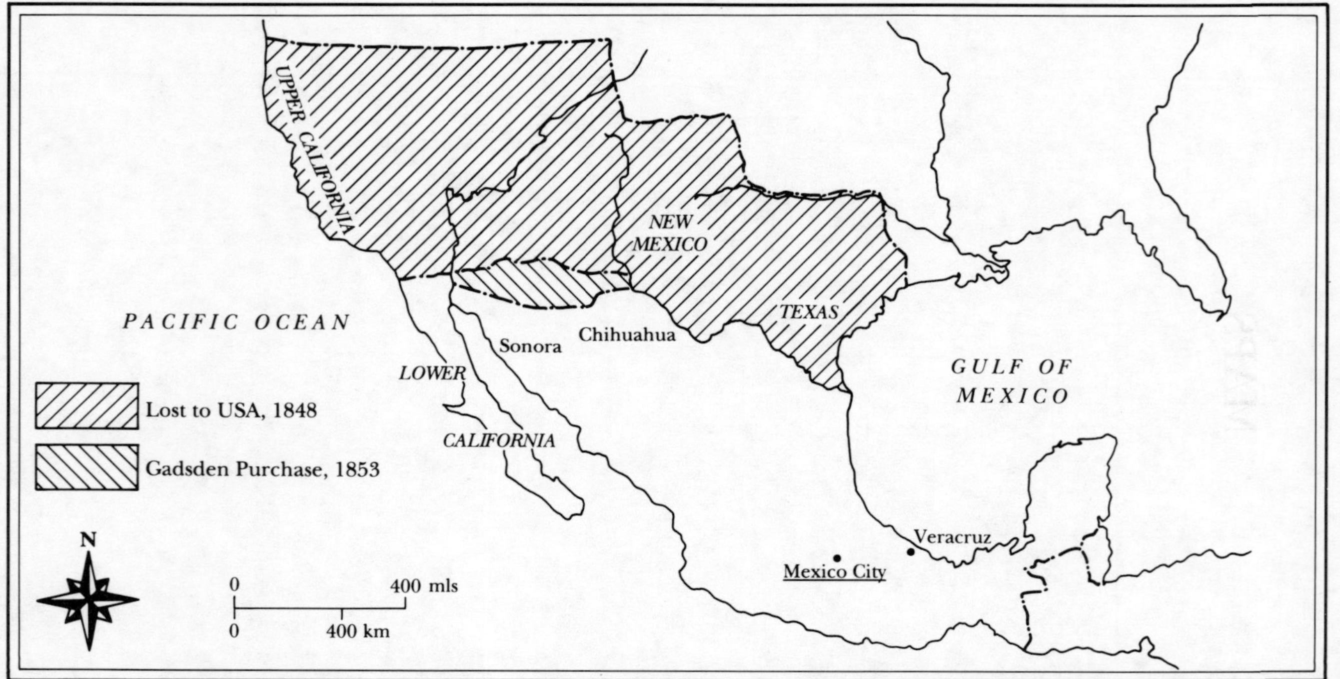

1. Mexico, 1821-53

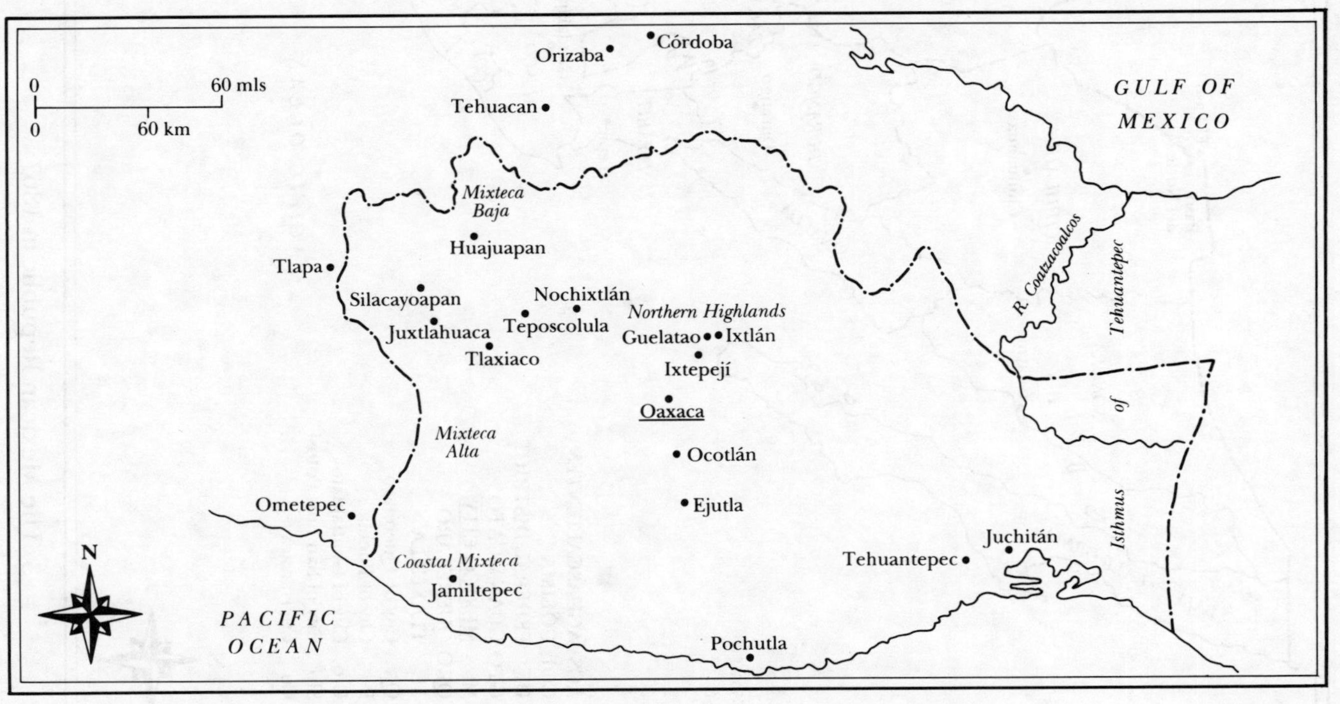

2. The State of Oaxaca, 1857

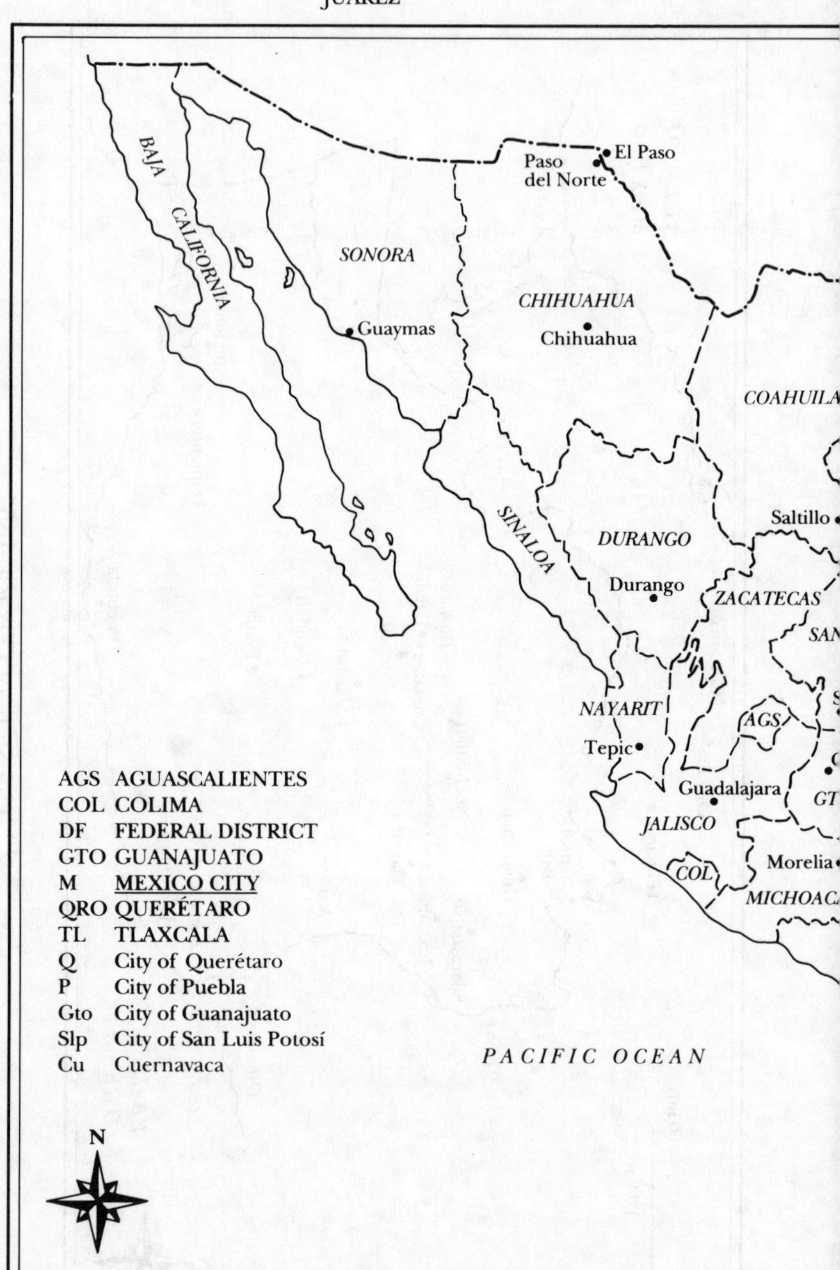

3. The Mexican Republic in 1867

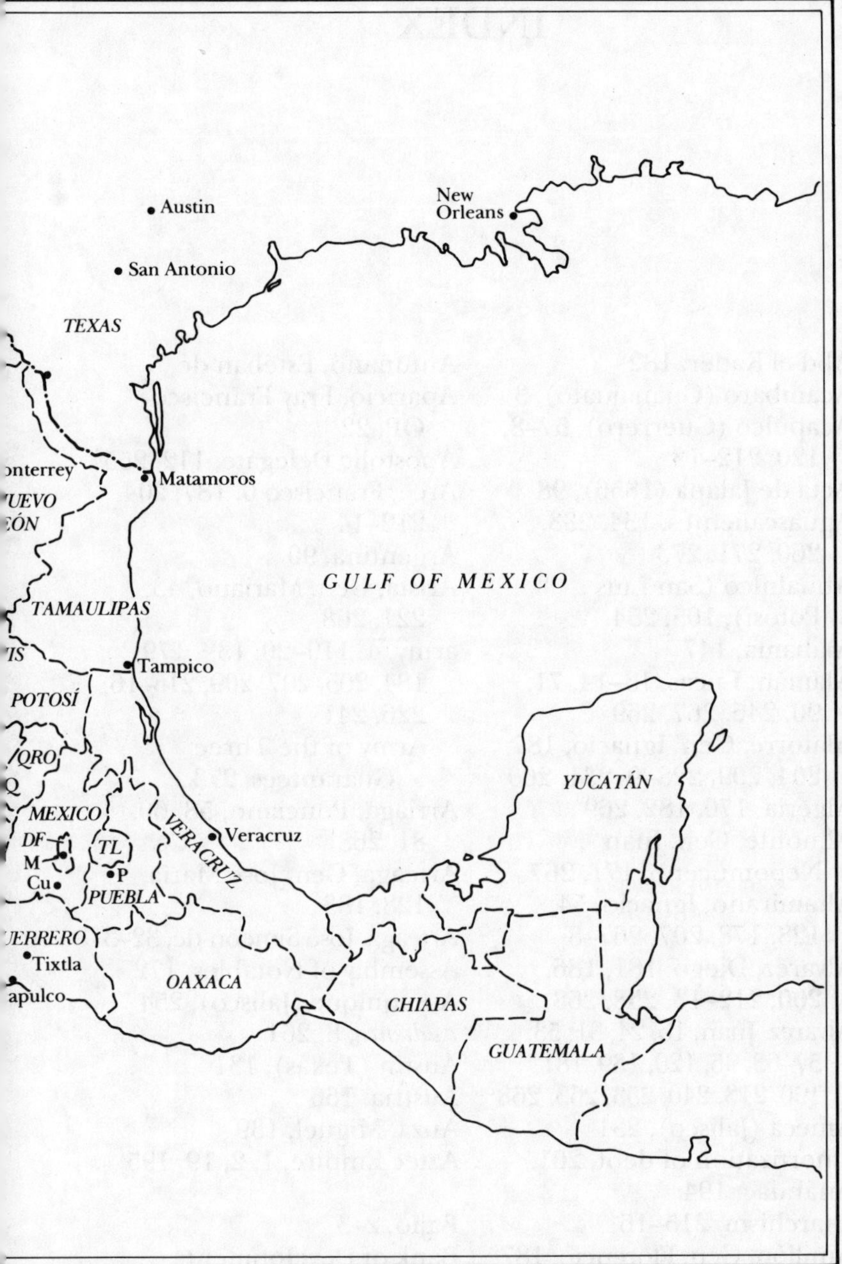
Austin
New Orleans
San Antonio
TEXAS
onterrey
Matamoros
UEVO
EÓN
GULF OF MEXICO
TAMAULIPAS
IS
Tampico
POTOSÍ
/QRO
Q
YUCATÁN
MEXICO
VERACRUZ
Veracruz
DF
M
TL
P
Cu
PUEBLA
UERRERO
Tixtla
OAXACA
apulco
CHIAPAS
GUATEMALA

INDEX

Abd-el-Kader, 182
Acámbaro (Guanajuato), 3
Acapulco (Guerrero), 57–8, 120, 212–13
Acta de Jalapa (1856), 98
Aguascalientes, 134, 233, 260, 271, 273
Ahualulco (San Luis Potosí), 105, 254
Alabama, 147
Alamán, Lucas, 13–14, 71, 90, 246, 267, 269
Alatorre, Gen. Ignacio, 187, 204, 209, 228–9, 231, 260
Algeria, 170, 182, 269
Almonte, Gen. Juan Nepomuceno, 171, 267
Altamirano, Ignacio, 54, 128, 178, 207, 267–8
Álvarez, Diego, 181, 186, 200, 212–13, 258, 268
Álvarez, Juan, 16, 24, 31, 53, 57–63, 96, 120, 139, 181, 190, 213, 240, 253, 263, 268
Ameca (Jalisco), 231
amortization of debt, 261
Anáhuac, 194
anarchism, 215–16
Antillón, Gen. Florencio, 187
Anton Lizardo Incident, 152
Antuñano, Estéban de, 5
Aparicio, Fray Francisco OP, 22
Apostolic Delegate, 112, 255
Arce, Francisco 0, 187, 204, 212–14
Argentina, 90
Arista, Gen. Mariano, 43, 221, 268
army, 4, 119–20, 139, 179, 184, 205, 207, 209, 215–16, 226, 241
  Army of the Three Guarantees, 273
Arriaga, Ponciano, 58, 60, 81, 268
Arteaga, Gen. José María, 128, 183
Arteaga, José Simeón de, 32–3
Assembly of Notables, 172
Atenquique (Jalisco), 254
audienca, 8, 261
Austin (Texas), 131
Austria, 166
Auza, Miguel, 139
Aztec Empire, 1, 2, 19, 195

Bajío, 2–3
Bank of Development (*Banco de Avío*), 267

Barron, Eustace, 217
Bases Orgánicas (1843), 15, 59, 261
Baz, Gustavo, 244
Baz, Juan José, 103, 194, 208, 268
Bazaine, Marshal François Achille, 169–86, 257–8, 268–9
Benítez, Justo, 64, 208, 269
bienes nacionales (nationalized properties), 174, 261
Bismarck, Count Otto von, xii, 166
Bolaños (Jalisco), 3
Bolívar, Simón, 15
Bolivia, 16
Bonilla, Gen. Juan Crisóstomo, 227–8
borlados, 54, 230, 261
Bourbon reforms, 8, 18
Bourbons, 11–12
Bravo, Nicolás, 13, 14, 269
Brazilian Empire, 191
Brownsville (Texas), 58, 156
Buchanan, James, 147, 149–50, 254
Buenos Aires, 168
Bulnes, Francisco, 25, 63–4, 75, 81, 83, 152, 244–6, 269
Bustamante, Gen. Anastasio, 14, 16, 23, 25, 27, 252, 269
Bustamante, Carlos María de, 27, 270

cacicazgo, 200, 261
caciques, 6, 54, 57–8, 74, 81, 228, 261, 268
caciquismo, 7, 25, 81, 262
Cajiga, Ramón, 55
Calderón, Estéban, 36
California,
  Alta (Upper), 146, 160
  Baja (Lower), 105, 147, 150–1, 155, 161
Calleja, Gen. Félix María, 268
Calles, Plutarco Elías, 220
Calpulalpan (Tlaxcala), 124
Canada, 239
Canalizo, Gen. Valentín, 29
Cañas, Lic. Tiburcio, 23–4, 27
capitation tax, 41
Capulalpan (Oaxaca), 22
Cárdenas, Gen. Lázaro, 90
Carlist War (1833–40), 182
Carranza, Jesús, 180
Carranza, Venustiano, 196 n.21
Cartas, Benigno, 229
Carvajal, Bernardino, 36, 101
Casavantes, J.J., 137
Cass, Lewis, 147
Castelar, Emilio, 175
Castellanos, Gen. José María, 34, 38–9, 43
Castillo, Florencio del, 25–6
Castillo, Velasco, José María, 81
Castro, Miguel, 21, 36, 45, 51, 54, 77, 118
  and Rebellion of La Noria, 222–30, 265
Catholic Church, 14, 25, 57, 60, 64, 88, 103
  and Empire, 173
  and French Intervention, 172
  and Juárez, 86–113
  and Reform Laws, 106–10, 265

and Restored Republic, 205–6
Catholicism, 3, 25, 80, 88–9
Cedillo, Saturnino, 21
Celaya (Guanajuato), 270
Central America, 172
centralism, 29, 31, 57, 59, 73, 237
Centralist Republic, 32, 253
Céspedes, Carlos Manuel, 53
Chacalapa, 230
Chalco, 214–15, 259
Charles V, Emperor, 194
Chávez López, Julio, 214–15, 259
Chiapas, 35, 124
Chihuahua, 5, 132–8, 140–1, 147, 149, 155, 157, 176, 178, 180, 184, 231, 247, 257
Chilapa (Guerrero), 41, 181, 213
Chile, 90
Chilpancingo (Guerrero), 269
  Congress of, 270
Chontal Indian group, 40
Churchwell, William, 150
citizenship, idea of, 37
civil marriage, 103, 108–9, 255
civil militia, 4, 37–8
Civil Registry, 98, 109, 255
Civil War (USA), 152–8, 170–1
Civil War of the Reform, *see* Reform Movement
Coahuila, 2, 6, 58, 64, 103, 119, 122, 130–2, 158, 176, 178, 180, 183, 231, 255, 257
Colima, 117, 122
Colombia, 151, 238
Comonfort, Gen. Ignacio, 40, 54, 57–64, 67, 75–6, 82–3, 90, 97, 101, 104, 117, 121, 125, 127, 132–3, 147–8, 199, 200, 202, 240, 246, 253–4, 270
  coup d'état of 1857, 83, 102
  Estatuto Orgánico Provisional (1856), 64
Confederacy, 131–3, 135, 153–9, 161, 170, 239
Congress, Mexican Federal, 53, 64, 74, 101, 104, 119, 125–30, 133, 175, 198, 207, 210, 213–14, 241, 256, 259
  in Restored Republic, 198–234
Conservative Party, 12, 16, 21, 57, 59, 68, 82, 97, 102, 104–5, 108, 110, 117, 121–2, 134, 152, 159, 267, 270
  attitude to USA, 149
  and French Intervention, 168, 170–95
  and Lozada, 199, 217
Constituent Congress,
  1822–23, 269–70
  1823–24, 269
  1856–57, 64, 71–5, 79–84, 253, 272
Constitution,
  1787 (USA), 71–2, 202
  1791 (France), 36, 74
  1812 (Spain), 10, 36, 73–4, 83, 87, 252, 263, 266
  1824 (Mexico), 3–4, 36, 63, 65, 74–5, 78, 83, 87, 93, 160, 220, 252, 265–6
  1857 (Mexico), 7, 55, 71–84, 100–1, 116, 118,

125, 139, 160, 176–7, 191, 240, 263, 266
issue of re-election, 220
reform of 1857 Constitution, 232–3
and Restored Republic, 199–234
1917 (Mexico), 7, 83, 220
constitutionalism, 9–12, 221
Convention of London, 154, 256
convocatoria (1867), 202–3, 210, 229, 259, 262, 272
Corona, Gen. Ramón, 139, 181, 186–7, 205, 217–18, 227, 258
corporate properties, 214
Imperial Decree (1856), 183, 258
see also, disamortization; Lerdo Law
Corpus Christi (Texas), 132
Cortés, Hernán, 40
cortes, 261
Cortes of Cádiz, 10–11, 13–14, 22, 25, 27, 71, 262, 271
Corwin, Thomas, 155
Cosijoeza, 34
Costa Chica, 57
Costa Rica, 25
Council of State, 173
counter-guerrilla force (French), 181
Cravioto, Gen. Rafael, 208–10
Creel, Ruben, 135
Crimean War, 160, 269
Cuauhtémoc, 242–3
Cuautla (Morelos), 31, 66
Cuba, 104, 146, 153, 273
Cubans, 51–3, 118, 250
Cuernavaca, 31, 41, 56, 66, 82, 186
Cuetzalan (Puebla), 209
Cuilapan (Oaxaca), 24
Davis, Jefferson, 132–3, 146, 155, 190
debt question, 123, 154–5, 167–8
Decrees of 8 November 1865, 138–41
Degollado, Santos, 59, 81, 119, 122–4, 134, 151, 256, 270
Dehesa, Teodoro, 230
Democratic Party (USA), 145, 149, 153
Díaz, Félix, 204, 210, 270
Governor of Oaxaca, 222–33, 260, 270
Díaz, Porfirio, 54–5, 58, 61, 73, 117, 126, 139–40, 181, 194, 243–4, 246, 251, 257–60, 263–4, 268, 270–1
in Rebellion of La Noria, 223–34
and Restored Republic, 201, 205, 207, 215–16
Díaz Ordaz, José María, 36, 76–7, 79
disamortization, 65, 67–8, 214–15, 217, 253, 262, *see also* Lerdo Law
Doblado, Manuel, 59, 62, 108, 117, 119, 122, 126–7, 133–4, 161, 179, 271
Dolores (Guanajuato), 272
Domínguez, Bishop José Agustín, 100
Dominican Republic, 168
Dominicans, 87, 93
Douay, Gen. Félix Charles, 217
Dublán, Manuel, 54, 64, 77, 96, 128, 179, 271

Dubois de Saligny, Alphonse, 168, 271
Dupin, Col, 181
Durango, 134, 137, 180, 226–7, 257–8, 260
dye trades (Oaxaca), 19, 78

Echeverría Álvarez, Luis, 248
Ecuador, 16
Ejutla (Oaxaca), 269
El Correo del Sur (Oaxaca), 270
El Globo (Mexico City), 208
El Paso (Texas), 157
El Republicano (Mexico City), 63
El Siglo XIX (Mexico City), 53, 63, 75, 213, 229, 272
Empire,
  First Mexican, 273
  Second French, 175, 251
  Second Mexican, 171–95
Enlightened Despotism, 11–12
Enlightenment (Spanish), 13–14, 22, 71, 88
Escandón, Pedro, 5
  family, 30
Escobedo, Gen. Mariano, 131, 139–40, 180–1, 186
  Hill of the Bells (Cerro de las Campanas), 187
  siege of Querétaro, 188–95
  in Restored Republic, 204–5, 227, 231
Esperón, Estéban, 67
Esperón, José, 54–5, 67, 77
Estancia de las Vacas, 122, 255
Estatuto Orgánico Provisional (1856), 64
Eugénie, Empress, 169
exaltados, 64–5, 262
extraordinary powers, granted to Juárez, 215, 229, 233, 254, 256, 259–60

Favre, Jules, 178, 251
federalism, 5, 31–2, 118, 240, 252, 270
  First Federal Republic, 8, 30, 74, 252
  Second Federal Republic, 253
Ferdinand VII, 10
Fernández del Campo, Col. Luis, 29, 31, 40, 76–7
Fischer, Fr. Agustín SJ, 185
Foreign Legion (French), 173, 182, 184
Forey, Marshal Élie Frédérick, 171, 256, 269
Forsyth, John, 147–8
France, 167–95
Francis Joseph, Emperor, 188
Franco-Prussian War, 182, 269
  siege of Metz, 182, 269
freemasonry, 86
  masonic lodges, 14, 262, 266, 269
French Intervention, 6, 8, 54–5, 132–42, 157, 159, 161–2
  and Juárez, 166–95, 242, 245–6, 251, 256
French Revolution, 10, 13, 22, 49, 112
  Constitution of 1791, 36, 74
Frías y Soto, Hilarión, 161, 245–6

fueros, 262
fuero eclesiástico, 96–7, 263
fuero militar, 263

Gadsden, James, 147
Gadsden Purchase (also Mesilla Treaty) 150, 160
Galindo y Galindo, Miguel, 245–6
Garay, José, 41
García, Genaro, 245
García, Gen. Julio, 181
García, Gen. Rafael J., 204, 208–9
García de la Cadena, Gen. Trinidad, 215, 227
García Granados, Ricardo, 246
García Salinas, Francisco, 4
Garibaldi, Giuseppe, 89, 194
Garza, Archbishop Lázaro de la, 110, 112
Goicuría, Domingo de, 52–3
Gómez Farías, Benito, 119
Gómez Farías, Valentín, 14, 16, 22–3, 26, 32–3, 57, 60, 88, 99, 119, 167–8, 252, 271–2
Gómez Pedraza, Manuel, 22
González, Gen. Manuel, 220–1, 227
González Ortega, Jesús, 103, 117, 124–8, 134, 139, 159, 179, 201–2, 207, 216, 221, 227, 257
Gran Círculo de Obreros Mexicanos, 216, 259
Great Britain, 167–8
Gregory XVI, Pope, 91
Guadalajara (Jalisco), 2–3, 8, 15, 83, 103–4, 117, 119–20, 186, 217–18, 227, 254, 256, 258, 268
Guanajuato, 2–3, 20, 83, 117, 119, 186, 231, 256, 267, 271
Guatemala, Kingdom of, 8, 18
Guaymas (Sonora), 120, 151, 257
Guelatao (Oaxaca), 2, 20, 29, 234, 248, 252
Guergué, José Joaquín, 23, 28, 33, 40
Guerra, Gen. Donato, 227
Guerrero, Gen. Vicente, 13–14, 16, 22–5, 29, 56, 237, 243, 252, 269, 272
Guerrero, State of, 52, 181, 198, 200, 258, 263
in Restored Republic, 211–14, 259
guerrilla bands, 181–4
Gutiérrez Zamora, Manuel, 121–2, 126
Guzmán, Gordiano, 58
Guzmán, León, 55, 63, 72, 120, 203, 240, 272

haciendas, 263
Hacienda de La Concepción (Oaxaca), 67
Hacienda de La Noria (Oaxaca), 225, 227
Hacienda del Rosario (Oaxaca), 76
Hacienda de La Providencia (Guerrero), 57, 212
Haro y Tamariz, Antonio, 59, 97
Havana, 152, 168
Hermosillo (Sonora), 258
Hernández, Fidencio, 204, 222, 228–9

Hernández, José Santiago, 23
Herrera, Gen. José Joaquín (de), 31–2, 36, 38, 147, 221
Hidalgo y Costilla, Miguel, 25, 27, 52, 237, 243, 267, 272
Hidalgo, State of, 209, 215
Holy See, 89, 99, 102, 248
Hoorics, M., 190
Huajuapan (Oaxaca), 26, 30
Huasteca, 181
Huatulco (Oaxaca), 94
Huauchinango (Puebla), 208
Huerta, Epitacio, 103
Huerta, Gen. Victoriano, 21
Hugo, Victor, 194

Iglesias, José María, 161, 272–3
Iglesias Calderón, Fernando, 161, 246
India, 194
Indo-China, 170
Iturribarría, Manuel, 23, 36
Iturbide, Agustín de, 273
Ixtaltepec, 43
Ixtepejí, 19–20
Ixtlán, 20, 222, 228
Izúcar (Puebla), 41

Jacobinism, 10, 54, 90–1, 263
  French Jacobins, 109–10
Jalapa (Veracruz), 44
Jalisco, State of, 3, 7, 80, 102–3, 180, 204, 216, 271, 272
jefes políticos, 73–4, 136, 180, 194, 204, 222–3, 263
Jiménez, Albino, 229
Jiménez, Vicente, 181, 200, 204, 213, 263
jimenistas, 211–14, 259, 263
Jiquílpan (Michoacán), 269
Johnson, Andrew, 158
Joseph II, Emperor, 86
Juárez, Benito, xi–xiii, 9, 13
  attitude to European Powers, 166–95
  and Catholic Church, 86–113
  and Constitution of 1857, 71–84
  and Díaz brothers, 220–34
  historiography of, 244–51
  Juárez Law (*Ley Juárez*), 60–1, 64, 96–8, 100, 240, 253
  last years, 198–218, 220–34
  and Liberalism, 49–68
  provincial origins, 18–45
  Rebellion of La Noria, 222–3
  relations with Álvarez, 58
  relations with Lozada, 216–18
  state governor (1847–52), 5, 6, 34–45, 91–6, 253 (1856–57), 75–9, 100-1, 253
  and state governors, 116–42
  supposed *coup d'état,* 138–42
  and USA, 145–63
juarismo, 129, 180, 199, 213, 244, 263
juaristas, 5, 21, 173, 179, 182–3, 222–3, 226, 230, 263, 264
Juchitán (Oaxaca), 41–2, 79, 264

and Félix Díaz, 224, 229–31, 259
juchitecos, 42–3, 264

La Bandera Roja (Morelia), 103, 268
Labastida, Bishop Pelagio Antonio de, 97–9
Archbishop of Mexico, 171
Regent, 171
in Restored Republic, 206
labour movement, 216, 259
La Cruz (*Mexico City*), 114 n.22
Lacunza, José María, 187, 273
Lafragua, José María, 61, 63, 68, 81, 234, 273
Lafragua Law, 98
Lares, Teodosio, 173, 187
latifundio, 264
Sánchez Navarro properties, 176–7
Terrazas properties, 136, 177
La Victoria (Oaxaca), 175, 223
Lee, Gen. Robert E, 158
León, Col. Antonio de, 21, 23, 26, 29, 31, 253
León, Lic. José María, 30
lerdistas, 221–2, 225, 229, 231, 264
Lerdo de Tejada, Miguel, 52, 65, 67, 79, 89, 103–6, 121, 123, 126, 133–4, 150, 167, 241, 255, 273
Lerdo Law (*Ley Lerdo*), 65–8, 77, 98–100, 217, 253–4, 262, 273
Lerdo de Tejada, Sebastián, 52, 55, 72, 80, 117, 133, 147, 157, 188, 264, 274
in Restored Republic, 199–234, 241, 246, 260, 274
trial of Maximilian, 191–5
Liberalism, Mexican, 5, 10–14, 16, 21, 25, 35, 50–1, 54, 61, 65–6, 82
and Catholic Church, 87–113
Juárez and Liberalism, 49–68, 71–84
Oaxacan, 22–3, 26, 36–7, 45, 54–5, 77
Spanish, 10–13, 71
state governors and Liberalism, 116–42
Liberals, Mexican,
admiration of USA, 122
moderates, 63, 79, 110, 240
radicals, 71–2, 81, 102–3, 224–5, 262
in Restored Republic, 200–34
Linares, Bishop of, 110
Lincoln, Abraham, 149, 153, 155–8, 164 n.18, 175
Llave, Ignacio de la, 121
Llave, Pablo de la, 101
London Bonds (1824), 30
López Mateos, Adolfo, 248
López Ortigoza, José, 20, 24, 26
Lorencez, Gen. Charles Latrille de, 171, 256
Louis XIV, 170
Loxicha (Oaxaca), 26, 45
Lozada, Manuel, 21, 66, 216–18, 230, 258, 259
Lucas, Juan Francisco, 204, 208–10, 228, 260

Madero, Francisco I, 21
Madrid, 145
Maghreb, 182
Malo, Gen. José María, 38–9
Manero Embides, Víctor, 23
Mantecón, Bishop Antonio, 92–6
Manzanillo (Colima), 230
Maqueo, Estéban, 28, 40
Maqueo, Roberto, 223
María Cristina, Regent of Spain, 182
Mariscal, Ignacio, 96, 112, 128, 274
Márquez, Gen. Leonardo, 117, 119, 126, 174, 187, 189, 199, 201, 255, 274–5
Martínez Pinillos, Gen. Ignacio, 43–4
masonic lodges, 14, 262, 266, 269
Mata, José María, 58, 148–9
Matamoros, 120, 132, 135, 156
Martínez de la Torre, Lic. Rafael, 189, 191–2
Matthews, George, 123
Mauleón, Joaquín, 223
Maximilian, Archduke and Emperor, 21, 86, 134, 141, 156, 158, 275
  capture, trial and execution, 189–95, 258–9
  Colonization Law, 158–9, 257
  Imperial Decree of 3 October 1865, 183, 257
  Imperial Decree of 26 June 1866, 214, 258
  Junta for the Protection of the Impoverished Classes, 214
  Second Empire, 170–95, 199, 240–1, 247, 256–9, 267
Maza, Antonio, 28
Maza de Juárez, Margarita, 28, 53, 141, 234, 250–1, 252, 259
Mazatlán (Sinaloa), 120, 151, 178
Mazzini, Giuseppe, 89
McLane, Robert, 150
McLane–Ocampo Treaty, 151–2, 157, 160, 248, 255–6
Meijueiro family, 21, 204
  Francisco Meijueiro, 222, 229
Mejía, Col. Ignacio, 40, 43, 45, 51, 55, 76, 118, 180, 205, 222, 234, 275–6
Mejía, Gen. Tomás, 21, 117, 119, 186–7, 276
  trial and execution, 190, 193, 195, 199, 258–9
Meléndez, José Gregorio, 41–4
Méndez, Gen. Juan Nepomuceno, 187, 203, 208–9, 227–8
Méndez, Miguel, 22–3, 265
Mesilla strip, La, 147
  Treaty (also Gadsden Purchase), 150, 160
mestizos, 264
Metz, 182, 269
Mexican Revolution (1910–11), 2, 67, 248
Mexico
  archbishop of, 96
  monarchy, 7, 152, 168, 246, 267, 273
  population, 1–2

Mexico City, 8, 79–80, 82, 87, 264
citadel, 227
French entry into, 171, 256
junta (1867), 186, 258
Maximilian and Carlota arrive in, 173, 257
siege of, 187
strike, 216, 259
Michoacán, State of, 12, 25, 52, 58–9, 66, 80, 96, 102, 110, 117, 119, 180, 183, 270, 272
Mier y Terán, Gen. Luis, 208, 229, 260
Miramar, 256
Treaty of (1864), 173
Miramón, Gen. Miguel, 97, 105, 117, 119, 122, 134, 149, 151–2, 168–9, 186–8, 199, 254–5, 258–9, 269, 276–7
capture, trial and execution, 189–95
Mixteca, 4, 58
Alta, 19–20, 229
Baja, 21, 30
Mixtecs, 19
Moctezuma, 27, 242
Mon-Almonte Treaty, 267
Monclova (Coahuila), 180
Monroe Doctrine, 158
Monterrey (Nuevo León), 119, 130–1, 135, 140, 184, 231, 257, 260, 271
Montes, Ezequiel, 68, 81, 102
Montluc, Armand de, 169
Mora, José María Luis, 13, 88, 90, 272, 277
Morales, José Ignacio, 22
Morelia (Michoacán), 258, 270, 272
Morelos, José María, 22, 25, 52, 56, 237, 243, 268, 269, 277
Morelos, State of, 4, 215
Morny, Duc de, 168
Munguía, Bishop Clemente de Jesús, 96, 99

Napoleon III, 55, 135, 156, 158–9, 161, 168–95, 237, 245–7, 258, 267, 271
National Guard, 4, 37, 42, 49, 58, 66, 76, 117, 136, 204, 208, 222, 224
nationalism, Mexican, 110–13, 248
nationalization of ecclesiastical properties, 103, 107
Nayarit, State of, 216–18
Negrete, Gen. Miguel, 139, 209–10, 259
neo-Liberalism, 249
New Mexico, 146, 158, 160
New Orleans, 25, 44, 51–2, 58, 147, 237, 244–5, 253, 268
New Spain, Viceroyalty of, 8
New York City, 141, 230, 234, 271
New York Herald, 160
Nochixtlán (Oaxaca), 229
North Africa, 168
North American Free Trade Area (NAFTA), 239, 248–9
North German Confederation, 239
Nuevo Laredo (Tamaulipas), 156
Nuevo León, State of, 6, 58, 64, 119, 122, 130–2, 135, 140, 158, 180, 226–7, 255, 257, 260

Oaxaca, city of, 2, 41
Conservative occupation, 180
French capture, 257
Institute of Science and Arts, 22–3, 25, 152, 237, 269, 271
insurgent occupation, 22
Liberal press, 170
seminary college, 21
Oaxaca, State of, xii, 2, 5, 7, 18, 120, 206, 244
caciques of the sierra, 21, 204
Department of, 27, 29
Department Assembly, 32
diocese, 26, 87, 91–6, 109, 174
Félix Díaz and, 225–30
Rebellion of La Noria, 204, 225–30, 260
Senate, 36, 101
State Constitution, 32, 37
State Court of Justice, 24, 27, 33, 36
State Legislature (Congress), 34–5, 77, 252
Obregón, Álvaro, 220
Ocampo, Melchor, 15, 25, 52, 55, 60, 63–5, 81, 89–91, 103, 105–6, 119–23, 150–2, 167, 241, 244, 256, 268, 270, 277
Ocotlán (Oaxaca), 93, 229
O'Donnell, Gen. Leopoldo, Duque de Tetuán, 169
Ogazón, Gen. Pedro, 217–18
Ometepec (Guerrero), 57
Oran, 182
Orizaba (Veracruz), 185, 256–8, 267
Orozco, José Clemente, 251
Orozco y Berra, Manuel, 173–4
Ortega, Lic. Eulalio, 190, 192
Ortiz, Máximo R, 42
Osollo, Gen. Luis, 97, 119, 254
Otero, Mariano, 33, 57, 74
Ottoman Empire, 194

Panama, Isthmus of, 59, 146, 151, 160
Papal Nuncio, 174
Papantla (Veracruz), 31
Parada, Petrona, 28
Paredes (y) Arrillaga, Gen. Mariano, 15–16, 25, 31–2, 262
Paris, 145, 185, 267
Parrodi, Gen. Anastasio, 103, 117, 119, 254
Partido Nacional Revolucionario (PNR), 220
Partido Revolucionario Institucional (PRI), 249
Paso del Norte (El), 135, 158–9, 178, 184, 207, 257
Patoni, Gen. José María, 134, 137
Pavón, Desiderio, 181
Payno, Manuel, 63, 82, 85 n. 21, 277
peasant movements, 214–18, 259
Pénjamo (Guanajuato), 272
peones, 264
Pérez, Marcos, 21–2, 34, 41, 64, 265
personalism, 6, 15
Peru, 16
Pesqueira, Ignacio, 181
Petapa (Oaxaca), 41, 79

Piedragorda, San Pedro (Guanajuato), 271
Piedras Negras (Coahuila), 132
Pierce, Franklin, 147
pintos, 57, 62, 264
Pius IX, Pope, 89, 99, 172, 206, 254, 259
Plan of Acapulco (1854), 57, 61
Plan of Ayutla (1854), 57, 59, 62, 147, 230
Plan of Iguala (1821), 268, 269, 272, 273
Plan of Jalapa (1829), 269
Plan of Jalisco (1852), 43
Plan of La Noria (1871), 210, 225–8, 231, 260
Plan of Tacubaya (1857), 82
Pochutla (Oaxaca), 38, 229
Poinsett, Joel Roberts, 278
Poland, 8
Polk, James, 146
polko rebellion, 33–5, 38, 41, 264
porfiristas, 207–8, 221–33, 244, 264
Prieto, Guillermo, 54–5, 60, 81, 89, 120, 139, 148, 278
Prim, Gen. Juan, Conde de Reus, 169, 195, 278
pronunciamientos, 264, *see also* Plans
Protestantism, 89, 111–13
Prussia, 9
Puebla, 2, 4, 7, 26, 53, 87, 98, 111, 171, 198, 213, 215, 246
  Battle of (1862), 171, 256
  business community, 5
  Díaz's capture of city, 187, 258
  Liberal recovery, 207
  in Restored Republic, 198, 201, 203, 208–11
  serrano caciques, 204, 228, *see also* Bonilla, Lucas, Juan Nepomuceno Méndez
  siege of (1863), 256
  sierra, 259, 260
pueblo, 264
Puerto Angel (Oaxaca), 229
Puerto Rico, 162
puros, 57, 265
Putla (Oaxaca), 31, 41

Querétaro, 3, 66, 83, 102, 117, 128, 183, 186, 271, 273
  defence and siege of, 187–93, 258
Quetzalcóatl, 236
Quezada, Manuel, 53
Quezada, Rafael, 53

Rabasa, Emilio, 73, 246
railway (Mexico City–Veracruz), 214
Ramírez, Ignacio, 55, 60, 64–5, 81, 127, 207, 267, 278
Ramírez, José Fernando, 173
Ramírez de Aguilar, Ramón, 20, 23–6, 29, 33
rancheros, 265
Rebellion of the Acordada, 14
Rebellion of La Noria, 201, 204, 208, 211, 225–33, 243, 269
Rebellion of Tuxtepec, 269
re-election, issue of, 138–9, 199–203, 220–8, 233, 260, 273

Reform Movement, Mexican (*Reforma*), 3, 12, 58, 60–1, 64, 86, 88, 90, 245, 253, 265
  Civil War of the Reform, 9, 52–3, 191–5, 110, 112, 117–25, 245, 254, 271
  Reform Laws, 104–10, 124, 136, 150, 160, 172, 176, 255
Regency Council (1863–64), 171–3, 178, 256 (1867), 187
regionalism, 6–7, 58, 74, 116–42, 216
Régules, Gen. Nicolás de, 181
'Republic of the Sierra Madre', 131
Republican Party (USA), 149, 153
  radical Republicans, 157
Restored Republic, 66, 86, 198–234, 259
Revolution of Ayutla, 16, 56, 58, 64, 66, 76–9, 81, 89, 97, 101, 117, 136, 226, 228, 253, 268, 270, 272
Richmond (Virginia), 145, 155
Riva Palacio family, 215
  Mariano, 128, 189–93, 215
  Vicente, 179–80, 187, 189, 208
Rivera, Aureliano, 187
Rivera, Diego, 251
Rocha, Gen. Sóstenes, 187, 204, 227, 231, 260
rojos, 54, 103, 265
Romero, Félix, 64, 77, 223, 228
Romero, Matías, 75, 79, 83, 118, 139, 152–9, 161–2, 188, 198
Romero Rubio, Manuel, 128
Romero Vargas, Ignacio, 204
Rosario (Sinaloa), 3
Ruiz, Manuel, 64, 82, 95, 102, 105, 107–8, 120, 121, 127, 139, 160, 179
Russia, 9

Salamanca (Guanajuato), 104, 119, 254, 273
Salas, Gen. Mariano, 33, 171
Salinas de Gortari, Carlos, 248
salt trade, 40
Saltillo (Coahuila), 53, 134, 256–7, 271
San Blas (Nayarit), 120, 217
San Diego (California), 146–7
San Germán, Lope, 23
San Luis Potosí, 2–3, 20–1, 53, 110, 216, 226, 231, 258, 268
  decree of 22 July 1863, 137, 265
  decree of 16 August 1863, 176
  Juárez in, 133, 137, 140, 186, 191, 273
  rebellion in (1870), 208
San Miguel el Grande (Guanajuato), 3
Sánchez, Juan, 244
Sánchez Navarro family, 176–7
  Carlos, 176
Santa Anna, Gen. Antonio López de, 14–16, 21, 23, 25, 30–1, 33, 39, 41, 44, 51, 57, 59, 61, 65, 71–2,

76, 78, 92, 147, 150, 228, 231, 240, 252–3, 261, 262, 265, 267, 278–9
Santacilia, Pedro, 51, 53, 58, 139, 182, 234
santanistas, 265
Senate (Mexican Federal), 36, 72, 232
Senate (USA), 151, 255
Serrano, Francisco, 52, 168–9
serranos, 22, 265
Seward, William H, 139, 153–6, 159, 161–2, 188
Sierra Gorda, 217
Sierra, Justo, 90, 245
Siete Leyes (1836), 14, 265
Silao (Guanajuato), 255
Siliceo, Manuel, 62, 80, 173, 199
silver mines, 2–4, 19–20, 238
Sinaloa, State of, 139, 155, 180
Siqueiros, David, 251
Solar Campero, Manuel del, 28
Sonora, State of, 139, 147, 149, 155, 180, 231
South Carolina, 153, 170
Southern Intelligence, 131
Spain, 195
Spanish merchants, 19
State Department (USA), 162
state governors, 116–42, 198–231
sub-prefects, 36, 41
Suez Canal, 170
sugar cultivation, 31
Supreme Court (Federal), 60–1, 79, 82, 127, 138, 140, 231, 234, 254, 271, 272
Supreme Executive Power (1823–24), 269
Supremo Poder Conservador (1836), 270

Tacubaya, *coup d'état* of, 79–84, 226, 254, 270
Tamaulipas, State of, 139, 226, 268
Tampico (Tamaulipas), 150, 260
Tavehua (Oaxaca), 101
Taylor, Zachary, 146
Tegetthoff, Vice-Admiral Wilhelm, 193
Tehuacán (Puebla), 26
Tehuantepec, Isthmus of, 5, 18–19, 28, 40–4, 78–9, 92, 146–7, 149, 170, 217, 231, 233
Tehuantepec (Oaxaca), 41, 93, 230–1
Tenango del Valle (Mexico), 272
Teococuilco (Oaxaca), 22
Teotitlán del Camino (Oaxaca), 38
Tepejí (Puebla), 210
Tepic (Nayarit), 66, 216–18, 230
Terrazas family, 5–6
Luis, 6, 132–8, 177, 180–1, 184, 247
Texas, 7–8, 32, 122, 131, 145, 151, 160, 168, 238, 252, 267 269
textile production, 3, 5, 19
and labour movement, 216, 259
tierras baldías, 137, 164, 265
Tixtla (Guerrero), 200, 213, 267

Tlapa (Guerrero), 41, 212, 270
Tlaxcala, 111, 209, 215, 246
Tlaxiaco (Oaxaca), 19–20, 67, 76
Tlemcen, 182
Toluca (Mexico), 216
Toombs, Robert, 132
Treaty of Guadalupe Hidalgo, 145–6, 253
Treviño, Gen. Jerónimo, 131, 187
  rebellion (1871–72), 227, 231
Trías, Gen. Angel, 137
Tripartite Intervention, 129–30, 154–5, 167–8, 175, 256
Tulancingo,
  Bishop of, 174
  Rebellion of, 13
Tuxtepec (Oaxaca), 38

unicameralism, 65, 83, 202, 266
United States of America,
  Civil War, 130–1
  Mexican Conservatives and, 148
  Juárez's attitude to, 145–63, 166
  population, 1
  Protestantism, 111–13, 122
  relations with Mexico, 8, 17, 103–5, 122, 125, 238–9, 245, 249
Uraga, Gen. José López, 62, 179
Uruapan (Michoacán), 183

Valladolid, 271–2, *see also* Morelia, Michoacán
Vallarta, Ignacio, 81, 103, 279
Valle, Gen. Leandro, 103
Velázquez, Lic. José María, 190, 192
Veracruz, 4–5, 66, 83, 103–4, 106–7, 109–10, 117, 129, 175, 230, 265
  allied naval demonstration off, 150
  Juárez régime in, 121–5, 148, 241, 250, 254
  sieges of, 149–55
  Tripartite Intervention, 155, 167–8, 256
Victoria, Guadalupe, 221
Vidaurri, Santiago, 6, 58–9, 64, 103, 117–22, 130–2, 179, 187, 255, 256–7
Vienna Settlement (1814–15), 170
Viesca, Andrés, 181, 183
Villa Alta (Oaxaca), 20
Villarreal, Col. Florencio, 57

War of Independence, 1, 3, 6, 41, 58, 248, 252, 267
War of 1846–47, 8, 15, 21, 32, 38, 42, 145–6, 150, 253
Washington, DC, 151, 153, 156, 161, 188
Washington, George, 154
Wydenbruck, Count von, 188
Wyke, Sir Charles, 154
Wyke–Zamacona Agreement, 154, 157, 256

Xindihuí (Oaxaca), 229–30, 260
Xochiapulco (Puebla), 210, 228

Yucatán, 7, 15, 35, 233

Zacapoaxtla (Puebla), 209
Zacatecas, 2–4, 7, 20, 103, 134, 138–9, 176, 180, 186, 215, 226, 231, 254, 260
rebellion (1870), 208
Zacatlán (Puebla), 209
Zamacona, Manuel María, 133, 154, 157, 208, 229, 279–80
Zapata, Emiliano, 62
Zapotec Indian groups, 5, 18–20, 22, 34–5, 41
Zaragoza, Col. Ignacio, 131, 255
Zarco, Francisco, 55, 64, 81, 112, 127, 133, 161, 280
Zavala, Lorenzo de, 13–14, 16, 22, 88, 280
Zenea, Juan Clemente, 52
Zimatlán (Oaxaca), 94
Zoochila (Oaxaca), 101
Zoque Indian group, 40
Zuloaga, Félix, 59–60, 80, 82, 101, 136, 148, 254, 280